MW00781958

A Fine Romance

A Fine Romance

Adapting Broadway to Hollywood in the Studio System Era

GEOFFREY BLOCK

OXFORD
UNIVERSITY PRESS

Oxford University Press is a department of the University of Oxford. It furthers
the University's objective of excellence in research, scholarship, and education
by publishing worldwide. Oxford is a registered trade mark of Oxford University
Press in the UK and certain other countries.

Published in the United States of America by Oxford University Press
198 Madison Avenue, New York, NY 10016, United States of America.

CIP data is on file at the Library of Congress
ISBN 978–0–19–750173–3

DOI: 10.1093/oso/9780197501733.001.0001

Printed by Sheridan Books, Inc., United States of America

To Dominic Broomfield-McHugh
Superb scholar, treasured colleague, and, best of all, friend

Contents

Illustrations

Figures

Musical Examples

Tables

Acknowledgments

It is to be expected that our predecessors might offer invaluable information and ideas in their writings that authors can use, credit, and build on. With *A Fine Romance*, the more I immersed myself, the more I became aware not only of my debt to my scholarly predecessors but also of the growing awareness that I was doubly blessed with the privilege of having worked with many of these fine and inspiring scholars, especially in my bystander role as general editor of Yale Broadway Masters and series editor of Oxford's Broadway Legacies.

I'd therefore like to begin these Acknowledgments by singling out some of the individuals I learned so much from and the works they wrote about that are discussed in this volume (see the Bibliography for more details): Stephen Banfield (*Show Boat* and *The Cat and the Fiddle*); Richard Barrios (*West Side Story*); Dominic Broomfield-McHugh (*Brigadoon, Silk Stockings*, and film adaptation more broadly); Tim Carter (*Oklahoma!*); Todd Decker (*Show Boat*); Kara Gardner (*Brigadoon* and *Oklahoma!*); Mark Eden Horowitz (*Show Boat*); James Leve (*Cabaret*); Jeffrey Magee (*Call Me Madam*); Ethan Mordden (stage and film more broadly); Carol J. Oja (*On the Town*); Howard Pollack (*Cabin in the* Sky); and Kevin Winkler (*Cabaret*).

Numerous other people and institutions provided invaluable kindnesses that made this book happen. First I'd like to express my gratitude to the indispensable theater and film collections (and their staffs) at the Library of Congress, the Margaret Herrick Library, the New York Public Library, and Boston Library, collections that fulfilled my desire for librettos and screenplays, lyrics and music drafts in various stages of completion, memoranda, letters, photographs, and production and censorship files. Sargent Aborn, Dominic Broomfield-McHugh, Judy Carlson Hulbert, Mark Eden Horowitz, and Howard Pollack generously provided me with unpublished librettos, screenplays, and letters. The library staff at the University of Puget Sound (Chris Dowd, Cassandra Palmore, and Debbie White) managed to locate obscure articles, reviews, and books. Thanks also to the anonymous reviewers who originally helped guide the volume based on an early prospectus and sample chapter and to the reviewer who read the completed manuscript and offered numerous additional helpful suggestions for improvement. Ken Zirinsky provided detailed and helpful proofreading.

I owe a special debt to Jinshil Yi and Shepherd Engle for providing expert technical assistance with the stage photos and screenshots. Thanks also to my capable and immensely helpful project editor Zara Cannon-Mohammed and project manager Jeremy Toynbee for taking such care with the production process. As an unexpected bonus, Jeremy teamed me up again with the meticulous and wise copy-editor Patterson Lamb who previously shared her editing expertise on the second edition of *Enchanted Evenings*. I was also thrilled to learn that Alexa Selph (aka Alexa "Indexa") was again available to prepare this superb index. Finally, my deep thanks to Senior Editor Norm Hirschy who supported and shepherded this book from first to last.

My good friend and colleague Andrew Buchman tirelessly read numerous drafts, offered detailed and helpful suggestions on every front and endless moral support and interest throughout the gestation and writing process. Dominic Broomfield-McHugh, an acclaimed musical theater and film scholar, treasured colleague and friend, and the dedicatee of this book, provided invaluable advice and encouragement from the book's inception and a thorough and perceptive reading of the final draft.

Thanks to my wife Jacqueline, our daughter Jessamyn Myers, and son Eli Block for supporting this project (and me) as they always do, and additional thanks to Eli for another superb job engraving the musical examples.

To all the people and institutions named above (and doubtless some I unfortunately overlooked) I offer my heartfelt gratitude.

Preface

Two Confessions

When I began to think of what to say in my Preface, for some reason I couldn't help thinking of Rousseau's famous lament divulged early in his *Confessions* (1781–1788), "My birth was the first of my misfortunes." Even knowing I can't top Rousseau, I begin this book on stage musicals and their screen adaptations with a confession of my own, Confession No. 1 (the first of three): Due, not to a misfortune but an accident of birth, I was born too late to see any of the first eleven (of twelve) stage works discussed in the pages that follow until *after* I had seen their film adaptations. To compensate for this deprivation, my prescient parents thoughtfully brought their Rodgers and Hammerstein–obsessed son along to see the newly arrived film versions of *Oklahoma!*, *South Pacific*, and *The King and I*. For the record, the *stage* version of *Oklahoma!* debuted five years before my birth and *The King and I* when I turned three. This leads to Confession No. 2: In my sheltered life (so far) I have yet to see a stage production of nearly half of the musicals explored in the book you are now reading (*The Cat and the Fiddle*, *Roberta*, *Cabin in the Sky*, *Call Me Madam*, and *Silk Stockings*). It provides small comfort to know that most readers of this volume will join me in this same crowded confessional.

The first edition of my first book on Broadway musicals, *Enchanted Evenings*, a survey that scrutinized such topics as the compositional genesis and the relationship between drama and music in more than a dozen stage musicals from *Show Boat* to Sondheim, appeared in 1997.[1] The survey didn't discuss film adaptations, but after issuing the usual caveats about how film musicals differed markedly and generally offered usually pale imitations of their stage models, these films proved useful for teaching purposes. For the second edition twelve years later, I added two new chapters, this time devoting attention to the film adaptations of the stage shows I wrote about from *Show Boat* to *West Side Story* and providing commentary on the film versions of *Sweeney Todd* and *The Phantom of the Opera* in an expanded Sondheim chapter and a new chapter on Andrew Lloyd Webber. With two exceptions, again *Show Boat* and *West Side Story*, this volume does not revisit stage shows and film adaptations considered in the earlier survey. When these shows and films are reprised here (along with two works previously discussed elsewhere), the goal is to say something new about them.[2]

The Chosen Ones

The central topic of *A Fine Romance: Adapting Broadway to Hollywood in the Studio System Era* is the symbiotic relationship between a dozen Broadway musicals and their Hollywood film adaptations.[3] Since I couldn't conjure up a sensible way to avoid doing so, I begin as I did in *Enchanted Evenings* with the Broadway opening of the pivotal *Show Boat* in 1927, but this time my story will conclude with *Cabaret*, a work that in its 1966 stage version arrived at the end of the Broadway era that began with *Oklahoma!* The multiple Oscar award–winning film version of *Cabaret* that followed in 1972 (although losing to *The Godfather* in the Best Picture category) marked a glorious valedictory moment that preceded thirty years of perceived decline. The curse was broken in 2002 when the film adaptation of *Chicago* captured the Oscar for Best Picture, a milestone that helped inspire a renaissance in the movie musical of all types that is continuing as of this writing.[4]

Here is my list of the twelve Chosen Ones, shows and films, arranged in the order they first appeared on the stage (performance run totals and film run times, respectively, follow the artworks' dates in parentheses):

1. *Show Boat*, 1927 (572); Universal 1936 (113 min.)
2. *The Cat and the Fiddle*, 1931 (395); MGM 1934 (92 min.)
3. *Roberta*, 1933 (295); RKO 1935 (105 min.)
4. *Cabin in the Sky*, 1940 (156); MGM 1943 (99 min.)
5. *Oklahoma!*, 1943 (2,212); Magna 1955 (145 min.)
6. *On the Town*, 1944 (463); MGM 1949 (98 min.)
7. *Brigadoon*, 1947 (581); (MGM 1954 (108 min.)
8. *Call Me Madam*, 1950 (644); 20th Century-Fox 1953 (117 min.)
9. *Silk Stockings*, 1955 (478); MGM 1957 (118 min.)
10. *West Side Story*, 1957 (732); Mirisch-Seven Arts 1961 (151 min.)
11. *Flower Drum Song* 1958 (600); Universal 1961 (133 min.)
12. *Cabaret*, 1966 (1,165); Allied Artists and ABC 1972 (124 min.)

These twelve stage shows and their film adaptations span a period of thirty-nine years (1927 to 1966) for the stage works, thirty-eight for the films (1934 to 1972). All but one of the original stage productions was at least a modest commercial hit in its era. In half the cases, they were either the longest-running show of their respective decade (*Oklahoma!*), or among the longest (*Show Boat, The Cat and the Fiddle, Brigadoon, West Side Story, Cabaret*). The exception is *Cabin in the Sky*, a major cultural milestone with its all-Black, all-star cast, both on Broadway and in Hollywood, stage and film, but only a *succès d'estime* on the stage. The films, which followed their stage predecessors by intervals between two years (*Roberta*,

Silk Stockings) and twelve years (*Oklahoma!*), were for the most part commercially successful and critically highly regarded in their day. Several have matched or overshadowed the acclaim of their stage predecessors and are widely regarded as film classics.

All but three of these film adaptations clocked in under two hours, and three flew by in less than 100 minutes. Since the average two-act stage musical lasts about two and a half hours, not including intermission, the length of a film adaptation constitutes a pre-existing condition that provides a starting point for many of the differences between stage and screen versions. With the exception of the period between the film versions of *Oklahoma!* in 1955 (145 minutes) and *Fiddler on the Roof* in 1972 (180 minutes), the decreed film length of screen adaptations before and after these milestones was no more than two hours. What this meant as a practical matter was that for most film adaptations, roughly thirty stage minutes of dialogue or music had to go.

Most of the stage musicals chosen for this study debuted during the twenty-year period between *Oklahoma!* (1943) and *Fiddler on the Roof* (1964), often designated as a Golden Age. It was the era of Richard Rodgers and Oscar Hammerstein II, Alan Jay Lerner and Frederick Loewe, Cole Porter, Frank Loesser, Leonard Bernstein, George Abbott, Agnes de Mille, and Jerome Robbins whose legacy included many of the most memorable and frequently revived shows of all time. Film historians have designated their own overlapping but also chronologically distinctive Golden Age of Hollywood (or more formally, Classical Hollywood Cinema in the Sound Era).[5] This era began before *Oklahoma!* with the earliest sound films of 1927 and continued briefly after the collapse of the studio system in the late 1950s, several years before the twilight of Broadway's Golden Age. While this extended time period fits the range, diversity, and artistic accomplishment of *original* film musicals (i.e., film musicals *not* based on stage works), *A Fine Romance* will argue that the Golden Age of film *adaptations* of Broadway shows did not begin in earnest until the 1950s and was nearly over by the mid-1960s, several years after the decline of the studio system.

On Adaptation

A common (and perhaps prevailing) critical position offered by stage and film critics is that adaptations are intrinsically inferior to "original" film musicals. For these critics, the idea of a Golden Age of Film *Adaptations* is an oxymoron. According to this critical consensus, film adaptations of stage classics, including *Oklahoma!*, *My Fair Lady*, or *West Side Story*, despite the Oscar-winning status of the latter two films, simply don't belong in the same league as original film musicals such as *Love Me Tonight*, *Top Hat*, *The Wizard of Oz*, *Singin' in the Rain*,

The Band Wagon, and *Gigi*. Readers might as well know sooner rather than later that I am not one of these critics. Based on anecdotal evidence and personal encounters, conventional wisdom, and my familiarity with vitriolic or snide film critics who regularly regard adaptations with disdain as deformations of stage musicals, I strongly suspect that until recently I have been in the minority. In fact, over the years I have come across few colleagues or published critics prepared to acknowledge that any but a handful of film adaptations approximate their stage sources in quality.

Adaptations most often lauded among this handful regularly include the 1936 version of *Show Boat*, *The Sound of Music*, *Cabaret*, *Chicago*, and sometimes a few others such as *Kiss Me Kate* (minus the comma), *The King and I*, *West Side Story*, *The Music Man*, *My Fair Lady*, *Sweeney Todd*, and *Into the Woods*, several of which are explored in *A Fine Romance*. But for the most part, despite their consistent commercial success and sometimes surprisingly high rankings in various polls, when it comes to film adaptations, a cognitive dissonance remains between popularity and critical respect.[6]

The tone and tenor of this book will thus differ from many (but by no means all) in its tolerance for and appreciation of the art of adaptation. In contrast to the conventional wisdom dating back to the origins of the species, I consider the adaptations discussed here as mostly worthy films, even (or perhaps especially) when they flaunt their infidelity and fool around with revered stage material. My critical position maintains that the collection of twelve stage musicals and film adaptations gathered here not only encompasses a wide range of stage shows and films but presents works in both genres that are historically and aesthetically significant. The chosen stage musicals feature work by some of the most prominent lyricists, composers, directors, choreographers, and costume, set, and lighting designers of their time. In their efforts to offer fresh media-appropriate approaches, the film adaptations employed some of the finest film talent available, including directors, other major off-camera creative figures, and stars that regularly repeat their stage successes. Moreover, beginning in the 1950s film adaptations more often than not thankfully leave their exceptional musical scores largely intact. As a fringe benefit, the retention of these scores helps preserve the *theatrical* legacy of shows such as *The Cat and the Fiddle*, *Roberta*, *Call Me Madam*, *Silk Stockings*, and *Flower Drum Song* which have become a vanishing presence in musical theater history.

Through the use of primary sources (libretti, screenplays, scores, recordings) and documentary materials such as production and censorship files and letters, the chapters that follow will focus on the connections between original Broadway shows and their Hollywood screen adaptations with the goal of illuminating the intricate and varied adaptation processes and interconnections between these genres. In keeping with the principles of adaptation theory and fidelity studies, the film adaptations will not be judged on the extent to which they follow their stage predecessors but as equally and mutually nurturing (or exploitative) romantic partners.[7] Adaptation theorist David L. Kranz persuasively argues that "there is no reason to replace the comparative analysis at the heart of fidelity criticism."[8] Instead, he sensibly suggests replacing the term "fidelity criticism" with "comparative criticism" thus "making the issue of fidelity (still important for economic, audience-response, and hermeneutic reasons) only one of several related questions in the comparative equation."[9] I agree and will follow Kranz's lead and stick mainly to "comparative criticism."

A Fine Romance does not wish to minimize the significant and fundamental differences between live stage and mediated film performances and the visual possibilities afforded by the latter. For example, most of the films explored here effectively employ the classic cinematic technique of montage (scene sequences made up of contrasting camera angles and actions, the latter often superimposed or overlapping). Several take their viewers on location to New York, New York in On the Town and West Side Story, Arizona for Oklahoma! (standing in for the Indian Territory of 1907), and the German countryside in Cabaret. Like most films of their era, most of the films in our list, however, including Brigadoon and Flower Drum Song, with their constructed replicas of the Highlands of Scotland and San Francisco's Chinatown, respectively, were filmed on elaborate studio soundstages. Also, in sharp contrast to the requirements of the stage, half of our films—On the Town, Call Me Madam, Brigadoon, Silk Stockings, West Side Story, and Flower Drum Song—feature vocal dubbing for at least one major character.

In "Twelve Fallacies in Contemporary Adaptation Theory," leading adaptation theorist Thomas Leitch asserts that "of all the explicitly stated fallacies that have substituted for theoretical principles in adaptation study," the fallacy that "literary texts are verbal, films visual . . . is the most enduring and pernicious."[10] Had Leitch been focusing on stage versus film musicals, he might have rephrased the fallacy to read that "stage works are theatrical, films cinematic." In elaborating how this fallacy plays out for literary texts versus films, Leitch makes the obvious but surprisingly often overlooked assertion that applies equally well to screen musicals: "Films are not strictly speaking visual."[11] Since the arrival of synchronized sound, films have been audio-visual, depending as they do on soundtracks as well as image tracks for their effects. Commentators who continue to brush aside synchronized sound as a mere appendage to the visual essence of cinema are impervious to several crucial and powerful developments in film history more broadly, but especially film musical history.[12]

As we will see, stage musicals often demonstrate a marked cinematic quality, and film musicals regularly adopt theatrical features to their arsenal of re-imaginings. Yet when the film adaptation of his Sweeney Todd (1979) was finally released in 2007, Sondheim stated in an interview with Jesse Green that "everyone who has attempted to translate a stage musical to film has underestimated the distance between the languages."[13] Sondheim is not alone in thinking that stage musicals are from Mars and their film adaptations from Venus.

Such a divide might be true of novels and films, but stage and film do in fact speak a common language. In particular, they both rely on sound as much as visual material to communicate their narratives. Consequently, many of the films examined here depend on music as much as visual imagery to tell their stories. Stage musicals and their adaptations may not use all the dialogue or all the music from their stage sources, and they regularly interpolate new musical possibilities and alter the libretto much as a stage revival of a musical might do, but both genres rely on sound as well as image to convey dialogue, lyrics, and melody.

As a musicologist who specializes in musical theater and musical film history, I will practice my trade here. Consequently, while I will try to contribute something meaningful about the visual component of film adaptations, which I consider of incalculable importance, I will place my central emphasis, without apology, on the aural component of films, the words the characters speak, the music they sing, and the ways film adaptors use and discard the words and music of their stage sources. Too often the music, especially in musical films, gets short shrift from scholars and critics. The present volume will travel in the opposite direction in its emphasis on the musical component of a stage musical or musical film, beginning with detailed considerations of how, and how much, the stage score was altered and then moving on to why.

In the 1930s and 1940s the film studio structure, commercial interests, and the tastes of the viewing public led to a conspicuous lack of fidelity in film adaptations of stage musicals. For reasons addressed in chapter 1, starting in the 1950s and continuing through the mid-1960s, fidelity became increasingly fashionable (and profitable). But even *Oklahoma!*, the film version discussed here that comes closest to its stage source in its retention of its dialogue, songs, and dance, removed one of the stage show's most powerful songs, Jud Fry's "Lonely Room." This liberty, however, was a far cry from what happened to *Cabin in the Sky* and *On the Town*, in which studios removed most of the original stage scores, instead offering new songs drawn from a pool of contracted composers and lyricists.

Show Boat, Call Me Madam, Silk Stockings, and *Cabaret* featured newly interpolated songs. But following one of the Commandments of film adaptation (introduced in chapter 1), producers and directors commissioned the original songwriters rather than studio composers to write them. *The Cat and the Fiddle* and *Roberta* retained most of their original scores but greatly altered their presentation, ordering, singer assignments, and dramatic contexts. *Flower Drum Song* and *West Side Story* retained nearly all of the music but made significant changes to the stage song order. The film versions of *Oklahoma!* and *West Side*

Story kept most of the original stage choreography by de Mille and Robbins, whereas the film adaptations of *Cabin in the Sky*, *On the Town*, *Call Me Madam*, *Brigadoon*, *Silk Stockings*, *Flower Drum Song*, and *Cabaret* discarded most of the original choreography.[14] Even in the Age of Fidelity, opportunities for cheating were seemingly endless.

A Fine Romance: The Condensed Version

The romance explored in *A Fine Romance* begins in 1927, the year *Show Boat* began its long "life on the wicked stage" (to steal a song title from that show). The birth of *Show Boat* coincides conveniently with the birth of the sound film, after which chapter 2 continues with a discussion of two more hit stage musicals with music by Jerome Kern from the 1930s, *The Cat and the Fiddle* and *Roberta*. In subsequent chapters film adaptations of four 1940s musicals (*Cabin in the Sky*, *Oklahoma!*, *On the Town*, and *Brigadoon*) and four 1950s musicals (*Call Me Madam*, *Silk Stockings*, *West Side Story*, and *Flower Drum* Song) offer significant opportunities to explore a fascinating variety of instructive case studies. In some cases, the Hollywood studios approached the process of adaptation with genuine love and even respect, but seldom, and in this case to their credit, with unwavering fidelity. The end of the affair arrives, at least in this volume, with Bob Fosse's cinematic 1972 re-envisioning of *Cabaret*, our sole stage representative from the 1960s.[15]

During the forty-five years encompassed between the stage debut of *Show Boat* and film debut of *Cabaret*, the relationship between Broadway and Hollywood was frequently turbulent, laden with disappointments and broken promises, mutual attempts at economic and artistic domination, and occasional irreconcilable differences. At other times, the stage and screen planets (and their bright stars) aligned, leading to well-crafted, artistic, entertaining, remunerative, magical, inspiring, occasionally even breathtaking films. Generations of Broadway musical and Hollywood film audiences, critics, aficionados, music, stage, and film historians, performers, and practitioners provide continuous proof that the two-way romance between the two genres can sometimes lead to commercial and artistic unions based on respect and love rather than merely marriages of commercial convenience.

For more than twenty years following *Show Boat*'s stage debut the institutional policies, corporate structures, and aesthetic attitudes practiced within the Hollywood studio system were determined by film executives who viewed the work of virtually everyone involved with a given stage production as expendable. Consequently, film adaptations of stage musicals in these earlier years took significant liberties with the narratives seen and musical scores heard during the

Broadway run. While usually profitable, with few exceptions the critical verdict on these films remains mostly negative.

After two decades of rampant infidelity, film studios had an about-face and decided that greater fidelity would better serve their greater interests. The resulting films beginning in the 1950s would soon be accused of being *too* faithful by not adopting a more original or cinematic approach to their stage sources. Despite the frequently impressive commercial successes of film adaptations of stage musicals in the 1950s and 1960s, original film musicals (i.e., film musicals not based on stage sources), continued to dominate the critical attention of film scholars.[16]

Following years of condescension and neglect from critics and scholars, critical attitudes on adapted film musicals began to soften.[17] As evidence of the increased attention paid to film adaptations, accompanied by a more accepting critical outlook, interested readers can turn to *The Oxford Handbook of Musical Theatre Screen Adaptations*, edited by Dominic McHugh, a collection that devotes twenty-seven chapters and 700 pages to the critical and scholarly scrutiny of film adaptations.[18] A few years prior to this milestone Ethan Mordden offered a sympathetic treatment of the topic and Richard Barrios conveyed positive critical verdicts in a survey of fifty film musicals that included nineteen adaptations.[19] I am grateful for the critical support as well as the insights these new perspectives offer.

While the discussion of these shows and films will focus on the connections between song and story, it also addresses questions related to the business underpinnings of Broadway and Hollywood, how the relationship between these rival yet collaborative entities evolved, and how the differing commercial and aesthetic models and goals of Broadway and Hollywood created both conflict and harmony. Although the emphasis will be on aesthetic and critical issues, the case studies, especially those focusing on *Show Boat*, *Cabin in the Sky*, *West Side Story*, *Flower Drum Song*, and *Cabaret*, will also engage crucial social issues such as race and ethnicity, class, gender, and sexual identity.

It was noted earlier that the central topic of *A Fine Romance* is the symbiotic relationship between a dozen Broadway musicals and their Hollywood film adaptations. To this end, each chapter addresses the symbiosis between Broadway and Hollywood through an examination of one to three significant, representative, and mostly hit stage musicals and their film adaptations. Throughout this process I have been guided by the ancient but timeless wisdom of musicologist Joseph Kerman, who encouraged scholars in my discipline to embrace critical positions without apology and to take to heart former Senator Daniel Patrick Moynihan's often-quoted assertion that humans are entitled to their own opinions but not to their own facts.[20] For each work, I will strive to address the following questions. What happened in the transfer from stage to film? How are the two versions similar and different? What pragmatic and critical criteria motivated decisions to alter or preserve stage elements in the transfer to film? Who made these decisions and why? What are the dramatic and musical consequences of these commercial and artistic choices and to what extent might they be considered successful ones?

Final Confession: Mea Culpa

In what follows I express the view that (for the most part) the adaptations under scrutiny offer something new and serve the newer medium without providing a disservice to the old. With the exception of *Brigadoon*, I will try to make the case that the film adaptations of stage musicals in this survey offer effective and successful artistic alternatives that coexist, without embarrassment, with their distinguished predecessors. This position brings me to my final and perhaps most heretical, confession, Confession No. 3: Although I am old enough to know better, I continue to harbor a special affection for these films, and even when I discovered that film versions more often than not fell short of what I saw and heard on stage, it didn't stop me from enjoying and appreciating these films.

   After confessing my sins as a musical theater and musical film historian I conclude with one last heresy. Much to my surprise, I am now prepared to espouse the unpopular critical position that most of the films discussed here merit admiration, and sometimes even love, more than they deserve scorn, pity, or neglect. I would go even further and assert my critical position that in their imaginative expansion of the dance component, four of the twelve film adaptations discussed in *A Fine Romance—Roberta*, *Call Me Madam*, *Silk Stockings*, and *Flower Drum Song*—go a long way to disprove Ralph Waldo Emerson's adage that "imitation cannot go above its model."[21]

1

The Hollywood Studio System and a Brief Survey of Film Adaptations from *Show Boat* to *Cabaret*

> You never give the orchids I sent a glance!
> No! You like cactus plants,
> This is a fine romance.
>
> —Dorothy Fields, "A Fine Romance"
> from *Swing Time* (1936)

The Studio System and the Broadway Musical in the 1930s

To understand how adaptation from stage to screen happened the way it did requires an explanation of the sometimes compatible and sometimes competing aims and goals of Broadway and Hollywood. The remaining sections of this introductory chapter offer a brief survey of how and why film adaptations evolved from their stage origins between *Show Boat* and *Cabaret*.

Whether for the stage or the screen, the business of mounting musicals has always been driven by the marketplace and the need to create an entertaining show or film that can reach its intended market. Sometimes attitudes and practices evolved in different ways from one medium to the other. A good example of this is the changing view of song interpolation (i.e., the introduction of film songs that were not in the original stage show). Broadway songwriters gradually achieved autonomy over their own material, but when George and Ira Gershwin, Richard Rodgers and Lorenz Hart, and Cole Porter began their careers in the 1910s and 1920s (Jerome Kern's career began in the early 1900s), song interpolation was a common practice that helped these famous future songwriters get their start when producers used their songs in someone else's show.[1]

The situation could also backfire—for example, when Rodgers and Hart discovered on an opening night in 1920 that half of the songs in what they thought belonged to their own Broadway show, *Poor Little Ritz Girl*, had been replaced with songs by Sigmund Romberg and lyricist Alex Gerber. By the 1930s, the days were far less common when Florenz Ziegfeld could insert Irving Berlin's "Blue

A Fine Romance. Geoffrey Block, Oxford University Press. © Oxford University Press 2023.
DOI: 10.1093/oso/9780197501733.003.0001

Skies" on opening night to boost the sinking prospects of Rodgers and Hart's *Betsy* (1926) without the principal authors' knowledge or permission.[2]

In contrast, until the 1950s, Hollywood executives and directors would continue the practice of replacing Broadway songwriters with studio songwriters who would produce new songs. As the Depression took hold and songwriters like Rodgers and Hart traveled to a financially more lucrative Hollywood haven to escape the economically troubled New York theater environment, they were regularly required to sign movie contracts that left them without the authority they were beginning to enjoy on Broadway.

As we will see in considering the film adaptations of *On the Town* (chapter 3) and *Cabin in the Sky* (chapter 4), even the most famous Broadway songwriters were often unable to decide which songs could stay in a film, which had to go, and which would be assigned to studio songwriters under contracts representing in-house publishers. The songs created by these songwriters under contract earned substantial profits for the studios and their music publishing companies as studio executives were contractually free to replace the work of Broadway composers with new songs written by a studio staff when the executives believed these could better reach what Ethan Mordden called the "American village."[3] To their financial, if not always artistic credit, the commercial results more often than not validated these decisions.

By the late 1910s and early 1920s, before the advent of sound, the studio system had established its hegemony over a vast commercial domain when independent film producers merged with theater chains and film distributors, creating an oligopoly. In 1928, one year into the sound era, RKO became the fifth major studio conglomerate, joining Metro-Goldwyn-Mayer (MGM), Fox Film Corporation (which merged with Twentieth Century in 1935 to become 20th Century-Fox), Warner Bros., and Paramount Pictures. Universal Pictures and Columbia Pictures employed similar production methods but owned fewer theater chains, while United Artists had access to ownership of production studios and mainly served as financial backers for independent film producers.

These were the eight companies known as the majors; collectively these companies produced the majority of films during the studio system era and also owned most of the 15,000 movie theaters in operation by the end of the 1930s.[4] The stable of contracted lyricists and composers whose songs were owned and distributed by the studios were joined on vast lots and soundstages by a large staff of screenwriters, set designers, technicians, prestigious directors, and the popular stars of the day, many of whom had also signed exclusive contracts.[5]

During the 1930s, 1940s, and 1950s, each major studio developed its own personality, specialties, and style. Although Paramount, MGM, and 20th Century-Fox specialized in the genre, all the studios made at least some memorable musicals. Paramount, a technological pioneer in the transition to sound, produced perhaps the most widely appreciated film musicals from sound's early years (1929 to 1934) in a series of five films directed by Ernst Lubitsch and one by Rouben Mamoulian starring Jeanette MacDonald and Maurice Chevalier, either alone or together.[6]

Near the end of the Lubitsch-Mamoulian-MacDonald-Chevalier reign, Warner Bros. released *42nd Street* (1933), the first in a series of spectacular dance musicals directed by Busby Berkeley that featured large ensemble dancing with kaleidoscopic military precision, often with overhead and other striking camera shots that couldn't be duplicated on a stage. The same year, RKO released *Flying Down to Rio*, the first of nine iconic 1930s films that featured the partnership of Fred Astaire and Ginger Rogers in a series that would include *Top Hat*, *Roberta*, *Swing Time*, and *Shall We Dance*, featuring timeless scores by Berlin, Kern and Dorothy Fields, and the Gershwins. Beginning in the 1930s, 20th Century-Fox offered superb sound, visuals in Technicolor, and a seemingly endless succession of female stars from Shirley Temple through Alice Faye, Betty Grable, June Haver, and Marilyn Monroe into the 1950s (later referred to as "the 20th Century-Fox blondes").[7] Universal, best known in the early 1930s for its horror films like *Frankenstein* and *The Bride of Frankenstein*, both directed by James Whale, surprised and delighted the skeptics when Whale was assigned to direct *Show Boat* in 1936.

The Big Five studios produced seven of the twelve film adaptations explored in *A Fine Romance*, including five films produced between 1934 and 1955 by MGM, the most prolific producer and distributor of musicals in the Studio Era: *The Cat and Fiddle*, *Cabin in the Sky*, *On the Town*, *Brigadoon*, and *Silk Stockings*. *Roberta* was the third in the Astaire-Rogers series of RKO films. *Call Me Madam* was produced by 20th Century-Fox. Twenty-two years after producing *Show Boat*, Universal (also among the top eight companies) added *Flower Drum Song*. Completing the dozen are three films produced outside of the studio system: *Oklahoma!* (Magna Theatre Corporation); *West Side Story* (The Mirisch Company); and *Cabaret* (Allied Artists Pictures and ABC).

While musicals are among the best-remembered films produced during the Studio Era, they represented only a small, albeit significant proportion, 4%, of the total number of films produced. MGM was by far the most prolific. As a sign of their productivity and dominance, during the post–World II years between 1946 and 1955, more than half the musicals made in Hollywood were MGM movies.[8] This came to about 25% of MGM's total output or eighty-one of their 316 films during this period.[9] The most consistently profitable musicals in their day and probably still the most memorable in ours are the forty musicals produced by Arthur Freed (1894–1973), who, after serving as associate producer of *The Wizard of Oz* (1939) headed his own team at MGM known as the Freed Unit until 1961, one year before he retired (see Table 1.1, "Musicals Produced by the Freed Unit").[10]

Table 1.1 Musicals Produced by the Freed Unit.

	Adaptations (15)	Original Musicals (25)
1939	*Babes in Arms* (Busby Berkeley)	*The Wizard of Oz* (Victor Fleming)
1940	*Little Nellie Kelly* (Norman Taurog)	*Strike Up the Band* (Berkeley)
1941		*Lady Be Good* (Norman Z. McLeod)
1942	*Panama Hattie* (McLeod)	*Babes on Broadway* (Berkeley)
1943	**Cabin in the Sky (Vincente Minnelli)**	*For Me and My Gal* (Berkeley)
	Du Barry Was a Lady (Roy Del Ruth)	
	Best Foot Forward (Edward Buzzell)	
	Girl Crazy (Taurog)	
1944		*Meet Me in St. Louis* (Minnelli)
1945		*The Clock* (Minnelli) [not a musical but included here because it starred Judy Garland and was directed by Minnelli]
		Yolanda and Thief (Minnelli)
1946		*The Harvey Girls* (George Sidney)
		Ziegfeld Follies (Minnelli)
1947	*Good News* (Charles Walters)	*'Till the Clouds Roll By* (Richard Whorf)
1948		*The Pirate* (Minnelli)
		Summer Holiday (Rouben Mamoulian)
		Easter Parade (Walters)
		Words and Music (Taurog)
1949	**On the Town (Gene Kelly and Stanley Donen)**	*Take Me Out to the Ball Game* (Berkeley)
		The Barkleys of Broadway (Walters)
1950	*Annie Get Your Gun* (Sidney)	*Pagan Love Song* (Robert Alton)
1951	*Show Boat* (Sidney)	*Royal Wedding* (Donen)
		An American in Paris (Minnelli)
1952		*The Belle of New York* (Walters)
		Singin' in the Rain (Kelly and Donen)
1953		*The Band Wagon* (Minnelli)
1954	**Brigadoon (Minnelli)**	
1955	*Kismet* (Minnelli)	*It's Always Fair Weather* (Kelly and Donen)
1956		*Invitation to the Dance* (Kelly)
1957	**Silk Stockings (Mamoulian)**	
1958		*Gigi* (Minnelli)
1959		
1960	*Bells Are Ringing* (Minnelli)	

• Musicals discussed in *A Fine Romance* are highlighted in bold.

• Directors are indicated in parentheses in each column.

Freed claimed to prefer original musicals to adaptations, and indeed the twenty-five musicals he produced in the former category are probably his best known, most notably *The Wizard of Oz, Meet Me in St. Louis, Easter Parade, An American in Paris, Singin' in the Rain, The Band Wagon*, and *Gigi*.[11] But although they have received considerably less attention, Freed also produced a significant number of film adaptations, fifteen between *Babes in Arms* and *Bells Are Ringing*. In both categories, one of the keys to Freed's success was his ability to assemble, sign, and in some cases discover a parade of outstanding directors, songwriters, screenwriters, choreographers (several of whom Freed groomed to become directors), and a pool of singers and dancers widely considered the most talented in the business.

Looking at Table 1.1, in the four Freed films included in this volume, two were directed by Vincente Minnelli, one by Gene Kelly and Stanley Donen, and one by Mamoulian. One film was choreographed by Hermes Pan (uncredited) and one each by Busby Berkeley (also uncredited) and Kelly.[12] Composers and lyricists include Vernon Duke and John Latouche, Leonard Bernstein, Alan Jay Lerner and Frederick Loewe, and Porter, with interpolations supplied by Harold Arlen and E. Y. Harburg to an abbreviated Duke-Latouche score and new music by Roger Edens set to words by the original stage lyricists Betty Comden and Adolph Green for an even-more-reduced Bernstein score. Although none of the four Freed adaptations showcase his great "discovery" Judy Garland, who appeared in fourteen Freed films, they boast the singing and/or dancing talents of Ethel Waters, Lena Horne, and John W. Bubbles (John Sublett) in *Cabin in the Sky*, Kelly and Vera-Ellen in *On the Town*, Kelly and Cyd Charisse in *Brigadoon*, and Astaire and Charisse in *Silk Stockings*.

The 1950s ended on a high note for MGM and the Freed Unit with *Gigi* (1958). With its screenplay and lyrics by Lerner, music by Loewe, and direction by Minnelli, this original musical was critically acclaimed, Academy Award–winning, and a commercial juggernaut that earned $10 million on a budget of $3.3 million. Unfortunately, the series would end anti-climactically two years later with a Freed-Minnelli collaboration, the modestly successful *Bells Are Ringing*.[13] According to Eric Hodgins, as a sign of their decline, by 1957, studios made only about 50% of the movies produced, with the other half created by independent producers.[14]

The fall of the studio system has been attributed to three main factors. The first blow was a case brought to the Supreme Court in 1948 that ruled against the studios' anti-competitive film distribution model and demanded that they sell their theater holdings, a major source of income and power over film distribution. Studios were also required to abandon the monopolistic practice known as block booking, which forced theater owners to purchase multiple films as a unit.[15] Since theaters were no longer required to screen their films, by the mid-1950s the major studios found it financially necessary to reduce their production output by more than a third and to cut their staff and budgets accordingly.[16] Earl Hess and Pratibha A. Dabholkar report that from 1948 to 1952, although enormously productive years for the Freed Unit, "the film industry [as a whole] lost close to 75% of its audience and 50% of its revenue.[17] In 1957, even MGM lost money for the first time and had laid off 345 of the 598 actors it had under contract in the previous decade.

The second challenge to the system was the rise of independent producers. This development led to fewer films but greater autonomy and more lucrative contracts for top stars, directors, and writers formerly controlled by the major studios. The third and final blow that led to the demise of the studio system was the rise of commercial television, a free entertainment that offered new audiences a reason to stay home rather than go out and pay to see a movie, even a movie using the trendy visual and song technologies Porter spoofs in his song "Stereophonic Sound" from *Silk Stockings*: "Glorious Technicolor/Breathtaking CinemaScope or/Cinerama, Vistavision, Superscope or Todd-AO and/ Stereophonic Sound."

Anything Goes: Stage and Film at Cross Purposes

Despite markedly different infrastructures and markets and contrary ideas about the best way to satisfy their mutual financial desires, Broadway and Hollywood danced cheek to cheek from the earliest days of sound films since they shared a common quest for commercial success. Nevertheless, in the 1930s and 1940s, conflicting procedures and values almost invariably led to film adaptations that departed significantly from their stage predecessors. Among the central issues to consider when taking stock of the "fine romance" between Broadway and Hollywood in the 1930s are the disparities between film studios' primary commercial interests and the critical verdicts of musical theater and film scholars, critics and commentators, and audiences.

Anything Goes, a hit musical in 1934 and a hit movie in 1936, admirably exemplifies these differences and how they led to contrasting outcomes. Following closely behind the 441 performances of *Of Thee I Sing* (1931), at 420 performances *Anything Goes* (1934) was the second-longest running book show of the 1930s.[18] After disappearing for nearly thirty years as a stage work (the songs remained popular), it re-emerged, first with a considerably revamped and modestly successful 1962 off-Broadway revival run (the basis of the 1969 London revival) and twenty years after that in a popular 1987 revival at the Vivian Beaumont Theater in New York. Unlike many revivals of 1930s shows and nearly all film adaptations, the Vivian Beaumont version, which also served as the basis for successful revivals on Broadway in 2011 and London in 1989, 2003, and 2021, retains all but one of the songs from the original 1934 production. On the other hand it also includes notable changes to the original book and a number of song interpolations from other shows by Porter, who wrote the music and lyrics.

The catalyst for the stage version was the failure of George and Ira Gershwin's *Pardon My English* the previous year, a flop that broke a string of hits produced by the team of Vinton Freedley and Alex Aarons, frequently with scores by the Gershwins and stars Fred and Adele Astaire.[19] Freedley and Aarons' (and the Gershwins') last major hit, *Girl Crazy* (1930), marked the spectacular Broadway debut of Ethel Merman singing "I Got Rhythm." After *Pardon My English* the Gershwins focused on the creation of *Porgy and Bess*, a collaboration with DuBose Heyward. To fill this gap, Freedley, without Aarons, enlisted Porter, who had been enjoying his own string of hit shows from *Paris* (1928) to *Gay Divorce* (1932), the latter Astaire's first show without his sister and his final Broadway show overall. To write the book for a musical set to take place aboard a ship, Freedley hired Guy Bolton and P. G. Wodehouse, the co-authors of books and lyrics to several historic Kern scores in the mid-1910s known as the Princess Theatre musicals.

Starting with Merman in her first major Broadway role after *Girl Crazy*, Freedley assembled an all-star cast for *Anything Goes* with William Gaxton as her leading man. Joining them was Gaxton's partner from *Of Thee I Sing*, the comic actor Victor Moore, who had delighted audiences in two of the Gershwin-Freedley-Aaron 1920s hits, *Oh, Kay!* and *Funny Face*. When Bolton and Wodehouse's libretto was deemed inadequate, Freedley commissioned a new libretto from the team of Howard Lindsay and Russel Crouse.[20] Several songs that Porter composed with Merman in mind would be discarded during rehearsals, one of which, "Buddie, Beware," was replaced by a reprise of "I Get a Kick Out of You" at Merman's request early in the run. Significantly, in sharp contrast to the fate that awaited him during the making of the film, Porter was asked to write the *entire* score. If a song didn't fit or the intended performer didn't like it, Porter himself would replace it with another.[21]

Although Broadway audiences appreciated Porter's sophisticated lyrics and music and the way Merman sang them, Paramount, immune to the delights of Porter and both oblivious and impervious to Merman's vocal and dramatic talents, came to a different conclusion about how to satisfy their film viewers. Consequently, Paramount greatly diminished the role Merman would play in her first film reenactment of a starring stage role.[22] Paramount's dim view of Porter's ability to create song hits became the rule rather the exception, beginning with RKO's decision to retain only one Porter song when transforming *Gay Divorce* into the newly titled film *The Gay Divorcee* (1934), the classic "Night and Day." The commercial wisdom of RKO's approach to success was reinforced when one of the added songs, "The Continental" (by Con Conrad and Herb Magidson), became the first song to win the Academy Award in the new Best Song category.[23]

Porter composed the scores to two more films in the 1930s, *Born to Dance* (1936), an original musical, and *Rosalie* (1937), the latter based loosely on a stage version composed by George Gershwin and Romberg with lyrics co-written by Ira Gershwin and Wodehouse. After *Anything Goes*, the most memorable film adaptations of Porter shows were delayed until the 1950s, *Kiss Me Kate* (1953) (unlike the stage version with no comma after *Me*), which in a rare exception was produced at MGM by Jack Cummings rather than by Freed, and the Freed Unit's *Silk Stockings* from 1957 as the Studio Era and MGM wound down (discussed in chapter 5). The 1936 film adaptation of *Anything Goes* retained only four of the eleven songs Broadway audiences heard in Porter's rich stage score. This amount of cutting remained par for the course until the 1950s, including the considerably altered dramatic scenario offered in the 1956 film remake.[24] What was unusual in 1936 was the film's retention, not only of the basic plot, but a considerable portion of the original stage dialogue, including many of the corny jokes.[25]

In an informative and nuanced study Allison Robbins uses *Anything Goes* to show the contrasting attitudes and needs of the Hollywood studio system and Broadway that led to a significantly altered end product expressly designed to serve Bing Crosby and Paramount's in-house songwriters.[26] The copyrights for the newly commissioned songs belonged to Paramount's publishing firm Famous Music Corp. and thus earned additional income for the studio through radio broadcasts, recordings, and sheet music sales. This system also saved money since the studios could now pay Porter less for fewer songs. A decade before attaining international fame for his rendition of "White Christmas," Crosby, already a recording superstar, was on the verge of becoming a major movie star as well when he was contracted to play the lead in Paramount's *Anything Goes*.[27] To fulfill studio expectations, Crosby needed songs that fit his voice and suited his personality. Paramount's stable of in-house songwriters was ready to supply them.

The four stage songs that Porter wrote to match Merman's vocal strengths were hits in their day and have maintained their classic status: "I Get a Kick Out of You," "You're the Top" (with Gaxton), and "Anything Goes" in Act I and "Blow, Gabriel, Blow" in Act II. One number was assigned to Gaxton without Merman, "All through the Night," an Act I duet Gaxton's character shared with his love interest, the wealthy ingénue Hope Harcourt.[28] The film dropped "Blow, Gabriel, Blow" entirely, retained only about twenty seconds of Merman singing "Anything Goes" (during the credits), and offered only a single verse and chorus of "I Get a Kick Out of You" near the beginning of the film.[29] Only Merman's duet, "You're the Top," significantly with Crosby, was given the full treatment (verse, multiple choruses, and a reprise). The only other Porter song retained in the film was the pseudo-sea chantey, "There'll Always Be a Lady Fair," first sung only by the Avalon Boys, a male quartet, then joined by Crosby in a reprise.

Paramount's stable of contracted composers proved extremely successful from the early days of sound film. Separately, but more often in collaboration, lyricist Leo Robin and composer Richard A. Whiting were responsible for six of Paramount's ten top-selling songs during these years, including three of the top four.[30] One of Robin's lyrics (with music by Ralph Rainger), the song "Please" from *The Big Broadcast* (1932), sung by Crosby in a purely singing role, sold the third most copies of any song during this period. Robin also set the lyrics to two of the three Crosby songs in the 1936 film version of *Anything Goes*, "Sailor Beware" with Whiting and "My Heart and I" with Friedrich Hollander. By contrast, Rodgers and Hart's "Isn't It Romantic?," originally sung by Maurice Chevalier in Paramount's *Love Me Tonight* (1932) and now regarded as one of the most memorable songs from any era, was only the eleventh top-selling song at 37,266 copies, far below that of "Please" (216,035 copies) and "Louise," the Robin-Whiting hit from *Innocents of Paris* (1929) which sold 385,058 copies and launched Chevalier into fame. Crosby's third song interpolation in *Anything Goes* featured music composed by Hoagy Carmichael with lyrics by Edward Heyman. Although Carmichael was by then well known for "Stardust" (1928), "Georgia on My Mind" (1930), and "Lazy River" (1931), "Moonburn" was the first of his many film songs.[31]

After the camera had already regularly shifted to view Crosby's antics while Merman performed "Shanghai-De-Ho" (lyrics by Robin and music by Frederick Hollander), an embarrassingly Orientalist diegetic (definition to follow) interpolated show number, Crosby gets on stage to join Merman toward the song's end with a few fragments of "You're the Top" thrown in. The addition of "Shanghai" in the film meant that Crosby was featured prominently in no less than six of the eight songs, only two of which were composed by Porter.[32] Despite this diminishment of Porter's contribution to the Paramount score, critics of interpolation can take some comfort that Crosby's three new songs not only suited the film star's vocal strengths but demonstrated their own intrinsic musical merits. Crosby, who began his career in the late 1920s as a pioneering jazz singer, recorded the added songs for Decca records in November 1935 (the film was released in February 1936) with a swinging instrumental trio of players taken from George Stoll and His Orchestra that included the jazz pianist Joe Sullivan, whose short but impressive solo in "Moonburn" resembles the usually inimitable Earl Hines.[33]

Although Porter was silent on the point, it is possible to imagine that Robin and Whiting's "Sailor Beware" might have even pleased the composer of "You're the Top" had they been placed in a different film musical. In addition to its intrinsic memorability, Robin and Whiting's song includes one overt borrowing (a reference to the opening of the traditional Scottish folk song "My Bonnie Lies over the Ocean") and one possible allusion. Whether intentional or not, the opening of the song's chorus unmistakably evokes the ascending scale and its rhythm in the opening phrase from Porter's "I Get a Kick Out of You."

House Rules in the 1930s (and the Man Who Broke Them)

The time period between *Show Boat* in 1927 and *Oklahoma!* in 1943 was mainly inhabited with stage musicals that did not survive beyond their era. Even the musicals that found a place in the repertoire, *Anything Goes* for example, usually did so with significant reworking of their books and scores. With the exception of Rodgers and Hart's *Pal Joey* (1940), revived with new orchestrations in 1952, it is a challenge to name a musical prior to *Oklahoma!* that returned to Broadway with its original book and score largely intact. In the case of *Show Boat*, after a virtually unaltered return engagement in 1932, future revivals, beginning with the significantly revised 1946 version supervised by Oscar Hammerstein II (with a new ending and a new final song by Kern), abandoned or replaced much of what viewers witnessed in 1927.

Porgy and Bess, with a book by DuBose Heyward, lyrics by Heyward and Ira Gershwin, and a score by George Gershwin, began its life on Broadway as a through-sung opera designed mainly for opera singers and remains a staple of the world's opera houses. When the work returned to Broadway in 1942, however, audiences witnessed a *Porgy and Bess* in which most of Gershwin's nearly continuous sung recitative was replaced with spoken dialogue. Operatic revivals of *Porgy* have generally exercised fidelity to the score and dramatic restraint, and even the newly conceived 2012 Broadway version of *Porgy and Bess* with an abbreviated and often rephrased libretto by Suzan-Lori Parks, new orchestrations by William David Brohn and Christopher Jahnke, and directed by Diane Paulus refrained from bringing in songs from other Gershwin stage works. *Crazy for You* (1992), based in part on Gershwin's 1930s hit *Girl Crazy*, exhibited a contrasting approach with the addition of a brand-new book based on the stage original and numerous song interpolations from other Gershwin sources. For the most part, the central legacy of shows that premiered between *Show Boat* and *Oklahoma!* more closely resembles what happened to *Girl Crazy/Crazy for You* rather than *Pal Joey* or even the Paulus revival: a treasure chest of autonomous songs from the Great American Songbook.

Although the majority of successful stage musicals were adapted into films, aside from a few prominent exceptions such as the 1936 *Show Boat*, it was the original film musicals such as those directed by Lubitsch (*The Love Parade*) and Mamoulian (*Love Me Tonight*), danced by Astaire and Rogers (*Top Hat*), or with songs performed by stars like Judy Garland (*The Wizard of Oz*) that gained the most critical distinction, popular appeal, and respect. Consequently, even the major Broadway songwriters were regularly forced either to compose songs for original films or to endure experiences similar to what happened to Porter's hit-filled *Anything Goes*. Now that we've witnessed the film adaptation fate of a Porter stage musical, here's a quick summary of what happened to Rodgers and Hart, the Gershwins, Berlin, and in the next section, more Porter shows and shows by Kurt Weill.

Three Rodgers and Hart stage scores in 1928 and 1929 were swiftly made into movies in 1930, *Present Arms* (retitled *Leathernecking*), *Spring Is Here*, and *Heads Up!*. None of these films included more than three songs from the stage versions. *Ever Green* (1930), a London musical that did not travel to New York, retained only two songs in its 1934 film adaptation (under the respelled title *Evergreen*). Perhaps even more disappointing, *Babes in Arms* (1937), arguably one of the richest stage scores of the 1930s, retained only two of its songs when transferred to film in 1939.[34] Although it presented the two George Balanchine ballets mostly unchanged, the film adaptation of *On Your Toes* (1936), also in 1939, found no use for *any* songs beyond melodic remnants relegated to orchestral underscoring. By then, Rodgers and Hart had redeemed their reputation in film with their original score to *Love Me Tonight* (1932), which remains widely regarded as one of the finest musical films ever made.[35]

At the dawn of the following decade, Gershwin's *Strike Up the Band* (1940) retained only its title song. In marked contrast to the lack of critical success enjoyed by the film adaptations of this and other 1930s stage musicals, however, the Gershwins created a memorable score for the Astaire-Rogers series (*Shall We Dance* in 1937) and another without Ginger (*A Damsel in Distress* also in 1937). Berlin achieved success by avoiding film adaptations of stage musicals altogether with his scores to three original Astaire-Rogers film musicals (*Top Hat*, *Follow the Fleet*, and *Carefree* between 1935 and 1938) and *Alexander's Ragtime Band* (1938). According to the Internet Musicals Database, the last, the first of the cavalcade or "jukebox" musicals based on older Berlin songs (and a few new ones), became the highest-grossing musical of any type the year it appeared.[36]

The career and reception of one composer, Jerome Kern (1885–1945), departs from this dismal disparity between the popularity and perceived quality of adaptations versus original film musicals. In fact, on more than one occasion the film adaptations of Kern's stage musicals survived the studio jungle intact, contradicting the fate suffered by his contemporaries. The next chapter will look at three successful films with music by Kern from among the eight film musicals adapted from thirty-eight stage works composed over the course of forty years. The three musicals are Kern's great 1927 hit *Show Boat* and two Kern hits from the 1930s, *The Cat and the Fiddle* (1931) and *Roberta* (1933). The film versions of all three shows managed to salvage a critical mass of songs as well as comparable narrative features of their stage sources at a time when film adaptations almost invariably elected to treat their stage sources with cavalier abandon.

The Commandments and Kern

The introduction of Kern provides a glimpse into a future still two decades away beginning shortly after the three sailors in *On the Town* (1949) completed their adventurous twenty-four hours on the town and returned to the Brooklyn Naval Yard. One might even be tempted to assert that the arrival in the 1950s of more faithful film adaptations of popular stage hits launched a new era that came with a new set of aesthetic principles. Ethan Mordden makes precisely this assertion in *When Broadway Went to Hollywood* and calls these principles Commandments, of which there are three:

1. Thou shalt cast by talent rather than by fame, if practical with the original Broadway star.
2. Thou shalt retain the original narrative structure and all or most of the score, without interpolations.
3. All right, thou mayest interpolate, but thou shalt let the original creators make the new numbers.

To which I propose a Fourth Commandment:

4. Thou mayest transform a singing character into a dancing one, but only if the metamorphosis is dramatically credible and enhances the narrative and the music.

While the changing approach to film adaptation began in earnest in the 1950s, it didn't begin *ex nihilo*. Just as the 1927 arrival of *Show Boat*, with its book and lyrics by Hammerstein and music by Kern, anticipated the Rodgers and Hammerstein *Oklahoma!* revolution in 1943, the 1936 Universal film adaptation of *Show Boat* anticipated Mordden's Commandments and future adaptations. For starters, it was cast by talent with several major roles duplicated by their original or touring actors and actresses, whose fame would arrive soon enough. Hammerstein's screenplay also closely followed the stage show, or at least the first three-fourths of it, and since Hammerstein was the author, the departures from the stage version in the remaining quarter possessed its own authorial authenticity. The original stage show contained too many songs to squeeze into a two-hour film, but most of the major songs were accounted for. Concerning interpolations, the original show itself, like other

Kern musicals, already contained several with Kern's blessing, most notably "After the Ball," Charles K. Harris's megahit from 1892. But as with most films in the 1950s in which the original songwriters supplied the interpolations, Hammerstein and Kern supplied all the new songs in the 1936 *Show Boat* film adaptation.

In *The Cat and the Fiddle*, Jeanette MacDonald was cast both for her fame and her talent. And in a major departure from pre-1950s norms, filmgoers get to hear most of the stage version's songs, albeit in newly conceived dramatic and musical contexts. When it came to *Roberta*, the film narrative was altered to accommodate the fame and dancing talents of Astaire and Rogers, thus anticipating (with varying success) a quintet of other films discussed in in *A Fine Romance*: *On the Town* (with Kelly and Vera-Ellen replacing stage stars), *Call Me Madam* (Donald O'Connor and Vera-Ellen), *Brigadoon* (Kelly and Charisse), *Silk Stockings* (Astaire and Charisse), and *Flower Drum Song* (Nancy Kwan and Reiko Sato).[37] Irene Dunne didn't star in the stage versions of either *Show Boat* or *Roberta* (although she did play the lead in a road company of the former), but as the female singing lead in both film adaptations she became indelibly associated with these and other film musicals with songs by Kern.[38]

In *Roberta*, some stage songs were cut or used as instrumental underscoring and two new Kern numbers replaced the lyrics of Otto Harbach with those of Dorothy Fields. Since Kern didn't mind interpolations, the insertion of "Indiana" did not constitute a sacrilege of Mordden's interpolation Commandment. This last point prompts me to offer a friendly amendment to his Third Commandment: that interpolations are permitted if film producers and directors are savvy enough to enlist composers and lyricists like Arlen (music) and Harburg (lyrics), Carmichael (music) with Heyman or Harold Adamson (lyrics), or Whiting (music) and Robin (lyrics), songwriters who could produce work that successfully complements the fine scores by Duke and Latouche, Porter, and Jule Styne.[39] Classic and dramatically appropriate interpolations such as "After the Ball" in *Show Boat* and "Indiana" in *Roberta* were also acceptable.

Although the three film adaptations with music by Kern examined in chapter 2 take greater liberties than *Oklahoma!* and *West Side Story*, it bears repeating that the relative fidelity to the stage narratives and scores demonstrated in these Kern films was the exception to the rule in their day. On the eve of a new decade, the film version of *On the Town* would continue to thrive under the old rules. Although it followed the basic outline of the stage narrative and its Broadway librettists, Comden and Green who wrote the screenplay, the film's casting was determined neither by the purported talents of the stage characters or the performers who played them. Unfortunately, in matching the vocal and dancing demands to new talent, Bernstein's score was suppressed and replaced by new songs with music by Edens, although fortunately these new songs employed the original lyricists, Comden and Green.

From Stage to Film in the 1940s: Some Preliminaries

When it came to the preservation of their musical stage legacies, the five Porter musicals among the sixteen 1940s films listed in Appendix 3, like *Anything Goes*, were doomed to an unhappy fate.[40] The three shows starring Merman—*Du Barry Was a Lady*, *Panama Hattie*, and *Something for the Boys*—as well as *Let's Face It!* and *Mexican Hayride*, were hits in their day and filmed within five years of their theatrical debuts. Four earned a healthy profit with *Du Barry* earning $2.2 million and *Hayride* $1.3 million. Since studios measured their successes mainly by profits, the ends justified the means, although the financial rewards came at the expense of Porter's scores obliged to share screen time with songs by in-house studio composers.

Let's Face It salvaged the most Porter songs, four (the same as Paramount's *Anything Goes* in 1936) to which were added three song interpolations by Styne.[41] *Hattie* and *Du Barry*, both without Merman, each used three Porter songs along with two by MGM's composer-in-residence Edens, who would later contribute songs to *On the Town* among many other musical films. *Something for the Boys*, also without Merman, used only the title song from the stage version, while *Hayride*'s film audiences heard *no* songs from the original show.

Film adaptations of Kurt Weill's musicals provide further evidence of how the studio system savaged the stage properties they purchased. Although rarely staged today, two musicals with scores by Weill were among Broadway's biggest hits in the early 1940s: *Lady in the Dark* (1941) and *One Touch of Venus* (1943). Both received film adaptations within a few years with severely slashed scores. *Lady*, the earlier adaptation (Paramount in 1944), retained long stretches of dialogue, which made up roughly half of the stage time. The extended musical dream ballets, for the most part devoid of dialogue, were cut mercilessly. These studio decisions resulted in the removal of most of the Glamour Dream and the Wedding Dream. The film of *Lady* also replaced "This Is New" with "Suddenly It's Spring" by James Van Heusen and Johnny Burke in the Wedding Dream and removed Danny Kaye's tour de force patter song based on Russian names, "Tschaikowsky," from the Circus Dream. Perhaps most regrettably, the film version inflicted a mortal wound to the stage work when it removed the song "My Ship," the song that provided the central key to the show's meaning. Despite (or because) of the major surgery performed on this wartime hit starring Gertrude Lawrence, the refashioned *Lady*, now with Ginger Rogers, achieved considerable financial success. The film's $4.3 million gross made it the fourth-largest grossing movie of 1944 of which $1.7 million was pure profit.

The eighty-two-minute Hollywood version of *One Touch of Venus* (Universal 1948), which type-cast Ava Gardner as Venus, removed still more material from its glorious stage version that featured Mary Martin in her breakthrough role as Venus with imaginative choreography by Agnes de Mille with the Broadway *On the Town*'s Sono Osato as featured dancer. Adding collateral damage, the film version of *Venus* preserved only three songs, "Speak Low, "That's Him," and "Foolish Heart," and viewers were made to wait for thirty-three minutes to hear any of them.[42]

Despite all these unkind cuts, in contrast to the 1940s Porter film adaptations, Weill's *Lady in the Dark*, and Bernstein's *On the Town*, the adaptation of *One Touch of Venus* contained no songs by *other* composers. The reason that *Venus* was spared this indignity can be traced to Weill's experiences with the film adaptations of *Lady* and *Knickerbocker Holiday* (1938), which motivated him to request a "non-interpolation clause," a clause that prohibited the use of music by other composers (Porter and Bernstein's contracts did not contain this clause).[43] As a result, the abbreviated *Venus* contained music only by Weill (with new lyrics for one of the three selected songs). The result was debatably not a musical at all but a straight play with isolated songs inserted sporadically to interrupt the dialogue.

Although at 156 performances the Broadway production of *Cabin in the Sky* was a *succès d'estime* rather than a commercial hit, its 1943 film produced by Freed, the first MGM musical directed by Minnelli, earned nearly $600,000. This leaves Freed's *On the Town* as the only bona fide 1940s hit on stage *and* film in which both versions were produced before the end of the decade. *Town* earned $2.3 million, more than the most profitable Porter or Weill film. Although location shooting dates back at least to *Applause* (Mamoulian's debut as a film director) in 1929, *Town* took fuller cinematic advantage of location filming, at least in the rapid montage of the film's iconic opening number, "New York, New York." Although *On the Town* has slipped in critical stature over the years, and despite its infidelity to the stage version, the first film to be co-directed by Kelly and Donen continues to be appreciated as a noteworthy film musical on its own cinematic terms, aided by a talented cast, terrific dance numbers, and even a few song classics here and there by Bernstein.

From the 1940s to the 1950s: Toward Great Fidelity

With the arrival of Rodgers and Hammerstein's *Oklahoma!* in 1943, Broadway creators began to acquire greater clout. For many historians, what followed was a Golden Age that extended to *Fiddler on the Roof* (1964) and perhaps as late as *Cabaret* two years later.[44] Soon film studios and their viewing audiences cultivated a taste for film adaptations that more closely approximated what they saw and heard on stage, read in published librettos, sang from the published vocal selections, and listened to on original Broadway cast albums that entered the marketplace on 78 rpm records starting with *Oklahoma!* and a few other shows. With the arrival of the LP (long-playing record) in the late 1940s, most shows were recorded, the popular songs were published, and published librettos became increasingly common.[45]

Through these channels Broadway directly entered the homes of millions of aficionados, many of whom had yet to see the shows in New York, in their home cities, or on the stages of their local high schools. In the 1930s, when only eight book shows (as opposed to revues) ran longer than 300 performances, stage musicals that ran nearly this long were most often adapted into films within three years of closing.[46] In large part due to their longer runs, a far smaller percentage of 1940s stage hits (9 out of 22) arrived on film by the end of that decade. A number of film versions of hit 1940s shows were delayed far longer, arriving in the 1950s or even later: *Brigadoon* (7 years); *South Pacific* (9 years); *Carmen Jones* (11 years); *Carousel* (11 years); *Oklahoma!* (12 years); *Pal Joey* (17 years); *Finian's Rainbow* (21 years); and *Song of Norway* (26 years).

Perhaps not surprisingly, the film versions of 1940s hits that appeared on stage before the decade was out, including *On the Town*, were for the most part less faithful to the Commandments than the 1940s stage shows whose film adaptations were delayed until the 1950s and beyond. Take for example Berlin's 1940 hit musical *Louisiana Purchase*, which at 444 performances was a marginally greater hit than the longest-running show of the 1930s, *Of Thee I Sing* (1931), the first Broadway show to win the Pulitzer Prize, which ran 441 performances. The movie version of *Louisiana Purchase*, which arrived at the end of the following year, retained three original cast members, including Moore, who played to perfection the sometimes shrewd and sometimes bungling Senator Oliver P. Loganberry, but replaced Moore's ubiquitous leading man partner Gaxton with Bob Hope, who had a greater film following.[47] At the same time, it removed, as did Paramount's *Anything Goes*, all but four of the stage songs as well as a major dance number. The film version of *Louisiana* also skewed the trajectory of the stage show by presenting most of the retained songs within a thirteen-minute section of the film, arriving after a nearly forty-five-minute gap that followed the film's opening number.

As with the adaptation of *One Touch of Venus*, the excruciating delay threatened to turn the film into a spoken play. In the absence of a cast album and a score that boasted only one well-known song, "It's a Lovely Day Tomorrow," the film chose to abandon most of it. The stage version was eventually reconstructed and resuscitated in New York for a limited six-concert performance engagement in 1996, leading to a welcome recording of an unjustifiably neglected Berlin score.[48]

Decades can be arbitrary. No one pressed a button on January 1, 1950, mandating that henceforward film adaptations would follow Mordden's Commandments and strive to be more faithful to their stage sources. Nevertheless, just as some film studios in the late 1920s soon realized the benefits of switching from silent to sound film and did so swiftly (ironically MGM was the last major to join in), studios were quick to rethink how to approach adaptation soon after the 1940s turned into the 1950s. *On the Town* and *Call Me Madam* (both discussed in chapter 3), offer instructive examples of what happened and why during the course of four years when, with some exceptions, film studios noticeably began to alter their modus operandi in adapting their stage sources. Clearly, studio executives realized by then that the most effective way to preserve their investment and achieve continued financial success was to produce adaptations that adhered more closely to the narratives, dialogue, and song content of the stage hits—and they were willing to pay more than a million dollars to secure the rights for some of these (*Oklahoma!*, *The Music Man*, *Cabaret*) and far more in the case of *My Fair Lady* ($5.5 million).[49] In short, when it came to film adaptations, it now paid to be faithful.

Note also that a number of 1950s film adaptations of hit musicals chose *not* to obey the teachings of the Commandments, and often these films also fared well financially. This is especially true for the belated film remakes of such 1920s and 1930s hit shows as the 1951 adaptation of *Show Boat*, the reworked version of *Roberta* (renamed *Lovely to Look At* in 1952), and the more extensively retooled *Anything Goes* in 1956. With the exception of MGM's 1951 remake of *Show Boat*, these adaptations largely ignored the corresponding stage narratives and song content. *Lovely to Look At* and *Anything Goes* also violated Holy Writ by inserting one or more interpolated songs not composed by Kern or Porter.

Before moving on to the more faithful adaptations of the 1950s and 1960s discussed in this survey, it might prove instructive to briefly consider two other non-faithful adaptations of 1940s stage musicals into 1950s films: *Brigadoon* (stage 1947; film 1954) and *Gentlemen Prefer Blondes* (stage 1949; film 1953). In the Preface, I stated my position concerning *Brigadoon* (chapter 4) with its pre-1950s approach to adaptation. Simply put, the decisions to cast dancers (Kelly and Charisse) instead of singers, to remove half of the integral stage songs, and to discard virtually all remnants of de Mille's choreography in the film version precluded me from making a strong case on its behalf.

In contrast, *Gentlemen Prefer Blondes* serves as a reminder that fidelity can be overrated. Despite its even more radical reworking of its stage material, including altering much of the plot and retaining only three songs from an excellent stage score with lyrics by Robin and music by Styne, I contend that *Blondes* should be considered a successful musical film adaptation. What makes it work are the fine performances by Jane Russell and Marilyn Monroe and their supporting cast, the imaginative direction by Howard Hawks and choreography by Jack Cole, and perhaps most surprisingly, two excellent interpolated songs by Carmichael and Adamson.

When discussing the well-considered decision to expand the dance component in *Call Me Madam* (chapter 3), or the more substantial re-imaginings in the film adaptations of *Silk Stockings* (chapter 5) and *Cabaret* (chapter 8), I support Barrios, who included the *Gentlemen Prefer Blondes* adaptation among his 50 *Must-See Musicals*. Barrios found the substantial departures "not so much distorting or reductive as they are transformational" and credited the transformation from stage to film as "one of the first 'reimagined' musical adaptations, like *Cabaret* (1972) or *Chicago* (2002)."[50]

Both *On the Town* (1944) and *Annie Get Your Gun* (1946) were stage hits. The latter enjoyed a far longer run, however, at 1,147 performances, one of the longest of the decade, more than double that of *On the Town*'s 463 performances. In December 1949 the MGM film version of *Town* arrived with its reduced Bernstein score. In April 1950 Berlin's *Annie* appeared in a version that more closely resembled its stage version and without song interpolations by interloping studio composers. Both films were commercial successes, although here too *On the Town*'s profit of $2.3 million was greatly surpassed by *Annie Get Your Gun*'s $4 million, enough to make it the most profitable musical film of the year. Once again, the studio system proved that it understood its market, this time by taking a new approach and preserving much from the stage model.

Despite exceptions like *Brigadoon* and *Gentlemen Prefer Blondes*, the trend in film adaptations of stage musicals in the 1950s and early 1960s moved in the direction of fidelity. In future chapters we will watch this play out in *Oklahoma!*, *Silk Stockings*, *West Side Story*, and *Flower Drum Song*. Freed, who produced the film versions of both *Brigadoon* and *Gentlemen Prefer Blondes*, shelled out $700,000 for the screen rights to *Annie Get Your Gun*, banking on the idea that a more faithful adaptation would be a good bet, especially since Berlin, unlike Bernstein, had demonstrated his success as a songwriter in a string of hit movies, most recently *Easter Parade* (1948), also produced by the Freed Unit.

The 1950 film adaptation of *Annie Get Your Gun* thus retained ten of the stage hit's original fifteen songs.[51] Compared with future adaptations, this amounts to a lot of deleted songs, but relative to adaptations produced by its 1930s and 1940s predecessors, including *On the Town*, it was a step in a new direction. The retention of *most*—and sometimes all or nearly all the songs from a stage score—along with the decision to preserve more of the stage plot and dialogue, would guide the majority of film adaptations during the final years of the studio system and throughout the 1960s.

Table 1.2 offers a list of thirty-one selected musical film adaptations from *Annie Get Your Gun* in 1950 to *The Sound of Music* in 1965. Fourteen of these films, including the five shows from this time frame explored in this volume (highlighted in bold), removed three or fewer songs from their stage source: *Kiss Me Kate*, *Damn Yankees*, and *The Sound of Music* (three deleted songs); **Oklahoma!**, *Carousel*, and **Silk Stockings** (two deleted songs); **Call Me Madam**, *The Music Man*, **Flower Drum Song**, and *Gypsy* (one deleted song); and *Carmen Jones*, *South Pacific*, **West Side Story**, and *My Fair Lady* (no deleted songs).[52] With three exceptions all the films in Table 1.2 that added new songs also religiously followed the Commandment to honor their stage parents and not interpolate the work of other song gods in their film manifestations.[53]

Other Continuities from Stage to Screen

The Commandment to retain a star on screen, if practical (or, as a corollary, other members from the original stage show) became an increasingly common practice during the 1950s and 1960s.[54] Here are a few prominent examples: *Call Me Madam* (Merman); *Guys and Dolls* (Vivian Blaine and Stubby Kaye); *The King and I* (Yul Brynner); *The Pajama Game* (John Raitt, Eddie Foy Jr., and Carol Haney); *Damn Yankees* (Gwen Verdon and Ray Walston); *My Fair Lady* (Rex Harrison and Stanley Holloway); *L'il Abner* (Peter Palmer, Howard St. John, Stubby Kaye, and Julie Newmar); *South Pacific* (Juanita Hall and Walston); *Bells Are Ringing* (Judy Holliday); *Flower Drum Song* (Miyoshi Umeki, Hall, and Jack Soo); and *The Music Man* (Robert Preston, Pert Kelton, and the Buffalo Bills).

Although not mentioned in the Commandments, the recycling of directors, choreographers, and director-choreographers from hit 1950s musicals also frequently provided a major continuity between the stage and film versions, a continuity demonstrated with particular force in the case of *West Side Story*. Ironically, unlike the other adaptations noted in the last paragraph, the film version of *West Side Story* retained only three members of the Broadway cast, all in smaller roles.[55] To ensure continuity, which more than compensated for Mirisch's decision to cast and then dub non-singing actors in most of the major roles, the film relied on director-choreographer Jerome Robbins to recreate the choreography that contributed so markedly to the work's artistry and power on stage. As we'll see in chapter 6, the importance of this decision was immense.

More examples of successful stage-to-film choreographic transfers include Bob Fosse's work in *The Pajama Game* and *Damn Yankees*, Michael Kidd's recreation of Runyonland in *Guys and Dolls*, and Onna White's River City in *The*

Table 1.2 Deleted and Added Songs in 31 Selected Musical Film Adaptations from 1950 to 1965.

1950

Annie Get Your Gun (MGM) [stage 1946]
> *Deleted:* "I'm a Bad, Bad Man"; "Moonshine Lullaby"; "I Got Lost in His Arms"; "I'll Share It All with You"; "Who Do You Love, I Hope"

1952

Where's Charley? (Warner Bros) [stage 1948]
> *Deleted:* "The Years Before Us"; "Serenade with Asides"; "Lovelier Than Ever"; "The Woman in His Room"; "The Gossips"; "My Darling, My Darling"

1953

CALL ME MADAM (20th Century-Fox) [stage 1950]
> *Deleted:* "Once Upon a Time Today"
> *Added:* "What Chance Have I with Love?" (replaced "Once Upon a Time Today"); Berlin's early hit "That International Rag"

Gentlemen Prefer Blondes (20th Century-Fox) [stage 1949]
> *Deleted:* All but three Styne and Robin stage songs ("A little Girl from Little Rock," "Bye, Bye, Baby," and "Diamonds Are a Girl's Best Friend") were cut.
> *Added:* "Ain't There Anyone Here for Love?"; "When Love Goes Wrong" (music by Hoagy Carmichael; lyrics by Harold Adamson)

Kiss Me Kate (MGM) [stage 1948]
> *Deleted:* "Another Op'nin, Another Show"; "I Sing of Love"; "I Am Ashamed That Women Are So Simple" (spoken only)
> *Added:* "From This Moment On" (from Porter's *Out of This World*)

1954

BRIGADOON (MGM) [stage 1947]
> *Deleted:* "The Love of My Life"; "Jeannie's Packin' Up"; "Come to Me, Bend to Me"; Sword Dance; "There But for You Go I"; "My Mother's Weddin' Day"; Funeral Dance; "From This Day On"

Carmen Jones (20th Century-Fox) [stage 1943]
> *Deleted:* none
> *Added:* none

1955

OKLAHOMA! (Magna) [stage 1943]
> *Deleted:* "It's a Scandal! It's a Outrage!"; "Lonely Room"

Guys and Dolls (MGM) [stage 1950]
> *Deleted:* "A Bushel and a Peck"; "My Time of Day"; "I've Never Been in Love Before"; "My Time of Day"; "More I Cannot Wish You"; "Marry the Man Today"
> *Added:* "Pet Me, Poppa" (replaced "A Bushel and a Peck"); "A Woman in Love" (replaced "I've Never Been in Love Before"); "Adelaide"

Kismet (MGM) [stage 1953]
> *Deleted:* "Rhymes Have I"; "Bazaar of the Caravans"; "He's in Love"; "Gesticulate"; "Was I Wazir"; "Rahadlakum"
> *Added:* "Bored" (cut from the 1953 Broadway production)

Table 1.2 Continued

1956
Carousel (**20th Century-Fox**) [**stage 1945**]
    Deleted: "Geraniums in the Winder" (and "Stonecutters Cut It on Stone"); "The Highest Judge of All"

The King and I (**20th Century-Fox**) [**stage 1951**]
    Deleted: "My Lord and Master"; "Shall I Tell You What I Think of You"; "Western People Funny"; "I Have Dreamed"

Anything Goes (**Paramount**) [**stage 1934**]
    Deleted: "Bon Voyage"; "There'll Always Be a Lady Fair"; "Where Are the Men?"; "Public Enemy Number One"; "Be Like the Bluebird"; "The Gypsy in Me"
    Added: "It's De-Lovely" (from Porter's *Red, Hot and Blue*); "Ya Gotta Give the People Hoke," "A Second Hand Turban and a Crystal Ball," and "You Can Bounce Right Back" were composed by Sammy Cahn (lyrics) and James Van Heusen (music).

1957
SILK STOCKINGS (**MGM**) [**stage 1955**]
    Deleted: "Hail, Bibinski"; "As on through the Seasons We Sail"
    Added: "Fated to Be Mated"; "The Ritz Roll and Rock"

The Pajama Game (**Warner Bros.**) [**stage 1954**]
    Deleted: "A New Town Is a Blue Town"; "Sleep-Tite"; "Her Is"; "The World Around Us"; "Think of the Time I Save"

Pal Joey (**Columbia**) [**stage 1940**]
    Deleted: "What Is a Man?"; "The Flower Garden of My Heart"; "Den of Iniquity"; "Take Him"
    Abbreviated: "Do It the Hard Way" (fragment); "Happy Hunting Horn" (brief orchestral statement); "Plant You Now, Dig You Later" (orchestral underscoring); "You Mustn't Kick It Around" (orchestra); "What Do I Care for a Dame?" (orchestral statement in Dream Sequence and Finale along with "Bewitched" and "I Could Write a Book")
    Added: "There's a Small Hotel" (from Rodgers and Hart's *On Your Toes*); "The Lady Is a Tramp" and "My Funny Valentine" (from Rodgers and Hart's *Babes in Arms*); "I Didn't Know What Time It Was" (from Rodgers and Hart's *Too Many Girls*)

1958
South Pacific (**20th Century-Fox**) [**stage 1949**]
    Deleted: none
    Added: "My Girl Back Home" (cut from the 1949 Broadway production)

Damn Yankees (**Warner Bros.**) [**stage 1956**]
    Deleted: "Near to You"; "The Game"; "A Man Doesn't Know"
    Added: "There's Something about an Empty Chair"

1959
Porgy and Bess (**Columbia**) [**stage 1935**]
    Deleted: "Jasbo Brown Blues"; "Leavin' for the Promis' Lan'"; "It Take a Long Pull to Get There"; "Buzzard Song"

(continued)

Table 1.2 Continued

L'il Abner (Paramount) [stage 1956]
　Deleted: "What's Good for General Bullmoose"; "Oh, Happy Day"; "Love in a Home";
　　"Progress Is the Root of All Evil"; "Society Party"
　Added: "Room Enuf for Us"

1960
Can-Can (20th Century-Fox) [stage 1953]
　Deleted: "Never Give Anything Away"; "If You Loved Me Truly"; "Never, Never Be an
　　Artist"; "Every Man Is a Stupid Man"; "I Love Paris" (sung over the credits)
　Added: "Let's Do It" (from Porter's *Paris*); "Just One of Those Things" (from Porter's
　　Jubilee); "You Do Something to Me" (from Porter's *Fifty Million Frenchmen*)

Bells Are Ringing (MGM 1960) [stage 1956]
　Deleted: "Bells Are Ringing"; "On My Own"; "You've Got to Do It"; "Is It a Crime?";
　　"Hello, Hello There"; "Long Before I Knew You"; "Mu-Cha-Cha" (significantly
　　reduced); "Salzburg"; "The Midas Touch" (abbreviated)
　Added: "Do It Yourself" (replaced "On My Own"); "Better Than a Dream" (replaced
　　"Long Before I Knew You")

1961
WEST SIDE STORY (The Mirisch Company) [stage 1957]
　Deleted: none, but the "Somewhere Ballet" was cut

FLOWER DRUM SONG (Universal-International) [stage 1958]
　Deleted: none, but "Like a God" was spoken only and abbreviated

1962
The Music Man (Warner Bros.) [stage 1957]
　Deleted: "My White Knight"
　Added: "Being in Love" (replaced "My White Knight," which shares the same musical
　　content in its middle verse)

Gypsy (Warner Bros.) [stage 1959]
　Deleted: "Together Wherever We Go"

Jumbo (MGM) [stage 1935]
　Deleted: "Laugh"; "The Sing of the Roustabouts"; "Women"; "Memories of Madison
　　Square Garden"
　Added: "Why Can't I?" (from Rodgers and Hart's *Spring Is Here*); "This Can't Be Love"
　　(from Rodgers and Hart's *The Boys from Syracuse*); "Sawdust, Spangles and Dreams"
　　(Roger Edens)

1963
Bye Bye Birdie (Columbia) [stage 1960]
　Deleted: "An English Teacher"; "A Normal, American Boy"; "Wounded"; "Hymn for a
　　Sunday Evening"; "What Did I Ever See in Him?"; "Baby, Talk to Me"; "Spanish Rose"
　Added: "Bye Bye Birdie" (sung over the credits)

1964
The Unsinkable Molly Brown (MGM) [stage 1960]
　Deleted: All but four stage songs were cut ("Belly Up to the Bar, Boys," "I Ain't Down
　　Yet," "I'll Never Say No," and "Johnny's Soliloquy")
　Added: "Colorado, My Home" (cut from the 1960 Broadway production); "He's My
　　Friend"

Table 1.2 Continued

My Fair Lady (Warner Bros.) [stage 1956]
  Deleted: none

1965
The Sound of Music (20th Century-Fox) [stage 1959]
  Deleted: "How Can Love Survive?"; "No Way to Stop It"; "An Ordinary Couple"
  Added: "I Have Confidence"; "Something Good" (replaced "An Ordinary Couple")

• Musicals discussed in *A Fine Romance* are placed in capital letters.

Music Man. Jack Cole, who choreographed *Kismet* on the stage, was also asked to recreate his vision of Middle Eastern exotic dancing in the film version. Other original stage directors who returned to direct the film adaptation include George Abbott (*The Pajama Game* and *Damn Yankees*) and Joshua Logan (*South Pacific*).[56]

In the case of *Oklahoma!* the decision to use de Mille's original stage choreography was a significant factor in the success of its film version. Its absence in *Brigadoon* was a critical flaw, unredeemed by the fine dancing of Kelly and Charisse and the latter's dialogue coach (both works are discussed in chapter 4). Likewise, the retention of Robbins's choreography in the film versions of *The King and I* and *West Side Story* (as opposed to *On the Town*) preserved some of the most memorable features of the stage versions in their new cinematic settings. But only in *West Side Story* did Robbins serve as *both* co-director and choreographer. The film is much the better for it.

The Sunset of a Golden Age: *West Side Story* and *Cabaret*

The stage and film versions of *West Side Story* (stage 1957; film 1961) and *Cabaret* (stage 1966; film 1972) are among the best-remembered and most discussed of any shows and musical films. By nearly every measure, these shows and the films based on them have enjoyed extraordinary popular and commercial success and critical acclaim. Although Robbins received the Tony Award for choreography and Oliver Smith for scenic design, the stage version of *West Side Story* was famously overshadowed by *The Music Man.* Facing less competition with shows like *I Do! I Do!* and *The Apple Tree*, *Cabaret* fared better, capturing eight Tony Awards, including Director (Hal Prince), Score (John Kander and Fred Ebb), Choreography (Ronald Field), Set Design (Boris Aronson), and Feature Actor (Joel Grey), capped off by the evening's biggest prize, the award for Best Musical. Both musicals also enjoyed runs that were among the longest of their respective decades, *West Side Story*, the twelfth longest-running 1950s musical at 734 performances, and *Cabaret*, the tenth longest-running musical of the 1960s with 1,165 performances.[57] Thirty-two years later, the 1998 *Cabaret* revival returned in a production directed by Sam Mendes that at 2,377 performances more than doubled its original run, making it the second-longest running musical revival of all time.[58]

Both film adaptations also enjoyed considerable commercial success. *West Side Story* earned $44 million, making it not only the highest grossing film of 1961 but the highest grossing musical film up to that time (surpassed a few years later by *The Sound of Music*). With its smaller initial budget of $4.6 million, *Cabaret*'s box office gross of $4.8 million surpassed *West Side Story*'s profit margin by a nose, $38.2 million to $37.5 million. Both films also enjoyed major triumphs on Oscar night. *West Side Story* won ten of its eleven nominations, including Best Picture, Best Direction (Robert Wise and Jerome Robbins), Best Supporting Actor (George Chakiris as Bernardo), and Supporting Actress (Rita Moreno as Anita), and is currently ranked #2 in the American Film Institute's (AFI) list of the Greatest Movie Musicals of All Time.

In a year when it was "fated to be mated" (to appropriate a song title added to the film adaptation of *Silk Stockings*) with Francis Ford Coppola's *The Godfather*, *Cabaret* did surprisingly well in its time and since. In fact, it was nominated for ten awards and won eight of them, including Liza Minnelli as Best Actress, Joel Grey triumphing over three Best Supporting Actor *Godfather* nominees, and Bob Fosse taking the prize for Best Director over the heavily favored Coppola. The only losses were in the Adapted Screenplay and Best Picture categories, falling short in the latter to *The Godfather,* its iconic contemporary rival. It was the first and only time a film that won so many awards did not win this high profile award. In the big picture, *Cabaret* also ranks nearly as high as *West Side Story* in the AFI's elite list of Great Movie Musicals at #5.

In addition to their craft and entertainment value, *West Side Story* and *Cabaret* introduced startling serious subject matter for a genre that for decades was labeled "musical comedy." As encapsulated by its librettist Arthur Laurents, *West Side Story* "was the beginning of it being OK to die, to be raped, [and] to be murdered in a musical."[59] Indeed, by the end of Act I audiences nightly witnessed a vicious (and well-choreographed) knife fight between rival gangs, the Jets and the Sharks in a "Rumble" that resulted in the murders of two major characters, Riff (a Jet based on Shakespeare's Mercutio) and Bernardo (a Shark based on Tybalt). The musical's central male protagonist, Tony (Romeo), was gunned down by Chino (Paris) near the end of the evening with barely enough time (or breath) to sing a couple of phrases of "Somewhere," the love song he had sung with his beloved Maria (Juliet) not long before.

Hal Prince, who directed *Cabaret* on stage, recalled that even without sexually outing Clifford, the central male love interest in *Cabaret*, as bisexual or gay, he "felt at the time that audiences had enough to handle—two doomed romances, Nazis, Sally's abortion—without inflicting Isherwood's homosexuality on them as well."[60] By the time *Cabaret* was adapted to film, viewers could accept a newly bisexual Brian (Clifford's screen name) who had sexual relations, not only with Sally Bowles, but with Maximillian van Heune. The musical was changing and *West Side Story* and *Cabaret* led the way, both on stage and film.

In *AFI's 101 Years . . . 100 Movies* honor roll, *West Side Story* ranked #41 in 1998 and #51 in 2007, while *Cabaret*, which didn't make the list in 1998, ranked #63 in the 10th Anniversary polling. The long-standing critical respect these films have received was to become still more dramatically evident when in 2006 the American Film Institute placed *West Side Story* second and *Cabaret* fifth in their exclusive list of 100 musicals.[61] *A Fine Romance* ends happily with the film version of *Cabaret*. For an encapsulated summary of highlights that followed *Cabaret*, readers are directed to the concluding remarks in the *Cabaret* chapter (chapter 8).

2

Surviving in the 1930s Movie Studio Jungle

Jerome Kern and *Show Boat, The Cat and the Fiddle,* and *Roberta*

The Outlier

In the early days of the sound film, one Broadway composer perhaps more than any of his contemporaries saw his musicals survive the Hollywood studio jungle intact: Jerome Kern (1885–1945). More remarkably, Kern did it twice, and a third film director almost pulled it off a third time. On the other hand, about half of the film musicals based on stage musicals with a score by Kern and his lyricists, usually Oscar Hammerstein II (1895–1960) or Otto Harbach (1873–1963), demonstrate Hollywood's attitude at the time toward song retention in adapting stage musicals to the screen. For starters, only two songs remained in the 1929 adaptation of *Sally* (1920), "Look for the Silver Lining" (lyrics by Buddy De Sylva) and "Wild Rose" (lyrics by Clifford Grey).[1] The 1930 film adaptation of *Sunny* (1925) used only one Kern song from the stage version, "Who?," while adding a new Kern song for the film, "I Was Alone," both of which shared lyric credit between Hammerstein and Harbach. At the end of his stage career, despite the film successes showcased in this chapter, the studio retained only one song from the film adaptation of Kern's final stage musical *Very Warm for May* (1939), retitled *Broadway Rhythm* (1944). This song was the classic "All the Things You Are" with lyrics by Hammerstein.

Other Kern films fared well for his era when it came to song retention. The film versions of *Sweet Adeline* (stage 1929; film 1935) and *Music in the Air* (stage 1932; film 1934), both with lyrics by Hammerstein, are a case in point. *Sweet Adeline* retained eight of the seventeen songs from the stage version. Only four songs were dropped from *Music in the Air*, although unfortunately (and surprisingly) one of these expunged songs was "The Song Is You," probably the show's greatest hit.

This chapter examines how Kern's film adaptations contradict the norms suffered by his contemporaries. It does this by focusing on three film successes among Kern's eight film musicals adapted from his thirty-eight stage works composed over the course of forty years. The chapter leaves unexplored the nine original film musicals that included a trio of bona fide film classics filled with

A Fine Romance. Geoffrey Block, Oxford University Press. © Oxford University Press 2023.
DOI: 10.1093/oso/9780197501733.003.0002

memorable songs, *Swing Time* (1936) (with its Academy Award–winning "The Way You Look Tonight"), *You Were Never Lovelier* (1942), *Cover Girl* (1944), and one *succès d'estime, High, Wide and Handsome* (1937).[2]

The three musicals explored here offer three divergent approaches to song retention. The 1936 film version of *Show Boat* (stage 1927) cut several songs but left the majority of the score intact and added three important new songs, all by Kern. The 1935 film version of *Roberta* (1933) kept only four songs ("Let's Begin," "Yesterdays," and "Smoke Gets in Your Eyes" with lyrics by Harbach, and "I'll Be Hard to Handle" with lyrics by Harbach's nephew Bernard Dougall). On the plus side, it also added one new Kern song ("Lovely to Look At") with lyrics by his new lyricist Dorothy Fields (1904–1974) and recycled a song he had previously composed with Hammerstein ("I Won't Dance") with mostly new lyrics by Fields. It also found a way to use most of the other songs from the stage work as underscoring. Remarkably, the 1934 film version of *The Cat and the Fiddle* (1931) managed to retain *all* the songs but at the same time seriously fiddled with the dramatic contexts and meaning of most of these songs.

The 1936 adaptation of *Show Boat* continues to enjoy, and deserve, high critical regard unsurpassed by its contemporaries and most future adaptations, despite justifiable concerns about its perpetuation of racial stereotypes and insensitivities. The film version of the all-but-forgotten *The Cat and the Fiddle* has far more to recommend it than its pioneering use of three-strip Technicolor in the final reel and deserves another (and closer) look. *Roberta*, the third film in the historic partnership between Fred Astaire and Ginger Rogers, while less known than some of the films that followed in the series, has continued to gain in critical stature, both as a film musical in its own right and as an adaptation. In fact, at least one commentator, besides the present author, singled out *Roberta* as the first film adaptation to surpass its stage model in imagination and execution.[3]

SHOW BOAT
(Broadway 1927; Universal 1936)

The historic operetta-musical comedy hybrid *Show Boat*, with a book and lyrics by Hammerstein and music by Kern, has undergone continuous transformations in numerous stage revivals in New York and London since its Broadway premiere in 1927.[4] It has also inspired numerous light opera and opera company productions since 1940, three film versions (1929, 1936, and 1951), and several high-profile television broadcasts.[5] Todd Decker, in his detailed study of the racial history of this work, goes as far as to assert that "the bold choice to put Black and white music, dance, characters, and themes into the same show. . . makes

Show Boat the most important musical ever made and also necessitated its remaking again and again."[6]

Show Boat was based on a popular novel by Edna Ferber, which took readers from the 1870s to the then-present when the book was published in 1926. Unlike most (if not all) musicals of its time, *Show Boat* was truly epic in scope, covering most of Ferber's half-century narrative saga. Even so, it was less epic than Ferber's novel, since it removed the childhood years of Magnolia, the female protagonist, and began when she was on the verge of eighteen. Perhaps even more significant was that a 1927 musical confronted the dismal aspects of life in the South with such seriousness—in particular laws and attitudes toward miscegenation and Blacks in Mississippi more generally—and made the multiracial dimension a crucial part of the plot.

The fact that even a drop of "Negro" blood fit the legal definition of a Black person at that time inspired Hammerstein to create a significant new element in the plot. Steve pricks the finger of his wife Julie, ingests her blood, and thus accurately, if deceptively, claims he has Black blood in him because perversely and absurdly he has metamorphosed into a Black man in the eyes of the law. Due to Steve's subterfuge, the marriage no longer technically fit the crime of miscegenation, which was grounds for criminal prosecution. Nevertheless, Julie and Steve must leave the show boat, a community not yet ready to harbor a mixed racial cast.

Show Boat, the first high-profile Broadway musical to feature a Black and white chorus on the same stage, took an additional leap when it became the first high-profile musical to feature Black actors in important speaking and singing roles along with whites. In the segregated world of Broadway prior to *Show Boat*, all-Black shows arrived as early as *A Trip to Coontown* and *Clorindy, or the Origin of the Cake Walk* in 1898 and *In Dahomey* in 1903, all of which were created, directed, and performed by Blacks. After a gap, the all-Black *Shuffle Along*, also created and performed entirely by Black artists (and produced by some of these same artists with the Nikko Producing Company) became a hit in 1921, inspiring several less successful followers. After *Show Boat*, a number of shows with all, or nearly all, Black casts appeared on Broadway, notably *Porgy and Bess* (1935), *Cabin in the Sky* (1940) (see chapter 4), *Carmen Jones* (1943), *Raisin* (1973), *The Wiz* (1975), *Ain't Misbehavin'* (1978), and *The Color Purple* (2005).[7] When it comes to successful *multiracial* musicals that feature significant Black parts, however, *Show Boat* appears at the head of a far shorter list along with *Lost in the Stars* (1949), *Golden Boy* (1964), *Dreamgirls* (1981), *Big River* (1985), *Hairspray* (2002), and *Memphis* (2009).[8]

In addition to its ambitious epic structure, *Show Boat* tackles the challenge of depicting relationships between five sets of couples: Cap'n Andy and Parthy Ann Hawks; their daughter Magnolia Hawks and future co-star and husband

Gaylord Ravenal; the star couple Julie La Verne and her husband Steve Baker (who preceded Magnolia and Gaylord); the comedians Ellie May Chipley and Frank Schultz; and the cook Queenie and her husband, the stevedore Joe. With one exception these relationships do not end well. Cap'n Andy's warm and generous nature doesn't suit stern and humorless Parthy, and from the beginning their marriage is a loveless one marked by mutual disdain.[9] Magnolia and Gaylord fall in love at first sight for real while "only" pretending to be in love ("Make Believe") as stage actors. Later, when they appear together on the show boat *Cotton Blossom*, the reality of their love comes across to audiences unaware that they aren't merely playing a "lover's part" (as the lyric goes). Her prescient friend Julie knows that once in love, Magnolia can't help loving her flawed man Ravenal until she dies.

Consequently, although Ravenal will leave Magnolia and their nearly eight-year-old daughter Kim and vanish for twenty-two years, Magnolia will welcome him back at the end of Hammerstein's (but not Ferber's) narrative. Steve loves Julie, but their marriage can't weather their expulsion from the *Cotton Blossom*. Playing comic roles on the stage, Frank also loves Ellie in real life, but the feeling is not mutual. Ellie sings that she might "fall back" on Frank if things don't work out, but her goal is to find someone more desirable.

This leaves a Black couple, Joe and Queenie, who alone manage to express genuine love, a love that transcends much bantering and bickering and Queenie's insults both on stage and on film. As Gary Giddins writes in his introductory essay to the DVD released in 2020, "It is a joy to watch the superb performers Robeson [Joe] and McDaniel [Queenie] undermine typecasting with chemistry, eye contact, and affection; of all the couples in the show, as in the novel, they are the most contented, suggesting an earthy bond that the others never achieve."[10] The film version adds heroism to Joe's character (thus contradicting stereotypes about his work ethic) when he risks his life on the turbulent river in a violent storm to locate and deliver a doctor to aid the precarious birth of Magnolia's daughter Kim.

Decker makes the case that *Show Boat* remains "the only 1920s operetta or musical comedy to remain part of the active musical theater repertory, the only old show to consistently win new audiences."[11] Although dated in some respects, including in its treatment of racial matters, the film version can lay claim to a similarly lofty position in the pantheon of musical film adaptations. With its screenplay by the original Broadway librettist Hammerstein, the 1936 film is widely acknowledged as the first memorable film adaptation of a stage musical and remains one of the handful of film adaptations to challenge a stage classic in critical acclaim. Among its many claims to fame, the film was directed by James Whale, known then and now for his *Frankenstein* (1931) and other horror films. *Show Boat* would be his first and last musical. Among the many to sing its praises, the film critic Jeanine Basinger wrote: "It is the 1936 *Show Boat* that shows what a movie musical could be—and should be. It adapts a cinematic point-of-view, lifting *Show Boat* off the stage and into the newer art form under the direction of the very talented and sensitive Whale. The 1936 *Show Boat* is not just the best of all the filmed *Show Boats*; it's also one of the very best examples of the musical format on film, one that has stood the test of time and will no doubt continue to do so."[12]

Faced with the inevitable decision to cut down the dialogue and the score to conform to the studio's self-imposed two-hour maximum, the question was not whether but what to cut. Nevertheless, the starting point remained the stage show. In a letter to the film's producer, Carl Laemmle Jr., shortly before filming began, Hammerstein acknowledged that "when I deviate from the structure of the play I get into trouble" and expressed his plan to follow "Whale's contention that the screen version should be as nearly as possible, a transcription of the stage version."[13] The only exception to this plan would be "the finish which we all agree was very weak."[14]

Portions of *Show Boat*, especially the first and second scenes of Act I, have remained constant throughout its many reincarnations. In sharp contrast, following Hammerstein's desire to strengthen the ending, future stage and film versions continue to offer new attempts to solve the "weak" finish. In his letter to Laemmle, Hammerstein thought he found a solution, and some commentators, most notably Stephen Banfield, have found Hammerstein's solution to the 1936 film ending preferable to any other. But for most critics and scholars none of the endings, including the film, are truly satisfactory. The essential unsolvable problem is that after Ravenal abandons his wife and family, his reappearance and reconciliation either in Natchez (stage) or on the New York stage (film) comes across as undeserved and contrived. In Ferber's *Show Boat*, Ravenal dies (as did Cap'n Andy and Parthy).

Magnolia, one of Ferber's characteristically strong and independent female characters, goes on to do well for herself professionally without a husband and doesn't need to be reunited with a loser like Ravenal. Miles Kreuger considers Ravenal's return after twenty-three lost years "an immature concession to musical comedy convention that in days to come Hammerstein himself would help abolish."[15] Considering the perceived dramatic necessity of a musical reconciliation, however contrived, Ravenal's sudden reappearance as a doorman in the film, his reunion with Magnolia and Kim at her Broadway debut at the theater where he works, ending with everyone singing "You Are Love," is probably as plausible a resolution as film viewers could expect in 1936.

As he explained to Laemmle, Hammerstein wanted to retain as much as possible of the dramatic structure that worked so well during the original *Show Boat*'s extraordinary run of 575 performances between December 27, 1927, and May 4, 1929, a run surpassed in the 1920s only by *The Student Prince in Heidelberg* in 1924 (608 performances). Only three years after it closed *Show Boat* returned for a virtually unprecedented six-month New York faithful revival beginning in May

1932 that retained most of the original 1927 cast with the added bonus of the popular Paul Robeson (1898–1976) as Joe, Hammerstein and Kern's first choice for the original production and the man who sang "Ol' Man River" to great adulation in the 1928 London production.

A successful US national tour and a West Coast production in 1933 introduced stage audiences to future stars of the 1936 film, including Irene Dunne (Magnolia), Hattie McDaniel (Queenie), and Allan Jones (Ravenal). The film also recruited Cap'n Andy (Charles Winninger), Julie (Helen Morgan), Frank (Sammy White), and Rubberface (Francis X. Mahoney) from the original Broadway production and most famously Robeson from the London 1928 and New York 1932 productions. In addition to the historical value of permanently capturing on film performances by many of the stars associated with the original show, these actors and singers offered superb performances.

Comparing the 1927 Stage and 1936 Screen Versions

So popular was Robeson in 1936 that Hammerstein and Whale decided to add a song for him, the duet with Queenie called "Ah Still Suits Me," that was historic for capturing a loving relationship in a Black marriage.[16] More so than in the stage original (and perhaps more so than any other film musical of the era), the 1936 film makes it clear in this song that Joe and Queenie truly enjoy each other's company and that Joe is right to conclude that no matter what she says, he knows she loves him. In fact, after the racial stereotypes in the stage work, "Ah Still Suits Me" broke new ground in depicting an intimate and positive connection between a Black husband and wife amid a story of four problematic white marriages. See Figure 2.1.

Hammerstein wrote (or planned) four other new songs, two of which were used. One was a duet between the budding lovers, Ravenal and Magnolia ("I Have the Room above Her"), that was placed between their initial meeting in which they pretended to be in love ("Make Believe") and the final declaration of their love near the end of the first act ("You Are Love"). The final new song used was a diegetic (definition to follow shortly) stage number for Magnolia and the *Cotton Blossom* company, "Gallivantin' Around," a song that has generated controversy as it was performed in blackface.

The addition of new songs for Joe and Queenie and Ravenal and Magnolia within an overall reduced time allotment meant that even more of the stage material had to go. Ellie and Frank suffered the main casualties with the removal of "Life on the Wicked Stage" for Ellie and a female chorus (Act I, scene 3, "Outside of a River-Front Gambling Saloon") and "I Might Fall Back on You" Ellie's duet with Frank in Act 1, scene 5 ("Box Office, on Foredeck of the *Cotton Blossom*"). In the absence of

Fig. 2.1 Paul Robeson (Joe) and Hattie McDaniel (Queenie) singing "Ah Still Suits Me" in the 1936 film of *Show Boat* [68:41]. Screenshot.

these musical numbers, Ellie's and Frank's musical contribution was reduced to a short song and dance at the Trocadero in Chicago on New Year's Eve 1904 (Act II, scene 6) with its interpolated "Good-Bye, Ma Lady Love" and "At a Georgia Camp Meeting."

Queenie lost two songs, "C'mon Folks" (or "Queenie's Ballyhoo") originally in Act I, scene 5, and "Hey, Feller" from Act II, scene 7. Another Hammerstein cut was Ravenal's "Till Good Luck Comes My Way," which, along with the removal of "Life on the Wicked Stage" virtually eliminated the scene outside the waterfront saloon. The 1936 film also nearly eliminated the opening of Act II, which took place at the Chicago World Fair in 1893. This in turn led to the removal of the opening chorus of white fairgoers. "Why Do I Love You?" for Ravenal and Magnolia was reduced to underscoring as the temporarily flush pair sing together on a country ride in their fancy new convertible.[17] "In Dahomey," performed in the stage version by a dancing chorus at the Fair masquerading as Africans, was completely eliminated. See Table 2.1, "*Show Boat* on Stage (1927) and Screen (1936)."

The musical contributions of the remaining characters were mostly unchanged. Parthy didn't sing in the stage version, and "Cap'n Andy's Ballyhoo," already more spoken than sung, was further reduced. Given the importance of Helen Morgan as Julie, Hammerstein and Whale made sure she kept her two

Table 2.1 *Show Boat* on Stage (1927) and Screen (1936).

Stage	Screen
Act I	
Opening: Cotton Blossom (Ensemble) (5)	Cotton Blossom (Ensemble) (1:21)
Parade and Ballyhoo (Winninger, Show Boat Troupe, Townspeople) (9)	Cap'n Andy's Ballyhoo (Winninger, danced by Smith and White) (5:00)
Where's the Mate for Me? (Marsh) (15)	Where's the Mate for Me? (Jones) (8:54)
Make Believe (Marsh, Terris) (17)	Make Believe (Jones, Dunne) (10:44)
Ol' Man River (Bledsoe, Jubilee Singers) (19)	Ol' Man River (Robeson, Black Chorus) (15:31)
Can't Help Lovin' Dat Man (Morgan, Gardella, Terris, Bledsoe) (23)	Can't Help Lovin' Dat Man (Morgan, McDaniel, Robeson, Black Chorus, danced by Dunne and Black dancers) (20:52)
Life on the Wicked Stage (Puck, Girls) (28)	
'Til Good Luck Comes My Way (Marsh, Men) (30)	
Misery (theme) (Jubilee Singers) (38)	Mis'ry's Comin' Aroun' (Instrumental) (35:12)
	I Have the Room above Her (Jones, Dunne) (40:56)
I Might Fall Back on You (Puck, White, Girls) (46)	
C'mon Folks (Queenie's Ballyhoo) (Gardella, Jubilee Singers) (48)	
	Gallivantin' Around (Dunne, Ensemble) (57:19)
	Ol' Man River (Reprise) (Robeson, Black Chorus [humming]) (59:42)
You Are Love (Marsh, Terris) (56)	You Are Love (Jones, Dunne, Ensemble) (61:25)
	Ol' Man River (Reprise) (Robeson) (64:43)
Finale (Ensemble) (58)	

(*continued*)

Table 2.1 Continued

Stage	Screen
Act II	
Opening: At the Fair (Sightseers, Barkers, Dandies) (62)	
Why Do I Love You? (Terris, Marsh, Winninger, Oliver, Chorus) (68)	
In Dahomey (Jubilee Singers, Dahomey Dancers) (69)	
	Ah Still Suits Me (Robeson, McDaniel) (66:08)
Bill (Morgan) (lyrics by P. G. Wodehouse and Hammerstein) (76)	
Can't Help Lovin' Dat Man (Reprise) (Terris) (79)	
Service and Scene Music, St. Agatha's Convent (81)	Service and Scene Music (Girls) (81:42)
	Make Believe (Reprise) (Jones) (83:05)
Apache Dance (Sidell Sisters) (86)	
	Washington Post March (John Philip Sousa) (Danced by Girls) (84:42)
	Bill (Morgan) (86:03)
	Can't Help Lovin' Dat Man (Reprise) (Dunne) (90:47)
	Can't Help Lovin' Dat Man (Reprise) (Dunne, danced by White) (93:41)
Goodbye, My Lady Love (White, Puck) (music and lyrics by Joseph E. Howard) (86)	Goodbye, My Lady Love (Smith, White, singing and dancing) (96:41)
	At a Georgia Camp Meeting (composed by Kerry Mills) (Smith White, dancing) (97:22)
After the Ball (from *A Trip to Chinatown*) (Terris) (music and lyrics by Charles K. Harris) (88)	After the Ball (Dunne, Ensemble) (99:45)
	Make Believe (Partial Reprise) (Jones) (103:17)
Ol' Man River (Reprise) (Bledsoe) (89)	
Hey, Feller! (Gardella, Jubilee Singers) (91)	
	An Old Fashioned Wife (partial) (O'Dea) (lyrics by P.G. Wodehouse) (103:54)

Table 2.1 Continued

Stage	Screen
	Gallivantin' Around (Reprise) (Black Chorus [humming], Black Dancers, and O'Dea) (106:57)
You Are Love (Reprise) (Marsh) (93)	You Are Love (Reprise) (Dunne, Jones) (111:34)
Kim's Imitations (Terris) (95)	
Eccentric and Tap Dances (Ensemble) (95)	
Finale (Ensemble) (97)	Ol' Man River (Partial Reprise) (Robeson) (112:58)

- *Numbers in parentheses in the stage column refer to page numbers in Hammerstein, "Show Boat" (See Appendix 2).*
- *The songs listed in bold in the screen column were not in the stage version.*
- *Numbers in parentheses in the screen column refer to film timings.*

MAJOR SINGING AND DANCING AND SELECTED ROLES

Stage: CHARLES WINNINGER (Cap'n Andy); Norma Terris (Magnolia); Howard Marsh (Ravenal); HELEN MORGAN (Julie); Jules Bledsoe (Joe); Edna Pay Oliver (Parthy); Eva Puck (Ellie); SAMMY WHITE (Frank); Tess Gardella (Queenie)

Screen: CHARLES WINNINGER (Cap'n Andy); Irene Dunne (Magnolia); Allan Jones (Ravenal); HELEN MORGAN (Julie); Paul Robeson (Joe); Helen Westley (Parthy); Queenie Smith (Ellie); SAMMY WHITE (Frank); Hattie McDaniel (Queenie); Sunnie O'Dea (Kim)

- *Names in capital letters indicate that a cast member appeared both on stage and in the film.*

big numbers, "Can't Help Lovin' Dat Man" (Act I, scene 2, in the stage version), and "Bill" at the Trocadero rehearsal sequence (Act II, scene 3), thus making the most of Morgan's relatively small amount of stage and now film time. Basinger considers Morgan's "credible but understated emotionalism" in "Bill" one of the film's "finest moments" and praises Whale's "perfection" in his ability to capture on film Julie's anguish "honestly without detracting from a lyrically beautiful song."[18]

Following Julie's song, the film adds a conversation between Julie and Sam the doorman (Charlie in the stage version) in which Julie explains that she is leaving the Trocadero to make way for Magnolia. The exchange provides an opportunity to feature the African American actor Clarence Muse, whose 150 film credits include the first starring role for a Black actor ("Hearts in Dixie" in 1929). Among Muse's other achievements, he served as the first African American director of a Broadway play (*Run Little Chillun* in 1933) and composed "When It's Sleepy Time Down South," a song indelibly associated with Louis Armstrong. Muse also appeared as the Honey Man in the 1959 film adaptation of *Porgy and Bess*.

Probably the best-remembered and iconic moment in the film is the striking photography used for Robeson's "Ol' Man River" with Joe sitting alone on the dock and the camera doing the rest. It was probably Whale's idea to insert a film montage of stevedores toting barges, lifting bales, and Joe's getting drunk and landing in jail, all in four uninterrupted minutes, but notes in the script and a letter from Hammerstein to Whale support a conclusion that the idea of rotating the camera 180 degrees around and behind Robeson and to cut away to a montage to illustrate the lyrics of "Ol' Man River" came from Hammerstein.[19]

By enhancing their dialogue and physical presence in the film and giving Joe and Queenie the song "Ah Still Suits Me," the 1936 film challenged white American racial norms. One of the censorship issues Whale had to confront in the transfer from stage to film was the fact that Tess Gardella, an Italian American actress known for playing roles in blackface, played the role of Queenie in blackface as well, both in the original production and in the 1932 revival. Joseph I. Breen, who headed the Production Code Administration (commonly known as the Hays Code) since 1934, put the kibosh on casting Gardella in the film, warning Universal to be "extremely careful . . . not to indicate any physical contact between the white woman and the negro man for the reason that many people know Aunt Jemima [Gardella] is a white woman and might be repulsed by the sight of her being fondled by a man who is a negro."[20]

In his essay "Notes on Lyrics" Hammerstein wrote that when he began his career in the early 1920s "it was never expected that the audience would understand the words" in the opening chorus, which in *Show Boat* began provocatively with the word "niggers," followed by "all work on the Mississippi."[21] Decker makes the point that while audiences and white critics seemed to have ignored these words, Blacks did take notice but accepted its use as the price to pay for lucrative theatrical work. One notable exception was Chappy Gardner, who wrote in an African American weekly that some performers resented the opening salvo because "it hurts their pride—it cuts into their dignity."[22]

The following year the London production altered the offending opening line to "coloured folks work on the Mississippi," thus employing a term considered more respectful at the time.[23] For the 1936 film, "colored" was changed to "darkies," at the time a more acceptable word than "niggers," if less so than "colored." Kreuger traces the subsequent evolution of the opening line: "In *Till the Clouds Roll By* [a *Show Boat* sequence lasting fifteen minutes at the opening of this 1946 Kern biopic] it was 'Here we all work' on de Mississippi: and by the 1966 revival *nobody* worked on the Mississippi, because the opening Negro chorus was omitted altogether."[24]

If a major offending word disappeared from the opening song, the film retained another racially controversial element: Magnolia's shuffle that follows the sung choruses of "Can't Help Lovin.'" In her novel Ferber relates that it was

Joe, not Julie, who taught Magnolia Negro spirituals when she was growing up in Queenie's kitchen and explains how these songs formed the basis of her musical tune box and subsequent fame. The film gives viewers a sense of this when Magnolia informs the owner of the Trocadero and the house pianist that she sings "Negro songs," before proceeding to audition with "Can't Help Lovin'" for the New Year's Eve 1904 show in Chicago. Since it forms a crucial component of the plot, the 1927 stage and 1936 film versions both note that it was *Julie* not Joe who taught her this song. To quote a lyric from "Make Believe," the "cold and brutal fact" is that it is Julie's knowledge of this song that reveals her blackness.

The stage version offers a strong foreshadowing of this revelation early in the story (scene 1) when Pete (an engineer) confronts Queenie about where she got the brooch he had given to Julie. Queenie refuses to answer Pete's question, but the underscoring speaks for her when it plays the chorus of "Can't Help Lovin'," even though its meaning won't be understood until the next scene in the kitchen pantry. The film replaced this important foreshadowing with Magnolia's less meaningful piano theme. In the stage version, audiences first hear Magnolia's piano theme later in scene 1 when Parthy confirms to a female admirer of Cap'n Andy that the "little girl" playing is her daughter, now nearly eighteen and "ain't so little anymore." By playing "Can't Help Lovin'" as underscoring to the exchange between Queenie and Pete, stage viewers, or in this case auditors, receive the first evidence of a connection between this song and Queenie. The decision to insert Magnolia's piano theme instead in the film removes both the connection and its meaning.

When the stage and film versions introduce Ravenal moments later with his first song, "Where's the Mate for Me?," originally written in AABA form, the film version omits the song's B section ("The driftwood floating over the sea"), which is based on Magnolia's piano theme. Thus only in the stage version does Ravenal hear Magnolia playing her theme and immediately incorporate it into his song which establishes his "love at first sound." Only when Ravenal asks "if she is a player" (i.e., an actress) does the film make a direct association between Magnolia and her signature piano tune. The film forfeits another chance for musical meaning during the conversation that leads to "Make Believe" with the omission of Parthy's theme, which by then was clearly associated with Parthy in the stage version. Consequently, when Magnolia suddenly explains that she needs to go, film audiences don't hear Parthy's theme, the presence of which would have enhanced the audience's understanding of Magnolia's sudden nervousness.

In a letter to Whale from March 16, 1936 (the film was released in April), Hammerstein asked the director to consider cutting the main refrain but to restore (and begin with) the B section of "Make Believe," the second of the song's five short contrasting sections that Whale wanted to remove.[25] This is the waltz section that begins with the words "You'll pardon I pray." By removing this musical consequence of Ravenal's declaration of love at the end of the opening refrain, film viewers aren't given enough information to understand the dramatic significance of a passage in which Ravenal apologizes for rashly admitting that his love is *not* make believe, and Magnolia responds that she knows he was only pretending to play a lover's part. The next day Whale stated his view that they needed both sections.[26] Nevertheless, in the end "Your pardon, I pray" was cut, a late decision if Kreuger is correct in claiming the entire song was recorded.[27]

The kitchen pantry scene (scene 2) where "Can't Help Lovin'" becomes a song, reveals the meaning of the earlier underscoring in the scene between Queenie and Pete. Julie prepares audiences for this song when she expresses her instinctive understanding that Magnolia is the kind of woman destined to love her man no matter what (i.e., the way Julie loves her man Steve). Julie knows what Magnolia does not yet realize: that she has fallen in love for real as opposed to "make believe." Queenie then confirms her connection with "Can't Help Lovin'" when she asks Julie, "How come y'all know dat song?" When Joe enters, he tells Julie that the song is his favorite, after which other Black workers appear and become immediately entranced by the song. The meaning is unmistakable. The only plausible way for Julie to know this song would be her direct knowledge of Queenie and Joe's world.

Not only has Magnolia learned the song from Julie, but she also knows the dance that goes with it, a dance described as a "coon shuffle" in the 1927 stage script. In the film, Robeson expresses appreciation for Magnolia's cultural appropriation: "Look at that gal shuffle!!" Clearly, Dunne's shuffle, after which she leads the Black ensemble in a cake walk, another dance with African American origins, was *intended* to demonstrate Magnolia's admiration and love for Black culture, not as a caricature. As late as 1989 Kreuger described Dunne's shuffle as "one of the film's delights."[28] In contrast to Joe and Kreuger, however, later writers find the scene offensive, especially the brief cut away to Queenie's (McDaniel's) eye rolling, which, for Decker, "conjures up the worst of Hollywood's preservation of minstrel tropes in the 1930s."[29] Giddins finds the "minstrel-style shuffling" in "Can't Help Lovin'" more troubling than the use of blackface in "Gallivantin' Around."[30]

The African American scholar Shana L. Redmond does not specifically mention McDaniel's eye rolling in "Can't Help Lovin'," but in "Recognizing Race in *Show Boat*" on the *Show Boat* DVD she addresses the cultural meaning of Magnolia's shuffle. While noting that it might be interpreted as a "mocking or caricature of blackness," she also acknowledges "the possibility that she's participating in ways that are actually an homage to her relationship with Joe and Queenie, and Julie has always been part of that acculturation as well."[31]

Even assuming that Magnolia and Hammerstein had more benign intentions than Whale (the eye rolling is not in the 1927 scene directions), Magnolia will appropriate this same Black song again years later when she auditions for the

Trocadero. Neither stage nor film audiences learn the extent to which Magnolia makes her career by singing "Negro" spirituals, but Ferber's novel makes it clear that her appropriation of Black music is what makes her a star. Both the stage and film versions minimize this influence when Magnolia becomes a star by performing an interpolated waltz with *white* associations, "After the Ball" (1892).[32] It is worth noting that Kern, who unlike many Broadway composers regularly used interpolated songs in his shows, chose to recycle someone else's famous tune for Magnolia's New Year's Eve opening in 1904 but wrote his own Black songs for Joe and Julie to sing in the late 1880s.

Although Giddins found the shuffle in "Can't Help Lovin'" especially disturbing, the greatest challenge to Black viewers then and now and racial sensitivities for present-day Black and white viewers of the 1936 film is probably Dunne's impersonation of African Americans in "Gallivantin' Around," the blackface number that followed as an encore in front of the curtain (known as an olio), unrelated to the *Cotton Blossom* players' dramatic performance of *The Parson's Bride*. The performance proper is forced to come to a halt when an armed backwoodsman unable to distinguish the make-believe theatrical performance from reality threatens the stage villain Frank and chases him off the stage. In order to let audiences know what they were missing, Cap'n Andy comes onstage as he did in the 1927 and 1932 stage versions and acts all the parts. Winninger's performance is a tour de force that ranks as one of the funniest in all of film. See Figures 2.2 and 2.3.

The scene then shifts to the cringe-worthy image of Dunne blacking up and going into her song. Before blackface receded from movies in the early 1940s, the practice was common. A surprising number of film stars, including Fred Astaire, Bing Crosby, and Judy Garland, performed at least one blackface number onscreen in their careers. Al Jolson, the star of *The Jazz Singer* (1927), one of the first talking and singing motion pictures, made blackface such a major component of his film persona that the changing attitudes toward this practice significantly contributed to the decline of his subsequent reputation.

In a letter he wrote to Whale shortly before filming, Hammerstein responded to the suggestion for the production number he referred to as "Magnolia's banjo number." This is the number that became "Gallivantin' Around": "I hope you will agree that a naïve, old-fashioned 'coon number' production is just the thing for the Show Boat, and it seems to us that having Dunne doing a number in blackface is novel and different from anything she's ever done. It 'loosens her up.' She herself is most enthusiastic about the idea. I think it is one of those things that is sure to be talked about by those who see the picture, and is all in all a good stroke of showmanship."[33]

This might be a good place to remind readers that the person who conceived "Gallivantin' Around" was the lyricist who would go on to write "Carefully

Fig. 2.2 Charles Winninger (Cap'n Andy) on stage in the stage version with the segregated balcony to the right in *Show Boat*. Photofest.

Taught" thirteen years later. It was also the same writer who served unceasingly as an advocate for racial tolerance outside of the theater, sat on the board of the NAACP, contributed generously both to this organization and the Negro College Fund, and was widely considered one of the most socially liberated and least racist figures in theater and film. Clearly, Hammerstein, like most of his contemporaries, interpreted Dunne's blackface number in a different light than did future audiences, not as an insult but as a transgressive and daring challenge for the regal (and hugely popular) Irish American, Kentucky-born Dunne. In 1989 Kreuger characterized "Gallivantin' Around" as a "delightful blackface

Fig. 2.3 The segregated audience in the rear of the *Cotton Blossom* auditorium in the 1936 film *Show Boat* [48:29]. Screenshot.

routine," a characterization Shana Redmond challenges when noting that "for those who were being portrayed on stage, it [blackface] was not innocent or sweet in the least.[34]

Peter Stansfield offers a contextualized position that interprets the blackface in *Show Boat* as a way to "represent America's theatrical and musical past."[35] In his more benign explanation, as time passes and the world begins to evolve after the 1890s, Magnolia, and *Show Boat*, will leave blackface behind as a memory, albeit an accurate one, of numerous outmoded American attitudes around race. Stansfield thus interprets blackface as "a marker against which the characters are able to judge their social progress."[36] He also regards it as significant that blackface occurs within the context of a biracial cast, thus "emphasizing the performance's artificiality and fabrication."[37] For good or ill, blackface, a practice humiliating to Blacks and used to reinforce cultural hierarchies, evolved into "an essential element in the evocation of an American vernacular."[38] Magnolia, singing her banjo number, in blackface and bewigged, rolling her eyes and impersonating a Black dialect, may be disturbing and something contemporary viewers may not want to witness or even think about, but it does offer a theatrical truth, another "cold and brutal fact" about life on a show boat in the South in the late 1880s.

Kern scholar Banfield praises the 1936 film, not only in comparison with the other two *Show Boat* films but also the many stage versions: "The new, tighter, closer-to-the-novel screenplay provided by Hammerstein together [i.e., with its revised score] offer the most satisfying, balanced, and compelling version of *Show Boat* as drama achieved up to the present day. In almost every way it is superior to the stage version and its variants."[39] At the same time, as discussed here, some of the musical decisions, especially in the opening scene, result in losses of dramatic meaning, while two of the three new numbers, "I Have the Room above Her" and "Ah Still Suits Me," add much to the musical and dramatic richness. Although the film also falls short by not avoiding racial stereotypes and offenses, the latter song offers a sympathetic picture of a married Black couple who truly love each other, and the film as a whole conveys a positive depiction of Joe's courage and humanity that transcends its time.

THE CAT AND THE FIDDLE
(Broadway 1931; MGM 1934)

In the dangerously prosperous 1920s, nine stage musicals ran longer than 500 performances. In the depressed 1930s not one book show attained this magic number. In the 1940s things went about as far as they could go when *Oklahoma!* (1943) transformed what constituted the criteria for a popular musical by running nearly six years, closing after a then-record-setting 2,212 performances. The good news for 1930s musicals was that the smaller running totals of hit shows did not necessarily result in financial failure. This apparent contradiction is explained by the simple fact that it could take less than a year and not many more than 200 performances for a 1930s musical to qualify as a hit.[40] Although two late 1930s revues, *Pins and Needles* (1937) and *Hellzapoppin* (1938), ran longer than a thousand performances, no fewer than fifteen shows from the 1920s surpassed the longest-running *book* musical of the 1930s, *Of Thee I Sing* (1931), 441 performances.

In this context *The Cat and the Fiddle*, with music by Kern, book and lyrics by Harbach, and starring Bettina Hall (Shirley Sheridan) and Georges Metaxa (Victor Florescu), was an impressive popular success in Depression Era Broadway.[41] Running three weeks shy of a year, October 15, 1931 to September 24, 1932, its total of 395 performances placed this musical below only *Of Thee I Sing*, *Anything Goes* (420), *and Du Barry Was a Lady* (408) as the fourth longest-running show of the decade. On March 4, five months before its Broadway close, a London production starring Peggy Wood as Shirley began a healthy run of 226 performances.[42] The Broadway cast toured in the Eastern portion of the US until mid-March 1933, while another touring company played the West Coast. The movie adaptation, which followed closely on February 1934, starred Jeanette MacDonald (1903-1965) as the popular American female songwriter in her first MGM film. Her co-star who played the Romanian longhaired composer was the former Mexican American silent screen icon Ramon Novarro. In contrast to the prolific pairings with Maurice Chevalier (1929-1934) and Nelson Eddy (1935-1942), the latter launched with *Naughty Marietta* in 1935, the year MGM did not renew Novarro's contract. Consequently, MacDonald's first joint film appearance with Novarro would also be the last. See Table 2.2, "*The Cat and the Fiddle* on Stage and Screen."

The outstanding score and its popularity on Broadway and the West End did not transfer into a Hollywood success story. Despite favorable reviews, the film lost $142,000.[43] And in contrast to the longevity enjoyed by *Anything Goes, On Your Toes,* and twenties perennial *Show Boat,* the stage version of *The Cat and the Fiddle* gradually drifted into obscurity as a dramatic entity, although it continued to be remembered for some of its songs. The denial of a license for re-release a few years later sounded the death knell for the film version, after which it too nearly disappeared.

Even during its initial New York run, *Cat* was overshadowed by the popular success and critical accolades accorded *Of Thee I Sing,* which opened three months later in December. *Of Thee I Sing,* with its book by George S. Kaufman and Morrie Ryskind and a score by George and Ira Gershwin, ran only about fifty performances longer, but this difference was sufficient to make *Sing* the longest-running book show of the decade and *Cat* the fourth. Adding to its higher profile in its day and doubtless future historical glory, the Kaufman-Ryskind-Gershwin political satire became the first musical to receive the Pulitzer Prize for drama and the first musical libretto to be published. Despite this contemporary success, neither *Of Thee I Sing* nor *The Cat and the Fiddle* has enjoyed an impressive revival history or recording legacy comparable with that of the Gershwins' *Porgy and Bess,* Kern and Hammerstein's *Show Boat,* or Kern and Harbach's *Roberta.* In the absence of a stellar studio cast recording, successful stage revivals, and a popular film, *The Cat and the Fiddle* virtually vanished from memory and received surprisingly sparse scholarly attention.[44]

Unlike Kern's *Sweet Adeline* (1929) and *Music in the Air* (1932), *The Cat and the Fiddle* has also not been heard at New York City *Encores!,* a long-running forum for under-the-radar musicals deemed worthy of reexamination.[45] The first (and to date only) significant revival of *The Cat and the Fiddle* was a six-performance unstaged concert version conducted by John McGlinn in 1990.[46] Unfortunately, despite his affinity and admiration for Kern, McGlinn recorded only the Entr'acte to Act II, which features two pianos (one representing Shirley and the other Victor).[47]

Table 2.2 *The Cat and the Fiddle* on Stage and Screen.

Stage	Screen
Act I	
The Night Was Made for Love (Meader) (1-1-5)	The Night Was Made for Love (MacDonald) (14:44)
She Didn't Say "Yes" (Meader) (1-1-5)	
She Didn't Say "Yes" (Hall) (1-1-17)	She Didn't Say "Yes" (MacDonald) (36:09)
The Love Parade (Meader, LeBreton) (1-2-28)	The Love Parade (Novarro, MacDonald) (42:47)
One Moment Alone (Metaxa) (1-3-37)	
	The Breeze Kissed Your Hair (Novarro) (turns into One Moment Alone as a waltz) (23:52)
Try to Forget (Hall, Foy, Carson) (1-4-48)	Try to Forget (Butterworth, MacDonald) (65:35)
Poor Pierrot (Chambers, Valsy) (1-6-60)	Poor Pierrot (Instrumental) (35:08)
Episode in Victor's Play, "The Passionate Pilgrim," (Myrtil, Valsy, Adams, Chambers) (1-6-61)	
Finaletto (Try to Forget) (Hall, Metaxa) (1-8-68)	
Act II	
She Didn't Say "Yes" (Reprise) (Hall) (2-1-10)	
A New Love Is Old (Metaxa) (2-3-14)	A New Love Is Old (Segal) (47:00)
The Breeze Kissed Your Hair (Metaxa) (2-3-20)	
One Moment Alone (Hall, Metaxa) (2-5-18)	One Moment Alone (follows The Breeze Kissed Your Hair above) (23:52)
Hh! Cha! Cha! (Hall, Others) (2-7-40)	Hh! Cha! Cha! (Segal and Chorus) (56:56)
Poor Pierrot (Meader, Metaxa (2-7-41)	
Finale (She Didn't Say "Yes" Reprise) (Meador, Metaxa, Hall) (2-7-43)	One Moment Alone (beginning and end) (Novarro, MacDonald) (86:38)

Table 2.2 Continued

- *Numbers in parentheses in the stage column refer to page numbers in Otto Harbach, "The Cat and the Fiddle" (unpublished).*
- *Numbers in parentheses in the screen column refer to film timings. Note the discrepancies in song placement between the musical and the film. For a song outline keyed to the published Vocal Score, see Table 2.3.*

MAJOR SINGING AND DANCING AND SELECTED ROLES

Stage: Georges Metaxa (Victor Florescu); Bettina Hall (Shirley Sheridan); Odette Myrtil (Odette/Pierrot); Eddie Foy Jr. (Alexander Sheridan); José Ruben (Jules Daudet); Lawrence Grossmith (Major Chatterly); Doris Carson (Angie Sheridan); George Meader (Pompineau); Constance Carrington (Margaret Adams); Flora LeBreton (Mazie Gripps); Peter Chambers (Jean Colbert/Compere); Lucette Valsy (Claudine/Commere); Margaret Adams (Constance Carrington)

Screen: Ramon Novarro (Victor); Jeanette MacDonald (Shirley); Frank Morgan (Clément Daudet); Charles Butterworth (Charles); Jean Hersholt (Professor Bertier); Vivienne Segal (Odette Brieux); Joseph Cawthorn (Rudy Brieux); Frank Conroy (Theatre Owner); Irene Franklin (Opera Singer Lotte Lengel)

Although it might be overly optimistic to expect a complete resuscitation of the worthy stage version or the underrated, if flawed, film adaptation, this chapter will explore what makes both neglected versions unusual and imaginative.[48] Before delving into a comparison between the stage and film versions, it might be helpful to examine two shared attributes, both of which are not only relevant to this show in particular but to other stage and film works that followed in the 1940s: integration and diegeticism. The first concept has generated more than its fair share of controversy in the scholarly and critical literature, while the second has experienced some misuse and confusion regarding its meaning.

In brief, in an integrated musical the songs regularly advance the plot, flow from the dialogue, and express the characters who sing them.[49] The use of orchestral underscoring in the stage version of *Show Boat* to complement and advance the action is another frequent characteristic. With some exceptions such as *On Your Toes* (1936), a prominent role for dance to advance the action and enhance the dramatic meaning of the songs was less common before the 1940s. The musicals of Kern were among those that pioneered the idea of integration. In fact, Kern spoke of his intentions as an integrationist as early as 1917.[50] Not all scholars agree on the merits of integration or even in its existence, but the evidence suggests that some Broadway composers, perhaps starting with Kern, aspired to the principle of integration long before *Oklahoma!* Further, when used well, integration can be a significantly positive attribute of a musical so long as the integration possesses dramatic meaning. In fact, integration is so directly observable in *The Cat and the Fiddle* that Ethan Mordden maintains that this show "may well be the most integrated musical of all time."[51]

Now for a few words about the term diegetic, a term already used in this chapter to describe the mode of performance in "Gallivantin' Around." Both the indispensable term diegetic and the concept of diegeticism have been misappropriated from their origins in ancient Greece.[52] In this and future chapters, rather than trying to explain the origins and nuances of the misappropriation, I will use the term as it has been used since about 1950, that is, a word indicating that the *characters* in an opera, musical, or film (and their stage and film audiences) are aware they are singing. Rather than using the term "diegetic" in a way that corresponds to its original Greek meaning, *A Fine Romance* will use the term (and its opposite, non-diegetic) as most theater and film scholars have by now long understood it. Despite the continued confusion, the word diegetic has served its evolved meaning well. It also offers one incontrovertible advantage in that so far no one has been able to come up with a satisfactory alternative.

Thus when Stephen Banfield, the author of the most rigorous analysis to date of *The Cat and the Fiddle*'s stage version, writes that Kern "sought a plot and a treatment in which all the musical performances would be diegetic," his point is that the characters—and in this case the two major characters who are also the composers of the music they sing—know they are singing their songs.[53] The characters are blithely unaware that Kern and Harbach and not Shirley Sheridan and Victor Florescu wrote the songs they sing, but this detail does not negate the concept of diegeticism. Banfield expands the notion of diegetic musical performance to encompass their "spectacular piano playing," which plays a dramatic role in the story, even though the characters are oblivious to the orchestral underscoring when it replaces their pianos. Although film musicals often employ a mode of performance that is solely diegetic (e.g., *42nd Street* and *Cabaret*), the degree to which *The Cat and the Fiddle* is diegetic may be unprecedented in a *stage* musical before 1931 and perhaps since. For the purposes of this text, if the characters know they are singing (not just thinking, as they do in "Twin Soliloquies" from *South Pacific)*, their songs will be described as diegetic. If the characters are unaware that they are singing, their songs will be described as non-diegetic.

In both its stage and film versions, a central conflict in *The Cat and the Fiddle* relates to the contrast between the catchy danceable popular songs of the day (usually in an AABA or related form) and a more formally complex operetta style, which is presented as an extension of the cultivated European art music tradition sometimes called "classical style" for short—in the course of the story. The composer of the popular music is the American Shirley Sheridan, whose song "She Didn't Say 'Yes,'" prior to the opening of the show, has been published and sung throughout Brussels by the street singer Pompineau played by the operatic tenor George Meader.[54] Representing classical style is the talented Romanian composer Victor Florescu.

The artistic and social conflict between Victor's pseudo-classical quasi-modern European music and Shirley's jazzy American popular style of the day dominates much of the score, most of which is sung, played, and composed by Victor and Shirley. Odette (Odette Myrtil), the violin-playing Pierrot, and several other singers also perform various portions of Victor's operetta *The Passionate Pilgrim* (composed with a little musical assistance from Shirley). See Figure 2.4.

The one remaining major singing character is Pompineau (the street singer mentioned a few sentences ago) who introduces "The Night Was Made for Love" in the first scene, leads "The Love Parade" in the second, and launches a reprise of "Poor Pierrot" in the Café Scene. The only other song not composed by either Shirley or Victor is probably "Hh! [pronounced "Hah"] Cha! Cha!" although it is possible that here too Shirley is singing one of her own songs. In a late change to the score, Shirley's brother Alec and sister-in-law Angie's song and dance "Don't Ask Me Not to Sing" became a dance only, a decision that deprives the song of the dramatic meaning embodied in its title. Another scene in Act II includes the Albertina Rasch Dancers playing jazz instruments accompanied by singers singing behind the curtain.

Fig. 2.4 "Poor Pierrot" from *The Passionate Pilgrim* in the stage version of *The Cat and the Fiddle*. White Studio (New York, NY). Museum of the City of New York 62.100.502 © The New York Public Library.

In addition to Pompineau's "The Night Was Made for Love," Shirley's ubiquitous song hit "She Didn't Say 'Yes,'" and perhaps "Hh! Cha! Cha!," the score contains four other major songs. Three of these are attributed to and sung by Victor ("The Breeze Kissed Your Hair," "A New Love Is Old," and "One Moment Alone"). The fourth is composed and sung by Shirley, "Try to Forget," a song inspired by her attempt to forget the sadness of her lost romance with Victor. Aside from their songs, Victor and Shirley express their respective styles at the piano. Victor favors waltzes to go along with his semi-classical modern-sounding harmonies; Shirley's piano music, like her songs "She Didn't Say 'Yes'" and "Try to Forget," resembles stride piano with a touch of Zez Confrey's "novelty piano" style that was popular in the 1920s.

The Stage Plot

The opening scene on stage begins on a July evening along a quay in Brussels where Shirley is sitting on a bench waiting for Alec and Angie. Pompineau's "The Night Was Made for Love" captures the romance in the air when Victor strolls by and joins Shirley in conversation. See Figure 2.5.

Shirley and Victor both attended the same conservatory. Although they hadn't met, Victor is well known to Shirley as "the prize pupil in composition," and she has even heard his symphony. Victor is quickly smitten, Shirley becomes increasingly interested, and they agree to exchange letters until one or the other no longer wishes to continue. Unfortunately, the budding epistolary romance comes to an abrupt end a few weeks later when Victor's assistant Biddlesby misplaces the letter that contains Shirley's new Parisian address. Consequently, all Victor's letters are returned, thus seemingly ending a potentially fine romance.

When Shirley returns to Brussels a month later, her apartment happens to be situated adjacent to Victor's studio, a coincidence that allows them to overhear each other's opposing piano styles. Among the highlights of an extremely rich score, the rival composers respond directly through music to each other's playing (Act I, scene 3). While Shirley enjoys Victor's music, the feeling is not mutual. Four weeks later they are brought together by the producer Jules Daudet, who is interested in Victor's operetta score but finds the song "A Moment Alone" "too somber" and in need of "lightening here and there." No sooner does Daudet utter these words, audiences (also Victor and Daudet) hear Shirley's jazz piano playing from her apartment, a good example of diegeticism at work. Shirley's music is precisely the kind of music Daudet is looking for to liven up Victor's score, which he basically likes: "In the main, it's good—but without the changes I've suggested, I'm afraid I can't consider it" (1-3-39).[55]

Fig. 2.5 Opening scene along the quay in Brussels. Georges Metaxa
(Victor), George Meader (Pompineau), and Bettina Hall (Shirley) in the
stage version of *The Cat and the Fiddle*. White Studio (New York, NY).
Museum of the City of New York 68.80.158 © The New York Public Library.

Shirley reluctantly agrees to help Victor achieve Daudet's demands, but not
wanting to infringe on Victor's creative autonomy, she tries to to find unobtru-
sive ways to enliven the score. The stage musical must also address additional
romantic complications when Daudet makes known his desire to move beyond
a professional relationship with Shirley. Odette almost ruins a reconciliation between Shirley and Victor when she shares with the latter her understanding that
Daudet had slept with the former after everyone else had left the party celebrating

the successful run-through of Victor's operetta. Audiences know the truth because they are direct witnesses as to how Shirley managed to escape Daudet's clutches in the early morning hours, but neither Victor nor Odette will learn that Shirley was faithful until near the end of the second act.

The Film Plot

When compared with the norms of song usage in most musical film adaptations of the 1930s, including Kern's *Show Boat* and *Roberta* films, the film musical version of *The Cat and the Fiddle*, remarkably, retained nearly every song from the stage score. It also maintained a virtually unprecedented practice from the stage version in which the songs are presented diegetically. By removing Pompineau as a composer, the songs in the film version are now all composed (often at the keyboard) by either Shirley or Victor, who also sing all the numbers with the exceptions of "A New Love Is Old" and "Hh! Cha! Cha!," now assigned to Odette. The catch is that despite the retention of the songs, changes in the *plot* significantly alter the contexts of these songs as well as their original meanings. See Table 2.3, "Musical Outline of the Film Version of *The Cat and Fiddle* Keyed to the Vocal Score [VS]."

Instead of a bench along a quay in Brussels and Pompineau's "The Night Was Made for Love," the film opens with Victor at the piano at a Brussels restaurant where he is playing for his supper. We eventually realize he is completing an excerpt from his operetta. When the owner demands that Victor pay for the wine that was not part of his contract, the impoverished composer runs away and jumps into a taxi occupied by Shirley. See Figure 2.6.

Victor impertinently and spontaneously asks Shirley if she believes in love at first sight. After Shirley fails to respond affirmatively the two musicians spend the rest of the cab ride bickering about whether the driver should stop at Pension La Fitte or Pension La Tour. The argument proves to be a moot point since the two hotels are located across the street (rather than placed adjacently as in the stage version) but still close enough for each to overhear the other's piano playing through their respective windows.

Instead of the rapport they demonstrate and Victor's consistently respectful manner toward Shirley in the stage version, the screen Victor is annoyingly insistent, a behavior that prompts Shirley to extricate herself as soon as possible. From this first unpromising meeting and throughout most of the picture, Victor demonstrates traditional toxic masculinity that makes Shirley uncomfortable and becomes increasingly unacceptable. In this respect he has much in common with a long list of importuning male leads in musical (among other) films of the era from Jack Buchanan in *Monte Carlo* (1930) to Nelson Eddy in *Maytime* (1937), to cite two other films that feature Jeanette MacDonald. Soon after they

Table 2.3 Musical Outline of the Film Version of *The Cat and the Fiddle* Keyed to the Vocal Score [VS], T.B. Harms, 1932.

1:13	Victor Florescu is playing the piano at a restaurant, playing a number from his new operetta. After refusing to pay for the wine, he dashes out of the restaurant, his bill unpaid.
2:37	He joins a parade in front of a band but is soon discovered and chased down the street. The faster he runs, the faster the band plays.
3:36	A taxi drives by and Victor jumps in. The taxi is occupied by Shirley Sheridan, who is not happy about Victor's arrival. Throughout the drive they argue about which pension they should be dropped off. Unlike the stage version, Shirley doesn't recognize Victor's name when he tells her he is a composer who has studied at the Conservatoire, and she considers him a pest. She wants the driver to take her to Pension La Fitte to which Victor counters she should stay at Pension La Tour.
4:56	When the driver stops, we learn that La Fitte and La Tour are directly across the street from each other. Victor is unable to pay the fare, and the driver takes his music portfolio as collateral.
8:31	Victor is over an hour late for his appointment with Professor Bertier. Victor has an audition with Daudet, but in the absence of his portfolio he has to play from memory.
9:40	Victor sits down and plays some waltz fragments and the chordal fanfare figure later heard under the title card of *Till the Clouds Roll By* (VS 75).
10:15	The Professor leaves and Victor sits down to practice. As he plays the opening of Edvard Grieg's "Morning Mood," he overhears Shirley playing her jazzy variation on this melody (VS 73-74). The camera shifts back and forth from Victor to Shirley at their respective pianos in their respective pensions, Victor playing Grieg and Shirley playing jazz and ragtime variations on Grieg (see Musical Example 2.3c which includes both versions). At one point they play the chordal change from G major and B minor (VS 76-77). The scene in the film contrasts with the stage version, in which neither Victor nor Shirley know who is playing in the other room.
14:44	"The Night Was Made for Love" (Shirley) (VS 14) Victor enters Shirley's room through the window. Shirley sits down at the piano and plays her novelty music (VS 73). Then Shirley begins her song, "The Night Was Made for Love." Victor interrupts after the first 2 measures and attempts to improve the next 2 measures. Shirley agrees: "It is better, I'm grateful." They then both sing in harmony after which Victor tries to kiss Shirley and gets a slap. Victor offers more improvements for the music: Shirley sings the first phrase, then Victor sings the second phrase twice. In a following film montage, viewers see Shirley's song published by Daudet.
23:52	"The Breeze Kissed Your Hair" (Victor) (VS 67). Song turns into "One Moment Alone" as a waltz.
26:30	"The day has eyes for" (in "She Didn't Say 'Yes'") (Shirley) (VS 135)
27:23	"The Night Was Made for Love" (Shirley) follows 26:30 directly on VS 134 in the opposite order.

(continued)

Table 2.3 Continued

29:47	Victor plays "One Moment Alone" as a waltz for a few seconds. Note from Daudet, "The Night Was Made for Love."
32:40	"The Night Was Made for Love" (Victor) (VS 134) (20 seconds)
34:28	Opening Chorus (instrumental with live musicians invited by Victor) (VS 11)
35:08	"Poor Pierrot" (instrumental from VS 11) (VS 96)
36:09	"She Didn't Say 'Yes'" (Shirley), i.e., after a proposal (VS 17)
39:10	"Don't Ask Me Not to Sing" (chorus) (VS 109) turns into the last phrase of "The Night Was Made for Love." "Don't Ask" is not sung in the stage version.
40:29	"The Night Was Made for Love" (VS 109) (chorus continues) (beginning of song)
	In a montage, viewers see Shirley's song becoming a huge hit and sung everywhere, including outside Victor and Shirley's room in Paris as Victor tries to compose his operetta. Even the clock and a water pitcher play the tune. Victor shuts his window to block the sound.
	Despite their professional tensions (and despite the Production Code), the film makes it clear that Shirley and Victor are living together outside marriage.
42:47	"The Love Parade" (chorus) (Victor and Shirley; Shirley sings the A section and Victor spontaneously composes the B section) (VS 49).
43:47	"The Love Parade" (verse) (VS 46)
47:00	"A New Love Is Old" (Odette) (VS 141) (verse)
	Victor starts to play "The Love Parade" for Odette who asks for one of his songs.
47:35	"A New Love Is Old" (Odette) (VS 140) (chorus)
51:00	"Breeze" underscoring while Victor talks to Daudet.
	The conversation with Daudet leads Victor to go back to Brussels without Shirley.
54:57	"A New Love Is Old" (Victor) (VS 140)
	Shirley asks Victor, "Will you marry me?" "Just something to remember the moment. Odette is thinking of backing my operetta." Victor plays "A New Love" for Shirley. After "And after a few thrills, your new love is old," he silently leaves their Parisian apartment. The chandeliers play against "The Love Parade" after he leaves.
56:56	"Hh! Cha! Cha!" (Odette and chorus) (VS 170)
	Rehearsal of operetta. "Breeze" underscoring. Odette's husband Rudy sees Victor and Odette kissing and threatens Odette if she doesn't abandon the show. After Odette leaves, most cast members agree to stay as they hum "One Moment Alone." But the leading man does leave, which means that Victor must find both a leading man and a leading woman.
65:39	"Try to Forget" (Charles plunks out the first four bars) (VS 85).

Table 2.3 Continued

	Charles, who is not present in the stage version, goes to see Shirley. She is to be married the next day to Daudet. Charles explains the dire situation and notes that there is only one new song ("You know most of the score"). Note: This doesn't make sense because when Shirley left Paris Victor had much left to compose. Before Charles starts to play "Try to Forget," he tells Shirley that "you were in his heart when he wrote this."
66:35	"Try to Forget" (Shirley starts to sing the chorus)
67:07	"Try to Forget" (Shirley) (verse)
67:47	"Try to Forget" (Shirley returns to the chorus)
	Shirley plays and sings the entire song in a freight elevator.
73:20	"Prologue" (Orchestra) (VS 7)
	The evening the show opens the leading woman (Lotte Lengel) gets drunk and can't go on.
74:40	"A New Love Is Old" (reprise) (Shirley) (VS 140) (verse and chorus)
75:44	"Love Parade" (underscoring)
77:00	Jeanette is in her underwear as in the majority of her early films.
80:00	"Don't Ask Me Not to Sing" (waltz version of vamp)
81:00	"Try to Forget" (underscoring, a reprise, first Victor then Shirley, ending with the last four bars on VS 86, same as the last four bars of the film, VS 88). Shirley arrives and saves the day.
84:32	"Love Parade" (Victor and Shirley) in three-strip Technicolor
85:14	"Poor Pierrot" (reprise) (Shirley, 8 bars then Victor, 8 bars)
85:41	"Try to Forget" (orchestra) (follows "Poor Pierrot")
85:48	"Poor Pierrot" (duet Victor and Shirley)
86:38	"One Moment Alone" (Victor and Shirley) (VS 177) (beginning and end) [starts as a waltz on VS 22]

arrive at the pension, Victor climbs through the window into Shirley's apartment where he joins her at the piano and rewrites the song she is composing, formerly Pompineau's "The Night Was Made for Love" from the stage version. When Shirley thanks him for improving her song, he kisses her.

Although this last action earns a slap, Victor's ardor improbably (from a modern perspective) succeeds in lowering Shirley's resistance. Shortly thereafter, following a montage that conveys the vast public success of Shirley's "The Night Was Made for Love" (the version with Victor's substituted second phrase), film viewers find the two unmarried lovebirds sharing an apartment in Paris in Pre-Code Hollywood. Unfortunately, the insecure Victor is both unable to accept playing second fiddle to his more successful girlfriend and unable to concentrate on completing his operetta. When the envious Daudet, now Clément Daudet (Frank Morgan) threatens to ruin Shirley's budding career in Paris, Victor decides to return to Brussels, leaving Shirley to her newfound but lonely stardom.

Fig. 2.6 Jeanette MacDonald (Shirley) and Ramon Novarro (Victor) exiting the taxi where they shared a ride during their acrimonious first meeting in the film version of *The Cat and the Fiddle*. Henry Armetta (the taxi driver) is demonstrating his taxi's distinctive horn [5:49]. Screenshot.

This plot summary already differs markedly from the stage version. Differences continue to mount while the music remains, albeit in altered dramatic contexts. Victor finishes his operetta, but a major setback occurs shortly before its premiere when Rudy (Joseph Cawthorn), the wealthy elderly husband of Odette (Vivienne Segal), the operetta's leading lady who is attracted to and pursues Victor, catches his wife kissing the young composer. To punish the flagrant lovers for their lapse in judgment, Rudy not only demands that Odette leave the show but he also withdraws his financial backing. Most of the cast, crew, and orchestra agree to stay on until opening night, but unfortunately the leading man abandons ship, now leaving the show bereft of both its male and female leads. To keep the show afloat by re-paying money due the show's backers and hiring new singers, the desperate Victor writes a check he can't cover, thus placing himself in legal jeopardy, including possible imprisonment.

Meanwhile back in Brussels, Victor's eccentric assistant and amateur harpist Charles (Charles Butterworth), an important film character who doesn't appear in the stage version, reads in the paper that Shirley will be marrying Daudet the following day. He immediately travels to Paris where he explains to Shirley Victor's dire financial, legal, and artistic situation. Before he leaves he gives her the music to "Try to Forget," the song Victor wrote while pining for her and the only song in the operetta that Shirley doesn't already know.

In response to Charles's plea to Shirley that she fill in as the leading lady to save her former lover from financial ruin, she doesn't say yes and she doesn't say no. But in a variation on the *42nd Street deus ex machina* trope where the young star saves the day, Shirley returns in the nick of time to replace the last-minute replacement for the female lead who has passed out in a drunken stupor.[56] After rehearsing a few details in the dressing room, Shirley is ready for her stage entrance. This last plot point provides the opportunity for MacDonald to appear in her underwear, a costume that audiences had come to expect after seeing her in this informal attire since her early films (what might be called the "the negligée period"), directed by Ernst Lubitsch and Rouben Mamoulian.

For the grand finale of Victor's operetta (the final reel), viewers are treated to five minutes in three-strip Technicolor, the first time this technique had been used in a film musical. To Daudet's chagrin, Victor and Shirley fall in love again while singing (diegetically) a medley that includes Shirley's "The Love Parade" and Victor's "Try to Forget," "Poor Pierrot," and "One Moment Alone," the latter duet, harmonies and all, closely matching the final three pages of the published vocal score.[57] In the stage musical, Shirley and Victor clear up everything with Daudet about what *didn't* happen and sing a diegetic duet reprise only of "One Moment Alone." In the Hollywood version, Shirley returns in triumph, the separated lovers reconcile as they perform together on the movie set stage (and in color), and together triumphantly save Victor's show. See Figure 2.7.

Fig. 2.7 Jeanette MacDonald (Shirley) and Ramon Novarro (Victor) together in Technicolor in the stage finale of the mostly black and white film version of *The Cat and the Fiddle* [87:28]. Screenshot.

New Song Contexts

In the film as well as the stage version, Shirley composed "She Didn't Say 'Yes'" and Victor composed "The Breeze Kissed Your Hair," "A New Love Is Old," and "One Moment Alone." In the film Shirley acquires ownership of Pompineau's "The Night Was Made for Love" and "The Love Parade." The composer responsible for "Hh! Cha! Cha" is unclear, but the fact that it occurs in a performance of *The Passionate Pilgrim* suggests that Victor was its composer, even though stylistically the song sounds more like something Shirley would have written. As stated earlier in the film summary, Shirley's "Try to Forget" is composed by Victor in the film.

The effect of assigning "The Night Was Made for Love" to Shirley (instead of to Pompineau or Victor) and "Try to Forget" to Victor rather than Shirley unfortunately means that their styles now contradict their respective musical languages. "The Night Was Made for Love" is a song that Pompineau could have overheard Victor sing in his studio and "Try to Forget," while a little less jazzy than "She Didn't Say 'Yes,'" could readily be recognized in a lineup as belonging to Shirley, less so to Victor. It should also be noted that no one asks Victor to alter Shirley's music in either the stage or screen version, but in the film Victor does just that. As she plays and sings her new song, "The Night Was Made for Love," Victor interrupts after only 2 measures and sings his idea for the next 2 measures, after which Shirley is free to go on with her song. After Shirley plays the A sections of "The Love Parade," a song in standard 32-bar song form (AABA), Victor sings (i.e., composes) the release (B) without having heard Shirely's version. As a result, the film asks viewers to believe that Shirley relied on *Victor's* casual improvisations to achieve hits as big as "The Night Was Made for Love" and "The Love Parade." This change in plot contradicts the point of the stage version, which makes it clear that Victor needs *Shirley* to create a popularly successful operetta. Clearly, Hollywood in 1934 wasn't yet ready for a self-sufficient female composer.

Similarly, while film viewers learn that Daudet wants Shirley to make changes to enliven Victor's score, they never witness this happening as they do in the stage version. In the latter, this important moment is revealed when audiences directly hear Shirley's attempt to make "One Moment Alone" less classical (i.e., less European) and more in the American popular vernacular. Also in the stage version, a foreshadowing of "One Moment Alone" appeared unannounced and unattributed after Pompineau offered to sell Shirley a copy of her own hit "She Didn't Say 'Yes.'" Pompineau sings 8 measures of Shirley's song before its composer surprises him by singing along for 2 measures and before singing the next 6 without further assistance. As her song continues with orchestral underscoring, Shirley formally acknowledges her authorship.

Victor then enters accompanied by a theme that attentive auditors may come to recognize as "Victor's Love Theme," one of numerous short melodies not attached to a particular song.[58] After more orchestral underscoring beginning with the "Street Vendors" theme, Pompineau sings the first 8 measures (same as the last eight) of "The Night Was Made for Love" before making his exit to allow for the message of the song to become a reality. Shirley and Victor then begin their underscored conversation to the strains of "Shirley's Love Theme." After a few measures of the "Flirtation Waltz," the orchestra introduces an instrumental melody in 6/8 time in the style of a Baroque siciliana.[59] It appears in the vocal score as underscoring to the conversation immediately prior to Shirley's explanation that she withdrew from the conservatory because of "a lack of woman's—*tuition*" (1-1-10). The rhythm, meter, and harmony may differ, but the *melody* of this passage is fundamentally the same as the first 8 measures of "One Moment Alone" (Musical Example 2.1a).

The underscoring returns to the "Flirtation Waltz" followed by another 8 measures of "One Moment Alone," the latter music corresponding to the place in the dialogue when Shirley tells Victor that "if for any reason you have lost interest, just stop writing. I'll understand" (1-1-14). Alec and Angie arrive and Victor leaves directly after Shirley's introductions. Following his departure, Angie asks Shirley what she said when he asked for her address. This is Shirley's cue to respond by singing in the third person, "She didn't say 'yes'/she didn't say 'no,'" a song that will be used in imaginative ways and at appropriate moments in both the stage and screen versions.

In Act I, scene 3, of the stage version (about twenty-four minutes into the film), Victor plays the final scene of his operetta *The Passionate Pilgrim* at Daudet's request. Odette, its lead singer (and violinist), explains that the work "was inspired by one of Victor's grand passions—The Glove Lady!" (1-3-36), a reference to Shirley, whose gloves Victor stole as a remembrance of their meeting one month earlier. Victor sits down at the piano and accompanies himself with the first (and only) 8 measures of "The Breeze Kissed Your Hair." In the stage version, but not the film, Victor directly moves from this abbreviated song to the first phrase of "Shirley's Love Theme" with the words "One moment there I sat with you/Then

Example 2.1a Foreshadowing of "One Moment Alone" in 6/8 time in *The Cat and the Fiddle*.

Example 2.1b Victor sings and plays "One Moment Alone" as a waltz in 3/4 time in *The Cat and the Fiddle*.

vanished from your view." Victor then plays a phrase of the "Flirtation Waltz," a reminiscence of two themes stage audiences heard when he first met Shirley.

Victor continues with his "One Moment Alone" as a waltz (Musical Example 2.1b). In the stage version the waltz replaces the siciliana from the opening scene. Unlike "Breeze," "One Moment Alone" is a full-scale song, the central love song on both stage and screen. After two leisurely 16-bar statements, Odette joins Victor on her violin for a contrasting 16-bar section, after which she continues with her muted violin obbligato to accompany Victor's final statement of the main tune.

After hearing "One Moment Alone" Daudet is not shy about expressing his disappointment: "Frankly, I had hoped for something a little more gay" (1-3-38). Daudet's reservations prepare audiences for Shirley's subsequent suggestions to make the tune less somber. The morning after escaping Daudet's attempted seduction, Shirley arrives at Victor's studio. Since she appreciates his music, she doesn't want Daudet's requested changes to overshadow the serious classical component with a more popular style without Victor's approval. Her solution is to demonstrate what she means by a "gayer rhythm" as she transforms Victor's waltz (triple meter) version of "One Moment Alone" into a swinging duple meter (Musical Example 2.1c). Shirley's swinging version replaces Victor's European

Example 2.1c Shirley transforms "One Moment Alone" into a swinging duple meter in *The Cat and the Fiddle*.

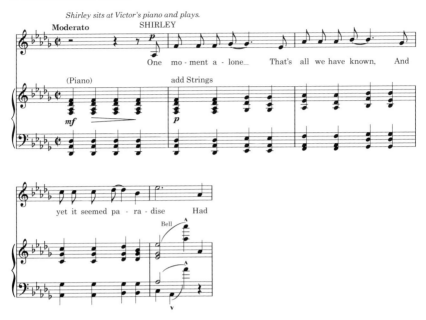

waltz in both the stage and film versions, but only in the stage version do audiences learn directly the nature of Shirley's small changes that made Victor's score more accessible or even what song she altered. Instead, in the film version, viewers only learn what changes *Victor* made to two songs attributed to Shirley, "The Night Was Made for Love" and "The Love Parade" (songs that belong to Pompineau in the stage version).

Victor's composition isn't the only classical music Shirley alters in the stage version. In their two-piano duel Shirley responds to Victor's pompous introduction of *The Passionate Pilgrim* with a ragged (as in ragtime) version of Edvard Grieg's "Morning Mood" from the *Peer Gynt* Suite No. 1, first in major and then in minor (Musical Examples 2.2a and b).[60] After some novelty piano she plays a varied, more virtuosic paraphrase of "Morning Mood," which Victor interrupts by playing Grieg's melody "furioso" and "fff" (i.e., as loudly as possible) while Shirley continues her jazzy version (Musical Example 2.2c).

In the Broadway version the scene directions confirm that the Grieg borrowing was intentional when Victor "turns a hanging portrait of Grieg toward the wall," a touch not included in the film's piano war. Interestingly, what Shirley does to Victor's "One Moment Alone" and Grieg's "Morning Mood" is similar to what happens in *Show Boat*, when Magnolia auditions at the Trocadero with

Example 2.2a "Morning Mood" from Edvard Grieg's *"Peer Gynt"* Suite No. 1, Op. 48 (beginning) in *The Cat and the Fiddle*.

Example 2.2b Shirley's jazzy paraphrase of "Morning Mood" (beginning) in *The Cat and the Fiddle*.

Example 2.2c Shirley's virtuosic paraphrase of "Morning Mood" (continued) interrupted by Victor's "furioso" version on Grieg's original melody in *The Cat and the Fiddle*.

"Can't Help Lovin' Dat Man" in a straight musical style that prompts the rehearsal pianist to suggest that she could transform the tune into something more suitable if she would "rag it" a little.[61]

The film version of *The Cat and the Fiddle* later suffered along with other Pre-Code films in response to the increasingly Draconian censorship practices enforced by Breen and the Production Code Administration (PCA) after 1934. Thus, in the months leading up to its initial release, *The Cat and the Fiddle* managed to avoid complying with a major suggestion offered by James Wingate, then the director of the Studio Relations Committee as the Pre-Code Production Code Administration office was called. Wingate concluded that *Cat* offered "the basis for a charming picture," but asked E. J. Mannix at MGM to follow "the recent decision of the Association to tone down such portrayals of loose sex relationships" in which an unmarried couple is seen living together and clearly sharing a bed.[62]

Given this breach of decorum, it is surprising to read in a later memo from Breen to Louis B. Mayer dated February 13, 1934, that the film "should meet with no censorship difficulties and that it meets the requirements of the Code with one minor exception."[63] Unfortunately, three years later Breen changed his tune when he denied MGM a certificate to reissue the film on the grounds Wingate questioned, an unmarried couple living together in sin. According to Breen and the PCA, "This immoral relationship is made to seem attractive and glamorous, and is not presented with any of the proper compensating moral values."[64] Fortunately for posterity, Breen's decision to stop the film's reissue was not a permanent setback, and the original uncut film is as of this writing available on DVD for anyone curious to watch an entertaining and worthwhile adaptation of an undeservedly overlooked musical. The song goes "Try to Forget." The purpose of this chapter is to try to help and encourage readers not to do so.

ROBERTA
(Broadway 1933; RKO 1935)

The stage show, *Roberta*, which opened on November 18, 1933, enjoyed a successful run of 295 performances before it closed on July 2, 1934, and was then followed by a tour. One week before the tour's end the film version debuted on March 8, 1935. It eventually became RKO's greatest moneymaker that year, earning the studio a profit of $770,000. While preserving much of the Aunt Minnie-John Kent-Princess Stephanie component of the plot and four of the stage show's five major musical numbers, the film also made significant changes. In what follows I will try to make the case that these changes resulted in a successful film that arguably surpasses its model, the first in a short list.[65]

The stage version had added two new characters not in the novel, one song man (Bob Hope) and one dance man (George Murphy). The film retained the idea of a song and dance man, but combined these two roles into a single character, Huck Haines, played by the incomparable Fred Astaire (1899–1987). The casting of Astaire naturally led to an expanded singing and dancing role not only for Astaire but also for his partner Ginger Rogers (1911–1995) cast as Scharwenka.[66] In the stage version, Scharwenka, played by Lyda Roberti, was one of three women competing for John's attentions. The film focuses exclusively on Scharwenka, the assumed name of a woman formerly known as the American Lizzie Gatz. In a newly conceived backstory, screenwriters Sam Mintz, Jane Murfin, and Allan Scott (uncredited) recreated Scharwenka as a character who could serve as a believable performing partner for Astaire, who naturally plays a professional entertainer; the attraction between them is designed to complement the developing romantic relationship between John, a former All-American football player who inherits his Aunt Minnie's elite Parisian dress salon called Roberta, and Stephanie, Minnie's capable assistant and an exiled Russian princess. The fine romance between Huck and Scharwenka starts with "I'll Be Hard to Handle," the first of the Astaire-Rogers duets, the number that Arlene Croce describes as "the big event of the film, the number (and the film) in which 'Fred and Ginger' became fixed screen deities."[67] See Figure 2.8.

Although the film version of *Roberta* retained only four major stage numbers as stand-alone songs, unlike *Music in the Air* it didn't remove the show's best-loved song in the process and thankfully retained the two big hits from the show,

Fig. 2.8 Fred Astaire (Huck) and Ginger Rogers (Countess Scharwenka) get to know each other through dance in "I'll Be Hard to Handle" in the film version of *Roberta*. [32:58]. Screenshot.

"Smoke Gets in Your Eyes" and "Yesterdays." The one significant number left on the cutting room floor was the difficult-to-sing "Something Had to Happen," sung on the stage by John (Ray Middleton). Its removal might be viewed as collateral damage as a consequence of assigning this role to the non-singing Randolph Scott.

As in the stage version, "Smoke Gets in Your Eyes" was sung in the film by Stephanie (Dunne), but in a new twist "Yesterdays," sung on stage by Minnie (Fay Templeton), was newly assigned in the film, also to Dunne.[68] Since it was standard in musical films of all types, original films or adaptations, to focus on two or three singers, the decision to make Minnie a non-singing role was par for the course. The film also added two Kern songs not found in the stage version. One of these, "I Won't Dance," had been introduced the previous year in Kern and Hammerstein's London production *Three Sisters*. In the film version of *Roberta* it served as the central solo dance number for Astaire with lyrics considerably reworked by Fields, who would contribute her first full set of lyrics for a Kern musical the following year in *Swing Time*. A brand new second inserted number, "Lovely to Look At," was conceived as a third song for Dunne. By enhancing Stephanie's vocal importance to represent the operetta side and Huck's combined vocal and dance role on the musical comedy side, the transformation from stage to film captured the best of both theatrical worlds.

"Something Had to Happen" may have been the only major song completely excised from the film, but three songs were relegated to supporting orchestral roles. One of these was the now aptly named "Don't Ask Me Not to Sing," which was sung as a diegetic show number in the stage version at the fashion show led by Huck and his band of musicians, the Collegians. Their tune is rhythmically catchy and slides easily between duple and triple meter.[69]

In the film the song's melody underscores Huck's diegetic spoken sales pitch, also at the fashion show. See Figure 2.9. The removal of "Don't Ask" as a singing number in the film was the second time the song was left unsung. As previously noted, the first time occurred in *The Cat and the Fiddle* when the sung portion was dropped in favor of a dance number for Shirley's brother Alec and sister-in-law Angie. In its new position in this show it launched the Act I finale prior to a duet reprise of "Try to Forget" for Shirley and Victor.

In the film version of *Roberta*, two other important songs are heard only in the orchestra, "The Touch of Your Hand" and "You're Devastating." When all is said and sung (or not sung), the only other song besides "Something Had to Happen" completely removed in the transfer from stage to film was "Madrigal," sung by John, Huck, Billy, the amateur college ensemble on stage (the Collegians) and the professional band (the Indianians) in the film. Another stage song for Scharwenka, "Hot Spot," had already been reduced to 23 measures. In exchange for the loss of "Madrigal" and "Hot Spot" were the two new songs with lyrics by

Fig. 2.9 Bob Hope (Huck) sings "Don't Ask Me Not to Sing" at the fashion show in the stage version of *Roberta*. Photofest.

Fields, "I Won't Dance" and "Lovely to Look At" and two interpolated numbers not heard in the stage version, "Indiana" and "Russian Song."[70]

The net result of song deletions and replacements of songs with underscoring led to a major transformation in the respective modes of presentation from stage to film, a move from the non-diegetic to the diegetic. To review, the stage and film versions of *Show Boat* maintain a clear division between these two modes. In some songs, the characters are aware they are singing—for example, "Can't Help Lovin'" on both stage and screen and the added screen number "Gallivantin' Around." Other songs such as "Make Believe" and "Ol' Man River" are presented non-diegetically on both stage and film. As discussed earlier, the nearly totally diegetic presentational mode of *The Cat and the Fiddle* in its stage version was largely preserved in the film adaptation, despite new dramatic contexts. The adaptation of *Roberta* took yet another approach. Diegetic stage songs such as "I'll Be Hard to Handle" remained diegetic in the film. What was unusual about the film version is that its creators looked for and discovered ingenious ways to *convert Roberta's* non-diegetic stage songs into diegetic film songs.

Here's a quick checklist of what happened with the major songs heard in the stage version and how they were altered in the film. The screen column in

Table 2.4, "*Roberta* on Stage and Screen." provides the order in which songs appear in the film. In addition to the sheer amount of diegeticism in the film (when compared with its stage counterpart), the variety of *new* diegetic purposes is notable. The expanded use of diegeticism supports a trajectory that begins with *auditions*, moves on to *rehearsals*, and culminates in *performances*. In the opening film song, the interpolated "Indiana" provides the material for an audition in which the Indianians fail to persuade the manager with five names (Alexis Petrovich Moscuyvitch Ivan Voyda) to hire the "pale face Americans" when he discovers that band members do not belong to the Wabash Indian tribe as he had assumed. The musicians redeem themselves in their successful second *audition* ("Let's Begin").

Sandwiched between the two serenades that Stephanie clearly presents as performances for Minnie, "Russian Song" and "Yesterdays," is "I'll Be Hard to Handle," in which Fred and Ginger *rehearse* a song and dance for their forthcoming performance. The next two numbers, "The Touch of Your Hand" and "You're Devastating," consist of orchestral underscoring that is diegetic because the participants associated with the fashion show let viewers know they can hear these songs. As a result, "I Won't Dance," "Smoke Gets in Your Eyes," and "Lovely to Look At" are now unmistakably diegetic *performances*.

At the same time, unlike many, if not most, films in the 1930s, all of these songs are demonstrably integral components of the plot. In the presentation of probably the best-known song in the stage show and film, a *performance* of "Smoke Gets in Your Eyes," which viewers might expect to hear uninterrupted, the exigencies of the plot necessitate a dramatic interruption, a confrontation between Stephanie and John. After the interruption, Stephanie returns to sing the release (or bridge). The release begins in a remote key (C-flat major in the key of E-flat major), which dramatically enhances Stephanie's disconcerted psychological state before she regains her composure at the return of the main section.

In his survey of film musicals from the 1930s to 1950s Roy Hemming states that despite converting "The Touch of Your Hand" and "You're Devastating" from full-blown songs with words and music to unidentified orchestral underscoring, "*Roberta* is, arguably, the first movie adaptation of a Broadway musical that turned out better than the original."[71] Hemming attributes this success to a great score by Kern and Harbach (and presumably Fields) and the timeless performances of Dunne, Astaire, and Rogers.

This chapter supports Hemming's assessment. I would also like to express my opinion that the high quality of the *Roberta* film adaptation goes beyond simply the fine singing performances of Kern specialist Dunne and the spectacular dancing of Astaire and Rogers, indispensable as they are. The larger critical context for this opinion is the widely accepted view (which I share) that relatively few film adaptations of Broadway musicals truly match their stage counterparts in

Table 2.4 *Roberta* on Stage and Screen.

Stage	Screen
PROLOGUE	
	Indiana (Huck, Indianians) (3:58) **New diegetic song for an audition**
Let's Begin (Murphy, Ensemble) (2) Non-diegetic song at a party	Let's Begin (Astaire, Candy, Sheldon) (20:23) Diegetic song and dance audition for the Indianians
Alpha, Beta, Pi ["Madrigal" in Vocal Score]	
(Hope, Murphy, Middleton) (5)	
You're Devastating (Hope) (8)	
Let's Begin (First Reprise) (Murphy, Middleton, Hope, Male Ensemble) (17)	
Act I	
	Russian Song (Traditional Song) (Dunne) (27:35) **New diegetic song**
You're Devastating (Reprise) (Tamara) (20)	
	I'll Be Hard to Handle (Rogers, Astaire) (song, 29:34; dance, 31:32) Diegetic song performed at a rehearsal. On stage it functions as a performance preview
Yesterdays (Aunt Minnie) (25)	Yesterdays (Dunne) (41:53) Diegetic serenade
Something Had to Happen (Roberti, Hope, Middleton) (37)	
The Touch of Your Hand (Tamara, Hain) (50)	The Touch of Your Hand (Instrumental) (50:36-53:23) Diegetic music for the in-house fashion show and the removal of Sophie's future dress
	Diegetic music for the in-house fashion show and the removal of Sophie's future dress
Fashion Show (You're Devastating) (66)	You're Devastating (Instrumental) (66:59-68:42) Diegetic music for the fashion show which includes Sophie's unveiling of the vulgar dress she finds "elegantly alluring"
I'll Be Hard to Handle (Roberti) (68)	
Finale (You're Devastating; I'll Be Hard to Handle) (73)	

Table 2.4 Continued

Stage	Screen
Act II	
	I Won't Dance (Astaire) (song, 68:52; dance, 71:55) **New diegetic song and dance for Huck**
Hot Spot (Roberti) (76)	
Smoke Gets in Your Eyes (Tamara) (83)	Smoke Get in Your Eyes (Dunne) (Begins 75:53; continues after dialogue at 81:26) for Huck and Scharwenka (Astaire and Rogers Diegetic song for Stephanie; later a dance for Huck and Scharwenka (Astaire and Rogers)
Let's Begin (Second Reprise) (Hope, Tamara) (91)	
Something Had to Happen (Reprise) (MIddleton) (106)	
Let's Begin (Third Reprise) (Hope, Middleton, Roberti, Lord Henry) (108)	
Don't Ask Me Not to Sing (Huck, California Collegians) (110-A)	Don't Ask Me Not to Sing (Astaire) (88:27) Diegetic orchestral accompaniment to Huck's spoken sales pitch
The Touch of Your Hand (Reprise) (Tamara, Ladislaw) (112)	
	Lovely to Look At (Dunne) (92:11) Sung performances
	Lovely to Look At and Smoke Gets in Your Eyes (Astaire and Rogers) (98:17) Dance performance
Finale (I'll Be Hard to Handle, Let's Begin) (Murphy, Roberti, Hope, Tamara, Middleton) (122)	I Won't Dance: Finale (Astaire and Rogers) (103:49) Dance performance

- *Numbers in parentheses in the stage column refer to page numbers in Otto Harbach, "Roberta" (unpublished script).*
- *The songs listed in bold in the screen column were not in the stage version.*
- *Numbers in parentheses in the screen column refer to film timings.*

MAJOR SINGING AND DANCING AND SELECTED ROLES

Stage: Lyda Roberti (Madam Nunez/Clementina Scharwenka); Bob Hope (Huckleberry "Huck" Haines, the Crooner); Faye Templeton (Aunt Minnie/Roberta); Tamara (Princess Stephanie); George Murphy (Billy Boyden, the Hoofer); Sydney Greenstreet (Lord Henry Delves); Ray Middleton (John Kent); William Hain (Ladislaw); Helen Gray (Sophie Teale); Fred MacMurray (California Collegian); Allan Jones (California Collegian)

Screen: Irene Dunne (Stephanie); Fred Astaire (Huck); Ginger Rogers (Scharwenka); Randolph Scott (Kent); Helen Westley (Roberta); Victor Varconi (Ladislaw); Claire Dodd (Sophie); Luis Alberni (Voyda); Candy Candido (Candy, Wabash Indianian); Gene Sheldon (Banjo-Playing Wabash Indianian); Lucille Ball (Fashion Model) quality, much less surpass them. The film adaptations of Kern's musicals explored here depart from conventional practices of their time and offer exceptions to the conventional wisdom. *The Cat and the Fiddle* may be a near miss, but *Show Boat* and *Roberta* remain among the few great film adaptations of stage musicals. Indeed, the latter in my view deserves a special place in musical film history as perhaps the first film adaptation "that turned out better than the original," a critical verdict later matched by only a handful among many valiant attempts.

3

Challenging the Hollywood Studio Model

On the Town versus *Call Me Madam*

The film version of *On the Town* (1949) not only ended a decade but nearly an era as well. Since the late 1920s when sound replaced silence, the studio system rightly did not regard the preservation of a stage musical's content as indispensable to popularity and financial success. In fact, as we have observed in the adaptation of *Anything Goes* in chapter 1 and will soon observe with *On the Town*, the original score might be considered a liability, a fixer-upper in need of in-house studio composers. Thus, for roughly the first twenty years of film adaptation, the *Anything Goes* model remained the studio's modus operandi. Though it occasionally persisted with later films such as *Gentlemen Prefer Blondes* (1953) and the second film adaptation of *Anything Goes* (1956), by the end of the 1950s the once ubiquitous way of looking at film adaptation was nearly over.

Starting in the early 1950s film studios began to change their tune, significantly by *not* changing the tunes. MGM led the way with three adaptations: *Annie Get Your Gun* (1950), *Show Boat* (1951), and *Kiss Me Kate* (1953), none of which inserted interpolations by other songwriters. Studio producers and directors now determined that the most effective way to achieve continued financial success (still the bottom line) was to cultivate greater allegiance to the musical content, narrative, and often the casting of the stage version. One cause of this change was the greater integration between song and story of the stage hits that studios were paying increasingly high premiums to secure.[1]

The new popularity of the cast album contributed to the new trend toward more faithful adaptations. Viewers familiar with the songs they heard in this format expected to see and hear the characters in the film sing the same songs they sang on the cast album (even if a dubbed voice might now inhabit their bodies) and in roughly the same dramatic context. Sometimes, as with Donald O'Connor in *Call Me Madam*, they would willingly adjust to and appreciate changes that gave the characters something to dance about. The film adaptation of *Call Me Madam*, which appeared only four years after *On the Town*, will serve admirably as Exhibit A for this altered set of norms as will most of the shows and films discussed in future chapters of *A Fine Romance*. With some exceptions, the studios' revised approach to film adaptation would hold sway until *Cabaret* arrived at the end our story in 1972.[2]

A Fine Romance. Geoffrey Block, Oxford University Press. © Oxford University Press 2023.
DOI: 10.1093/oso/9780197501733.003.0003

ON THE TOWN
(Broadway 1944; MGM 1949)

One year after Rodgers and Hammerstein launched their collaboration with the revolutionary and game-changing musical *Oklahoma!*, four talented young descendants of Jewish immigrants joined the legendary director George Abbott (1887–1995), known as "Mr. Abbott," to put on a show. The result was *On the Town*, which premiered on December 28, 1944, and ran until February 2, 1946. The ambitious quartet of novices consisted of choreographer Jerome Robbins (1918–1998), composer Leonard Bernstein (1918–1990), and co-librettists-lyricists Betty Comden (1917–2006) and Adolph Green (1914–2002). Separately and sometimes together, Robbins, Bernstein, and Comden and Green would go on to create some of the most memorable and acclaimed musicals and movies of their era. A highly selective list among the many Broadway and film highlights of these illustrious careers would include the following: Robbins: *The King and I*, *West Side Story*, *Gypsy*, and *Fiddler on the Roof*; Bernstein: *Wonderful Town*, *Candide*, and *West Side Story*; Comden and Green: stage musicals, *Wonderful Town*, *Bells Are Ringing*, *Applause*, *On the Twentieth Century*, and *The Will Rogers Follies*; and film musicals, *The Barkleys of Broadway*, *Singin' in the Rain*, and *The Band Wagon*.

Prior to their first major breakthrough in *On the Town*, Comden and Green, along with the future Hollywood star Judy Holliday (with Bernstein occasionally joining in), formed a cabaret ensemble in 1938 called The Revuers. Over the next few years, the future Broadway librettist-lyricist duo performed at the Village Vanguard in Greenwich Village, gaining indispensable experience writing skits and song lyrics, training that would serve them in their collaborative stage and film work for another six decades. Bernstein got the world's attention on November 14, 1943, when at the age of twenty-five he conducted the New York Philharmonic on short notice, replacing the ill Bruno Walter in a performance that was broadcast nationally on radio and made front page news in the *New York Times*. The following year, an annus mirabilis, Bernstein conducted his first symphony ("Jeremiah") in January, celebrated the mounting of the highly successful ballet *Fancy Free* with choreography by Robbins and music by Bernstein in April, culminating with the debut of his first Broadway musical *On the Town* in December.

The musical created by these exuberant and talented Broadway newcomers with its iconic opening number, "New York, New York," did not possess the immediate impact and broad long-term influence of *Oklahoma!*, and the MGM adaptation starring Gene Kelly (1912–1996) and Frank Sinatra (1915–1998) remains far better known. Still, at 462 performances, *On the Town* was a solid hit in a decade that could boast only about a dozen shows that ran for more than 500 performances and only four that ran over a thousand. The show has been revived several times in New York and London, and Bernstein's concert work, "Three Dance Episodes from *On the Town*" (constituting about a third of what might be an unprecedented amount of dance music in a musical), continues to enjoy a firm place in the orchestral literature.[3]

Though barely noticed at the time, *On the Town* also made history as the most thoroughly racially integrated musical of its era starting with its star dancer, the Japanese American Sono Osato (1919–2018). Osato's father, a Japanese immigrant and American citizen, was separated from his Irish French Canadian wife and children and incarcerated in an "internment camp" for the duration of World War II while was daughter was appearing on Broadway. After the Broadway run, the show had a limited national tour in 1946 that lasted three months and traveled as far west as Chicago. On this tour, Osato was replaced by Allyn Ann McLerie, then newly married to Adolph Green; most of the other leading players also left the touring company (except for Comden and Green). In addition, the cast featured interracial dancing couples and chorus and African American actors in small but non-stereotypical roles. Performances during the later months of the show's run were conducted by the African American conductor Everett Lee.

The ballet *Fancy Free* may have provided its scene designer Oliver Smith the inspiration for *On the Town* (which he also designed), but in the end the only significant common denominators between their plots are the three sailors and their twenty-four hours of shore leave. Even here they differ since in *Fancy Free* the sailors are in competition over a woman whereas in *On the Town* two grateful sailors (Chip and Ozzie) try to assist Gabey, who rescued them from imminent wartime danger, in locating the poster woman of his dreams, Miss Turnstiles of June 1944. In another major distinction, the three women companions in *On the Town* were assertive, smart, and funny. As for any *musical* connections between his ballet and his first Broadway show, Bernstein emphatically and repeatedly asserted "there was not a note of *Fancy Free* music in *On the Town*."[4]

Not only were the composer, librettist-lyricists, choreographer, and scene designer new to Broadway, but none of the stage actors had established credentials as major stars.[5] Among the men, neither Cris Alexander (Chip) nor Green (Ozzie) had any Broadway experience. John Battles's short life on the Broadway stage had begun in the chorus of *Something for the Boys* the previous year and continued in *Follow the Girls* earlier in 1944. Three years later Battles would star as Dr. Joseph Taylor in Rodgers and Hammerstein's ill-fated *Allegro.* Comden (Claire) and Green's success on Broadway and in Hollywood was still a few years in the future. Nancy Walker (Hildy) played the role of Blind Date in both the Broadway and Hollywood versions of *Best Foot Forward* in 1941 and 1943, respectively. At the time of *On the Town*, Walker was a rising comedic dynamo at 4'11". She would go on to appear in numerous future musicals on Broadway, twice earning Tony Award nominations. Walker also achieved considerable success on television beginning in the 1950s, and readers of a certain age might remember her in the popular 1970s sitcom *Rhoda* as Rhoda's comically neurotic mother who vacuumed obsessively whenever she was upset.

The best-known leading player in *On the Town* was Osato, the lead dancer cast as Miss Turnstiles (Ivy Smith), the central dramatic female role. Regular theatergoers had seen Osato the previous year as the critically acclaimed featured dancer in the three major ballets showcased in the hit musical *One Touch of Venus*, choreographed by Agnes de Mille. Osato was a natural choice for the role of Miss Turnstiles, the exotic woman on the subway poster whom Gabey searches for all over the city and eventually catches up with at her singing lesson in a Carnegie Hall studio. As in *Venus*, Osato in *On the Town* was the featured dancer in three ballets: (1) the elaborate "Presentation of Miss Turnstiles" (Act I, scene 4); (2) the short and jazzy dance that concludes her duet with her boozy singing teacher Madame Dilly in "Carnegie Hall Pavane" (Act I, scene 8); and (3) a romantic pas de deux with Battles's dream double in the "Dream Coney Island" ballet (Act II, scene 3). Remarkably for a female lead in a musical (in Venus she is labeled only as Première Danseuse), it is only in the duet with Madame Dilly that Ivy sings, mainly in unison and with few exposed notes. Ivy also doesn't get to talk much. In the "Presentation of Miss Turnstiles," she conveys her surprise, "Who, me?" with a hand gesture and relies on simulated rather than audible speech when she learns she has been selected. Although she has some dialogue with Gabey prior to "Pavane," her main communication takes place in pantomime such as in Gabey's "Dream Coney Island."

The five singing members of the sextet of main characters dance about as much as Ivy sings. Instead, a dancing chorus provides most of the extensive choreography. In contrast to Ivy, with the exception of Gabey's strong male vocal presence the women dominate the singing as well as the personal dynamics with their respective partners. The amorous taxi driver Hildy takes the lead with Chip in "Come Up to My Place" and doesn't let her new boyfriend sing at all in "I Can Cook Too." In the former song, Hildy does her best, with mixed success, to take Chip's mind off the New York tourist attractions that have disappeared in the years since his 1934 guidebook was printed. In Act II, Hildy introduces "Ya Got Me" at the Latin-themed nightclub, the Conga Cabana, before being joined in song by Claire, Chip, and Ozzie.

Although Claire doesn't get a song of her own, she sings a lot. In Act I she shares the stage in a mock-operatic duet with Ozzie at the Museum of Natural History in Act I, in which the pair acknowledge their compatible predilection to get "Carried Away," despite their best efforts to remain in control of their passions. In Act II, Claire follows Hildy with a complete verse and chorus of "Ya Got Me," and in the quartet with Hildy, Ozzie, and Chip, "Some Other Time" (added during the Boston tryouts), she sings the entire opening verse and chorus before Hildy follows with the first two A sections of the second chorus. This poignant song then evolves into a harmonized quartet for the B section of the traditional AABA song form, after which, with the exception of Ozzie's solo 6 measures of the final A, the four will continue in harmony until the song's end.

Just as Miss Turnstiles is alone among the female leads to play a major dance role and a virtually non-singing role, Gabey, her male counterpart, barely dances. On the other hand, Gabey was given the two major romantic solo ballads of the show. Both occur in Act I, "Lonely Town," in which Gabey sings of his loneliness before locating Miss Turnstiles, and "Lucky to Be Me" in the final scene of Act I, when he expresses his joy and sense of good fortune at finally finding Ivy and eagerly awaits his rendezvous with this girl of his dreams. In a role that disappeared in the move from stage to screen, Claire's mentor and platonic (or perhaps simply passionless) boyfriend Pitkin (Robert Chisolm) sings a solo song, "I Understand." After allowing himself to be taken for granted and taken advantage of his entire life (and the entire musical), Pitkin finally reaches his breaking point, both with Claire and the world at large, concluding emphatically, and operatically, "I hereby do not understand!!" See Figure 3.1

Adapting *On the Town* from Stage to Film

In assessing the central decisions and premises of the adaptation process from stage to film, remember that in the 1940s, as in the 1930s, fidelity was not the objective. Even in the late 1940s, the goal was to mine (and plunder if necessary) a stage source for the opportunities it offered to serve the needs of the studio production team and the established and emerging stars on the studio payroll and to reach a sizable audience and make a large profit. With *On the Town*, the negotiations for a film version had begun years earlier—in fact, not long after Abbott agreed to direct the original stage show. The pre-production agreement with MGM was $250,000, twice as large as the entire operating budget for the stage version.[6] Such an agreement was unprecedented at the time, and according to Green's recollection, it was "the last pre-production deal of a musical for many years."[7] Apparently, after signing the contract, Louis B. Mayer (the second M in MGM), put off by both the score and the tone of the show, developed a case of buyer's remorse. By the time producer Arthur Freed expressed his personal dislike of much of Bernstein's score, the deal was sealed. Four years later Freed launched their work on a film that greatly altered the show, a film that served studio tastes and bottom lines, with a familiar *Hollywood* cast who possessed

Fig. 3.1 Adolph Green (Ozzie), Betty Comden (Claire De Loone), and Robert Chisolm (Pitkin W. Bridgework) in the stage version of *On the Town*. Vandamm. Museum of the City of New York. F2013.41.4930 © The New York Public Library.

the right combination of marketable and desirable talents. See Table 3.1, "*On the Town* on Stage and Screen."

In the years between the stage and screen versions of *On the Town*, Green and Comden joined the MGM team as scriptwriters and lyricists and contributed screenplays, lyrics, or both to several musical films that appeared shortly before *On the Town*: *Good News* in 1947 (an adaptation of the 1927 Broadway hit) and two original film musicals that appeared earlier in 1949, *Take Me Out to the Ball Game*, and *The Barkleys of Broadway*.[8] *On the Town* (released in December 1949) reunited a number of familiar faces from *Ball Game* (released in April) both on screen and behind the scenes. Freed produced all three films for MGM, and Roger Edens (1905–1970) co-produced. Gene Kelly (1912–1996) and Stanley

Table 3.1 *On the Town* on Stage and Screen.

Stage	Screen
Act I	
I Feel Like I'm Not Out of Bed Yet (Sameth) (8)	I Feel Like I'm Not Out of Bed Yet (Hoffman) (2:20)
New York, New York (Battles, Alexanders, Green) (9)	New York, New York (Kelly, Sinatra, Munshin) (3:35)
Gabey's Comin' (Green, Alexander, Battles) (14)	
Presentation of Miss Turnstiles (Ballet) (Osato) (18)	Presentation of Miss Turnstiles (Ballet) (Vera-Ellen and Ensemble) (10:00) Mainly based on The Great Lover but with one theme from the Miss Turnstiles stage ballet
Come Up to My Place (Walker, Alexander) (21)	
Carried Away (Comden, Green) (32)	**Prehistoric Man (Miller, Green, Kelly, Sinatra, Garrett) (21:47)**
	Come Up to My Place (Garrett, Sinatra) (29:44)
Lonely Town (Battles) (36)	
High School Girls (Ballet) (36)	
Lonely Town Pas de Deux (36)	
Carnegie Hall Pavane (Osato, Steele) (43)	**When You Walk Down Main Street with Me (sung by Kelly; danced by Kelly and Vera-Ellen) (40:04)**
I Can Cook Too (Walker) (53)	**You're Awful (Sinatra; sung to Walker) (47:51)**
Lucky to Be Me (Battles, Chorus) (55)	
Times Square Ballet (Act I Finale) (61)	
	On the Town (Kelly, Vera-Ellen, Sinatra, Garrett, Munshin, and Miller) (55:27)
Act II	
So Long, Baby (Diamond Eddie's Girls) (64)	
I Wish I Was Dead (Diana Dream) (65)	
You Got Me (Walker, Comden, Munshin, Alexander) (68)	Count on Me (Sinatra, Garrett, Munshin, Miller, and Pearce; sung to Kelly) (72:20)
I Understand (Chisolm) (74)	
The Subway Train to Coney Island and the Great Lover (Ballet) (77)	**A Day in New York (Ballet) (77:23) Incorporates material from New York, New York; Lonely Town; Times Square Ballet; The Great Lover; High School Girls; I Feel Like I Can't Get Out of Bed Yet, and Some Other Time**

(*continued*)

Table 3.1 Continued

Stage	Screen
Some Other Time (Comden, Walker, Green, Alexander) (79)	
The Real Coney Island (Rajah Bimmy) (Lorenz) (81)	Pearl of the Persian Sea (89:50) Cooch dance performed by Kelly, Sinatra, and Munshin dressed as ladies of a harem
Finale: New York, New York (Reprise) (Green, Battles, Alexander, Walker, Comden, Osato, Three Sailors, and Entire Company) (84)	New York, New York (Reprise) (95:30)

- *Numbers in parentheses in the stage column refer to page numbers in Betty Comden and Adolph Green's On the Town, in The New York Musicals of Comden & Green (New York: Applause, 1997).*
- *The songs listed in bold in the screen column were not in the stage version.*
- *Numbers in parentheses in the screen column refer to film timings.*

MAJOR SINGING AND DANCING AND SELECTED ROLES

Stage: Sono Osato (Ivy Smith); Nancy Walker (Hildy Esterhazy); Betty Comden (Claire de Loone); Adolph Green (Ozzie); John Battles (Gabey); Cris Alexander (Chip); Robert Chisolm (Pitkin W. Bridgework); ALICE PEARCE (Lucy Schmeeler); Marten Sameth (Workman); Susan Steele (Madame Dilly); Robert Lorenz (Bimmy)

Screen: Gene Kelly (Gabey); Frank Sinatra (Chip); Betty Garrett (Hildy); Ann Miller (Claire); Jules Munshin (Ozzie); Vera-Ellen (Ivy); PEARCE (Lucy Schmeeler); Carol Haney (Principal Dancer); Bern Hoffman (Shipyard Builder)

- *Names in capital letters indicate that a cast member appeared both on stage and in the film.*

Donen (1924-2019) shared directing and choreographic duties in *Ball Game* and *On the Town*, with Donen focusing on the camera work and Kelly mainly in charge of the dancing. The ball-playing singing and dancing trio of Kelly, Sinatra, and Jules Munshin metamorphosed into the three sailors on twenty-four-hour shore leave in *Town*, and once again Betty Garrett, cast as Hildy, chased after Sinatra (Chip) as she did to a lesser extent in the earlier film.

The studio knew at the outset that the film version of *On the Town* needed considerable reworking to fit a new set of personalities and talents. From Freed's perspective, to make the film successful, most of Bernstein's score had to go, a decision that has remained controversial. For Thomas S. Hischak, the result was "probably the butcher job of the decade."[9] On the other hand, Clive Hirschhorn considered *On the Town* "the freshest, most invigorating and innovative screen musical of the decade" and a film that "pushed the Hollywood musical out of its claustrophobic confines in search of new ideas, and was a landmark of its time."[10] Whatever we might think about the decision to gut the film musically, it should be noted that Bernstein had not insisted on a non-interpolation agreement. Consequently, his only other option was to write new, more film-friendly songs, an option that none of the principals—Freed, Edens, or Bernstein—wanted to exercise.

In a retrospective panel discussion of *On the Town* in 1981, the panelists Bernstein, Comden, Green, Robbins, and Smith gave the more experienced Abbott considerable credit for guiding the talented but still green youngsters through the creation and rehearsal of this show. To their surprise, Abbott, at the time still a relative youngster at fifty-seven and considered a long-shot to accept the project, had readily agreed, providing they could put things together in ten days.[11] Abbott had seen *Fancy Free*, enjoyed it, and was impressed when he met Comden and Green. Although he referred to Bernstein's complex and dissonant music as "that Prokofieff stuff," Bernstein lost no future opportunity to point out that in the end Abbott didn't cut a single measure, "not a bar of it."[12]

When it came time to prepare the film version, however, not only Mayer but also Freed expressed distaste for Bernstein's score. Mayer was reportedly put off more by the show's multiracial dance ensemble than the "Prokofiev stuff," while Freed's reservations were based as much on pragmatic as aesthetic factors. In a 1986 interview with John Kobal (quoted in chapter 1), Freed acknowledged that he preferred to produce original film musicals rather than adaptations and tried to limit adaptations to musicals he was required to put on because MGM owned the rights to them.[13] A few years later, Gene Kelly recalled what he thought was the conventional studio wisdom about Bernstein's inability to produce hit songs: "You know the moguls. They want hit songs. The moguls heard the score to *On the Town* and they didn't hear any hits."[14]

The moguls weren't alone. Bernstein may have written the score to a hit show on his first attempt in 1944, but five years later in the absence of a reasonably complete cast album, few potential film viewers would have seen or heard *On the Town*.[15] Signs of change would arrive in the following decade, the original 1957 cast album of *West Side Story* sold reasonably well, the same year that Sinatra recorded "Lonely Town." In 1958, jazz pianist Bill Evans issued the first of ten recorded renditions of "Some Other Time." He would reuse its vamp in "Peace Piece" on the album *Everybody Digs Bill Evans*, also in 1958, and again in "Flamenco Sketches" on Miles Davis's album *Kind of Blue* one year later.

Once Freed made the decision to cast Kelly and Ann Miller, dancers rather than singers like John Battles and Betty Comden, it would prove an insurmountable challenge to give Kelly ballads like "Lonely Town" or Miller a tune like "Carried Away" that required considerable vocal but virtually no dancing skills. Sinatra biographer Will Friedwald relates that it was on account of "Lonely Town" that Sinatra agreed to put on a sailor suit again for *On the Town*, and he was angered when he learned on the last day of shooting that he wouldn't be singing the song.[16] According to Donen biographer Stephen M. Silverman, the removal of "Lonely Town" also "proved a particular bone of contention with

Comden and Green, who pleaded with Freed through telegrams right up to the starting date of production that the ballad be retained."[17]

In the end, the only songs that made the transition from stage to film were the bluesy workman's song that opened the show (and the film) at the Brooklyn Naval Yard, "I Feel Like I'm Not Out of Bed Yet," the famous opening musical number for Gabey, Chip, and Ozzie that immediately follows, "New York, New York" (now a "wonderful" rather than a "helluva town") and "Come Up to My Place," Hildy's bold and bawdy proposition to Chip. The film also retains the "Presentation of Miss Turnstiles" ballet that follows the stage plot closely but with significant changes in musical content. With the exception of the ballet "A Day in New York," which displays a considerable amount of Bernstein's musical material, albeit rearranged and reconceived, the remaining songs in the film were composed by associate producer Edens with lyrics by Comden and Green.

Roger Edens was probably the main studio composer (and most often recruited MGM on-call studio lyricist) to serve Freed and his "Unit" from the late 1930s through the 1950s. Although his songs are professionally well crafted, it's probably not unfair to say that few Edens songs are enshrined in the Great American Songbook. Although his work as the composer or lyricist appeared in numerous films at MGM, he is probably most remembered for the lyrics or music he wrote during his longtime association with Judy Garland: the new lyrics for the then-rising star to the tune of "You Made Me Love You" (1937), two years prior to *The Wizard of Oz*; the once-popular "Our Love Affair" (with a lyric by Freed) in *Strike Up the Band* (1940); and a big showcase number in *A Star Is Born* (1954), "Born in a Trunk." Two years before the film version of *On the Town*, Edens also wrote the music for "The French Lesson" to Comden and Green's lyrics in *Good News*.

In most of these films, Edens usually added a single song or other material to film scores mainly created by such noted songwriters as Harold Arlen and E. Y. Harburg (*Cabin in the Sky*, MGM 1943), B. G. DeSylva, Ray Brown, and Ray Henderson (*Good News*, 1947), and Richard Rodgers and Lorenz Hart (*Jumbo*, MGM 1962). A few months before *On the Town*, Edens collaborated with Comden and Green on four songs and contributed the words as well as music for a fifth included in the score to *Take Me Out to the Ball Game*, which featured *On the Town*'s sailor trio plus Garrett. Filling in this score were two other songs, one of which was the famous title song published in 1908 with music by Albert von Tilzer and lyrics by Jack Norworth. In *Funny Face* (1957), a film inspired by George and Ira Gershwin's 1927 Broadway score that retained the title but discarded the plot, Edens contributed three songs, "Think Pink," "Bonjour, Paris!," and the charming "On How to Be Lovely," to a score packed with Gershwin standards such as "How Long Has This Been Going On?," "Funny Face," "Let's Kiss and Make Up," and "He Loves and She Loves."

"Probably the Butcher Job of the Decade":
Adapting a Classic Score

At six songs, Roger Edens's contribution to the musical score of *On the Town* exceeds that of even *Take Me Out to the Ball Game.* The Bernstein material is front-loaded within the film's first thirty minutes when Bernstein buffs are treated to "I Feel Like I'm Not Out of Bed Yet," "New York, New York," the reworked "Presentation of Miss Turnstiles," and "Come Up to My Place."[18] After that, Freed & Co., tired of "that Prokofieff stuff," removed the rest of Bernstein's songs and most of his score. All that remained was the rearrangement and reconceived stage ballet of Bernstein's "Times Square Ballet" that metamorphosed into the film's most extended ballet, "A Day in New York."

Let's look at the Bernstein songs the Freed Unit discarded in the transfer from stage to screen and how Edens's songs altered the meanings and contexts of these abandoned songs. The first film song not by Bernstein, "Prehistoric Man" (21:47), introduced about eight minutes before "Come Up to My Place," replaced "Carried Away," the duet between Claire de Loone and Ozzie that *followed* "Come Up to My Place" on the stage. "Carried Away," clearly a parody of operatic indulgence, required, if not actual opera singers, singers with strong voices. Claire also needed to be able to flaunt a range from the F below middle C (the first time she sings "away") to a high C two octaves above at the end of the song, naturally also on the word "away." The duet also needed singers who could negotiate counterpoint and harmony. On the other hand, minimal dancing skills were required.

Both Betty Comden on stage and Ann Miller in the film version worked in the Museum of Natural History (renamed the Museum of Anthropological History in the film), but unlike the stage Claire, Miller was required to come to work in tap shoes in case she came across a man (Ozzie) who bears an uncanny resemblance to the museum's statue of a prehistoric man that would inspire her to sing and dance. Despite their stylistic differences, both "Carried Away" and "Prehistoric Man" are in the minor mode, a mode generally used sparingly by Bernstein and most of the popular composers of the day with the conspicuous exception of Cole Porter.[19]

Probably few members of the stage audience had difficulty figuring out that the expression "carried away" meant casting aside sexual inhibitions. Somewhat surprisingly in the light of potential Production Code Administration (PCA) infractions, "Prehistoric Man" makes this meaning more rather than less explicit. The Production Code censors did ask MGM to excise as unacceptable the word "hot" in "Lots of guys are hot for me," the word "libido" in "healthy happy libido" and "I love that libido," and the lyric "they sat all the day just beating their tom toms."[20] Curiously, when the film was released, while "hot" and "libido" had been expurgated, the suggestion to remove the line about tom toms was disregarded. Instead, Claire not only emphasizes the point that she "*really* loves tom toms" but still more suggestively that she loves "bear [think bare] skin." Just as the Production Code didn't seem to mind the unmistakable implications of Hildy's invitation to Chip to come up to her place, they apparently either never got around to screening the final cut of the film or imagined how a lyric about loving bear skin might be construed. Miller's suggestive delivery makes it a challenge to miss the word's intended spelling, but to their credit the PCA overlooked the transgression.

After "Carried Away," the next stage song was Gabey's "Lonely Town." Even if the Freed Unit liked this song and wanted to include it, the breath control required would have demanded too much of Kelly, although it would have suited Sinatra well. Indeed, Comden and Green found a place for Sinatra to sing "Lonely Town" in his assigned role as Chip to lead into an earlier version of "A Day in New York," but the song was removed when the ballet was reconceived. Eight years later Sinatra included "Lonely Town" on his studio album *Where Are You?*, the only Bernstein song the prolific singer recorded outside of the film soundtrack.[21] In place of "Lonely Town" the film added a new Edens song for Gabey to sing to Ivy at Symphonic Hall (Carnegie Hall in the stage version), "When You Walk Down Main Street," which led into a soft shoe duet.

The "Main Street" song and dance replaced Ivy's vocal duet with Madame Dilly, "Carnegie Hall Pavane," which was followed on stage by Ivy's solo dance. In the dialogue leading up to the new song, Gabey admits that he grew up in the small Indiana town of Meadowville (population 18,000) and is not the sophisticated New Yorker he pretended to be to impress a celebrity like Miss Turnstiles. Ivy, who also feigns a worldliness she doesn't possess, almost gives the game away when Gabey quotes a phrase uttered by his high school teacher Miss Hodges, who happens to have been Ivy's teacher as well, and Ivy can't resist expressing delighted surprise. Ivy's veneer vanishes, however, when Gabey informs her that he has to get back to his ship the next morning. The news prompts Ivy to cancel her attendance at "a big society party" in order to go out with Gabey that evening.

Near the end of the film Ivy admits she has been earning her living as a cooch dancer at Coney Island and that like Gabey she, too, is from Meadowville and not a "New York glamour girl." She even acknowledges that she had Miss Hodges for American history and grew up just two blocks away from Gabey. For a Production Code that would have prohibited the potential miscegenation between Battles and Osato, Vera-Ellen's Ivy was perfectly cast as the girl next door in Middle America. "Main Street," a conventional song about the idyllic life in a small town, may not be nearly as interesting and clever as "Carnegie Hall Pavane," but it does fit the newly conceived characters, the enhanced dancing skill set for Gabey, and the dramatic context reimagined by Comden and Green.

Carol Oja summarized the changes between stage and film that were made in order to conform to Main Street America expectations: the leading female roles were reduced in importance and the three sailors became the stars; New York City was magically transformed into a white settlement, with the exception of exotic dancers at nightclubs and sideshows enacting cultural stereotypes; and Ivy metamorphosed into a small-town white girl.[22] Since Gabey and Claire in the stage version were cast as singers rather than dancers, and since casting determined content, the film version had to accommodate the dancing talents of Kelly and Miller and modify the musical material of their revised roles accordingly. The casting of Sinatra and Betty Garrett did not create a similar need to rewrite their songs. Since "Come Up to My Place" fit the characters cast as Chip and Hildy, it was possible to keep it in the film, providing the Production Code didn't object. "I Can Cook Too" posed a greater challenge to the Code since its lyrics go beyond the suggestive when Chip, upon learning that Hildy can cook, asks her to tell him the specialty of the house and she replies, "Me!!"

Garrett possessed the personality and vocal chops to sing this rousing boogie-woogie number, but the words to the song, attributed to Bernstein by those in the know, were so provocative—not unlike Bessie Smith's lyric to "Empty Bed Blues" which suggestively asks her man to grind her coffee and boil her fresh cabbage—that Freed likely realized the futility of testing Joseph I. Breen at the Production Code office.[23] Perhaps MGM was discouraged after being asked to replace the description of New York as a "helluva town" with "wonderful town."[24] The decision to omit "I Can Cook Too" might also have been a byproduct of Sinatra's greater stardom and the need to give him a song of his own, since otherwise he only shares one song, "Come Up to My Place," which Hildy dominates. Whether due to censorship or Sinatra's star status, or a combination of both, Freed, Kelly, and Donen made the decision to give the larger share of screen time to Sinatra rather than to Garrett.

The song Edens composed for Sinatra, "You're Awful," follows a date with Hildy during which Chip resists her advances and hurts her feelings by showing greater interest in the New York sights than in establishing a romantic relationship. Chip feels remorse for his behavior, has a change of heart, and throws his treasured, if dated, guidebook over the railing of the Empire State Building observation deck. This last gesture prompts Chip to sing a traditional love ballad, with a twist, in which insults (e.g., "you're awful," "you're nothing," "you're fright'ning," "you're boring," and "you're cheap") become endearments. For example, "awful" becomes "awful nice to look at" and "to be with" and "you're cheap" becomes "cheap at any price, dear,/Cheap for such a diamond" or "for such a pearl." The word "*pearl*" brings Comden and Green back to the original endearment "You're awful" and prepares for the final rhyme, "awful nice to be my *girl*." Unfortunately, although we know that he was miffed at not being allowed to sing "Lonely Town," Sinatra remained circumspect about what he really thought about the "Awful" song assigned to him instead.

On stage, the second act begins with five members of the sextet nightclub hopping, first at a white club, Diamond Eddie's, where the clientele in the original stage version included two African American women, then at a Spanish club (Conga Cabana), and finally the Slam Bang Club, a Black club, renamed the Dixieland in the film. Ivy's absence is due to Madame Dilly's threats to inform Ivy's parents about her questionable place of employment. Madame Dilly's blackmail causes Ivy to break her date with Gabey and to instead keep her appointment as a cooch dancer in Coney Island. All the music performed at the three nightclubs disappears in the film, including songs performed by singers at the various night clubs, "I Wish I Was Dead" (regularly identified by the opening words "I'm Blue") sung by Diana Dream at Diamond Eddie's and a Spanish variation of this song with the same title sung by Señorita Dolores Dolores at the Cabana.

At this second stop of their nightclub stage adventures, Hildy introduces a lively rhumba "numba," "Ya Got Me," with its Latin-tinged rhythmic metrical accents (3 + 3+ 2). The purpose of the song is for Hildy, later joined by Claire, Chip, and Ozzie, to cheer up Gabey, who is pining at the loss of Ivy. Instead of a musical number in a style with African American signifiers, the final musical leg of their nightclubbing consists of Pitkin's song "I Understand." In a mixture of Gilbert and Sullivan (think "When I Was a Lad") and Boris Godunov's coronation acceptance speech to the Russian folk, Claire's cuckolded boyfriend explains in the minor mode (until the final chord) that he has had enough.

Since the operatic Pitkin has been removed as a character from the film there was no need to replace his song, and it disappeared along with all the other club music. Instead, the quintet sings another interpolated Edens song, the lively new title tune, "On the Town," as they begin their clubbing. At the Club Dixieland the film introduces yet another new Edens song "Count on Me" in place of "Ya Got Me."[25] Even a superficial comparison between "Ya Got Me" and "Count on Me" (a lyrical if not a musical variation on a parallel theme) might explain what was lost in the translation from Bernstein's sophisticated score. Written in a pseudo-country western vein, the energetic but predictable (even the first time) and repetitive "Count on Me" is only partially redeemed by Kelly's energetic choreography featuring his signature use of stage props. We can only infer what Gerald Mast thought of "Count on Me," but he did offer harsh specific assessments of other Edens replacements before summarizing, "Every Edens song for the film ('Prehistoric Man,' 'Main Street,' a vapid title tune, and 'You're Awful') is hackwork—the kind of musical garbage that proved the inferiority of Hollywood musicals to Broadway buffs."[26]

"A Day in New York"

Although the film replaced the all-singing no-dancing Battles and Comden with the superstar dancers Kelly and Miller, the overall dance component in the film was actually less than the four major ballets along with various shorter dances seen in the stage version. Nevertheless, in addition to the interpolated new dance numbers, "Main Street" and "Prehistoric Man," the film managed to retain a considerable amount of Bernstein's *ballet* music, mainly in two numbers, "Presentation of Miss Turnstiles" and "A Day in New York," although in both cases staff arrangers greatly altered the ordering of Bernstein's musical material.

The *music* of the ballet "Miss Turnstiles" in the film that was composed by Bernstein was mainly derived from "The Great Lover Displays Himself," which occurs far later in the stage version. In fact, the only music retained from the original "Miss Turnstiles" six-minute stage ballet is the loud and discordant theme heard at the outset and the bustling figure that starts in the sixth measure. But despite a minimal musical connection, the "Turnstiles" film *scenario* does correspond relatively closely to the stage pantomime as it acts out "Gabey's fanciful projection of what Ivy Smith must be like." As in its stage source, the film ballet depicts the range of Ivy's interests and personal qualities described on her subway poster. Film viewers also witness her dancing a pas de deux with four different men, the home-loving type, the soldier, the artist, and the athlete.

Even more musically substantial is the seven and one-half-minute-long central ballet in the film titled "A Day in New York." Unlike "Miss Turnstiles," "A Day in New York" corresponds only loosely to the dramatic content of a stage ballet. Perhaps the closest to it is "Subway Ride and Imaginary Coney Island." And although it relies on musical material heard *somewhere* in Bernstein's score, its connection to "Coney Island" in its musical structure and ordering is even more tenuous. Like the tripartite "Coney Island" stage ballet (no. 21 in the 1997 published vocal score), much of the ballet in "A Day in New York" occurs in Gabey's imagination. In the film, Gabey (Kelly) and Ivy (Vera-Ellen) dance to the reworked music to "The Great Lover Displays Himself" (21a); also in the film, Kelly dances with Vera-Ellen in their Pas de Deux (21b), whereas in the stage version Osato (Ivy) danced with Ray Harrison, the dancing body double for Battles (Gabey).

The published stage script provides detailed summaries of these three ballets. In all of them Battles is a spectator rather than a participant, much in the way de Mille had used body doubles for both Curly and Laurey in the Act I dream ballet in *Oklahoma!* the previous year. The musical content of "Subway Ride and Imaginary Coney Island" derives mainly from the verse of "Some Other Time" (no. 21), a song otherwise absent from the film. Although "Lonely Town" was not sung in the film, the "Pas de Deux" borrows liberally from the "Lonely Town" ballet along with new material not related to other songs or dances.

To sum up, although the musical material used in the culminating ballet "A Day in New York" was *composed* entirely by Bernstein, the *organization* of Bernstein's music does not match the music he composed for the stage show. Instead, its content consisted of passages from no fewer than seven songs and dances located in various places in the stage score that were chosen mainly in response to *Kelly's* ballet scenario. From Bernstein biographer Humphrey Burton and Comden's recollections, it is possible to get an idea about some of the steps that led to "A Day in New York." Accounts concur that the starting point of the ballet was the scenario presumably prepared jointly by Kelly and Comden and Green and its corresponding choreography prepared by Kelly, perhaps with some input from his assistant, Carol Haney, who would also be featured as one of three female dancers in the number as a dancing double in the film.

This process was virtually the opposite of the modus operandi agreed on between choreographer George Balanchine and composer Richard Rodgers during the preparation of *On Your Toes*, a pioneering Broadway dance musical from 1936, only eight years before *On the Town*. In his autobiography, Rodgers recalls what Balanchine said to him when they first discussed the jazz ballet "Slaughter on Tenth Avenue" that combined the talents of the jazz and tap dancer Ray Bolger and classical ballerina Tamara Geva and gained a place in musical theater history for the way it connected to the show's plot. As Rodgers tells the story, before they got to work he "was unsure how we should go about it." When he asked the choreographer whose work should come first, Balanchine famously responded, "You write, I put on."[27]

In contrast, before Bernstein arrived to work on "A Day in New York" in June, Burton reports that "Saul Chaplin [the vocal arranger] had already cut and pasted various sections of the original dance number to fit Gene Kelly's choreographic wishes."[28] This action doesn't mean that Bernstein didn't have any input in what portions of his music would best suit Chaplin's cutting and pasting suggestions. He did. The question is the extent of Bernstein's input. Bernstein's contract required that he, not Chaplin, would supply the appropriate music to be orchestrated. When the promised scenario was delayed, an anxious Bernstein traveled to Los Angeles, arriving on June 3, 1949. In Comden's recollection, Bernstein "came out and worked on the film and put the ballet music together for Sollie Chaplin."[29]

Kelly adds that when Bernstein arrived they worked together at the dancer's home until the two agreed on the musical content and how it fit with Kelly's choreographic conception. Freed adds still more to this picture when he recalled that he "brought Lenny Bernstein out to conduct the ballet music," a recollection that leaves open the possibility that Bernstein was the conductor on the soundtrack.[30] Remarkably, although the musical content of "A Day in New York" was derived collaboratively from seven songs and dances dispersed throughout the stage score, the final result possesses its own integrity and Bernstein's touch. In fact, I would contend that the musical choices in the reconceived ballet to Kelly's scenario "A Day in New York" constitute Bernstein's major new contribution to the film.

Table 3.2 outlines the musical and dramatic content of "A Day in New York," the culminating dance of the film as recorded on June 24, 1949.[31] Although staged theatrically and not filmed on location, for many the number ranks as the film's highlight. Earl Hess and Prathibha A. Dabholkar go as far as to proclaim "A Day in New York" "the most effective film ballet Kelly ever created."[32] The final film sequence was shot on July 2. Between rehearsals and the final filming, the original scenario had changed considerably. In Comden and Green's February 24, 1949, screenplay, the entire ballet scenario consisted of "a thrilling love duet [between Gabey and Ivy] on the roof [of a skyscraper] which in its climax transcends space and they are lifted into the air and dance exultantly over the city."[33] An extant published photograph based on this deleted scenario shows Kelly and Vera-Ellen literally dancing in the clouds.[34]

In Comden and Green's February version, not only does Chip appear before and after the ballet, but Gabey's remark about a town that now appears strange and empty to him in his present dejected state "cues Chip into a song about the lonely town."[35] The February screenplay is significant because it confirms Comden's memory quoted earlier about her desire to incorporate "Lonely Town" into the film and to provide an opportunity for Sinatra to sing the song that initially enticed him to sign up for the project. The early scenario for this ballet concludes with "Chip finishing the 'lonely town' song as Gabey comes out of his reverie back into reality."[36] The rehearsals and filming of the deleted "Lonely Town ballet" experiment wasted some time but only set MGM back $13,265 of its $2,111,250 budget.[37] More significantly, from Sinatra's perspective the removal of this ballet permanently eliminated his chance to sing "Lonely Town."

Despite the omission of "Lonely Town" as a vocal number, "A Day in New York" opens with a recurring four-note oscillating motive (B-C#-B-C#) from near the opening of the "Lonely Town" ballet (#7b, measure 12). Later in "A Day in New York," Bernstein (probably) inserted "High School Girls" (#7a), heard earlier in the "Lonely Town" ballet, and the opening verse of "Some Other Time." "High School Girls" wasn't part of a vocal number in any event, but "Lonely Town" and "Some Other Time" are pivotal Bernstein ballads that if not heard in "A Day in New York" would have been completely absent from the film.

The oscillating motive serves as a framing melody for "A Day in New York" in Kelly's scenario first heard before the dancing commences and returning at the ballet's end. The actual dancing begins with two and one-half minutes of musical

Table 3.2 *On the Town*: "A Day in New York" (MGM 1949).

77:03	#7b: Lonely Town (oscillating motive, B-C-sharp-B-C-sharp, mm. 12-17). *Gabey standing alone looks at a poster that reads "A Day in New York—A Comedy in Three Acts with Music."*
77:42	#2a: New York, New York (opening motive, mm. 44–50). *Two sailors standing in for Sinatra (Chip) and Munshin (Ozzie) join Kelly (Gabey) in a ballet on the rooftop of a skyscraper. The dancers are Alex Romero (left) and Gene Scott (right) joining Kelly in the center.*[a]
77:51	#2a: New York, New York, the recurring unsung jazzy "New York, New York" counter-melody above the four-note motive on the words "New York, New York" (mm. 15-26).
78:08	#2a: New York, New York (opening of the main chorus, mm. 63-68).
78: 28	#12: Times Square Ballet (based on New York, New York) (mm. 53–100). *Carol Haney and Marie Grossup, standing in for Miller (Claire) and Hildy (Garrett) arrive and dance with the three sailors.*[b] *One sailor kicks Kelly which makes him slide on his knees across the rooftop where he lands in front of a poster of Ivy (Vera-Ellen) as Miss Turnstiles.*
79:32	#26: I Feel Like I Can't Get Out of Bed (variation). *The four stand-in dancers leaving Vera-Ellen in leotard at a ballet.*
80:52	#22: Some Other Time (verse). *Kelly and Vera-Ellen kiss during a moment of silence.*
81:09	#7b: Lonely Town (oscillating motive B-C-sharp-B-C-sharp)
81:21	#12: Times Square Ballet (mm. 120–155). *Vera-Ellen departs and Kelly returns to the poster which becomes his dancing partner.*
81:49	#7a: High School Girls. *Kelly continues his dance with the poster of Miss Turnstiles.*
82:10	#12: Times Square Ballet (mm. 122-99). *Kelly kisses the poster.*
82:38	#21: The Great Lover *Vera-Ellen returns, now wearing a red dress. Again they kiss. The four professional stand-ins for Chip, Ozzie, Claire, and Hildy return and the six dancers dance together. The stand-ins depart and Kelly and Vera-Ellen dance a pas de deux.*
83:37	#2a: New York, New York, the recurring unsung jazzy "New York, New York" counter-melody above the four-note motive on the words "New York, New York" (mm. 15-26), alternates with 21a (mm. 11-13) [same music as Times Square Ballet, rehearsal B, mm. 15-25]. *Kelly and Vera-Ellen pick up the pace with a jazzy version based on the unsung jazzy "New York, New York" counter-melody above the "New York, New York" motive below that precedes the main chorus of "New York, New York" heard a few seconds after the dancing began six minutes ago at 77:51.*
84:16	#21a: Pas de Deux (beginning). *Vera-Ellen disappears and Kelly returns to the poster.*
84:24	#7b: Lonely Town motive; #22: Some Other Time (verse). *Kelly is alone once again, joined by Sinatra when the music stops.*

[a] Romero, who bears a familial resemblance to Sinatra, had an impressive film resume as a dancer and choreographer and can be seen in Kelly's *An American in Paris*. He is perhaps best known as Elvis Presley's choreographer in *Jailhouse Rock* (1957).

[b] A few years later Haney would achieve acclaim for her dancing with Bob Fosse in the film adaptation of *Kiss Me, Kate* (1953). Her performance on stage in *The Pajama Game* (1953) would earn Haney a Tony for the best featured actress in a musical as Gladys, a role she would repeat in the 1957 film version.

material based on "New York, New York." This includes the iconic four-note "New York, New York" motive consisting of two successive perfect fourths (E-A, and B-E) that announces the city's name, one note for each syllable (Musical Example 3.1a). Between 2009 and 2020 and probably unknown to most, millions of computer users who signed in to Microsoft Windows 7 heard these four notes as the startup sound.[38] In the musical, the four notes are followed by a variation of the opening motive, a few measures of the main chorus of the tune, and still more variations of the chorus derived from the "Times Square Ballet."[39] In the ballet's climax one minute before the end, the orchestra repeats the "New York, New York" motive in the bass below the invariably accompanying unsung jazzy counter-melody (Musical Example 3.1b). This was the unsung melody introduced prior to the big moment when Gabey, Chip, and Ozzie announce the four-note "New York, New York" motive in overlapping entrances. The melodic combination of the "New York, New York" motive in the bass below the jazzy counter-melody returns early in the "Times Square Ballet."

Although he might have used the names Gabey and Ivy, MGM chronicler Hugh Fordin is correct in stating that the "Day in New York" ballet scenario "is a reflection of Kelly's experience of that day" that "shows his love for Vera-Ellen" and that the action "in essence is a repeat of the over-all story of the film."[40] Fordin doesn't mention that the ballet is not what *has* happened so far that day but what Gabey *hoped* would happen. Indeed, in the first part of the ballet, Gabey imagines himself back in Symphonic Hall where he first met Miss Turnstiles and she agreed to meet him for a date that evening, but only in his ballet dream do they kiss after a pas de deux that is both tender and erotic. When she returns for the date in the final two minutes, another outcome that happens only in Gabey's dream, they dance with joyful abandon. At this moment the song "New York, New York" truly becomes Gabey and Ivy's New York City. They're not just on the town, they're on top of the town and in the clouds. Fortunately, the film-maker concluded prior to filming that a literal image of this blissful metaphor-ical euphoria outlined in the February 24 screenplay would not be necessary. See Figure 3.2.

In discussing "A Day in New York," dance scholar Beth Genné notes that Kelly's dancing and choreographic style "assimilates and amalgamates many influences," including those of Jerome Robbins, Fred Astaire, Agnes de Mille, and Michael Kidd, in its combination of classical ballet and modern dance.[41] She notes that what Kelly added to these influences and styles was "a particu-larly American flavor in its freer and more relaxed port de bras [carriage of the arms], its rhythmically intricate coordination with the popular music to which it is danced, and, most of all, the distinctive energy and vitality that animates the dancers."[42] In her description of the use of lighting (and darkness) and shadows and colors, Genné also remarks that the ballet was filmed within a shallow

Example 3.1a Gabey, Chip, and Ozzie's overlapping entrances of the four-note "New York, New York" motive in *On the Town*.

Example 3.1b The "New York, New York" motive repeated in the bass line below the recurring unsung jazzy counter-melody in *On the Town*.

Fig. 3.2 "A Day in New York." Gene Kelly (Gabey) and Vera-Ellen (Ivy) in the film version of *On the Town* [83:40]. Screenshot.

performance space and is therefore "almost theatrical in effect," which presents a sharp contrast to the frequently touted cinematic approach to actual New York locations in the "New York, New York" montage that opens the film.[43]

One might empathize with Freed and Kelly and agree that songs like "Lonely Town" and "Some Other Time" had to vanish from a film half the length of a stage show. There was simply not enough time for the moments of reflection that occasionally arrive in the stage version to offer a respite to the frantic pacing. Not only that, but in the case of "Some Other Time," some members of the film cast might have found it an insurmountable challenge to negotiate the extended vocal and contrapuntal lines and the song's rich harmonies. Still, the film suffers from the song's absence, an absence that calls attention to the significant fact that the show appeared in the middle of a world war with an uncertain outcome. For its contemporary audiences, it was all too imaginable that the three sailors savoring their twenty-four hours of shore leave might not be returning to their girlfriends and that they might never meet again "some other time" or any other time.

In the stage version "Some Other Time" stops the show, and is meant to, as it offers four and a half minutes of breathtaking poignancy. "Oh, well, we'll catch up/Some other time." Perhaps not. By the time MGM produced the film, the war had been over for four years and the three sailors no longer faced the same degree of danger and uncertainty. MGM had a point, but by removing "Some Other Time" it diminished the film's emotional range. Only nine years later, some other time (and some other place), had arrived, a new time when it would be unthinkable for a studio to remove a song like "Some Other Time" from Bernstein's *West*

Side Story, or for that matter lyrical and reflective songs like "One Hand, One Heart," "I Have a Love," or "Somewhere."

CALL ME MADAM
(Broadway 1950; 20th Century-Fox 1953)

"Now we understand each other. I'm the Madam and you're—just one of the *girls*." Stage version.

"Now we understand each other. I'm the Madam and you're just one of the *boys*." Film version

Sally Adams in *Call Me Madam*

Stage versus Film

Call Me Madam arrived on Broadway in 1950. Its film adaptation arrived in March 1953. A little less than a year before the film's release, July 1952, the screen version of *Where's Charley?*, Frank Loesser's hit first Broadway musical from 1948, honored Ethan Mordden's adaptation Commandments introduced in chapter 1 by retaining the show's leading stars Ray Bolger and Allyn Ann McLerie, Horace Cooper (another major player), and eight of the thirteen principal musical numbers. Before *Where's Charley?* and *Call Me Madam,* screen adaptations of musicals seldom rehired stage casts and rarely retained the complete (or nearly complete stage score). For example, even the relatively faithful 1950 film adaptation of *Annie Get Your Gun* replaced Ethel Merman (1908–1984) and cut five of the fifteen original stage songs. *Call Me Madam* went a step further toward fidelity than either *Where's Charley?* or *Annie Get Your Gun*. In fact, the film adaptation of *Call Me Madam* from 1953 arguably exhibited greater fidelity to a stage original than perhaps *any* previous musical film adaptation up to that point. If this wasn't sufficiently novel, this chapter will attempt to make the case that its departures from the 1950 stage original constituted improvements rather than concessions. See Table 3.3, "*Call Me Madam* on Stage and Screen."

The film's starting point was the pivotal decision to cast the stage diva Merman in the starring role of Sally Adams, the "hostess with the mostes'," a fictional character based on a real person named Perle Mesta. Both the historical Perle and the fictional Sally were appointed by President Harry S Truman to serve as the ambassadress to a small European country, Luxembourg for the real-life Mesta and the imaginary Lichtenburg for the fictional Sally. Twenty years earlier Merman brought down the house singing "I Got Rhythm" in the Gershwins' *Girl Crazy*. When the film version of *Call Me Madam* arrived, Merman was in her prime at the age of forty-two and as famous as any stage star in the Broadway firmament. Along with the decision to retain nearly all of Irving Berlin's score, allowing Merman to reprise her stage role was probably the single greatest factor in the eventual success of the film adaptation.

The decision was not a slam dunk. Merman was far less well known for her film roles and 20th Century-Fox was taking a risk. As noted in chapter 1, despite her onstage acclaim in *Anything Goes* (1934), Merman's lack of film star status compared with Bing Crosby led to a reduced status in the film version two years later (including far fewer songs). In 1938 she was again cast as second fiddle, this time to Alice Faye in *Alexander's Ragtime Band*, the first cavalcade film musical with songs by Berlin (1888–1989), but at least she was given her fair share of songs.[44] In the 1940s, Merman's film work was limited to a specialty number in *Stage Door Canteen*, but one year after her success in *Call Me Madam* she was cast as the lead in the third Berlin cavalcade, *There's No Business Like Show Business*.

Regrettably, *Call Me Madam* turned out to be the last film in which Merman reprised a starring stage role. In violation of the Commandments, three years earlier Merman had been cast aside, first for Garland, then for Betty Hutton, the eventual choice to play Annie Oakley in the film version of Merman's *Annie Get Your Gun*. Nine years after *Madam*, Warner Bros. would compound what Miles Kreuger in his audio commentary on the *Madam* DVD described as the "crime against posterity" when it cast Rosalind Russell instead of Merman as Mama Rose in the movie version of *Gypsy*.

The *Call Me Madam* film version adhered faithfully, but not slavishly, to the song retention and interpolation clauses of the Commandments. There was also a fair amount of dialogue and even song reordering, but only two songs were cut outright. One was "They Like Ike," Ike being the popular nickname of General Dwight D. Eisenhower. On stage "They Like Ike" was sung by two fictitious senators and a congressman who came to Lichtenburg to negotiate a government loan.[45] The backstory behind this song began in 1948, the year President Truman appointed Mesta, the daughter of an Oklahoma oil baron and now a wealthy and merry widow, for the Luxembourg post. It was this appointment that gave co-librettists Howard Lindsay and Russel Crouse the idea to develop a musical for Berlin in which Merman was cast as Sally, the fictitious daughter of an oil baron, now a widow, who became Truman's appointee as the ambassadress to the fictitious country of Lichtenburg.

At the time, Eisenhower, the popular US armed forces commander in Europe in World War II, had not declared a party affiliation nor even voted, but this didn't stop people from trying to draft him for president. Concerned about losing the election of 1948 (after a Republican landslide in the 1946 midterm election),

Table 3.3 *Call Me Madam* on Stage and Screen.

Stage	Screen
Act I	
Mrs. Sally Adams (Company) (6)	
The Hostess with the Mostes' on the Ball (Merman) (11)	The Hostess with the Mostes' on the Ball (Merman) [4:20]
Washington Square Dance (Merman and Company) (15)	Washington Square Dance (instrumental) (7:02)
Lichtenburg (Lukas, Company) (17)	Lichtenburg (Company) [10:53]
Can You Use Any Money Today? (Merman) (24)	Can You Use Any Money Today? (Merman) [21:15]
Marrying for Love (Lukas, Merman) (26)	Marrying for Love (Sanders) [26:45]
The Ocarina (Talva, Company) (30)	
It's a Lovely Day Today (Nype, Talva) (34)	It's a Lovely Day Today (O'Connor) [31:16]
It's a Lovely Day Today (Reprise) (36)	It's a Lovely Day Today (Reprise) (Vera-Ellen and (O'Connor) [34:00]
The Best Thing for You (Would Be Me) (Merman) (42)	
	Ocarina as a waltz (instrumental) [42:42]
	That International Rag (Merman) [46:20]
	That International Rag (dance, starting with Merman and Sanders) (48:15)
	It's a Lovely Day (dance between O'Connor and Vera-Ellen) (49:08); continued as a waltz (52:48)
	You're Just in Love (O'Connor, Merman) [56:50]
Act II	
Lichtenburg (Reprise) (Lukas, Company) (45)	
	The Ocarina (Vera-Ellen, Company) [60:00]
	What Chance Have I with Love? [O'Connor] [71:00]
Something to Dance About (Merman, Rall, Bentley, Company) (48)	Something to Dance About (O'Connor, Vera-Ellen) [82:00]
Once upon a Time, Today (Nype) (51)	
They Like Ike (Harrington, Ralph Chambers, Jay Velice) (54)	

Table 3.3 Continued

Stage	Screen
It's a Lovely Day Today (Reprise) (Nype and Talva) (57)	
You're Just in Love (Merman, Nype) (57)	
The Best Thing for You (Would Be Me) (Reprise) (Merman) (58)	The Best Thing for You Would Be Me (Merman) [90:00]
It's a Lovely Day Today (Reprise) (Nype, Talva) (61)	You're Just in Love (Reprise) (Merman, O'Connor) [105:00]
Mrs. Sally Adams (Merman, Company) (62)	Mrs. Sally Adams (Female Trio) [108:00]
Finale: You're Just in Love (Merman, Company) (64)	Finale: You're Just in Love, It's a Lovely Day, Something to Dance About (Sanders, Merman, O'Connor, Vera-Ellen) (112:40)

- *Numbers in parentheses in the stage column refer to page numbers in Howard Lindsay and Russel Crouse "Call Me Madam" (London: Irving Berlin, Ltd., 1956).*
- *The songs listed in bold in the screen column were not in the stage version.*
- *Numbers in parentheses in the screen column refer to film timings.*

MAJOR SINGING AND DANCING AND SELECTED ROLES

Stage: ETHEL MERMAN (Mrs. Sally Adams); Paul Lukas (Cosmo Constantine); Russell Nype (Kenneth Gibson); Galina Talva (Princess Marie); Pat Harrington (Congressman Wilkins); Alan Hewitt (Pemberton Maxwell); Ernst Ulman (Prince Hugo); LILIA SKALA (Grand Duchess Sophie); Tommy Rall (Principal Dancer); Muriel Bentley (Principal Dances)

Screen: MERMAN (Mrs. Sally Adams); George Sanders (Cosmo Constantine); Donald O'Connor (Kenneth Gibson); Vera-Ellen (Princess Marie); Billy DeWolfe (Pemberton Maxwell); Helmut Dantine (Prince Hugo); Walter Slezak (August Tantinnin); Ludwig Stössel (Grand Duke Otto); SKALA (Grand Duchess Sophie)

- *Names in capital letters indicates cast members who appeared both on stage and in the film.*

Truman wrote in his private diary that in a meeting with Eisenhower in 1947 he made the astonishing offer asking Eisenhower to join him on the *Democratic* ticket as *president*, with Truman as vice president.[46] Prior to the October 12, 1950, stage premiere of *Call Me Madam*, Truman's unpopularity was such that a serious draft Eisenhower movement had begun in earnest. Consequently, the idea of a song about liking Ike for president in 1952 would have been topical rather than provocative during the run of the show. After the show closed on May 3, 1952, a hit in its day at 644 performances, Eisenhower declared himself a Republican and won the presidency in a November landslide, an outcome that made "They Like Ike" unsuitable as well as anachronistic for a 1953 film wanting to eschew politics.

Another Merman song, "Washington Square Dance," was not *sung* in the film version but instead served as dance music at the Washington, DC, send-off ball before Sally assumed her post in Lichtenburg. To ensure that Merman would not be deprived of a song, Berlin and director Walter Lang gave her a new old song to sing later at the Lichtenburg ballroom scene added in the film. The new diegetic Lichtenburg song was an interpolation, but in compliance with the Commandments, it was one composed by Berlin, who received an additional $75,000 ($831,941 in 2022 money) for its reuse. The lead-up to the song is Sally's question to the orchestra leader, "Got anything hot, boys?" and the leader's response that his group can play the "up-to-date" American song by Berlin, "That International Rag," one of the composer's earliest hits. When Sally sees that the song is nearly forty years old (the film takes place in 1951), she quips, "HMM—1913. . . . Well, that's *fairly* up-to-date. . . . Let's give it a whirl."

Film audiences had already had two opportunities to hear "That International Rag." The first was in *Alexander's Ragtime Band* where it was assigned to Alice Faye. Ten years later the song returned, but in the orchestra only, in the second Berlin cavalcade musical film, *Easter Parade*. When Sally sings the song in *Call Me Madam*, she may *think* she's singing a song that was unchanged from 1913, but in fact Berlin added some new lyrics in 1953 to make the song more topical—for example, replacing "Russian czars" with "commies."[47]

Besides "They Like Ike," the only other song entirely removed from the film was Kenneth Gibson's stage solo, "Once Upon a Time, Today," sung to Sally, with lyrics that match the lovesick attaché's despair that the fates have conspired against a happy ending with Lichtenburg's Princess Maria. The song doesn't have a wide range, but it does display a number of large leaps and a high tessitura (i.e., where the largest percentage of notes fall) with long notes on D-E-flat-E and the occasional F. The song matched the talents of Russell Nype and the lyrics and music fit a character who imagines his fairy tale dreams are shattered by reality. A new film context and a new singer-dancer (Donald O'Connor) called for a different song—Berlin's own "What Chance Have I (with Love)?" borrowed from *Louisiana Purchase* where it served as a character song for Victor Moore who played Senator Oliver P. Loganberry. "What Chance?" was one of the many songs cut from the film version of that show, although viewers can still observe Moore parading at Mardi Gras in his toga, the stage setting for the song.

Moore may not have been much of a singer, but neither Moore nor Nype were dancers, a central change from the stage to screen version in *Call Me Madam*. What sets up "What Chance?" is a conversation with Princess Maria in which Kenneth learns that she must go through with a loveless arranged marriage. Kenneth's response is to drink himself into a stupor and to wreak physical havoc on a local tavern, popping a multitude of balloons along the way. The lyrics of "What Chance?" compare Kenneth's plight with the situation of famous lovers, [Marc] Antony, Romeo, Samson, Bonaparte, and even Adam. The punchline is that if these great lovers failed, Kenneth might ask himself, "What chance have I, an ordinary guy,/What chance have I with love?"

Perhaps the most significant change between stage and film was the transformation of the role of Kenneth, recently hired by Sally to serve as her attaché as she embarks on her adventures as Lichtenburg's new ambassadress.[48] The film expanded Kenneth's role by making him a worthy dancing partner for Princess Maria as well as the principal singer of the pair, while the princess remained primarily a dancer. Making Kenneth a dancer provided choreographer Robert Alton (1897–1957) new dramatic opportunities to showcase dance not available to the show's stage choreographer, *On the Town*'s Jerome Robbins, whose principal male and female dancers Tommy Rall and Muriel Bentley were unnamed and undeveloped as characters.[49]

Although his most familiar and acclaimed work remained ahead of him when he became a director as well as a choreographer, by the time Robbins became the choreographer for *Call Me Madam* he was already highly regarded for his innovative contributions to *On the Town* and imaginative dance numbers such as the "Mack Sennett Ballet" in *High Button Shoes* (1947). The year before *Call Me Madam*, Robbins had choreographed *Miss Liberty*, also with a score by Berlin. Always looking for sensational ideas for dance numbers, Robbins was frustrated when the stage director George Abbott (who also directed *On the Town*) dismissed some of his choreography ideas for *Madam* as unworkable. One of these ideas was a number, "The Wild Men of Lichtenburg," that Abbott later recalled was "a big number about the wild men from the mountains coming down and dancing in the village" that "had to be jettisoned."[50]

Another cut dance number was "Mr. Monotony," a song already cursed with a problematic history. Berlin had written the song for Judy Garland to sing in *Easter Parade* (1948), and the number, directed and choreographed by Charles Walters, was recorded and filmed but subsequently cut. One year later, Berlin and Robbins tried to resuscitate the song in *Miss Liberty*, and another year after that Berlin and Robbins tried to recycle "Mr. Monotony" for a third time in *Call Me Madam*, where according to a Robbins biographer, it "was jammed into the script as a cultural artifact that Sally Adams was importing to introduce Lichtenburg to American jazz."[51] Robbins's dance assistant Donald Saddler recalled that Merman's vocal rendition and Rall, Bentley, and Arthur Partington's dance "went like gangbusters" and stopped the show with applause. This may have been a welcome reception for Merman, but Robbins correctly realized that the song's success would seal its doom. As Robbins told Saddler, "Watch, Don, it's going to go out."[52] Much as he loathed to discard the fruits of his work, Robbins would likely have done the same thing had he been the director. In his future role as director-choreographer of *West Side Story* and *Fiddler on the Roof* he reluctantly but willingly discarded sensational numbers that either stopped or didn't fit the show.[53]

Hugh Fordin encapsulates the history of "Mr. Monotony" in his survey of MGM, starting with its removal from *Easter Parade*: " 'It slowed the picture,' says Berlin, 'and Arthur [Freed] and I were sorry to see it go because we both liked it, a very unusual song based on a phrase.[54] I later used it in the theatre, in *Miss Liberty* (1949) and it stopped the show and stopped everything else. Then I put it in *Call Me Madam* (1950); Ethel Merman sang it and it stopped the show again; but it didn't belong in that show and I took it out.' "[55]

The removal of "The Wild Men of Lichtenburg" and "Mr. Monotony" necessitated a late addition for the second act, a song inadvertently inspired by Robbins when he asked the composer to "just give him something to dance about."[56] Berlin thought this was a "damned good title," and a new song was soon born in which Berlin's references in his lyrics to various dances (fox-trot, tango, waltz, and rhumba), matched by their respective musical styles, certainly gave Robbins something to dance about. Nevertheless, compared with Robbins's future opportunities to make dance a central dramatic component of a show, in the end Robbins's last show with Berlin failed to provide enough substantive material to dance about. In addition to "Something to Dance About," which also featured Rall and Bentley in Act II, the show only allowed for three dance numbers in Act I, "Mrs. Sally Adams," "Washington Square Dance," and "The Ocarina." Of these, only the latter, a charming folk dance led by Princess Maria, was retained in anything like its stage context in the film.

The career of Robert Alton highlights the ephemeral nature of preserving what was danced in hit stage shows of the 1930s and 1940s. During these years, Alton choreographed five musicals with scores by Porter (*Anything Goes, You Never Know, Leave It to Me, Du Barry Was a Lady*, and *Panama Hattie*), and four with scores by Rodgers and Hart (*Too Many Girls, Higher and Higher, Pal Joey*, and *By Jupiter*). In the 1950s he choreographed Rodgers and Hammerstein's *Me and Juliet*. Several of these shows were major hits, but Alton's cavalier attitude toward documenting his work and the fact that he didn't establish a choreographic vision and stylistic persona to match his major contemporaries George Balanchine, Busby Berkeley, Agnes de Mille, and Jerome Robbins, inhibited the recognition of his stage work.

On the other hand, Alton's record on film is there for everyone to view. Among an impressive series of movies are the five he choreographed for Berlin (*Easter Parade, Annie Get Your Gun, Call Me Madam, White Christmas*, and *There's No Business Like Show Business*), Berlin's entire film output between 1948 and 1954. Both O'Connor and Vera-Ellen starred in two of these films as well as in other Alton films containing scores by other composers. *Call Me Madam*, regrettably the only film in which O'Connor and Vera-Ellen danced together, vividly reveals two of his claims to Broadway and Hollywood fame. The first was his practice of "breaking up the regimented platoons of dancers that had dominated Broadway in the 1920s" and for featuring individual soloists briefly within smaller groups.[57]

"The Ocarina" number in which Vera-Ellen leads a dancing chorus is a particularly expressive example of this practice. Alton's second claim to fame (an original approach to combining ballet and tap) is on full display in the song and pas de deux between O'Connor and Vera-Ellen that takes place in a wine cellar hidden underneath the passageway between the embassy and the palace in "Something to Dance About." In the stage version the number was sung by Merman in the embassy garden and was followed by a dance for the entire company.

Alton was not the first to combine classical ballet with jazz tap. A famous earlier example, Balanchine's choreography for Rodgers and Hart's *On Your Toes* mentioned earlier in this chapter, offered a substantial classical ballet in the first act, the satiric "Princesse Zenobia." The second act included a contrasting production number named after the show's title, in which a Russian ballet company and a jazz company alternated between classical and tap, and the show concluded with the substantial climactic jazz ballet "Slaughter on Tenth Avenue" featuring Tamara Geva and Ray Bolger. Interestingly, Alton (along with Kelly) co-choreographed the generous "Slaughter" segment in the Rodgers and Hart biopic *Words and Music* (1948), which featured Vera-Ellen, this time reunited with Kelly. As early as the Broadway revue, *Two for the Show* (1940), Alton had arranged a dance routine for Eunice Healey in which Healey herself combined the two styles. John Martin, probably the most influential dance critic of the day, criticized this oil and water approach to dance as "inherently antagonistic in virtually every way from considerations of style to those of actual technique."[58] In evaluating Healey's dance, however, Martin found that on this occasion the stylistic "contradiction has been advantageous."

In *Call Me Madam*, instead of combining ballet and tap within a single dancer, Alton adopted the approach Balanchine used in "Slaughter." But in contrast to Balanchine's alternating between the styles, he had Vera-Ellen (ballet) and O'Connor (tap) *combine* their contrasting aesthetic worlds into a harmonious wedding of the two. Joining the lovebirds in the wine cellar is the cameraman Leonard Shamroy, who deftly follows the dance partners to a series of rapidly changing nooks and crannies before they conclude their dance within a more confined space, similar to the Kelly/Vera-Ellen finale to "A Day in New York."

Unfortunately, O'Connor and Vera-Ellen's ballroom dancing to the music of "It's a Lovely Day" after "That International Rag" and their pas de deux in "Something to Dance About" were the only opportunities O'Connor and Vera-Ellen were given to dance together about something in a film musical. They made the most of it, and even jaded viewers might be moved to imagine that these two attractive and likable young people, one royal and one plebeian, will overcome the social distance between them and never stop dancing together. The decision to cast Vera-Ellen as Princess Maria and O'Connor as Kenneth and to make the latter character a dancer as well as a singer made this felicitous outcome possible. See Figure 3.3.

Fig. 3.3 "Something to Dance About." Donald O'Connor (Kenneth) and Vera-Ellen (Princess Maria) in the film version of *Call Me Madam* [84:48]. Screenshot.

The stage and film versions also differ in the circumstances of the first meeting between the commoner and the princess. In the stage version they meet in the scene that begins with "The Ocarina," when Kenneth enters during a conversation between Sally and the Princess Maria.[59] After Sally makes a diplomatic exit, Kenneth somewhat superciliously reveals that he knows more about Lichtenburg than the princess, who appreciates her country's physical beauty rather than the facts about its industrial complex. The conversation ends abruptly when Maria points out that she has "many, many things to do," a remark that Kenneth incorporates into the first stanza of "It's a Lovely Day Today" when he sings "And I hope whatever you've got to do/Is something that can be done by two." The song wins Maria over and when she sings the next chorus she realizes that "perhaps whatever I've got to do,/Is something that can be done by two." At the end of the song Kenneth raises the possibility they might meet again in the secret passage that links the embassy and the palace, and Maria acknowledges that this idea had occurred to her as well.

In contrast to the stage version, when Kenneth and Maria meet in the film their respective identities are unknown to each other. Kenneth is shopping in a department store for a top hat to wear to a ball that doesn't take place in the stage version. When the clerk goes to get a hat box, Kenneth hears an orchestral arrangement of "It's a Lovely Day" in the music department nearby. A customer (the Princess) approaches and asks about the song and Kenneth explains it was from a hit Broadway show that ran for a couple of years. For viewers who may not recognize the song, Kenneth takes out the sheet music with Irving Berlin's name and photograph on it. When the customer asks if Kenneth knows the words, the film takes advantage of this opportunity to convert what was a charming musical non-diegetic "intrusion" on the stage into a diegetic film song. After finishing singing the first stanza, Kenneth reveals that he doesn't work at the store. Right on cue a clerk comes over, bows to Maria, and addresses her as "Your Highness!" Maria sings a reprise of Berlin's hit tune and Kenneth follows with another abbreviated reprise. The princess leaves Kenneth to join the equerries who are waiting at a respectful distance, after which Kenneth concludes the scene with still another short reprise.

"You're Just in Love"

In the stage version, Russell Nype, who played Kenneth, was so winning in the role that during tryouts the powerful Ethel Merman, whose star quality practically made her a co-equal creative partner, asked Berlin to write a duet for Sally and Kenneth to sing in the second act. Berlin agreed and Mr. Abbott gave his blessing. Four or five days later Berlin had composed "You're Just in Love," which brought down the house and remains the best-known song of the score. It's a counterpoint song, a Berlin specialty, a song-type that presents two (usually) contrasting melodies and lyrics successively before combining them simultaneously.[60] In "You're Just in Love" one melody is a lyrical tune about love sung by Kenneth, the other is a more rhythmic and faster-moving counter-melody sung by Sally, who believes that Kenneth doesn't need to analyze his emotions because, "you're not sick, you're just in love." (See Musical Example 3.2 and Figures 3.4 and 4.5).[61] See Figures 3.4 and 3.5.

On the stage, "You're Just in Love" functioned as an "11 o'clock number," a show-stopping song designed to wake up an audience toward the end of an evening about 11:00 P.M. (in the days when musicals started at 8:30 P.M. and ended about 11:30 P.M.). It's the last new song in the show, followed only by a series of reprises of "The Best Thing for You" (Sally and Foreign Minister Cosmo Constantine), "It's a Lovely Day Today" (Kenneth and Maria), "Mrs. Sally Adams" (Company), and an additional snippet of "You're Just in Love" (Sally and Company in counterpoint). What sets up "You're Just in Love" is Kenneth's preoccupation with Maria, which is so overwhelming that he starts singing a short reprise of "their song," "It's a Lovely Day," instead of fulfilling his duty to write a letter to the State Department in Washington. Kenneth is not only preoccupied, he is also despondent at the thought that he won't be able to marry Maria. In this vulnerable state he imagines he hears Maria "singing and there's no one there" (she *is* actually singing off-stage). This gives Kenneth the first line of the song. At this point in the stage version, matters between Sally and Cosmo remain

Example 3.2 "You're Just in Love" when Sally and Kenneth's melodies combine in
Call Me Madam.

unresolved, but they haven't yet ended their romance. This means that only
Kenneth is despondent while the hopeful Sally assumes a motherly role based on
her life experiences and her empathy for the lovesick attaché.

In the film "You're Just in Love" occurs twice, the first time much earlier in
the story (56:40) a few minutes after "It's a Lovely Day." It then returns near the
end of the film (105:00). In contrast to the stage version, the screenplay sets up a
dramatic situation that precipitates a double despondency to match the double
song. The earlier occurrence also parallels the stage version in that Kenneth is
totally preoccupied with Maria, whom he has impertinently kissed after dancing
to a waltz version of "Lovely Day" at the ball and afterward imagines he hears
singing. As in the stage version, Kenneth can't focus on the missive (now a cable-
gram) Sally has asked him to send to President Truman.[62] In contrast to the stage
Sally, the film Sally is also in low spirits after her conversation with Pemberton
Maxwell, the scheming chargé d'affaires, who has deliberately planted the false
rumor that a duplicitous Cosmo was pretending *not* to want a US loan as a ruse

Fig. 3.4 Ethel Merman (Sally Adams) and Russell Nype (Kenneth Gibson) singing "You're Just in Love" in the stage version of *Call Me Madam*. Photofest.

Fig. 3.5 Ethel Merman (Sally) and Donald O'Connor (Kenneth) singing "You're Just in Love" in the film version of *Call Me Madam* [58:40]. Screenshot.

to actually receive it. The truth is that Maxwell knows well that Cosmo doesn't desire the loan but instead wants to guide Lichtenburg toward self-sufficiency. Rather than feeling gratitude, Cosmo finds Sally's loan offer offensive. By believing Maxwell, Sally fails to realize that her generosity has compromised Cosmo's pride and integrity, even as he is smitten by the brash ambassadress. This misunderstanding, set in motion by Maxwell, is the source of their romantic conflict.

By the time they reprise "You're Just in Love" forty minutes later in the film, both Sally and Kenneth have reached a new low. Cosmo has become the prime minister, and in this capacity refuses the American offer for a loan, which ironically becomes increasingly generous the more he claims that his country doesn't want it. In fact, when they misinterpret Cosmo's refusal as playing hard to get, the senators double their offer. Put into an impossible position, Cosmo reluctantly accepts the loan, but immediately resigns as prime minister and explains to Sally, whose intentions were generous but misguided, that "Lichtenburg is *not* for sale." Cosmo then ends the romance and says good-bye to the hostess with the mostes'.

Moments later Maria and Kenneth meet again in the secret passageway. In another irony, with the loan going through, the royal family now has the money for the dowry, which means that she must marry the shallow and controlling Prince Hugo. Kenneth tries to persuade her to relinquish the throne and move to America but understands that she must marry for political reasons rather than for love. When Kenneth and Sally meet later that evening, viewers don't need the scene directions to know that they are both "the picture of gloom."

> SALLY: You know what happened, Ken . . . ?
> KENNETH (nodding): She's getting married.
> SALLY (bitterly; after a pause): Me and my big mouth.
> KENNETH (shaking his head; he hasn't been listening either): There's nothing I can do about it.[63]

In the reprise it is a despondent Sally who hears the lyrical "singing and there's no one there" and Kenneth who sings the wise and lively counter-melody, but even this joyful song isn't nearly joyful enough to cheer either of them out of their mutual despair. Spoiler alert: *Call Me Madam* is a fairy tale so take heart.

A Film That Surpasses Its Model?

Call Me Madam was conceived as a star stage vehicle for Merman, and so was the film; within three years the latter followed its model dutifully but imaginatively, keeping Merman front and center. Although the film removed the vocal component of Sally's "The Washington Square Dance," reassigned "Something to Dance About" to Kenneth and Maria, and cut Sally's response to Cosmo's "Marrying for Love," Merman remained the star and sang the majority of the songs. These include "The Hostess with the Mostes'," "Can You Use Any Money Today?," and "The Best Thing for You" along with new opportunities for Merman to shine in the newly added "That International Rag" and a full-scale duet reprise of "You're Just in Love."

Thankfully, 20th Century-Fox gave Merman a fine cast to work with. On the musical side, only Vera-Ellen, who in *On the Town* was cast solely for her dancing prowess, does not do her own singing in the film version. Interestingly, a decade earlier Vera-Ellen did do her own singing on the Broadway stage when she played the second female lead in the 1943 revival of Rodgers and Hart's *A Connecticut Yankee.* Her voice, which can be heard on two songs from the cast recording, "On a Desert Island with Thee" and "I Feel at Home with You," might persuade listeners that dubbing wasn't such a bad idea. The voice is a combination of thin and grating, and her approach to the songs seems more suitable for the Grand Old Opry than Broadway (no offense intended). In contrast, the ballerina Galina Talva, who played Princess Maria on stage, managed to do her own singing, but unlike Vera-Ellen, did not enjoy a film career. Once in Hollywood Vera-Ellen, invariably dubbed, would be seen and not heard. To her credit, in *Call Me Madam* she lip synchs impeccably to the voice of Carol Richards, whose voice over the next few years would inhabit the body of Cyd Charisse in the film versions of *Brigadoon* and *Silk Stockings*, both of which are discussed in future chapters of this book.[64]

On stage, the role of Cosmo was played and sung by Paul Lukas, born in Budapest. His role in *Watch on the Rhine* earned him an Academy Award in 1943, but *Call Me Madam* was his first and only singing role. Lukas's counterpart in the film, George Sanders, born in St. Petersburg, was likewise known mainly as an actor. After appearing in two Alfred Hitchcock films (*Rebecca* and *Foreign Correspondent* both in 1940), Sanders acquired iconic stature as the acerbic and manipulative theater critic Addison De Witt in *All About Eve*, a role for which he earned a Best Supporting Oscar in 1950. Just as Cosmo was Lukas's only singing role on stage, it would be Sanders's only singing role in a film musical. With a bass-baritone voice that sounds more like Ezio Pinza's operatic bass in *South Pacific* than a conventional lyric baritone, Sanders offers a musically as well as dramatically credible and charming performance as Lichtenburg's foreign secretary and by the end of the film his country's American ambassador.

Although not a singing role, the pompous and fussy Chargé d'Affaires Maxwell, played by Billy De Wolfe, is wickedly funny in his condescending exchanges with Merman over diplomatic protocol. His look of shock and horror when he observes Merman vigorously throw the train of her gown under her legs offers a particularly fine example of his priceless facial expressions and body language. One of Sally's exchanges with Maxwell prompted a warning from the Hollywood censors. It occurs on stage after Sally establishes her authority and insists that Maxwell "Call me Madam!" "O.K. now we understand each other. I'm the Madam and you're—just one of the girls." In a memo to Fox, censorship czar Joseph Breen found this comment in the April 23, 1952, draft "unacceptably pointed."[65] For the September 5 shooting final and the final cut Fox changed the last word to "boys" (a remark that makes less sense than "girls" for a "madam" to make), but this change was apparently compatible with the Production Code, despite the possibility (if not likelihood) of also conveying a gay subtext.[66]

In addition to the quality of the material and the talent they had to work with, the creative team was clearly at the top of their game. In 1945, Walter Lang directed Rodgers and Hammerstein's *State Fair*, their one and only original film musical. After *Call Me Madam* he directed *There's No Business Like Show Business*, with a score by Berlin and starring Merman and O'Connor. Over the next few years he directed the critically acclaimed film adaptation of *The King and I* (1956) and the less successful *Can-Can* (1960). The screenwriter, Arthur Sheekman, known for his work with the Marx Brothers in the 1930s, received an Oscar nomination for *Call Me Madam* but lost to Comden and Green's *Singin' in the Rain*. Sheekman's screenplay, flexible yet respectful, is a model for how to create a film script that alters but does not damage the language and structure that made Lindsay and Crouse's version so effective on the stage. Leonard Shamroy's camera work also managed to convert the stage version from the theatrical to the cinematic without calling attention to itself. In particular, the newly added ballroom scene is stunningly filmed with its overhead crane shots and dancing camera movements. The costume designs of Irene Sharaff also live up to her reputation for creating gorgeous evening gowns and spectacular dresses designed for dancing.[67]

In the stage version, Grand Duke Otto and Grand Duchess Sophie (Maria's aunt and uncle) eventually accept the idea that Kenneth might make a worthy marriage partner for Maria. What wins them over is that Kenneth has decided to remain in Lichtenburg to build a hydro-electric dam farther up the river so as not to compromise the scenic beauty of Hammersburg Falls. But before leaving the two lovebirds alone to sort out their future, Sophie reminds her niece that, according to ancient custom, the princess must be the one to do the proposing. In the stage version Maria makes her proto-feminist marriage proposal promptly. After that, Kenneth and Maria sing a snippet of "It's a Lovely Day" then disappear from the show to live happily ever after. In the film Maria insists that she must be the one to ask Kenneth to dance and later commands him to kiss her as well, but saves some suspense for later, as we'll shortly see.

After the proposal in the stage version the chorus sings a reprise of "Mrs. Sally Adams," heard initially as the first song of the show before the scene shifts to

Sally's living room in Washington.[68] The congressmen try to cheer Sally up with the good news that Lichtenburg refused the $200 million loan. The actor playing Dean Acheson, Truman's secretary of state from 1949 to 1953, announces the new prime minister of the Grand Duchy of Lichtenburg, Mr. Cosmo Constantine, who bestows on Sally the title of Dame. Borrowing from a song, "The Best Thing for You (Would Be Me"), Constantine gets the last word: "Mr. Secretary, the Grand Duke thought it was the best thing for Lichtenburg, and –unofficially—it is the best thing for me."[69] All that's left is for Sally to sing a few lines of "You're Just in Love" with the chorus adding the second half of the counter-melody.

Sheekman's screenplay prolongs the fairy tale ending with some new twists after Sally and Kenneth return to America when their respective romances were both seemingly over. A cinematic collage reveals a female trio of phone operators singing and swinging "Mrs. Sally Adams" for the first (and only) time, with their jazzy invitation to a supper and dance from the "hostess with the mostes'" home again in Washington, DC. As in the stage version, the senators (sans Acheson, who does not appear in the film) congratulate Sally for saving the United States $200 million. Kenneth comes over to Sally and informs her that Constantine is the new ambassador from Lichtenburg and that he is bringing his female sailing companion to the party. When he arrives, Cosmo tells Sally (to her relief) that his charming companion is Maria. He then awards Sally the coveted "promotion" to Dame, while Maria, who had said good-bye to Kenneth in Lichtenburg without proposing to him, does so now after explaining that she has renounced the throne and has received her Uncle Otto's blessing to marry the man of her choice, the man she loves.

After affirming that things have turned out well for both Lichtenburg and for him, Cosmo sings a reprise of the central melody of "You're Just in Love" with Sally singing the counter-melody, after which they switch. Kenneth and Maria enter with a singing and dancing reprise of "It's a Lovely Day," and the film ends with everyone singing, then dancing, to "Something to Dance About." The screen directions describe the final image: "The camera moves to Sally and Cosmo. They are both dancing; and just before the climax, when Cosmo holds out his arms to Sally, she removes the pointed decoration from his chest and puts herself there instead."[70]

Merman, a victim of a "crime against posterity" when denied the leading stage role in the film adaptations of *Annie Get Your Gun* and *Gypsy*, left her greatest film legacy in *Call Me Madam*. In this silly but clever and ultimately touching fairy tale of a film, posterity can fortunately preserve and savor the way Merman demonstrates her superb comic verbal timing and physical humor as well as her stellar singing with her celebrated vocal power that can be appreciated by theater patrons sitting in the third-floor balcony, but now sufficiently toned down for film consumption. It is the central argument of this chapter that Merman's performance and that of her exemplary supporting cast, the superb dance partnership of O'Connor and Vera-Ellen, and the uniformly inspiring creative level from top to bottom place *Call Me Madam* in a rare category as one of the handful of film adaptations that surpasses its stage source.

Postscript: Two Good Movies

The market side of the New Fidelity equation became readily apparent as soon as film executives saw the $4.7 million of gross rentals for MGM's *Annie Get Your Gun*. This was the third highest total for *any* 1950 film. Clearly it now paid to be faithful. Had *On the Town* arrived in 1959 instead of 1949 perhaps viewers would be treated to more of Bernstein's score or new songs by Leonard Bernstein rather than by Roger Edens.

The relative artistic merits between the contrasting studio approaches exhibited in *On the Town* and *Call Me Madam* are subjective and endlessly debatable. But after *Annie Get Your Gun*, the lure of fidelity was hard to ignore. Still, I haven't forgotten my promise in the Preface that "film adaptations will not be judged on the extent to which they follow their stage predecessor." When it comes to evaluating the film version of *On the Town*, the absence of Bernstein's music makes it difficult to fulfill this promise, but by imagining *On the Town* as an *original* film musical rather than an adaptation of a stage musical, it becomes easier to appreciate the results on its own terms. According to these terms, *Town* was an entertaining film with a remarkable cinematic opening number followed by fine singing and outstanding dancing along with delightful comic touches. It also showcased some of the greatest film stars of their time and ours. Isn't this more than enough to ask of an original film musical?

In discussing the adaptation of her novel *Notes on a Scandal* (2003) into a movie three years later, Zoë Heller wrote that "there are no sensible generalizations to be made about what we're 'meant to get' from film adaptations—other than, perhaps, good movies."[71] Heller went on to question whether we should burden films with the obligation to be faithful to their source texts. Eventually she comes down on the side of audacious "chutzpah" (Disney's *Mary Poppins*) rather than tedious "reverence" (Peter Jackson's *The Hobbit*). This divide applies equally well when considering imaginative musical film adaptations that take considerable liberties with their sources and films that offer slavish imitations of their stage models. While it may fall short of *West Side Story*, which as we will observe retained nearly all of Bernstein's music *and* Robbins's choreography, I think it's fair to end this chapter by placing *On the Town* alongside *Call Me Madam* in the "good movie" column.

4

1940s Stage Musicals and Their Screen Adaptations

Cabin in the Sky, *Brigadoon*, and *Oklahoma!*

This chapter will explore three historically and artistically significant stage musicals from the 1940s and their film adaptations: *Cabin in the Sky* (stage 1940; film 1943); *Brigadoon* (stage 1947; film 1954), and *Oklahoma!* (stage 1943; film 1955). *Brigadoon* and *Oklahoma!* have since remained in the center of the musical theater mainstream and repertoire, and despite (or because of) continuing cultural and aesthetic controversies, all three film adaptations continue to be viewed and argued about. The central focus here will be what happened in the move from stage to screen, why these changes happened, and what was gained and lost in translation.

The sole member of this 1940s trio to be filmed in the 1940s, *Cabin in the Sky*, like *On the Town*, and for that matter most film adaptations of '40s musicals, took the greatest liberties. Due to these liberties, the neglect of the stage show, and its subsequent absence from the Broadway repertoire much of *Cabin*'s book, score, and choreography was irrevocably lost. The film version of *Brigadoon* also took its share of liberties, including casting the original singing leads with star dancers Gene Kelly (1912–1996) and Cyd Charisse (1921–2008) while eliminating most of Agnes de Mille's choreography. It also removed a considerable number of songs, although in contrast to difficult-to-obtain basic sources for *Cabin*, *Brigadoon*'s book has been published, most of its music is readily accessible on cast and studio albums, and de Mille's choreography is available for those who want to use it. *Oklahoma!*, like the majority of other 1950s adaptations, was more faithful to its still-popular stage source, including the retention of nearly its entire book, score, and choreography, the latter also by de Mille.

A Fine Romance. Geoffrey Block, Oxford University Press. © Oxford University Press 2023.
DOI: 10.1093/oso/9780197501733.003.0004

CABIN IN THE SKY
(stage 1940; MGM 1943)

The First Major Film Musical to Be Adapted from
an All-Black Stage Show

When *Cabin in the Sky* arrived on Broadway on October 25, 1940, probably no all-Black stage musical was better known than *Porgy and Bess* (1935).[1] Unlike these two shows, the first full-length Black musical, *In Dahomey* (1903), briefly mentioned in chapter 2, which preceded both of these musicals by more than thirty years, was created as well as performed by Blacks. In 1921, *Shuffle Along*, as also noted in chapter 2, was created by Black talent, ran an impressive 504 performances, and inspired a number of imitators. Other earlier notable Black shows included *Hot Chocolates* (1929) and two reasonably successful all-Black adaptations of W. S. Gilbert and Arthur Sullivan's *The Mikado*, *The Swing Mikado* and *The Hot Mikado*, both appearing one year before *The Cabin in the Sky*.

None of these shows entered the Broadway repertory, although *The Hot Mikado* received regular restagings regionally throughout the United States and in London. Only *Cabin in the Sky* was filmed, remarkably the first major film musical to be adapted from an all-Black stage show. All-Black musical films remained even rarer than all-Black stage shows. In fact, the film adaptation of *Cabin* (MGM, 1943) was preceded only by King Vidor's pioneering *Hallelujah* (MGM, 1929). In addition to its important historical role as the second all-Black Hollywood film musical, *Cabin* was only the fourth all-Black major studio film of *any* type.[2]

Although the libretto of *Cabin* remains unpublished (unlike those for *Brigadoon* and *Oklahoma!*) and the show appeared several years before cast albums became the norm, we are fortunate that its star Ethel Waters (1896–1977) recorded four songs in 1940, the year of *Cabin*'s stage premiere.[3] Miller Music published ten songs, although few remain easily accessible (see Appendix 2). *Cabin* has also been revived in smaller venues over the years, including a brief forty-seven-performance run at New York's Greenwich Mews Theater in 1964. On the other hand, it has received no significant Broadway exposure prior to a New York City *Encores!* concert performance in 2016, a performance unfortunately not released on CD.[4]

Also nearly stricken from the record is the choreography created by George Balanchine (1904–1983) and Katherine Dunham (1909–2006), the latter also featured on stage as the devil's seductive accomplice Georgia Brown. Curiously, while the show's billing stated "production staged by George Balanchine," it did not indicate a choreographer. According to the unofficial, uncredited, and belatedly acknowledged co-choreographer Dunham and those involved in rehearsals, the choreography was fully collaborative. Talley Beatty, a dancer in Dunham's company, went further when he stated that "Dunham did all of the choreographing" with the exception of the "Hell Scene" that opened Act II.[5] Unfortunately, the choreography was not filmed, although the costumes are preserved in stage photographs such as those for the "Egyptian Ballet," the big dance number in the second act. The choreography for "Lazy Steps" and "Boogy Woogy," also in Act II, was apparently borrowed from previous Dunham dances such as *Le Jazz Hot* and is also no longer extant. See Figures 4.1 and 4.2.

Nevertheless, other than a few significant changes, including an imaginative new opening, the film version shares the plot, the dramatic structure, and the majority of the stage dialogue spoken in the scenes common to both. In order to obtain Black support, associate producer Al Lewis, who directed the stage dialogue, asked the choral conductor Hall Johnson (1888–1970) to evaluate the screenplay for its racial content. Johnson responded that the script "may be offered to the general public without reservations—needing neither explanations nor apologies" in sharp contrast to "the slanderous misrepresentations of *The Green Pastures*."[6] Nevertheless, despite its attempt not to give offense, the film preserves the demeaning dialect and atrocious grammar of Lucifer Jr. (identified as Head Man in the stage libretto) and his assistants that became increasingly problematic for future viewers.

Figs. 4.1 and 4.2 "The Egyptian Ballet." Katherine Dunham (*center*) with the Katherine Dunham Dancers in the stage version of *Cabin in the Sky*. Photofest.

Figs. 4.1 and 4.2 Continued

   While fundamentally a decent man, Little Joe Jackson exhibits traits frequently associated with Black stage and film characters of the era such as an ad-
diction to gambling, the use of razors, illiteracy, laziness, and a susceptibility to
the charms of a beautiful and sexy woman, in this case, Georgia Brown, who has
taken a fancy to him. Little Joe's devoted wife Petunia also demonstrates a degree of religiosity that borders on stereotype, and sometimes she wears a racially
coded headscarf. At the same time, Petunia's prayers and her faith are portrayed
sympathetically under the direction of Vincente Minnelli (1903–1986), as in her
prayer at Joe's bedside after he is shot (13:10). The moments of tastefully scary
cinematic magic, such as the relighting of the lantern at Joe's bedside (14:35) by

the arriving Devil, which casts a sharply defined shadow of his horned profile on the wall, make this a family-friendly fantasy as well as a record of an important Broadway show.

The Production Code Administration led by Joseph I. Breen requested that MGM remove a few unacceptable words, including nine "hells," and that the filmmakers avoid sexual suggestiveness, such as the "improper exposure of Georgia where she crosses her legs" or when she is taking a bubble bath while singing "Ain't It de Truth." When it came to the song lyrics, with the exception of a single line in "Li'l Black Sheep," a couple of lines in "Ain't It de Truth," and "Jezebel Jones," the latter rejected outright as "unacceptable by reason of sex suggestiveness," Breen was "happy to report" that everything else met the Code requirements.[7]

At the beginning of the stage version Little Joe is on his deathbed after being stabbed by Domino Johnson in a gambling quarrel. The devil's son, Lucifer, is about to carry Joe off to Hell, but Petunia's "powerful prayer" summons the Lord's General, who agrees to let Joe return to life and a six-month period in which to reform. In both the stage and film versions Joe starts his redemption well and gets a steady job. He also fends off Georgia's advances *before* he learns that Lucifer has arranged for him to miraculously receive the winning ticket to the Irish Sweepstakes. When he learns about this unexpected windfall, Joe's first impulse is to use the money to give Petunia a better life. Unfortunately, also in both versions, Petunia returns at the precise moment Little Joe is innocently hugging Georgia and offering to buy her a diamond bracelet to thank her for discovering the crumpled ticket and reading its contents.[8] Faced with this incriminating scene, Petunia angrily throws Joe out without giving him an opportunity to explain the extenuating circumstances. See Figures 4.3 and 4.4.

By the end of his sixth and final month of probation Little Joe, now separated from Petunia, has spent nearly all of his sweepstakes money, half on Georgia and half on his nightlife activities such as gambling. On the last night of his six-month trial, Joe and Georgia confront Petunia and Domino at Henry's night club. Petunia has shed her matronly clothes for a lavish and revealing dress. Soon her dancing and flirting with Domino get out of hand, prompting Joe to attack his former assailant, who quickly gets the upper hand and shoots Joe and Petunia. The violence summons the Lord's General who uses his power to destroy the club.[9] The final scene takes place in Heaven. To their relief, Joe and Petunia learn that Georgia has repented, found the Lord, and donated Joe's money to the church, actions that prompt the Lord to permit Joe to join Petunia in a Heavenly "cabin in the sky."

A major change in the film was the decision to alter the opening of the story. The stage version begins outside, then inside, the Jackson home where Little Joe has been stabbed and is at death's door. To great effect, the film allows viewers

Fig. 4.3 Shown from left: Ethel Waters (Petunia), Dooley Wilson (Little Joe), and Katherine Dunham (Georgia Brown) in the stage version of *Cabin in the Sky*. Photofest.

to witness the events leading to Joe's near-death experience: Joe and Petunia in their home getting ready to go to church; Joe and Petunia inside the church and the congregational singing of the spirituals, "Li'l Black Sheep" and "Old Ship of Zion"; Joe's reluctant departure from church with Dude and Jim Henry who force him to go to the latter's club to pay off his gambling debts; and Domino's stabbing of Joe moments before Petunia arrives on the scene. In neither the stage nor film versions is Joe granted the ability to recall the battle between the General and Lucifer Jr. over his soul, but only in the film do the deaths of Little Joe and Petunia turn out to have been only a dream.[10]

Fig. 4.4 Ethel Waters (Petunia), Lena Horne (Georgia Brown), and Eddie Anderson (Little Joe) in the film version of *Cabin in the Sky* [64:30]. Screenshot.

The star on both stage and screen was Ethel Waters (1896–1977), whose career as a singer goes back to the 1920s. In the 1930s she became the first Black actress to appear on Broadway, and by the time *Cabin in the Sky* opened, she was the most highly paid. Ten years before Lena Horne (1917–2010) made the song her own in the film *Stormy Weather*, Waters had introduced Harold Arlen's "Stormy Weather" at the Cotton Club and recorded it. The same year, 1933, Waters introduced Irving Berlin's torrid "Heat Wave" and poignant "Supper Time" from the popular Broadway revue *As Thousands Cheer*.[11] One reason Arthur Freed selected Minnelli to direct *Cabin* for his movie debut was his success directing the Broadway revue *At Home Abroad* (1935), which featured Waters and future MGM movie star Eleanor Powell. One year before starring in *Cabin*, her first book musical on Broadway, Waters added to her acclaim as an actress when DuBose and Dorothy Heyward created a starring role for her in a 1939 adaptation of DuBose's 1929 novel *Mamba's Daughters*.

Waters's film work prior to *Cabin* was less distinguished. In 1942 she co-starred with Paul Robeson in a scene from his last Hollywood film, an anthology called *Tales of Manhattan*. Despite the participation of the Hall Johnson Choir, the demeaning stereotypes in their vignette outraged rather than entertained Black audiences.[12] Growing interest in producing a significant all-Black film musical led Freed to offer Waters the opportunity to reclaim her stage role in *Cabin*. This was considered a risky move, since the stage version was a *succès d'estime* rather than a box office sensation, and Waters's success with both Black and white urban audiences was no guarantee of success in a nationally distributed Hollywood film. To offset these uncertainties, Freed allotted fewer financial resources for *Cabin* than he did for his other films.[13] On the plus side, MGM supported Waters with outstanding Black talent, including such great jazz musicians as Duke Ellington (1899–1974) and Louis Armstrong (1901–1972), John W. Sublett (1902–1986) known as Bubbles, the Hall Johnson Choir, newcomer Horne, and Eddie "Rochester" Anderson (1905–1977).

Waters had vetoed Anderson for the stage version, which instead featured Dooley Wilson as Little Joe.[14] Had *Cabin* been released a few months later, Wilson might have made the transfer to film since by then he had gained recognition in *Casablanca* (released in November 1942) as the piano player who reluctantly played "As Time Goes By" when Ingrid Bergman insisted that he "Play it, Sam."[15] Anderson was nearly as well known as Waters from his regular appearances as comedian Jack Benny's valet and chauffeur Rochester, first on national radio broadcasts in 1937 and then in movies and television well into the 1970s. Anderson was also the *only* Black actor then under contract at MGM. He managed to sing on pitch and with reasonable lyricism in his unmistakable raspy voice during his chorus of "Cabin in the Sky," but the duet "Life's Full of Consequence" forces him to sing (and sometimes screech) well above his range as he fends off Georgia's advances.[16]

Minnelli had worked the previous year with Horne when he staged her two musical numbers in the film version of *Panama Hattie*. Soon she became the first Black actress to sign a long-term (seven-year) contract with a major Hollywood studio (MGM). She was also featured in 20th Century-Fox's *Stormy Weather*, which followed one month after *Cabin*, an all-Black film musical also packed with talent.[17] Slender and of light complexion, Horne embodied a physical type that appealed to both Black and white audiences. Nina Mae McKinney in *Hallelujah* in 1929 and Dorothy Dandridge, the latter's voice dubbed in the film adaptations of *Carmen Jones* and *Porgy and Bess* in the 1950s, presented a similar physicality.[18]

The *Cabin in the Sky* Screen Score

In contrast to the relatively modest changes in the screenplay, the film's musical departures from the stage version are considerable and far-reaching. The most all-encompassing changes stemmed from the decision to replace Dunham with Horne in the role of Georgia and to eliminate the Dunham Dancers, who made an incalculable contribution to the style and content of the stage version. The metamorphosis of Georgia from a role that emphasized dance (but also required considerable acting and singing) to a role that required no dancing resulted in the removal of more than a few songs and dance numbers. The following section will look at what was salvaged from the score, what was altered, and how Minnelli transformed the stage version into the film, which to all practical purposes remains the only version of *Cabin in the Sky* known today.

The Broadway show consisted of songs with lyrics by John Latouche (1917–1956) and music by Vernon Duke (1903–1969), shown in the left-hand column of Table 4.1, "*Cabin in the Sky* on Stage and Screen," along with interpolated

Table 4.1 *Cabin in the Sky* on Stage and Screen.

Stage	Screen
Act I	
(Chorus) "Wade in the Water" (Traditional spiritual)	
The General's Song (Duncan, Saints)	**Li'l Black Sheep (Waters and Chorus) (6:08)**
	Old Ship of Zion (Chorus) (8:09)
Pay Heed (Duncan and Saints)	
	Happiness is a Thing Called Joe (Waters) (25:45)
Taking a Chance on Love (Waters)	
Cabin in the Sky (Walters, Wilson)	**Cabin in the Sky (Waters and Anderson (34:00)**
	Taking a Chance on Love (Waters, with Bailey, Dancer) (48:00)
Holy unto the Lord (Waters, Wilson, Johnson, Churchmembers) (Chorus) (Traditional gospel hymn)	
Dem Bones (Waters, Dowdy, Churchmembers) (Traditional spiritual)	
Do What You Wanna Do (Ingram, Savage, Moxzer, Ohardieno, McDonald)	
Taking a Chance on Love (Reprise) (Waters, Wilson)	
Act II	
Fugue (Duncan, Saints)	
My Old Virginia Home on the Nile (Waters, Wilson)	
[Vision] Egyptian Ballet (The Dunham Dancers)	
	Life's Full of Consequence (Horne, Anderson) (60:56)
It's Not So Good to Be Bad (Duncan)	

(continued)

Table 4.1 Continued

Stage	Screen
Love Me Tomorrow (Dunham, Wilson)	
Love Turned the Light Out (Waters)	**Happiness Is a Thing Called Joe (Reprise) (66:55)**
Lazy Steps and Boogy Woogy (The Dunham Dancers) (music not by Duke)	
	Things Ain't What They Used to Be (Duke Ellington and His Orchestra (68:20)
	Going Up (Duke Ellington and His Orchestra) (69:47)
	Shine (Bubbles) (73:50)
Honey in the Honeycomb (Dunham, Boys)	**Honey in the Honeycomb (Horne) (78:41)**
Savannah (Waters)	**Honey in the Honeycomb (Reprise) (Waters) (83:50)**
Dance (Waters, Savage)	
	Cabin in the Sky (Reprise) (Chorus)
Finale (including a reprise of Cabin in the Sky)	Taking a Chance on Love (Reprise of final A section) (Waters) (97:55)

- *The songs listed in bold in the screen column were not in the stage version.*
- *Numbers in parentheses in the screen column refer to film timings.*

MAJOR SINGING AND DANCING AND SELECTED ROLES

Stage: ETHEL WATERS (Petunia Jackson); Todd Duncan (The Lawd's General); Dooley Wilson ("Little Joe" Jackson); Katherine Dunham (Georgia Brown); REX INGRAM (Lucifer Jr.), J. Rosamond Johnson (Brother Green); Katherine Dunham Dancers; J. Rosamond Johnson Singers; Helen Dowdy (J. Rosamond Johnson Singers); Archie Savage (Imp/Katherine Dunham Dancer); Dick Campbell (Domino Johnson).

Screen: WATERS (Petunia); Eddie "Rochester" Anderson ("Little Joe"); Lena Horne (Georgia Brown); INGRAM (Lucius/Lucifer Jr.); Kenneth Spencer (The General/Reverend Green); John W. Sublett ("Bubbles") (Domino Johnson); Louis Armstrong (The Trumpeter); Bill Bailey (Bill); Ford Buck (Messenger Boy); Mantan Moreland (First Idea Man); Willie Best (Second Idea Man); Butterfly McQueen (Lily); Duke Ellington Orchestra; Hall Johnson Choir

- *Names in capital letters indicate that a cast member appeared both on stage and in the film.*

spirituals and recycled material culled from the repertoire of the Dunham Dancers. The stage score featured Waters (Petunia) in nine musical numbers, Dunham (Georgia) and her Dancers in six, and Wilson (Little Joe) in five. See Figures 4.1, 4.2, 4.3, and 4.5.

From this rich assortment of songs Minnelli retained only three: Waters's "Taking a Chance on Love," the show's biggest hit; "Cabin in the Sky," the title song, a duet for Waters and Wilson; and Georgia's "Honey in the Honeycomb."[19]

Fig. 4.5 Dooley Wilson (Little Joe) and Ethel Waters (Petunia) in the
stage version of *Cabin in the Sky*. Photofest.

To replace the remaining Duke melodies and Latouche lyrics and to create a new
spiritual to open the film Minnelli hired Harold Arlen (1905–1986) and E. Y.
("Yip") Harburg (1898–1981) to compose eight new songs, three of which were
eventually used: "Li'l Black Sheep," "Happiness Is a Thing Called Joe," and "Life's
Full of Consequence."[20] The film soundtrack also includes two Ellington instrumental tunes, an interpolated song composed in 1910, a considerable amount
of effective (if occasionally intrusive) symphonic underscoring by Roger Edens,
and music that was recorded but not used. Fortunately, the nearly seventy-six-
minute soundtrack released in 1999 includes nearly all of this music.[21] The

following paragraphs will discuss the musical material that appears in the film as released and commercially available on DVD since 2006:

- 6:08   "Li'l Black Sheep" (Arlen and Harburg) [3:47 min.]

The stage version began with the sounds of the traditional and popular American spiritual, the somber "God's a-Gwineter Trouble de Water" (more commonly known as "Wade in the Water"), heard in the distance. Balanchine, who directed as well as co-choreographed with Dunham (both uncredited), wanted to begin with a Russian dirge but was vigorously outvoted by the Black cast. "Wade in the Water" came as close to a Russian dirge as Balanchine could find. To replace it in the film, Arlen composed a lively pseudo-spiritual about a black sheep, which, like Little Joe, strayed from the fold but has now returned. Instead of being heard outside of Joe's house, the film's "Black Sheep" is effectively heard and cinematically experienced at Jackson's church with Little Joe present to repent of his sins and celebrate his newly reformed life.

As the spiritual begins, the camera, mounted on a crane, starts at the front of the church and gradually moves to the rear as various soloists in the congregation sing the song's verse answered by the full congregation singing the chorus (sung by the magnificent Hall Johnson Choir).[22] Eventually the camera finds Little Joe sitting in the back to Petunia's right with her friend Lily (Butterfly McQueen) to her left. The music comes to a close when Petunia stands up and proclaims in a rhythmically free unaccompanied melody that the little black sheep (i.e., her husband Little Joe) is "safe in the fold once more."[23]

The notion of a white composer writing in a traditional Black genre, perhaps most controversially in George Gershwin's invented spirituals in *Porgy and Bess*, is a fraught topic that cannot be resolved here.[24] The Ghanaian British American philosopher Kwame Anthony Appiah makes a serious attempt to place the controversy in perspective by offering a contextualization in which "disrespect and exploitation are worthy targets of our disapproval, but the idea of cultural appropriation is ripe for the wastebasket."[25] A more recent example that has received more praise than blame for its eclectic and respectful appropriation of spirituals, blues, Motown, as well as klezmer and classical styles, is Jeanine Tesori's score for *Caroline, Or Change* (2004; revival, 2021).[26] For Appiah, simply borrowing ideas from another culture does not constitute a "property crime." Although this line of argument, even when voiced by a noted scholar of color, may not alter negative views on cultural appropriation, the fact remains that throughout his career Arlen wrote more famous songs and shows expressly for Black singers than any other white composer.[27] It was previously mentioned that one of his best-known songs, "Stormy Weather" has been indelibly associated with both Waters and Horne.[28] It might also be recalled that Arlen's adoption of Black culture appeared at a time when Black artists were largely excluded as creators for the Broadway stage. In any event, for what it's worth, Waters called Arlen "the Negro-est white man" she knew.[29]

- 8:09 "Old Ship of Zion" (Traditional) [3:06 min.]

The film directly followed Arlen's pseudo-spiritual at the church service with "Old Ship of Zion," a Christian hymn composed in 1889 by Daniel B. Towner to the words of M. J. Cartwright, the only traditional spiritual sung in the film.[30] Leading the congregation and the Hall Johnson Choir is Reverend Green (Kenneth Spencer), who later doubled as The General, the Lord's assistant.

- 25:45   "Happiness Is a Thing Called Joe" (Arlen and Harburg) [3:03 min.]

When Little Joe miraculously recovers from death's door in the stage version, Petunia sings the joyful hit song of the show, "Taking a Chance on Love." The film delays this exuberant moment for twenty minutes. Instead, Petunia sings a meditative, almost prayerful, new song (unfortunately in dialect) by Arlen and Harburg, "Happiness Is a Thing Called Joe," with characteristic dramatic power. "Happiness" is in the tradition of Julie's "Bill" from *Show Boat*, but instead of emphasizing her man's less-endearing qualities such as Little Joe's susceptibility to various temptations, Petunia's song emphasizes the positive reasons she loves her husband and her knowledge that Joe loves her deeply as well.[31]

During the repeat of the chorus the camera effectively dissolves from Little Joe's bedside to the Jackson backyard where we see Petunia taking down the laundry and seemingly improvising a counter line to the original melody. The song closes with a new second ending based exclusively on the two-note phrase (twice on the words "Little Joe" and once on "Mm Mm Mm") that marked measures 12–15. The ensuing dialogue clarifies that a month has transpired between the first and second choruses, implying that Petunia has been singing this slow but joyful song frequently since her beloved husband came back from the dead.

- 34:00   "Cabin in the Sky" (Duke and Latouche) [4:30 min.]

More than one-third of the film's ninety-eight minutes has passed before viewers hear the first Duke and Latouche song from the original stage version, the title song "Cabin in the Sky." In the stage version, Little Joe has just successfully resisted the Head Man's efforts to tempt Joe with thoughts of Georgia, and the song establishes a response to the General's optimism that Petunia and Joe will someday share a cabin in the heavenly sky. The song's form is the standard 32-bar AABA preceded by a verse sung by Petunia.

The film removes the stage skirmish between the Head Man and the General. It also moves the song from the Jackson backyard to a pastoral meadow on a river bank. After the verse, Petunia sings the first chorus, Joe the second, and in the third a group of picnickers arrive to the sounds of the Hall Johnson Choir. In the B section Petunia "calls" and the choir "responds," and during the final A section Petunia again provides a quasi-improvised counter line over the choral melody. Without apparent prompting from the Production Code, the lyrics underwent a few changes in the transfer to film, most notably the change in the B section of the first and third choruses when the film's Petunia sings "all we'll do is sing and pray" instead of "eating fried chicken every day" as she did on stage. Both Petunia and Little Joe also now invariably replace "baby" with the more family-friendly "mister" and "lady," starting with the opening phrase, "There's a little Cabin in the Sky, mister."

- 48:00   "Taking a Chance on Love" (Duke and Latouche) [4:20 min.]

As previously noted, the stage version introduces "Taking a Chance on Love," the unequivocal hit of the stage show, far earlier in the story when Petunia non-diegetically expresses her joy on learning that Little Joe's life has been spared. The song returns with an ironic twist at the end of the first act when Joe and Petunia go off to church unaware that the Head Man has arranged for Joe's sweepstakes ticket to win, a plan that will allow Petunia's flawed husband more than enough money to run afoul of the Lord and keep himself out of Heaven.

Four minutes before we hear "Taking a Chance," film viewers meet Georgia (Horne) for the first time as she exits her bubble bath, dresses, and allows Lucifer Jr. (the stage's Head Man) to get inside her head and plant the idea that now's a good time to seduce Little Joe. Inspired by Lucifer, the film's Georgia immediately goes to look for Joe at his place of work, finds the sweepstakes ticket he had thrown on the ground, and heads out to the Jackson home. We are now forty-four minutes into the film, almost exactly halfway through. In contrast, in the stage version Georgia (Dunham) was introduced in the opening minutes outside the Jackson home where the doctor treating Joe asked her to leave in order to avoid trouble with Petunia and her critically wounded husband.

Ironically, Georgia's initial actions in the film occur at precisely the same moment the Jacksons are celebrating their marital bliss with a reprise of "Taking a Chance." Now gainfully employed at hard labor and exuberantly tossing heavy bags of sugar, Little Joe has earned enough money to purchase a washing machine as a birthday present for Petunia. Overlooking the reality that they haven't yet installed the electricity needed to use this luxury, Petunia is ecstatic and proclaims that "there ain't nobody got no right being happy as I am." This prompts Joe to ask Petunia to "sing us a little song" to which Petunia responds with a diegetic performance of "Taking a Chance on Love."[32]

The film lavishes four full minutes on the song's four 32-bar AABA choruses. The first and second choruses belong entirely to Petunia.[33] Appropriately, the lyrics of the B section contain gambling images (cards, playing the numbers, and a rabbit's foot for good luck) to reinforce the idea that Petunia is taking a chance (on love). In the third chorus Petunia is joined by Little Joe's friend Bill (Bill Bailey) who had helped move the washing machine to the front porch and then stuck around to play his guitar, whistle, and tap dance. The introduction of tap contradicts the choreographic vision Balanchine and Dunham fought for in the stage version. In his autobiography, Duke recalls how producers Vinton Freedley and especially Martin Beck tried without success to fire Balanchine for refusing to incorporate tap into the show and his support of Dunham's efforts to combine the richness of African and Afro-Caribbean dancing styles with traditional ballet and modern dance idioms.[34] Although Balanchine and Dunham's vision in the end ruled the stage version, Minnelli and Freed chose to satisfy the film public's desire (and their own) for tap and added it to "Taking a Chance on Love." In Bubble's song and dance in "Shine" at Jim Henry's, the only interpolated sung number not composed by Arlen, tapping steps are also seen but only subtly heard.

Near the end of the final chorus Petunia gets so caught up in the moment that she lets out a wicked vocal growl. A shocked Little Joe calls out "PETUNIA!" which settles her down enough to sing a slow final statement of the song's title, not unlike the way she concluded "L'il Black Sheep." The final four bars of the last A section ascend to the highest note of the song sounding three times on the words "happy ending," before Petunia joyously sings "taking a chance on love" one last time to conclude the song an octave higher than the high note of the second A section.

- 60:56 "Life's Full of Consequence" (Arlen and Harburg) [1:50 min.]

As we have seen, the film's Georgia took the crumpled winning sweepstakes ticket and went directly to find Little Joe and begin her seduction. This sets up the third and final Arlen-Harburg song, "Life's Full of Consequence," during and after which Joe heroically defends himself against Georgia's advances. The song matches the sentiment of the song it replaced, "Love Me Tomorrow," which was sung on the stage *before* Georgia saw the discarded ticket in the Jackson backyard. Joe's lyrics in the stage's "Tomorrow," such as "you can come around in a year or two" and "ask me next Christmas," fall short of the firm resolve he expresses in the rhymed couplet of "Consequence": "I've been burned more than twice/and I ain't payin' the price." Between the stage and film versions Little Joe has matured at least a little.

- 66:55 "Happiness Is a Thing Called Joe" (reprise) [1:25 min.]

The film's Georgia infers that the reason Joe is playing hard to get is because of the ticket. When she realizes he hasn't seen it, she informs Petunia's faithful (albeit illiterate) husband of his good fortune. To express his gratitude, Joe gives Georgia a hug and offers to buy her a diamond bracelet, a fur coat, even her own nightclub. This is the unfortunate moment Petunia returns, sees the two embracing, and angrily kicks Little Joe out without giving him an opportunity to explain, an action that prompts a shocked Lord's General to exclaim, "You didn't even give him a chance." A disconsolate Petunia goes into the house, accompanied by the (invisible) orchestra playing the traditional spiritual "Nobody Knows the Trouble I've Seen," and sings a mournful reprise of "Happiness Is a Thing Called Joe."

In a nearly identical stage context, Petunia sang the ballad "Love Turned the Light Out," one of the four songs Waters recorded in 1940. It is a sophisticated and touching ballad, one of the finest songs in the Duke-Latouche score with lyrics that simply but eloquently capture how Petunia's love for Little Joe has turned into darkness and loveless shadows. The music of "Love Turned the Light Out" perfectly fit Petunia's somber mood and its disappearance is a considerable loss. On the other hand, the words lacked the specificity and direct emotional appeal of "Happiness Is a Thing Called Joe." Since the latter was a reprise, the substitution also reinforced the happy (not poignant) memory when Petunia first sang the song after her husband's miraculous recovery.

- 68:20 "Things Ain't What They Used to Be" [1:26 min.] and "Goin' Up" [3:38 min.]

The film immediately dissolves into Jim [John on stage] Henry's Café, now with Duke Ellington's name on the marquee. Instead of seeing the band, however, viewers hear it play two 12-bar blues choruses of "Things Ain't What They Used to Be" (a popular jazz chart composed by the Duke's son Mercer). Instead of showing the band, the camera homes in on the dancers, first outside and then inside the club. When the music abruptly shifts to Ellington's "Goin' Up," film viewers and Whitey's Lindy Hoppers now observe the Duke at his piano. The Hoppers stand still long enough to savor Lawrence Brown's rhythmically free (out-of-tempo) trombone solo. They then resume their vigorous athletic dancing to the steady beat of Ellington's band featuring two more top soloists, Ray Nance on violin and Ben Webster on tenor sax. If you're committed to removing the Dunham Dancers from the film, you could do worse.

- 74:50 "Shine" (music by Ford Dabney and lyrics by Cecil Mack) [2:51 min.]

Domino, the man who nearly killed Little Joe prior to the time the stage show begins, has just been released from jail and appears shortly after Georgia and Little Joe's arrival. The stage Domino does not sing, but in the film he performs a song composed in 1910 called "Shine," a tune that had been performed and recorded by jazz artists for decades. In addition to the historical value of seeing Bubbles's accomplished singing and dancing on film, more than any other number in the film "Shine" addresses racial stereotypes directly in the lyrics with references to curly hair, pearly teeth, and "shady" coloring. The song's punch line, "makes no difference, baby/That's why they call me 'Shine,'" obscures the probable origins of the word "shine" as a racist nickname for the Black shoe shiners prevalent in American society in the first half of the twentieth century.

The performer, John W. Sublett, who performed under the name of Bubbles since the early 1920s with his partner Ford L. "Buck" Washington under the name Buck and Bubbles, is probably best known today as the original Sportin' Life in *Porgy and Bess*.[35] His performance of "Shine," one of the film's finest moments, offers ample evidence of what Bubbles brought to this famous role eight years earlier and supports Bubbles's reputation as one of the finest stage dancers of the day, admired by all, including Fred Astaire.[36] New lyrics replace "Shine's" published verse but retain most of the words and chord changes of the chorus. Unlike most jazz instrumentalists since the 1940s who usually abandon the original tune after an initial statement and then use the chords to support their improvisations, jazz singers like Ella Fitzgerald usually paraphrase the tune in a recognizable manner when singing the words and then scat improvisationally against the harmonies without the words. Unlike most jazz singers, Bubbles alters the melody beyond recognition at the outset, while at the same time preserving the harmonies and, more remarkably, the text. See Figure 4.6.

- 78:41 "Honey in the Honeycomb" (Duke and Latouche) [1:54]

Little Joe and Georgia arrive at Henry's Café in their flashy clothing, and in the case of Georgia, equally flashy underwear, which to the horror of the Production Code (and several film distributors) she displays to an attentive male audience, provocatively noting that "the accessories are even cuter."[37] She then sings a chorus of the third and final Duke-Latouche contribution to the film version. Although the Code had some objections to Georgia's sexual suggestiveness,

Fig. 4.6 Shown from *left:* Ethel Waters (Petunia), John W. Sublett (Domino Johnson), Eddie Anderson (Little Joe), and Lena Horne (Georgia Brown) at Jim Henry's Paradise in the film version of *Cabin in the Sky* [82:29]. Screenshot.

somehow they didn't mind her character singing lyrics about "jelly in the jelly roll" and equating honey with what she has to offer. In the unfortunate absence of "Ain't It de Truth," aside from her short duet with Joe, "Life's Full of Consequence," "Honey in the Honeycomb" is all Georgia gets to sing in the film.

- 83: 50 "Honey in the Honeycomb" (reprise) [1:22]

After Georgia's "Honey" number, a confrontation ensues with Petunia. Georgia asserts that Petunia is "just jealous because she ain't got what I got," to which Petunia, decked out in a tightfitting evening gown that presents a startling contrast to the loose-fitting dresses topped by bandannas she has previously worn, replies, "Not only have I got everything you got, but a whole lot more." She then sings and dances suggestively with Domino to prove it. In the stage version she sings "Savannah," a lively Latin number about the desirability of Savannah, Georgia (the state), over Havana, Cuba. Like "Love Me Tomorrow" and "Love Turned Out the Light," the exuberant show stopper reinforces why this lost stage musical deserves a worthy revival and a complete recording. Instead of "Savannah," the film's Petunia reprises "Honey in the Honeycomb," repeating the words and music of Georgia's chorus but omitting her verse. Not only was Horne not a dancer, a broken ankle made it necessary for her to sing her version of the "Honey" song sitting at the bar. Horne's misfortune provided the opportunity for Waters to upstage her rival and demonstrate that she indeed has got everything

Georgia has (and more), including an arsenal of flashy hip moves, high kicks, and an extra song.

Concluding Remarks

On stage, Todd Duncan, the first Porgy in *Porgy and Bess*, played the Lord's General who sang "The General's Song" and "Pay Heed" in Act I and "It's Not So Good to Be Bad" in Act II. His film counterpart Kenneth Spencer retained much of his Heavenly and Earthly dialogue but was not assigned any songs to sing. His nemesis, Lucifer Jr. played by Rex Ingram on both stage and screen, sang "Do What You Wanna Do" in Act I on stage, but although the role is substantial and followed the stage libretto closely, it too is musically silent in the film remake. By the time the movie arrived in theaters only four characters sang: Petunia, Little Joe, Georgia, and Domino.

One of these characters, Georgia, ended up with less to sing in the film than originally intended. Her big solo number, "Ain't It de Truth," made it as far as the filming stage but no further. Its eventual elimination despite its toned down "exposure of Georgia's person" and adherence to the Code-endorsed lyric, significantly altered the musical balance with Petunia, especially since the latter was allowed the opportunity to sing a reprise of "Honey in the Honeycomb."[38] Ellington and some of his instrumental soloists have their moments to shine in "Going Up," but unfortunately, no place could be found for even an abbreviated version of Armstrong's rendition of "Ain't It de Truth," the longest cut in the soundtrack at more than five minutes.[39] In the film version, Armstrong, the Trumpeter in Lucifer's Hollywood Idea Department's vision of Hell, is musically reduced to a jazz lick or two followed by Lucifer's demand to "Stop that noise!" But although his playing is silenced, Armstrong gets a fair share of new dialogue in which we learn that it was the Devil's trumpeter who at the beginning of his career conceived the idea about Eve getting Adam "to nibble on that apple." As they contemplate how best to undermine Little Joe's chances of getting into Heaven, it is also the Trumpeter who hatches the idea of corrupting Joe by giving him the winning sweepstakes ticket.

It was previously noted that Minnelli removed all but three of the Duke-Latouche songs. This amounts to roughly the same amount of damage MGM inflicted on Bernstein's songs for the film version of *On the Town*. This time, unlike Edens's serviceable but by general agreement uninspired replacements in the earlier film, Minnelli managed to hire the composer and lyricist of "Over the Rainbow" who could approximate the original songwriters in quality. One of these new Arlen-Harburg songs, "Happiness Is a Thing Called Joe," became so associated with *Cabin* that it was retained in the New York City *Encores!* 2016 reconstruction of the otherwise Duke-Latouche score. The decision to remove the Dunham Dancers and their distinctive choreography based on African American and Caribbean dance styles proved to be decisive in expunging the staged *Cabin* from the historical record. In the end, the artistic fruition of Dunham's anthropological studies of early African American dancing, studies that led to her earning a PhD in the field, virtually vanished when Minnelli, in the first of his many films at MGM, brought his alternative vision to bear.

The choreography for the stage version of *Cabin in the Sky* is nearly lost, but present-day viewers wishing to get a sense of how Dunham may have carried herself as Georgia can watch "Sharp as a Tack" from *Star Spangled Rhythm* (1942) on YouTube, in which Dunham jitterbugs with Anderson, the same Anderson who played Little Joe in the *Cabin* film. The Dunham Dancers are also featured in the "Stormy Weather Ballet" from *Stormy Weather*, a popular film that appeared closely on *Cabin*'s heels and remains in wide circulation. Instead of Dunham's combination of balletic, modern, and authentic Caribbean dancing, the film version of *Cabin* offers Bill Bailey's taps and Rochester's novelty steps in "Taking a Chance on Love," a memorable song and tap dance number by Bubbles, and some exuberant jitterbugging from Whitey's Lindy Hoppers at Jim Henry's Café, dancing styles that Balanchine and Dunham were determined to exclude. As noted earlier, Balanchine's insistence on not including traditional Black popular styles nearly got him fired.

For contemporary Black audiences, the superb performances throughout the film of exceptional music and movement, the sympathetic portraits of a loving couple and a caring community, and Minnelli's generally sensitive, imaginative direction weren't enough to redeem the recycled stereotypes still present in the screenplay and lyrics. Perhaps the harshest response to the film came from the Black newspaper *Amsterdam News*: it was "the sort of thing that keeps alive misconceptions of the Negro" and that "it's too bad the actors didn't have the courage to refuse to make the film in the first place."[40] While *Variety* acknowledged that "some of the box office limitations of *Cabin* are inherent in the original work," namely, the fantasy element and the limited commercial appeal of an all-Black show, the reviewer also faulted the film for lacking "the imagination and skill that such a subject should have."[41] On the other side of the critical ledger, the *New York Times* found the screen version "as sparkling and completely satisfying as was the original stage production."[42] Fifty years after *Cabin* closed, James Naremore ended a critical but balanced study of the work on a positive note that might still resonate in an altered cultural climate when he concluded that despite its flaws, *Cabin in the Sky*'s historic representation of an imperfect cultural past remains "arguably the most visually beautiful picture about black people ever produced at the classic studios."[43]

BRIGADOON
(stage 1947; MGM 1954)

Choreography: Essential or Expendable?

When *Cabin in the Sky* and *On the Town* were adapted into film in the 1940s, not long after their stage expiration dates, neither had achieved the stature of *Oklahoma!* and *Brigadoon*, both of which were firmly established in the Broadway canon long before the film versions were released in October 1955 and September 1954, respectively. The latter pair of shows were created by different librettist and songwriting teams: Richard Rodgers and Oscar Hammerstein II for *Oklahoma!* and Alan Jay Lerner and Frederick Loewe for *Brigadoon*. But they did share a crucial common denominator in the choreographer Agnes de Mille (1905–1993), a pioneer in the creation of dance that enhanced both plot and the psychological dimensions of their characters.[44]

Unfortunately, while de Mille's contributions to these and other shows are widely viewed as essential elements in the success of the original productions and regularly used in subsequent productions, the art of dance never attained the perception of indispensability enjoyed by Hammerstein's and Lerner's librettos and lyrics and Loewe's and Rodgers's songs. Worse, for future stage and film directors and producers who might want to include the original choreography of a musical, this decision was often no longer an option. In the case of de Mille, the choreography to only three of her best-known shows has fully survived: *Brigadoon*, *Oklahoma!* and *Carousel*.[45]

According to Colin McArthur, *Brigadoon*, which opened on March 13, 1947, and closed 581 performances later on July 31, 1948, has since become "among the most popular shows to be mounted by amateur groups, averaging 40 revivals annually."[46] In contrast, appearances on the New York stage were limited to brief runs lasting at most 133 performances (in 1980). Earlier New York stagings used de Mille's choreography, but subsequent productions, such as those in the West End in 1988 and the four-day staged concert engagement at the New York City Center in 2017, replaced de Mille's work.

Oklahoma!'s artistic association with de Mille lasted longer. In fact, for fifty years, professional revivals were choreographed either by de Mille herself (limited 1951 and 1953 engagements) or recreated by her protégé Gemze de Lappe (Broadway 1979, West End 1980, and Australia 1982).[47] The acclaimed 1998 London National Theatre production directed by Trevor Nunn, transferred to Broadway in 2002 (each production running eleven months), broke the string of de Mille revivals when Susan Stroman created new choreography for the "Dream Ballet" and tinkered with de Mille's other major dance numbers ("Kansas City,"

"Many a New Day," and "The Farmer and the Cowman"). A successful Broadway revival in 2019 featured new choreography by John Heginbotham.

In contrast to *Brigadoon* and *Oklahoma!*, future *Carousel* choreographers were ready to abandon de Mille's vision sooner rather than later. As early as 1967, Edward Villella created the choreography for a network television broadcast of *Carousel*. After that, Peter Martin choreographed productions at the New York City Opera (1985) and Kennedy Center (1986), Kenneth MacMillan created new choreography for the popular West End (1992) and Broadway revivals (1994) directed by Nicholas Hytner, Adam Cooper did the choreography for a London production in 2008, and Justin Peck created it for the 2018 Broadway revival.

The film adaptations of *Carousel* and *Oklahoma!* also responded in different ways to the option of presenting de Mille's original choreography. For the 1956 film of *Carousel*, choreographer Rod Alexander expanded the dance component to include a newly choreographed dance that followed the singing of "June Is Bustin' Out All Over." He also removed the "Hornpipe" and created new dance steps for the extended second act ballet. Alexander's decisions raise the question of what choreography *means*. If choreography is defined by dance steps, movements, and formations, Alexander clearly replaced de Mille's choreography. But beginning in earnest with *Oklahoma!* something changed. Increasingly, choreography became part of the printed script and dance became so thoroughly integrated into the plot that Broadway *stories* such as the "Dream" ballet sequence known as "Laurey Makes Up Her Mind" remain an integral component of the show (and the film version), even if the specific steps do not. Rodgers and Hammerstein may have decided not to retain most of de Mille's version in the film adaptation, but as Kara Gardner points out, Louise's ballet also "uses much of the music from the original production," and "much of de Mille's original narrative for the ballet, as it appeared in the published script, was preserved."[48] For these reasons, de Mille arguably deserves to share the credit as co-choreographer of the film version of *Carousel*, and indeed she is so listed.

The treatment of choreography in the film version of *Brigadoon* offers yet another response to de Mille's original vision: the removal of both the steps *and* the stories they were intended to tell. The misleading perception that the staged *Brigadoon* was not a dancer's show was allegedly first expressed by the film's choreographer Kelly when according to Minnelli he characterized "the movie version of *Brigadoon* as a singer's show on Broadway that had to be made as a dancer's show."[49] A more nuanced characterization is that dance *did* play a crucial part in the stage version but was encompassed primarily in a crucial secondary character, the outsider Harry Beaton. Unlike the rest of the town folk, Beaton felt imprisoned and embittered by *Brigadoon*'s destiny as a town privileged (but also condemned) to escape the march of time and civilization by sleeping a century at a time before being allowed to enjoy a single day in a waking state. Finding life in Brigadoon hopeless after being rejected in marriage by "Bonnie" Jean, Beaton decides to escape, an action that if successful would result in the permanent disappearance of the town and the death of all its inhabitants.

This intolerable and dangerous situation became the central source of dramatic conflict that de Mille attempted to explore through dance, most dramatically in a Sword Dance and The Chase. With the exception of Beaton's role (played by James Mitchell), the central protagonists, the Brigadoonian lass Fiona and the lost urban-American Tommy who finds meaning and purpose in this mysterious small Scottish town, were cast on the stage as singers, not dancers. The alluring Meg Brockie, who sings a substantial narrative song in each act, also did not dance, nor did the only other singer, Charlie, who later that day will marry Fiona's younger sister, Jean. In the original stage version, Harry and Jean dance but do not sing, and Tommy's cynical friend and traveling companion Jeff neither sings nor dances (in the film he does a little of both).

Although the Beaton cast in the film version, Hugh Laing, was a ballet star, most recently in the New York City Ballet, Kelly and Minnelli cut his Sword Dance after partially filming it, thus reducing a prominent stage role as a dancer to a small speaking part in the film. Instead, Tommy, played by choreographer Kelly, and Fiona, played by Hollywood's premiere female dancer at the time, Cyd Charisse, teamed up to transform the "singer's show" into a "dancer's show." Kelly, who sang, danced, and choreographed, also carried most of the vocal load, while Charisse, not a singer, was dubbed by Carol Richards.

Librettist-lyricist Alan Jay Lerner (1918–1986) and composer Frederick Loewe (1901–1988) had the option but chose not to write any new songs. Instead of bringing in a studio songwriting team for this purpose, as was done for the film version of *On the Town*, Minnelli and Kelly decided to remove many of the songs in the stage version and expand several of the remaining songs into more elaborately filmed dance numbers. Filmgoers familiar only with the incomplete original cast album (recorded by RCA Victor and released on LP), more than likely would not have missed Meg's "The Love of My Life," the female chorus's "Jeannie's Packin' Up," or the dance numbers deleted from the film (The Sword Dance, The Chase, and the Funeral Dance), since none of this music was included on this album. See Table 4.2, "*Brigadoon* on Stage and Screen."

The *Brigadoon* Film Score

The songs that didn't make it to the cast album were not the only songs to disappear, like Brigadoon itself, from the film's soundtrack. The removal of these other songs can be traced to the original decision to reassign the romantic

Table 4.2 *Brigadoon* on Stage and Screen.

Stage	Screen
PROLOGUE	
Once in the Highland (Chorus) (166)	Once in the Highlands (Dick Beavers and the MGM Studio Chorus) (1:42)
	Down on MacConnachy Square (Townsfolk and the MGM Studio Chorus (4:39)
Act I	
Brigadoon (Chorus) (168)	Brigadoon (MGM Studio Chorus) (10:40)
Down on MacConnachy Square (Gordon, Britton, Townsfolk) (168)	
Waitin' for My Dearie (Bell) (174)	Waitin' for My Dearie (Richards [Charisse]) (12:44)
I'll Go Home with Bonnie Jean (Anderson, Townsfolk, Dancers, including Mitchell) (178)	I'll Go Home with Bonnie Jean (Gustafsen, Thompson, Kelly, Johnson, and the MGM Studio Chorus) (25:55)
The Heather on the Hill (Brooks, Bell) (181)	The Heather on the Hill (Kelly, dance Kelly and Charisse) (37:40)
The Love of My Life (Britton) (184) [not in Oct. 14, 1953, screenplay]	
Jeannie's Packin' Up (Girls) (186) [Oct. 14, 1953, screenplay, p. 8]	
Come to Me, Bend to Me (Sullivan, Dancers, including Bosler) (187) [Oct. 14, 1953, screenplay, p. 34]	Come to Me, Bend to Me (Gustafsen) [Outtake filmed but not shown]
Almost Like Being in Love (Brooks, Bell) (189)	Almost Like Being in Love (song and dance by Kelly) (51:20)
The Wedding Dance (Dancers, including Bosler, Sullivan) (196)	The Wedding Dance (dance, Thompson and Bosler) (74:44)
The Sword Dance (Mitchell, Dancers) (196) [not in Oct. 14, 1953 screenplay, but filmed]	The Sword Dance danced by Hugh Laing [Outtake filmed but not shown]
Act II	
The Chase (Men of Brigadoon) (196)	The Chase (Men of Brigadoon) (79:18)

Table 4.2 Continued

Stage	Screen
	The Heather on the Hill (Reprise) [Kelly and Charisse dance] (87:23)
There But for You Go I (Brooks) (200) [Oct. 14, 1953, screenplay, p. 57]	There But for You Go I (Kelly) [Outtake not filmed; vocal outtake on Motion Picture CD Soundtrack]
My Mother's Weddin' Day (Britton, Townsfolk) (201) [not in Oct. 14, 1953, screenplay]	
Funeral Dance (Franklin) (203)	
From This Day On (Brooks, Bell) (204) [not in Oct. 14, 1953, screenplay]	From This Day On (Kelly and Richards [Charisse]) Duet, and pas de deux] [Outtake filmed but not shown]
Brigadoon (Reprise) Oct. 14, 1953 (205) [Oct. 14, 1953, screenplay, p. 61]	Brigadoon (MGM Studio Chorus) [not recorded or filmed]
Come to Me, Bend to Me (Reprise) (Bell) (208)	
The Heather on the Hill (Reprise) (Bell) (209)	The Heather on the Hill (Reprise) (99:54)
	Waitin' for My Dearie (Reprise) (101:22)
I'll go Home with Bonnie Jean (Reprise) (Sullivan) (209)	I'll Go Home with Bonnie Jean (Reprise) (102:25)
From This Day On (Reprise) (Brooks, Bell) (209)	
MacConnachy Square (reprise) (Townsfolk) (210)	
Brigadoon (Reprise) (Chorus) (211)	

- *Numbers in parentheses in the stage column refer to page numbers in Alan Jay Lerner,* Brigadoon, *in* Great Musicals of the American Theatre, *vol. 1, ed. Stanley Richards (Radnor, PA: Chilton, 1973).*
- *Numbers in parentheses in the screen column refer to film timings.*

MAJOR SINGING AND DANCING AND SELECTED ROLES

Stage: David Brooks (Tommy Albright); Marion Bell (Fiona MacLaren); Pamela Britton (Meg Brockie); Lee Sullivan (Charlie Dalrymple); George Keane (Jeff Douglas); James Mitchell (Harry Beaton); William Hansen (Mr. Lundie); VIRGINIA BOSLER (Jean MacLaren); Elliott Sullivan (Archie Beaton); Lidija Franklin (Maggie Anderson)

Screen: Gene Kelly (Tommy Albright); Cyd Charisse [dubbed by Carol Richards (Fiona Campbell); Van Johnson (Jeff Douglas); Jimmy Thompson [dubbed by John Gustafsen (Charlie Dalrymple); Barry Jones (Mr. Lundie); Hugh Laing (Harry Beaton); BOSLER (Jean Campbell); Elaine Stewart (Jane Ashton)

- *Names in capital letters indicate that a cast member appeared both on stage and in the film.*

principal roles, Tommy and Fiona, to actors known mainly (Kelly) or entirely (Charisse) for their dancing prowess. Consequently, Minnelli and Kelly greatly reduced what was widely regarded as an excellent score by removing Tommy's "There But for You Go I," and Tommy and Fiona's "From This Day On." They also removed Charlie's "Come to Me, Bend to Me" and Meg's "My Mother's Weddin' Day." All of these songs appeared on the original cast album. In fact, of the seventeen songs and dances heard and seen on the stage, the film that was released contained only *five* of the major songs, plus two short choral numbers and two dances.

- **Retained Solo Songs and Dances**

  "Waitin' for My Dearie" (Charisse [Fiona], dubbed by Carol Richards; dance by Charisse and Women Folk)
  "The Heather on the Hill" (song by Kelly; dance for Kelly and Charisse)
  "Almost Like Being in Love" (song and dance by Kelly)

- **Retained Ensemble Songs and Dances**

  "Once in the Highlands" (MGM Chorus)
  "Brigadoon" (MGM Chorus)
  "Down on MacConnachy Square" (Townsfolk and the MGM Chorus)
  "I'll Go Home with Bonnie Jean" (Townsfolk led by Jimmie Thompson [Charlie, dubbed by John Gustafson], with vocals and dancing by Kelly [Tommy] and Johnson [Jeff])
  The Wedding Dance (featuring Thompson and Virginia Bosler ["Bonnie" Jean]) See Figures 4.7 and 4.8.
  The Chase (Men of Brigadoon, choreographed song)

- **Deleted Musical Numbers (Songs and Dances)**

  "The Love of My Life" (Dodie Heath [Meg])
  "Jeannie's Packin' Up" (Women Folk)
  "Come to Me, Bend to Me" (Thompson [dubbed by Gustafson])
  Sword Dance (danced by Hugh Laing)
  "There But for You Go I" (Kelly, song only)
  "My Mother's Weddin' Day" (Heath)
  Funeral Dance (Maggie, in love with Harry Beaton, characters and dance also removed from the film)
  "From This Day On" (Kelly and Charisse)

Fig. 4.7 The Wedding Dance in the stage version of *Brigadoon*. Vandamm. Museum of the City of New York. 68.80.11904 © The New York Public Library.

Fig. 4.8 The Wedding Dance in the film version of *Brigadoon* [77:07]. Screenshot.

The decision to remove six vocal numbers and two dance numbers created a film adaptation more in keeping with a 1940s or even a 1930s approach to a stage work. The result stands in marked contrast to the approach exemplified by *Call Me Madam* (see chapter 3 and *Oklahoma!* discussed in this chapter). The removal of fondly remembered material by those who recalled the stage version and the original cast album did not go unnoticed. The next few paragraphs will explore why Minnelli and Kelly might have decided to remove such a large number of highly regarded songs and the consequences for doing so.

Although he continued to make changes, Lerner's screenplay of October 14, 1953, offers a useful snapshot of how things stood two months prior to the shooting that began on December 9.[50] This Final Screenplay reveals that by October, Minnelli and Kelly had made several decisions about which songs to cut. First to go were Meg Brockie's two songs, "The Love of My Life" in Act I and "My Mother's Weddin' Day" in Act II. The removal of "The Love of My Life" is explained in a June 5 letter from Production Code Administration head Breen to MGM's head of operations Dore Schary. Breen found the lyrics to the former song "an unacceptably light treatment of illicit sex."[51] Based on the extant correspondence in the Production Files at the Margaret Herrick Library, MGM chose not to fight for the song's inclusion or adapt the lyrics to mollify the censors.

The production files are also silent as to whether Schary proposed Meg's second song for consideration, but if he had, the response more than likely would have been the same. Another communication between Breen and Schary from November 2 discusses changes Lerner made to a dramatic scene between Meg and Jeff after October 14. As with Meg's song lyrics, this scene does not appear in that script. Breen found Lerner's changes "unacceptable" because the dialogue "deals with the effort of Meg to seduce Jeff."[52] Perhaps salvaged by Minnelli's emphasis on a prospective marriage rather than a quick roll in the proverbial hay, the end of the scene was filmed.[53] The resulting disproportionately long new scene between Meg and Jeff usurped all but four of the seven musical minutes saved by silencing Meg's musical voice.

Another character from the stage version, Maggie Anderson, the woman who loved Harry Beaton unrequitedly, was entirely removed prior to the October screenplay. Her role had primarily involved dancing, her big moment occurring when she expressed her mourning over Harry's death with a Funeral Dance to the music of a traditional Scottish melody played on the bagpipes. Although Beaton's film role was reduced mainly to a speaking one, he did dance briefly before violently disrupting the wedding of *his* unrequited love, Fiona's younger sister Jean. Beaton is also seen intermittently in The Chase as he tries to escape Brigadoon and dies when Jeff mistakes him for a bird and shoots him.[54] Beaton's biggest stage moment, the Sword Dance, not found in the screenplay, was filmed but not released. With the removal of the brief and dramatically expendable "Jeannie's Packin' Up," Jean's film role was also reduced prior to the October screenplay.

This leaves three iconic songs removed sometime between October and December 1953: "Come to Me, Bend to Me," "From This Day On," and "There But for You Go I." The decision to eliminate these songs was not an easy one; "Come to Me" and "From This Day On" were filmed, and "There But for You Go I" was audio-recorded (released on the 1996 CD). The film outtakes were included among the special features on the 2005 DVD, along with the Sword Dance. As we have already observed, it is not uncommon for secondary characters to be diminished in the transfer from stage to screen. Nevertheless, preview audiences justifiably complained about the removal of the memorable "Come to Me," in which for a charmingly filmed three and a half minutes, Charlie is allowed to serenade (but not permitted to see) the woman he will soon wed.[55]

The removal of "From This Day On" is more surprising because this song constitutes the only duet between Tommy and Fiona in the latter portion of the musical and allows the lovers a poignant opportunity to express their love through dance. The song was replaced by a dance with instrumental accompaniment, an erotic pas de deux set to the music of "The Heather on the Hill" heard in Act I on stage that shows how their romance has evolved from playfulness to passion. See Figure 4.9.

The stage version of "Heather," entirely sung, begins with Fiona, then Tommy, each singing a 32-bar AABA chorus.[56] After some underscored dialogue to the music of the B section, the stage Fiona finishes the song with a final A section capped by the two highest notes of the song. In the film version Fiona sings the first two A sections and Tommy the B, and in the final A section they sing in harmony, a nice touch that the stage version does not allow. Placing Fiona in the lead of "From This Day On" also serves to balance Tommy's earlier vocal solo "There But for You Go I." The conventional wisdom is that the addition of dance provides Tommy and Fiona with a way to express their feelings unburdened by words, but the serenity and harmony of the *vocal* component of "From This Day On" creates a moving moment, without high notes, that makes the dance that follows seem superfluous.

In a thoughtful and well-argued essay, Susan Smith discusses what was gained and what was lost by the decision to design a classic stage show around dancers instead of singers.[57] To make her argument Smith focuses on two contrasting case studies. In the first, "Heather on the Hill," Smith argues on behalf of "the creatively enriching effects arising from the incorporation of dance." In the second, she views the deletion of Tommy's serious song, "There But for You Go I" as a missed opportunity. The main reasons usually offered for not filming this slow song were that it would bog down the action and that Kelly didn't possess the vocal equipment to sing a lyrical and sustained song that did not lead into a dance.[58] Smith contradicts the conventional wisdom by pointing out that Kelly's less assertive vocal instrument

Fig. 4.9 "The Heather on the Hill." Gene Kelly (Tommy) and Cyd Charisse (Fiona) in the film version of *Brigadoon* [41:16]. Screenshot.

paradoxically serves the dramatic needs of a character who has become deeply transformed by love and a new sense of purpose and vulnerability (qualities not usually associated either with Kelly or in this case the character he is playing).

Smith concludes by asserting that the inclusion of "There But for You Go I" "would have prevented the stage show from simply being recast into (and typecast as) a film musical for dancers, signaling MGM's ability to see beyond the dominant attributes of its stars' screen personae and to understand that fidelity to the source play may not necessarily be a barrier to creativity."[59] I agree and continue to wonder why in a film that barely removes a word from Mr. Lundie's (Barry Jones's) nine-minute explanation about the origins of Brigadoon, it was not possible to film Kelly singing even one chorus of "There But for You Go I."

It's probably fair to say that despite earning a profit, the film version of *Brigadoon* has long been generally regarded as less satisfying than *An American in Paris* (1951), directed by Minnelli and starring Kelly, or *Singin' in the Rain* (1952), co-directed by Kelly and Stanley Donen, starring Kelly and featuring Charisse.[60] A combination of factors led MGM to decide to convert a popular and critically acclaimed song *and* dance stage musical into a dance musical that deleted a substantial number of key songs, along with most of the de Mille choreography that made the stage version so successful and memorable. For starters, Minnelli "was never in love with the show."[61] Kelly biographer Alvin Yudkoff highlights the conflicts between Minnelli's "singing musical" conception of the show and Kelly's focus on the work as a "dancing musical."[62] He attributes Kelly's decision to toss out de Mille's stage choreography as a response to the threat of being overshadowed by her but also to his dislike of the "strong-minded" de Mille's "conservative politics and her homophobic prejudices."[63]

Another factor that led Minnelli and Kelly to reconceive a bona fide hit musical as a dance musical and then remove most of its ballads was the lapsed contract of MGM's star singer Kathryn Grayson, originally intended to play Fiona.[64] After the loss of Grayson, instead of trying to find another singer, Minnelli and Kelly decided to sign the non-singing Charisse and to emphasize Kelly's dancing over his singing, sealing the film's fate. The deliberation process also highlighted an essential difference between the studio system and Broadway in how each approached a musical, especially the question of why people sing in a stage musical versus why they dance in a film musical. The simple answer is that although Kelly and Charisse were cast as the main *singing* characters, in real life they were primarily *dancers*, so they had to dance the fictional roles they played in their films.

The next chapter will take a longer look at the director Rouben Mamoulian, who, in preparing the film version of *Silk Stockings* and in welcome contrast to most film directors (including Minnelli), carefully drafted a plausible explanation for how Ninotchka acquired her expertise as a ballerina. Minnelli concluded that viewers of the MGM *Brigadoon* did not need to know how Fiona managed to become such an accomplished dancer. Although her extraordinary dancing acumen may be nearly as far-fetched as the story of a town that awakens from a deep and ageless sleep for one day every hundred years, we can infer that from Minnelli's perspective the mere presence of Charisse provides all the justification viewers need.

As Cassie sings in "The Music and the Mirror" from *A Chorus Line*, "God, I'm a dancer, a dancer dances." After all, no one asked how the main character in *An American in Paris*, the painter Jerry Mulligan (Kelly again), learned to dance beyond the fact that he had an MGM contract.[65] And just as stagegoers might become uncomfortable if they thought too much about the underlying implications of *Brigadoon*, perhaps it's preferable to simply enjoy Minnelli's skillfully executed film conception (including the beautiful and unfairly maligned simulated reconstruction of Brigadoon) and not ask too many questions.

OKLAHOMA!
(stage 1943; 20th Century-Fox 1955)

Toward a More Perfect Union

The longest-running Broadway show in the 1940s, in fact by far the longest-running show in Broadway history up until then, was *Oklahoma!* With a book and lyrics by Oscar Hammerstein II (1895–1960) and music by Richard Rodgers (1902–1979), it ran 2,212 performances between March 31, 1943, and May 29, 1948. For reasons widely discussed by scholars, critics, and journalists, the show's popularity was matched by critical acclaim and influence.[66]

The central plot line is seemingly inconsequential. Who will Laurey, the attractive young farm girl, choose to accompany to the box social? Will it be the handsome, cocky, cowboy Curly, who loves her but who is not quite ready to tell her? Or will it be Aunt Eller's capable but menacing hired hand Jud, who lusts after her niece? The musical also conveys a larger theme, the conflict and eventual resolution of the two ways of life embodied in the song "The Farmer and the Cowman" and why they "should be friends," especially when Curly's life as a cowhand is giving way to the farming life while the Indian Territory of Oklahoma in 1907 rests on the verge of statehood.[67] From a late twentieth- and early twenty-first-century social perspective, the musical falls short by ignoring the plight of Native Americans who were forced to settle in Oklahoma as decreed in President Andrew Jackson's Indian Removal Act of 1830. This lack of acknowledgment is ironic at best, given that the name of the future state, repeated many times in the title song, is the Choctaw word that translates as red (*okla*) people (*humma*). In 1943 (and still today), the new state would be joining an imperfect union.

If *Oklahoma!* like most musicals fails to meet modern expectations for a more inclusive society, the show was historically and artistically cutting edge and impactful and remains so. Todd S. Purdom reinforced "these truths" when on the seventy-fifth anniversary of the show's stage debut he wrote that "*Oklahoma!* was as radical and innovative in its day as Lin-Manuel Miranda's *Hamilton* is in ours—and for many of the same reasons: it seamlessly blended story, song, and dance, in the service of realistic character development."[68]

While by no means the first musical to integrate the elements that make up a musical (primarily, but not limited to the book, the songs, and the choreography), *Oklahoma!* offered an approach that musicals of the next several decades strove to emulate. Rodgers encapsulated the show's integration this way: "When a show works perfectly, it's because all the individual parts complement each other and fit together. No single element overshadows any other. In a great musical, the orchestrations sound the way the costumes look."[69] Gleaned from their writings and interviews, the two central collaborators developed what might be called Rodgers and Hammerstein's Principles of Integration.[70]

1. *The songs advance the plot*: In "The Surrey with the Fringe on Top" Curly improvises an enticing description of the surrey he plans to use to take Laurey to the box social. Laurey and Aunt Eller become caught up in Curly's extravagant scenario, and by the end of the song—before it is interrupted by dialogue—the young couple have arrived at a deeper place in their still-unacknowledged but inevitable fine romance. In his introduction to *The Rodgers and Hammerstein Song Book* and again in his autobiography, Rodgers described his musical intentions in capturing the "clip-clop" rhythm suggested in Hammerstein's lyric, "chicks and ducks and geese better scurry."[71] To simulate this image, Rodgers describes a "melody in which the straight, flat country road could be musically conveyed through a repetition of the straight, flat sound of the D note, followed by a sharp upward flick as fowl scurry to avoid being hit by the moving wheels."[72] By the time Curly finishes pitching his imaginary surrey, a song has clearly moved the relationship between Curly and Laurey to a new place in the story.

2. *The songs flow directly from the dialogue*: By the time Ado Annie's beau Will Parker tells Aunt Eller, Ike Skidmore, and the assembled cowboys that he arrived in Kansas City "on a Frid'y," the song "Kansas City" has already begun. A little later, Annie explains to Laurey the problem she has saying no, and within a few words, the dialogue has merged almost imperceptibly with the music of "I Cain't Say No."

3. *The songs express the characters who sing them*: Ado Annie's "I Cain't Say No" expresses her flirtatiousness in language and music utterly foreign to Laurey. Similarly, it would be implausible for Annie to address Will in a song remotely like Curly and Laurey's "People Will Say We're in Love" or in a song as lush and romantic as Laurey's waltz "Out of My Dreams."

4. *The dances advance the plot and enhance the dramatic meaning of the songs that precede them*: Dance in *Oklahoma!* is most conspicuously exemplified by the historic dream ballet "Laurey Makes Up Her Mind," which is largely based on de Mille's stage choreography. See Figures 4.10 and 4.11.

   The dancing that follows other songs is also "integrated" musically and dramatically within the fabric of the show. The dance styles mentioned in the lyrics of "Kansas City" are executed in the accompanying dance, and Laurey's friends dance out the independence they extol in the words and music to "Many a New Day."

5. *The orchestra, through accompaniment and underscoring, parallels, complements, or advances the action*: In the reprise to "People Will Say We're in Love," it is the orchestra, not the singers, that initiates the musical development of this important dramatic moment. It does this by underscoring the kissing and affectionate banter between Laurey and Curly for nearly half of the song's chorus *before* Curly sings "Let people say we're in love." See Table 4.3, "*Oklahoma!* on Stage and Screen."

Fig. 4.10 "Laurey Makes Up Her Mind" in the stage version of *Oklahoma!* Vandamm. Museum of the City of New York. 48.210.1838 © The New York Public Library.

Fig. 4.11 "Laurey Makes Up Her Mind" in the film version of *Oklahoma!* [74:38]. Screenshot.

Table 4.3 *Oklahoma!* on Stage and Screen.

Stage	Screen
Act I	
Oh, What a Beautiful Mornin' (Drake) (7)	Oh, What a Beautiful Mornin' (MacRae) (2:37)
The Surrey with the Fringe on Top (Drake, Roberts, Garde) (10)	The Surrey with the Fringe on Top (MacRae) (7:00)
Kansas City (Dixon, Garde, Boys) (15)	Kansas City (Nelson, Greenwood, Male Ensemble) (19:05)
I Cain't Say No (Holm) (21)	I Cain't Say No (Grahame) (28:05)
Many a New Day (Roberts, Girls, Dancers: McCracken, Friedlich, DeKova) (29)	Many a New Day (Jones and Female Ensemble) (39:45)
It's a Scandal, It's a Outrage! (Buloff, Boys, Girls) (33)	
People Will Say We're in Love (Drake, Roberts) (36)	People Will Say We're in Love (MacRae, Jones) (51:25)
Poor Jud Is Daid (Drake, Da Silva) (41)	Poor Jud Is Daid (MacRae, Steiger) (58:35)
Lonely Room (Da Silva) (47)	
Out of My Dreams (Roberts, Girls) (49)	Out of My Dreams (Jones and Female Ensemble) (70:04)
Laurey Makes Up Her Mind Ballet (Sergava, Platt, Church, Dancers) (49)	Dream Ballet (Linn, Mitchell, Steiger, Ensemble) (72:00)

Table 4.3 Continued

Stage	Screen
Act II	
The Farmer and the Cowhand (Riggs, Garde, Drake, Dixon, Holm, Clay, Ensemble; Dancer: Platt) (51)	The Farmer and the Cowman (Whitmore, Greenwood, Flippen, Ensemble) (89:18)
All er Nuthin' (Holm, Dixon; Dance: McCracken, Friedlich) (65)	All er Nuthin' (Nelson, Grahame) (108:54)
People Will Say We're in Love (Reprise) (Drake, Roberts) (72)	People Will Say We're in Love (Reprise) (MacRae, Jones) (119:29)
Oklahoma (Drake, Roberts, Garde, Shiers, Clay, Ensemble) (75)	Oklahoma (MacRae and Ensemble) (125:36)
Oh, What a Beautiful Mornin' (Reprise) (Roberts, Drake, Ensemble) (84)	Oh, What a Beautiful Mornin' (Ensemble) (138:54)

- *Numbers in parentheses in the stage column refer to page numbers in "6 Plays by Rodgers and Hammerstein" (New York: Modern Library, 1959).*
- *Numbers in parenthesis in the screen column refer to film timings.*

MAJOR SINGING AND DANCING AND SELECTED ROLES

Stage: Alfred Drake (Curly McLain); Joan Roberts (Laurey Williams); Lee Dixon (Will Parker); Celeste Holm (Ado Annie Carnes); Betty Garde (Aunt Eller); Howard Da Silva (Jud Fry); Joseph Buloff (Ali Hakim); Ralph Riggs (Andrew Carnes); Joan McCracken (The Girl Who Falls Down); Marc Platt (Dream Curly); Katharine Sergava (Dream Laurey); BAMBI LINN (Aggie); George Church (Jess); Armina (Kate Friedlich); Paul Shiers (Mike); Margin DeKova (Singer); Edwin Clay (Singer)

Screen: Gordon MacRae (Curly); Shirley Jones (Laurey); Gene Nelson (Will Parker); Gloria Grahame (Ado Annie); Charlotte Greenwood (Aunt Eller); Rod Steiger (Jud); Eddie Albert (Ali Hakim); James Whitmore (Andrew Carnes); James Mitchell (Dream Curly); LINN (Dream Laurey)

- *Names in capital letters indicate that a cast member appeared both on stage and in the film.*

The Film Version

Due to its long stage run and tour, *Oklahoma!* had the longest gestation from stage to screen of any major hit musical of the 1940s: twelve years. As soon as they realized the magnitude of its stage success, film studios vied for the opportunity to make the movie, but content to wait until the national touring company completed its natural course, Rodgers and Hammerstein delayed serious discussions until 1954.[73] Consequently, the film was not released until October 11, 1955. Determined to maintain complete artistic control, Rodgers and Hammerstein joined the board of directors of an independent new film production company called the Magna Theatre Corporation (later purchased by 20th Century-Fox), which was in the process of creating a new widescreen 70 mm. film technology called Todd-AO developed by Mike Todd and Robert Naify in 1953.[74] The idea was to come up with a movie experience sufficiently

spectacular to provide viewers a good reason to temporarily abandon their television sets and attend "roadshow" versions of selected films in special theaters
invested in the new technology.[75] *Oklahoma!* was the first to use it. In anticipa-
tion of the potential need to serve theaters without the technology to screen the
film in Todd-AO, Magna shot the film twice, once in Todd-AO and a second time
in CinemaScope, a less expensive technology that enjoyed the widest distribution in its day (and remains the best known).[76] The most expensive film to date,
Oklahoma! cost a staggering $6.8 million to produce, an amount that consumed
most of the $7.1 million profit.

Like *Call Me Madam*, the film adaptation of *Oklahoma!* to a large extent
followed the Commandments summarized by Ethan Mordden (introduced in
chapter 1). In contrast to the casting of Ethel Merman in *Madam*, however, the
film version of *Oklahoma!* retained only one significant character from the stage
version: Bambi Linn as Dream Laurey. The stage Dream Curley, James Mitchell,
had also been *Brigadoon*'s original Broadway Harry Beaton.[77] Fred Zinnemann,
directing his first and only film musical, most definitely cast for talent rather than
fame in offering the featured roles to Shirley Jones in her film debut as Laurey,
and to Gordon MacRae as Curly; MacRae, well-established but not a star of the
magnitude of Marlon Brando, was cast that year as Sky Masterson in *Guys and
Dolls*. Gloria Grahame, a fine film actress but not known as a singer, nevertheless
managed to do justice to Ado Annie's two songs, while her beau, Will Parker, was
cast to perfection with one of the finest tap dancers of the day, the underrated
and underutilized Gene Nelson.[78] No one was dubbed, not even Rod Steiger who
played Jud. Since Jud's song "Lonely Room" was cut, Steiger's total singing assignment was limited to a few phrases of "Pore Jud," which was dominated by
Curly, but Steiger sang with such authority that both Theodore Chapin and Hugh
Fordin, the experts on the audio commentary of the CinemaScope version of the
50th Anniversary DVDs, assumed that he was dubbed.

In addition to its uniformly strong cast, Rodgers and Hammerstein preserved
nearly all of the original score, including the dances that followed songs and the
Dream Ballet, even if this meant extending the length of the film to the then virtually unheard of length of 145 minutes. The most significant deleted song, Jud's
"Lonely Room," was a deeply psychological song that reveals and humanizes the
complexities and anxieties of this otherwise unlikable character. Also eliminated
was the Persian peddler Ali Hakim's more peripheral "It's a Scandal! It's a
Outrage!," its removal depriving Eddie Albert of a song he was perfectly capable
of singing.

Although the Production Code's requests for script changes fall short of
Draconian, they do further confirm the reality that you can say, do, and reveal
less in a 1950s film than was possible in a 1940s musical. On April 9, several
days after receiving a screenplay on March 29, 1954, Breen sent producer Arthur

Hornblow Jr. three pages of requests to make the film more compliant with the Code.[79] The expressions "Lord," "Great Lord," and "Great Lordamighty" had to be dropped and the three uses of the word "damn" could be appealed to the Board of Directors, but most of the requests related to references or suggestions of sex or nudity. For example, in both the 1943 libretto and March 1954 screen- play, Ali Hakim tells Annie that he wants to take her to a hotel in Claremore so that they can find Paradise in its bedrooms. In response to Breen's suggested rewording (which was followed in the June 1 screenplay), Ali mentions the up- stairs *view*, but not that the unmarried couple will find Paradise there. Another Breen request led to a change in the lyrics of "Kansas City." At the "burleeque" "theayter" in both the stage and screen versions Will saw a woman he thought "was padded from her shoulder to her heel" and in both he learned that that "ev'rythin' she had was absolutely real." The June screenplay replaced the phrase "when she begun to peel" with a more innocuous and oblique reference to the dancer's body, what little Will saw of it ("And then she started dancin' and her dancin' made me feel").

The *Oklahoma!* film went far beyond the innovative opening scene of *On the Town* ("New York, New York") by filming *all* of the outdoor scenes outdoors, mostly on location in Nogales, Arizona, near the Mexican border, which despite the mountains in the background more closely resembled the state of Oklahoma of 1907 than the correct state did in 1955.[80] The decision to film *Brigadoon* the previous year on a soundstage rather than on location in Scotland had been a major disappointment to Kelly and for years was considered a major factor in the film's failure even though most of the successful musicals of the 1940s and 1950s were also filmed primarily on soundstages and backlot outdoor sets.[81] *Oklahoma!* bucked this trend.

On the proscenium stage, *Oklahoma!* begins with Curly out of sight singing "Oh, What a Beautiful Mornin'." The film opens with Curly riding and singing on horseback over the countryside and through the middle of the cornfields, planted a year earlier to ensure they would have time to grow as high as an elephant's eye in compliance with Hammerstein's lyric. In the next song, film viewers see Curly's imaginary surrey with the fringe on top come to life. They are even granted an eyewitness perspective known as POV (the abbreviation of point of view) from underneath its wheels as the surrey makes the chicks and ducks and geese scurry out of the way and a hard-to-shoot reflection of the surrey traveling next to a river in open country. On stage, the second act opens directly at the box social dance. Film viewers get to see the men and women of Claremore before this grand event as they travel in horse-drawn buggies, and through the magic of camera placement we are able to participate in the wild buckboard ride that was caused by Laurey's whipping Jud's horses in an attempt to escape from his unwel- come advances.

Film historian Richard Barrios offers an enthusiastic assessment of the film which he appreciatively describes as "beautifully cinematic and musically glorious," concluding that "between the locations, the cinematography, the dancing, and the musical arrangements, this is one of the most impressive musical productions ever."[82] Similarly, Mordden writes that "everything turned out well," especially the cast, in a film "Fred Zinnemann directed to fill the eye without adding much visual coloratura to what was a very simple story."[83] Not everyone shares the enthusiasm of Barrios, Mordden, or the present author for this film. The most frequent complaint voiced by film scholars is displeasure at what they consider to be an overly reverential approach to the show's stage version, which prompts the criticism that this lushly photographed film is paradoxically too theatrical.

One of these film scholars, Rick Altman, bemoans what was lost between the 1930s and the 1950s when he writes that "the freedom from scenic construction achieved by Lubitsch and Mamoulian a quarter-century earlier is here abandoned in favor of a staginess that testifies more to a poverty of taste than to any limitations of means."[84] In a surprising defense of backlot pseudo-locations Altman also espouses the position that "even the most undistinguished studio productions created a sense of visual and aural space that far surpassed the simple unity of the proscenium stage."[85] Unfortunately, it is unclear what Altman means by this last observation, as he cites no specific shots in the film as static or stagey. Gerald Mast disparagingly labels all the Rodgers and Hammerstein films, with the exception of *The Sound of Music* ("as good as any film adaptation of a stage musical" between 1958 and 1972), as "opera films," desperately "reverential attempts" that fail to heed the important lesson "that space need not remain constant while characters sing."[86] For both Altman and Mast, *Oklahoma!* is part of a more ubiquitous problem: that dialogue plays a more important role in most stage works than images do.

If the worst you can say about a film that mainly takes place outdoors is that it is *theatrical*, it might be a sign of a broader critical bias. Jeanine Basinger, who has something positive (and usually insightful) to say about *original* films, readily concedes that many of them are not good movies. Despite this admission, only rarely does she find something positive to say about a film *adaptation*.[87] Foremost among her complaints about the film adaptations of Rodgers and Hammerstein's *Oklahoma!*, *Carousel*, *South Pacific*, and *The King and I* are that they convey "the look of the stage set as it would be seen by a theater's viewing audience." The facts don't support this generalization. For example, not only does the filming of the Dream Ballet in *Oklahoma!* clearly eschew the "dominant horizontal line" that Basinger complains about, but it also includes the use of expressive close-ups and a three-dimensionality that would be invisible to a theater audience. Indeed, it would be foolhardy for a theater company to attempt to recreate on stage the effects of the location shots in most of the Rodgers and Hammerstein films.

True, the filming of the *songs* in *Oklahoma!* shows a respect and trust for Rodgers and Hammerstein's dialogue and songs and the actors who speak and sing them.[88] The camera work consequently avoids Donen- or Kelly-esque flourishes of cinematic "coloratura"—exuberant camera motions or spectacular crane shots—that attempt to salvage the less memorable songs that frequently inhabit original film musicals.[89] Still, in every song of the *Oklahoma!* film adaptation the singers move and the camera follows, even in the absence of the rapid cutting found in *Flashdance* (1983), the film adaptation of *Chicago* (2002), or the extraneous backstories prevalent in the 2004 film version of *The Phantom of the Opera* that interrupt Andrew Lloyd Webber's songs. Dismissing the *Oklahoma!* film version as theatrical seems misguided, especially at a time when filming all the outdoor scenes on location (or even filming on location at all) was extremely rare.

Like Mast (and nearly everyone else), Basinger concedes that the spectacular opening scene in the film adaptation of *The Sound of Music* with its overhead circular shot of Julie Andrews standing in a meadow in the Austrian Alps should persuade viewers at the outset "that this will not be a horizontal recreation of a stage play."[90] Why doesn't the cinematic opening of *Oklahoma!* with its hills and cornfields or the lush vegetation displayed in *South Pacific* filmed on location on the Hawaiian island of Kauai not qualify as comparably cinematic? It also should probably be noted that although Basinger finds unwelcome theatrical qualities in all but a handful of film adaptations, the same qualities go unnoticed (or at least unmentioned) when they occur in an original film musical such as *An American in Paris*. After reading Basinger's for the most part insightful and generous film history, readers may want to see every musical film they can find from Bing Crosby to Barbra Streisand and from Sonja Henie to Esther Williams, among scores of other screen originals. On the other hand, when it comes to film adaptations, Basinger's faithful readers are likely to come away motivated to avoid them altogether with the exception of the admittedly superior 1936 *Show Boat* adaptation directed by James Whale (discussed in chapter 2) and the opening minutes of *The Sound of Music*, two adaptations that Basinger does appreciate.

It is difficult to escape the double standard inherent in much musical theater and film criticism, a standard in which theatrical elements are regarded as bad in a film and cinematic qualities invariably valued as positive. For a refreshing minority view that may not signal a new consensus, I conclude with a quote from *New York Times* theater critic Jesse Green, who in a 2020 review of film adaptations argued that "the best adaptations today relish the theatricality of their sources and try to enhance it."[91] In their own way, each of the three adaptations explored in this chapter follow Green's directive. *Cabin in the Sky*, the historic all-Black musical on stage and screen, took considerable liberties with its stage source in its film adaptation which nevertheless largely succeeds on its own terms. For conceptual reasons *Brigadoon* falls short as an adaptation but remains a beautiful film to watch and features several fine dance performances. And even though it discarded an important song, the mostly faithful film version of *Oklahoma!* offers an entertaining balance of theatricality and cinematic excellence, a superbly cast adaptation that will continue to remind viewers why this stage show is both classic and timeless, even revolutionary.

5

More Than a "Chemical Reaction"

The Romance between *Ninotchka* and *Silk Stockings* on Stage and Screen

> Heretically, and despite Garbo, the Lubitsch touch, and the laughing scene, I enjoy *Silk Stockings* more than I enjoy *Ninotchka*.
>> —Robin Wood on *Ninotchka* versus the film version of *Silk Stockings*.

A New Beginning

Most hit musicals that arrived on stage between *Call Me Madam* in 1950 and *Silk Stockings* in 1955 were soon adapted into reasonably faithful and mostly successful films. Highlights include *Guys and Dolls* (1950; Goldwyn 1955), *The King and I* (1951; 20th Century-Fox 1956), *The Pajama Game* (1954; Warner Bros. 1957), and *Damn Yankees* (1955; Warner Bros. 1958). Among this parade of memorable shows, *Silk Stockings* (1955) experienced the quickest turnover from stage to screen, two years. Most adaptations through the mid-1960s dutifully follow Ethan Mordden's Commandments introduced in chapter 1, in particular the retention of most of the stage songs and the practice of using Broadway principals in key roles. Dominic Broomfield-McHugh writes that "by this point [the early 1950s], a new culture of adaptation had emerged, and the liberal films of *Gentlemen Prefer Blondes* (1953) and *Pal Joey* (1957) were exceptions to the rule."[1]

In addition to making a case on behalf of *Silk Stockings* as an accomplished and entertaining film adaptation of a stage musical, this chapter will introduce a new phenomenon: the choice of a film, a non-musical film at that, as the source for a stage adaptation. By the end of the century, non-musical films would become the default source type for film transfers, replacing the previous nearly ubiquitous reliance on literary sources. *Silk Stockings* may not deserve credit (or blame) for this eventual take-over, but it does deserve to be acknowledged as the first successful stage musical to take advantage of what was in its day a new resource for adaptation.

A Fine Romance. Geoffrey Block, Oxford University Press. © Oxford University Press 2023.
DOI: 10.1093/oso/9780197501733.003.0005

The Lubitsch Touch

In an early scene in the classic 1939 film *Ninotchka* directed by the German immigrant Ernst Lubitsch (1892–1947), viewers witness a stationary camera-shot of the door to the Royal Suite in a posh Parisian hotel. While the camera fixates on this door, the film's male protagonist, the free-loading Count Leon d'Algout, and three newly arrived Russian commissars mark the delay of a jewelry sale with "a little lunch." Two waiters wheel caviar and sumptuous hors d'oeuvres into the room behind the door, followed by a cigarette girl. Still more waiters bring in bottles of champagne and glasses. The cigarette girl runs out of the room to fetch another two cigarette girls, which will make three cigarette girls and three Russians.

After each new entrance, viewers hear increasingly loud shouts of approval from within. The screenplay states, "The CAMERA REMAINS ON THE DOOR as we SLOWLY DISSOLVE INTO EVENING."[2] Only after a band of Hungarian musicians carrying national instruments enter the suite does Lubitsch finally allow his viewers inside the room to witness the loud and raucous party directly, where one of the Russians has collapsed on the floor next to a cigarette tray. Film scholars and film buffs alike realize that they have just seen an example of what is widely referred to as "the Lubitsch touch."[3]

In the 1955 stage adaptation of Lubitsch's film, *Silk Stockings*, co-produced by Cy Feuer (1911–2006) and Ernest Martin (1919–1993), with lyrics and music by Cole Porter (1891–1964), and a book initially written by George S. Kaufman (1889–1961) and Leueen MacGrath (1914–1992) before they were unceremoniously replaced by Abe Burrows (1910–1985), there is no door and no lunch. Instead, the three Russians join the new incarnation of Count d'Algout, Steve Canfield, now a theatrical agent, who is trying to find a way to keep the famous Russian classical composer Peter Ilyitch Boroff in Paris to compose the music to a popular musical.[4] The problem is that Boroff must "go back to Moscow." This unpleasant development prompts Boroff, the hotel manager, the doorman, and various other hotel employees, but not the commissars, to introduce "Too Bad" in the Hotel Lobby early in the show (Act 1, scene 1, p. 4) reprised with the commissars (Act 1, scene 1, pp. 13–14).

Two years later, MGM adapted *Silk Stockings* into a film musical. For this version, the director Rouben Mamoulian (1898–1987) dropped the earlier rendering of "Too Bad" without the commissars and changed the location from the Hotel Lobby to the room *behind* Lubitsch's door. Instead of staring at a closed door, film viewers now observe Steve and Boroff, along with the commissars, sitting next to three attractive French actresses (who happen to be terrific dancers) at a table loaded with food, glasses filled to the brim with champagne, and a pile of tell-tale empty bottles clearly in view. Steve is now played by Fred Astaire

(1899–1987) in his last film role as a featured dancer, replacing the non-dancing Don Ameche (1908–1993) from the Broadway version. To take advantage of this casting switch, Mamoulian offers a preview of coming attractions when Astaire pairs off briefly with MGM dance regular Barrie Chase, soon to be his dancing partner in several live television broadcasts. Even Peter Lorre, the miscast commissar, does a silly dance in which he dangles his feet while holding on to two chairs. His fellow Russians, Jules Munshin and Joseph Buloff, dance in a more polished fashion.

These transformations of the commissar's dangerously bourgeois hotel party demonstrate the ways two of the most significant and gifted film directors of Hollywood's early Golden Age (Lubitsch and Mamoulian) romanticized and enhanced a political satire, while the powerful studio system injected inimitable star power into the story in the form of Greta Garbo (1905–1990), Fred Astaire, and Cyd Charisse (1921–2008). In his last outing as a film director, Mamoulian romanticized a classic film directed by the peer he is often compared to, Lubitsch, restoring scenes (albeit with renovations) that the intervening musical stage version had omitted. See Table 5.1, "*Silk Stockings* on Stage and Screen."

NINOTCHKA versus SILK STOCKINGS

Ninotchka was both a critical and commercial success in its day, earning not only great notices but $2.2 million, a return of nearly a million.[5] In the years since, the combined romantic comedy (or rom-com) and political satire has maintained its high stature. A biographer of co-screenwriter Billy Wilder went as far as to praise the film as "the most sublime and passionate political picture ever made in Hollywood."[6] Lubitsch himself reflected in an interview that "as for satire, I believe I probably was never sharper than in *Ninotchka*, and I feel that I succeeded in the very difficult task of blending a political satire with a romantic story."[7]

The origins of *Ninotchka* can be traced to three sentences supplied by the Hungarian playwright and screenwriter Melchior Lengyel: "Russian girl saturated with Bolshevist ideals goes to fearful, capitalistic, monopolistic Paris. She meets romance and has an uproarious good time. Capitalism not so bad, after all."[8] Lubitsch promptly paid $15,000 for the right to transform Lengyel's pitch into the first romantic comedy to feature Garbo, the popular Swedish actress.[9] Soon Lengyel was replaced by screenwriters S. N. Behrman, Jacques Deval, and Samuel Hoffenstein, all of whom in turn were replaced by the combined talents of Charles Brackett, Billy Wilder, and Walter Reisch.

The main action in the film begins in Paris with the arrival of an austere female Russian official, Ninotchka (Garbo). Ninotchka has been assigned to clean up the mess created by the ineptitude of three comical Russian trade representatives

Table 5.1 *Silk Stockings* on Stage and Screen.

Stage	Screen
Act I	
Overture (Hail Bibinski, All of You, Too Bad, Silk Stockings, Stereophonic Sound)	Main Title (Instrumental) (mainly All of You) (0:04)
Too Bad (Lascoe, Belasco, Opatoshu, Hotel Staff)	Too Bad (Astaire, Buloff, Lorre, Munshin, and Chorus) (9:21)
Paris Loves Lovers (Ameche, Neff)	Paris Loves Lovers (Astaire, Carol Richards [for Charisse]) (28:07)
Stereophonic Sound (Wyler, Three Reporters)	Stereophonic Sound (Astaire, Paige) (converted to a duet) (35:00)
It's a Chemical Reaction, That's All (Hildegarde, Ameche)	It's a Chemical Reaction, That's All (Richards [for Charisse]) (45:05)
All of You (Ameche)	All of You (Astaire) (46:07)
	Dance with Charisse (48:57)
Satin and Silk (Wyler)	Satin and Silk (Paige) (61:56)
	Silk Stockings (dance for Charisse) (65:31)
Without Love (Neff)	Without Love (Richards [for Charisse]) (75:00)
All of You (Reprise) (Steve)	
Act II	
Entr'acte (Paris Loves Lovers, Without Love, Stereophonic Sound)	
Hail, Bibinski (Opatoshu, Lascoe, Belasco, and French Comrades)	
As on through the Seasons We Sail (Ameche, Neff)	**Fated to Be Mated (Astaire, Charisse) (followed by a danced reprise of Paris Loves Lovers and All of You) (82:09)**
Josephine (Wyler and Chorus)	Josephine (Paige) (reduced from 4:49 to 1:23) (87:23)
Siberia (Lascoe, Belasco, and Opatoshu)	Siberia (Lorre, Munshin, Buloff) (92: 41)
Silk Stockings (Ameche)	
The Red Blues (The Russians)	The Red Blues (Sonnveld, Bill Lee, Munshin, the MGM Chorus, and the dancing of Charisse) (98:56)

Table 5.1 Continued

Stage	Screen
	The Ritz Roll and Rock (song and dance number for Astaire) (108:41)
Finale: Too Bad (Reprise) (Company)	Finale: Too Bad (Reprise) (Munshin, Lorre, Buloff) (23 seconds) (117:00)

- *The songs listed in bold in the screen column were not in the stage version.*
- *Numbers in parentheses in the screen column refer to film timings.*

MAJOR SINGING AND DANCING AND SELECTED ROLES

Stage: Hildegarde Neff (Ninotchka); Don Ameche (Steve Canfield); Gretchen Wyler (Janice Dayton); GEORGE TOBIAS (Commissar Markovitch); Leon Belasco (Brankov); Henry Lascoe (Ivanov); David Opatoshu (Bibinski); Julie Newmar (Vera)

Screen: Fred Astaire (Steve); Cyd Charisse (dubbed by Carol Richards) (Ninotchka); Janis Paige (Peggy Dayton); Peter Lorre (Brankov); Joseph Buloff (Ivanov); Jules Munshin (Bibinski); TOBIAS (Markovitch); Wim Sonneveld (Peter Ilyitch Boroff)

- *Names in capital letters indicate that a cast member appeared both on stage and in the film.*

(Iranoff, Buljanoff, and Kopalski) sent to Paris to negotiate the sale of jewelry confiscated by the Bolshevist government from the so-called White Russian Grand Duchess Swana now luxuriating in Parisian exile.[10] Swana's lover Leon (Melvyn Douglas), intends to steal the jewels first, but before he can execute this plan he meets Ninotchka by chance outside the hotel as she is studying a map to the Eiffel Tower where they will soon meet again. Looking over the city of Paris and later in Leon's room the playboy and the comrade establish a mutual "chemical reaction," an attraction initially more than offset by their fundamental political differences and warring cultural attitudes.

An overheard phone conversation reveals Leon's identity to Ninotchka and initiates the conflict the film will eventually resolve. Despite their ideological differences about the relative merits of capitalism versus communism and their differing objectives about the future of the grand duchess's confiscated jewels, Ninotchka and Leon fall in love. In time, the Russian learns to accept beauty for its own sake and even surreptitiously purchases a frivolous and silly-looking hat she formerly viewed as the reason the West would fall to Russian revolutionary culture. In future musical adaptations the hat will metamorphose into silk stockings and a song. See Figure 5.1.

Meanwhile, Leon also learns much from his Russian lover. He is even inspired to read Karl Marx's *Das Kapital* which motivates him to make his own bed. His butler, Gaston, disapproves of both decisions. When Leon asks Gaston whether he looks forward to the day they can adopt communist principles and "share and share alike," the butler's response comes as a surprise: "Emphatically not, sir. The

Fig. 5.1 Ninotchka (Garbo) puts on her stylish new hat in the film *Ninotchka* [52:48]. Screenshot.

prospect terrifies me. Now, don't misunderstand me, sir, I don't resent your not paying me for the past two months, but the thought that I should split *my* bank account with *you* . . . that you should take half of *my* life's savings . . . that is really too much for me."[11]

Along with most references to class distinctions, this exchange between the parasitic Leon and his hard-working butler Gaston does not appear in *Silk Stockings*, the musical stage adaptation of *Ninotchka*. The musical does, however, consider political distinctions between Russia and the West. Another decision facing a potential stage adaptation was how (or whether) to attempt to capture on stage one of the film's most iconic moments: Garbo's laugh. See Figure 5.2. This was the scene, vigorously hyped in its day, when the characteristically somber Swede laughed, allegedly for the first time in a film, and demonstrated an unexpected talent as a screwball comedian. Since the makers of *Silk Stockings* concluded that Garbo's legendary laugh would not translate well, stage (and later film) audiences will look in vain to see Ninotchka's spontaneous reaction when she sees an aristocrat stumble and fall down in a proletarian restaurant. Instead, Ninotchka, now a character in a musical, herself begins to fall in love when Steve serenades her in the song "All of You."

Changing times precipitated several significant plot changes in the Broadway version. In 1920s and 1930s Paris, Russian émigrés formed a visible subculture (recall *Roberta*), but by the 1950s, most had either vanished or assimilated. In response to this new reality, the stage adaptation removed conspiring White Russians from the plot line. This decision resulted in the elimination of the Grand Duchess Swana (played by Ina Claire, then forty-six), who was keeping Leon

Fig. 5.2 Greta Garbo laughs at Melvyn Douglas in the film
Ninotchka [49:27]. Screenshot.

financially afloat in exchange for his romantic attentions well before Ninotchka's
arrival and now must compete with the younger and potentially more desirable communist played by Garbo (then thirty-four). Swana's disappearance also
necessitated the change in Leon's profession.

Consequently, instead of arriving in Paris to sell the grand duchess's
confiscated jewels, in the stage version the three Russian emissaries in the film
version travel to the city that "loves lovers" in order to retrieve the reluctant composer ("Too Bad"). Not only do they fail to fulfill this directive, but the Russians
quickly adapt to Parisian high life and demonstrate behavior that prompts the
new Commissar of Art Markovitch to send his no-nonsense envoy Ninotchka
to end their insubordination. More than a fringe benefit of these changes is that
by making Steve a theatrical agent and replacing a duchess with a composer, the
stage version brought music naturally into the plot.

Leon's counterpart Steve solicits the help of a character who does not appear
in *Ninotchka*, Janice Dayton, an attractive, non-intellectual ex-swimming film
star. Unlike Swana, Janice is not in competition with Ninotchka.[12] Instead, her
dramatic task is to use her beauty and charm to persuade Boroff to adapt his
serious and ideologically Soviet ballet *Ode to a Tractor* into a popular musical.
This new turn in the plot provides the opportunity to address cultural and artistic conflicts that divide Western and Soviet societies in addition to the political
differences addressed in *Ninotchka*. The aesthetic rift is revealed in the second
act when audiences witness the rehearsal of a number from Boroff's new version of *War and Peace*, a mock striptease number named after Napoleon's wife
called "Josephine." The new version butchers Boroff's ballet to such an extent

that only the first seven notes (a mini-cadenza, technically a melisma, on the word "Josephine") bear any musical resemblance to it. The musical content of this opening will be described and illustrated later in Musical Example 5.1.

Ninotchka considers "Josephine" a sacrilege both to Boroff and to Russian culture. As she explains to Steve, "This silly musical number, as you call it, is a travesty—of music that belongs to the Russian people."[13] From Ninotchka's perspective, their contrasting positions regarding this song embody "the essence of our ideological conflict."[14] Instead of Swana's offer to hand over the stolen jewels in exchange for Ninotchka's immediate return to Russia, which was the plot catalyst in Lubitsch's film, Ninotchka and Steve temporarily part ways over aesthetic and cultural incompatibilities. Since *Silk Stockings* opened a couple years before *West Side Story* paved the way for an unhappy ending in a musical, it shouldn't be too much of a spoiler alert to disclose that Ninotchka and Steve will reconcile these differences before the end of the evening and live happily ever after.

Another revealing difference between *Ninotchka* and its stage adaptation occurs early in the film, when the three commissars ask Ninotchka about "things in Moscow." Ninotchka responds with the following, seemingly without irony: "The last mass trials were a great success. There are going to be fewer but better Russians." This remark is in keeping with Lubitsch's and especially Wilder's unsparing criticism of the Soviet dark side.[15] In the tamer stage musical and its screen adaptation, both conceived after Joseph Stalin's death in 1953, Ninotchka refrains from making this provocative remark, despite the ongoing tensions of the Cold War. Consequently, Ninotchka's approving assessment of Stalin's purges of the 1930s was removed.

For the most part, criticism has been kind to *Ninotchka*. In addition to the strong acting performances and imaginative direction, the film has had a lingering positive reception, possibly because even without the kind of hostility between the West and the Soviets that emerged after World War II, it attains a remarkable balance in equal opportunity satire. For example, concerning American capitalism, Lubitsch biographer Joseph McBride quotes the commissar's response to the Parisian jeweler who tells them he expects to take a loss on their transaction: "Capitalistic methods. . . . They accumulate millions by taking loss after loss."[16]

The cultural historian Nick Smedley articulates further how Lubitsch achieved this balance: "Lubitsch satirized the excesses of Stalinist totalitarianism, while remaining respectful of the communists' genuine commitment to social equality and welfare. Similarly, while he made it clear that the personal freedom and decadence of the West was vastly preferable to the stultifying politics of the Soviet Union, he took care to criticize unprincipled capitalism and the old order in Russia. His overall aim was to show the triumph of human bonds over conflict; his metaphor was, as always, a love story."[17]

SILK STOCKINGS: THE MUSICAL

The Genesis

Silk Stockings opened on Broadway on February 24, 1955, and closed on April 14, 1956. A bona fide but unspectacular stage hit at 478 performances, the show inspired no Broadway revivals.[18] When it was reintroduced in 2005 in London as part of Ian Marshall Fisher's "Lost Musicals" season, the sobriquet truly fit. In its original run, *Silk Stockings* garnered four raves and two favorable reviews in the New York papers against only one unfavorable notice.[19] It introduced one major song hit, "All of You," along with other highly regarded songs, including the cleverly satiric "Siberia," a fine title number, and Ninotchka's excellent but embarrassingly sexist love song, "Without Love (What Is a Woman?"). Overall, *Silk Stockings* was a well-crafted romantic musical comedy with a strong score and a palatable dose of political satire regarding communism and capitalism. It also offered topical cultural satire in its treatment of the trendiness of the film industry ("Stereophonic Sound") and the appropriation of high art into superficial popular entertainment ("Josephine").

Discussion of *Silk Stockings* regularly notes the valedictory historical position of both the musical and the film, which arrived at the end of Porter's long and prolific stage career and nearly the end of his film career.[20] His final musical was Porter's third hit after *Kiss Me, Kate* (1948) (1,070 performances) and *Can-Can* (1953) (892 performances), against one flop, *Out of This World* (1950) (157 performances). Joining Porter's exodus from a lifetime on the stage was Kaufman, the playwright and director with a comparably long resume going back, like Porter, to the late 1920s, including numerous hit plays such as *You Can't Take It with You* with Moss Hart and the Pulitzer Prize–winning *Of Thee I Sing* with George and Ira Gershwin. Kaufman's most recent triumph was as the director of Feuer and Martin's greatest success, *Guys and Dolls* (1950). Before he was fired, Kaufman was slated to direct and, along with his wife Leueen, to co-write *Silk Stocking's* stage libretto, and the two retained their writer's credit even after they were replaced by Burrows. The stage version was also the only Broadway musical to star the film actor Don Ameche as Steve. Hildegarde Knef (more commonly known by her Americanized stage spelling, Neff) (1925–2002), also in her first and only Broadway show, played Ninotchka. See Figures 5.3 and 5.4.

As consistently portrayed in books on Porter, Kaufman, and the autobiographies of Feuer and Burrows, the genesis of *Silk Stockings* was not a smooth process.[21] The documentary record supports this consensus. Perhaps the major turning point occurred when Feuer and Burrows took over as director and writer, respectively, after the dismissal of Kaufman and MacGrath. Ironically,

Fig. 5.3 Don Ameche (Steve Canfield) and Hildegarde Neff (Ninotchka) in the stage version of *Silk Stockings*. Photofest.

this situation repeated what happened five years earlier when Feuer and Martin rejected Jo Swerling's draft of *Guys and Dolls* and hired Burrows to write a new libretto based on Frank Loesser's songs that had already been written.[22] Steven Suskin notes that Feuer and Martin had also fired the director of *The Boy Friend* the previous year and a few years later would fire the librettist and choreographer of *How to Succeed in Business without Really Trying*, another hit musical with lyrics and music by Loesser.[23] Two decades later Feuer and Martin fired Martin Scorsese, the original director, and Ron Lewis, the original choreographer of Kander and Ebb's *The Act*.[24]

Fig. 5.4 Hildegarde Neff and Don Ameche rehearsing with Cole Porter at the piano for the stage version of *Silk Stockings*. Photofest.

The starting point of *Silk Stockings* was Feuer's desire to acquire a property that could serve as a fifth successive hit, a string that began with *Where's Charley?* (1948), Loesser's first Broadway show, and *Guys and Dolls* (1950). Since he had supplied the lyrics and music to Feuer and Martin's third hit *Can-Can*, it was not unexpected that when Loesser was unable to take on *Silk Stockings* due to his immersion in *The Most Happy Fella*, Porter's name would come up. Several letters convey Porter's enthusiasm for the script. In a letter to his musical amanuensis Albert Sirmay July 9, 1953, Porter found Kaufman and MacGrath's script to be "much funnier" than its film source, "with an excellent love story."[25] At the end of this letter he informs Sirmay he has agreed to write the show and will "go back into slavery on August 1st, scared but happy."

One year later (August 25, 1954) Porter reported to Moss Hart about his progress on the score: "*Silk Stockings* has a fine script and it seems to me that I have done a good job on the music and lyrics, although one never knows."[26] A few weeks before tryouts (November 11, 1954) Porter wrote to his Hollywood friend Sam Stark that "at the present moment it all looks like a howling flop," but in another letter to Stark two days after the Philadelphia opening Porter was happy to report "that at least hundred people wired me: 'May your Silk Stockings run forever'" (November 29).[27] Shortly before the show moved on to Boston on January 4, 1955, the second of the three out-of-town tryout cities (the third was Detroit on February 1), Porter wrote to thank Noël Coward for sending him additional lyrics to "Siberia" (December 23).[28] Although Porter assures Coward that "some of them will come in most handy," no one seems to know which Coward lyrics or suggestions for lyrics may have turned up in the final version.

While we have no reason to doubt that Coward sent Porter "Siberia" lyrics, the Porter Collection at the Library of Congress only offers tangible evidence that Porter received considerable lyrical assistance on this song from *Kaufman*, who sent Porter suggestions for material in two undated letters.[29] Kaufman's suggestions also clearly support the central idea in the song, which is to show that Siberia isn't so bad. According to Feuer, who along with Martin came up with the idea for this song, Porter thought Siberia "overwhelmingly beautiful" and had a pleasant experience there as the guest of a grand duke.[30] Since his personal experience so contradicted the standard image of Siberia, Porter resisted the premise of the song and wrote the lyrics reluctantly.

One among many examples of Kaufman's input appears in his second letter when he lauds the fact that in Siberia "you never run out of ice at your cocktail parties." Porter adopted this suggestion in his "Siberia Notes": "When it's cocktail time, it will be nice/To know you'll not have to phone for ice." In the end, while Porter deserves credit for transforming prose into poetry, there is barely a lyric in the four published refrains of "Siberia" that can't be traced to an idea posed by the original co-librettist. Although most of the rhymes are Porter's, Porter's reliance on his lyrical co-partner for ideas that could be transformed into sophisticated and funny rhyming lyrical lines is pervasive. It's difficult to imagine what Porter could have derived from Coward.

An informative (and entertaining) recollection of the rehearsal process appears in the 1970 memoir by the German film actress and singer Hildegard Knef, who as an author had returned to her native spelling rather than using Neff, her American stage spelling. Here's a sample: "Whole scenes are thrown out and replaced by new ones. Songs from the first act are moved to the second and the other way around. I start to say a line and somebody bawls, 'That's been cut since yesterday, for Heaven's sake.' Kaufman whispers his directions as though he were slipping hot tips on the races. Porter hasn't been in the theater for days; they say he's writing new songs and will come when we run through with ballet and chorus."[31]

The main reason for the lengthy (and sometimes turbulent) out-of-town tryout saga was the firing of Kaufman and MacGrath, who were replaced by Burrows.[32] The change in book writers led to many song changes, which meant that the lyricist and composer Porter was on constant call to create new material. Two Library of Congress (LOC) lists in the Porter Collection (see Tables 5.2 and 5.3) reveal the extent to which the songs evolved during the gestation of the show. The first, in Porter's hand labeled "Music Lay Out Act 2" (Table 5.2), although not dated, was inserted with Act II of the Kaufman-MacGrath libretto (Box 25, Folder 2) dated January 19, 1954. Most of the songs on this list are numbered, but more important, Porter offers references to specific pages in the January 19 libretto which match either directly by song title or by inference with a designated page in the libretto. Ten months later, a single page with a typed list of scenes and songs (with a few handwritten changes) for both acts labeled "Music Line-Up" (Table 5.3) was inserted among the "Miscellaneous" Porter papers in Box 25, Folder 6, with a handwritten note that reads "complete copy as of Oct 8/54."

Table **5.2** *Silk Stockings*: Porter's "Music Lay Out Act 2," January 19, 1954, Cole Porter Collection, Library of Congress, Box 25, Folder 2.

12	What a Ball (instr[umental])	2-1-1
13	"Under the Dress"	2-1-9
14	Reprise Without Love	2-2-13
15	Give Me the Land	2-3-14
16	Silk Stockings	2-3-20
17	What a Ball vocal	2-4-27
	Reprise—Paris Loves Lovers	2-4-27
18	Possible Number	2-5-30
	If Ever We Get Out of Jail	2-5-33
		2-5-38
	Finale--Give Me the Land	2-6-40

Cole Porter is responsible for all the strikeouts.

Table 5.3 *Silk Stockings*: Porter's "Music Line-Up," Acts I and II, October 8, 1954, Cole Porter Collection, Library of Congress, Box 25, Folder 6.

Act I	
Scene 1	Commissar's Office: Ballet to *Ode to Energy*
	"ART" (Commissar and Guards)
Scene 2	Royal Suite:
	1. "Too Bad" (Ivanov, Brankov, Bibinski)
	2. "Paris Loves Lovers" (Ninotchka and Steve duet)
Scene 3	Hotel Lobby or Corridor: "There's a Hollywood That's Good" (Janice)
Scene 4	Canfield's [Steve's] Suite:
	1. "All of You" (Canfield)
	2. "It's a Chemical Reaction, That's All" (Ninotchka)
Scene 5	Exterior Couture: "Hail Bibinski" (Ivanov, Brankov, and Bibinski)
Scene 6	Interior Couture: ~~"Under the Dress" or "Perfume"~~ (Janice) and Crossed out by Porter replaced by the handwritten title "Satin and Silk"
Scene 7	Stepladder
Scene 8	Royal Suite
	1. "Without Love" (Ninotchka)
	2. Possible Reprise of "All of You" (Canfield)
Act II	
Scene 1	Motion Picture Studio:
	1. "Josephine" (Janice and Girls)
	2. "As on through the Seasons We Sail" (Canfield and Ninotchka)
Scene 2	Elsewhere in Studio: "Why Should I Trust You" (Ivanov, Brankov, and Bibinski)
Scene 3	Split Stage: "Without Love" (reprise) (Ninotchka); "Silk Stockings" (Canfield)
Scene 4	Dancer Practice Bar [*sic*]: (no music)
Scene 5	Soviet Apartment:
	1. Choreographic Spot?
	2. "What a Ball" (Ninotchka and Boys)
Scene 6	Jail:
	1. "If Ever We Get Out of Jail" (Ninotchka and Canfield)
	3. "Too Bad" (reprise) (Ninotchka, Canfield, and Commissars)

It is a challenge to determine the precise number of completed *Silk Stockings* songs that went unused, but the Porter Collection contains the music and lyrics to more than a dozen unfinished or unused songs. In most cases the content makes the location of these songs clear, many of which are early versions of reconceived or retitled songs. A good resource for information and placement of these unfinished and unused songs can be found in Robert Kimball's introductions to the lyrics of these songs in *The Complete Lyrics of Cole Porter*.[33]

SILK STOCKINGS: THE FILM

Negotiating the Transition from Stage to Film

The success of *Silk Stockings* on stage made a film adaptation virtually inevitable, and MGM purchased the rights and started working on the adaptation soon after the show closed on April 14, 1956. One of the first orders of business was to resolve the issue of Porter's potentially controversial lyrics in order to gain Production Code approval. Since the world of Broadway was far less restrictive than the world of film, and since a number of Porter's lyrics to the stage version of *Kiss Me, Kate* in 1948 had been problematic for the film version only a few years earlier in 1953, there was legitimate reason for concern.[34] Indeed, a letter dated May 7 from Geoffrey Shurlock, the director of the Motion Picture Association of America and guardian of the Production Code, to MGM production chief Dore Schary indicates four controversial lyrics.[35] Not surprisingly, three of these belonged to Peggy (formerly Janice) Dayton, the sexy newly invented swimming film star.

But compared to the lyrical indignities suffered by Porter in the transfer of *Kiss Me, Kate* to film, *Silk Stockings* emerged relatively unscathed. Porter was asked to replace two lines in "Stereophonic Sound" (now a duet with Astaire), one of which referred to Marilyn's behind (a reference to the derriere of "sex symbol" Marilyn Monroe) and another to an unspecified woman whose bosom was five feet wide on the large screen.[36] Porter complied with both requests. The deletion of the Monroe reference necessitated a new lyric; the second request was easily remedied by substituting the word "bosom" with "mouth." An unacceptable lyric in "Satin and Silk," "shake like hell," prompted Porter to create a new stanza. Whether "*make* a friend" was problematic would "depend primarily on the manner in which it is sung." The only other problematic song was Astaire's "All of You." As with "make a friend," MGM was advised that Steve's tour of Ninotchka's body parts "must be delivered in a non-suggestive manner." Anyone watching the film today will notice that both Astaire and MGM disregarded this request.

Enter Mamoulian

While Schary was setting the stage for the production of the film on the legal front, Freed, the film's producer, was looking for a director. After years of successful films with his Freed Unit (see chapter 1), Freed's work as producer on *Silk Stockings* was his first project under the newly created, fully independent Arthur Freed Productions. One of Freed's first decisions was to pick Mamoulian to direct.

Freed's choice of Mamoulian was neither expected nor particularly welcome. The director's most recent film, *Summer Holiday* (1947), a musical adaptation of Eugene O'Neill's uncharacteristically bucolic comedy *Ah! Wilderness*, was a box-office flop. It was also an expensive failure that ran considerably over budget. Prior to *Summer Holiday*, however, Mamoulian had earned recognition as one of the most original and often successful stage and film directors of the past two decades. Highlights of Mamoulian's stage career began with his acclaimed direction of the play version of *Porgy* (1927) when he was still in his twenties, followed by its transformation into the opera *Porgy and Bess* (1935), the game-changing *Oklahoma!* (1943) (see chapter 4), and *Carousel* (1945). In the later 1940s, Mamoulian directed the less remunerative *St. Louis Woman* (1946) and *Lost in the Stars* (1949), and by the 1950s his career, both as a director of new stage musicals and as a film director, was at a virtual standstill.

The sixteen films that Mamoulian directed are collectively historic. Fourteen appeared between 1929 and 1942 followed only by *Summer Holiday* and *Silk Stockings*, both musicals. Prior to 1943, only three of the first fourteen films were musicals: *Applause* (1929); *Love Me Tonight* (1932); and *High, Wide and Handsome* (1937).[37] Of these, *Love Me Tonight*, starring Jeanette MacDonald and Maurice Chevalier with a score by Richard Rodgers and Lorenz Hart, occupies a central position among early film musicals and continues to enjoy a lofty critical stature. For example, Tom Milne asserted that *Love Me Tonight* "was one of the most enchanting musicals ever made, the Lubitsch film that Lubitsch was always trying to pull off but never quite did."[38]

Mamoulian's first feature film (and first musical), *Applause*, with its powerful performance by *Show Boat* star Helen Morgan, liberated cinematographers from their crowded and stifling camera booths. Early in the sound era Mamoulian also made technological film history, again in *Applause,* when he persuaded his studio bosses to allow him to record on two microphones simultaneously to add to the quality (and complexity) of the dialogue soundtrack. *Becky Sharp* (1935) was the first three-color Technicolor film. Mamoulian also brought out the best in actors and actresses as diverse as Fredric March, Marlene Dietrich, Greta Garbo, and Cyd Charisse. These many virtues earned Mamoulian a major following among film critics, and despite his lesser efforts, there remains a general consensus that his achievement as a film director was comparable in technical scope and artistry to his stage accomplishments.

Despite Mamoulian's long list of technical and artistic accomplishments, the failure of *Summer Holiday* had considerably decreased his desirability. In some circles, Mamoulian had not only passed his prime, but he was also considered washed up. Mamoulian biographer Mark Spergel raises the possibility that Freed's decision to hire Mamoulian was a response to pressure from their financial backers, Loew's Inc., who were hoping to lower costs, i.e., that Freed's decision was not only "an artistic decision but also a financial one."[39] Spergel goes further into why the somewhat tainted Mamoulian was both a risky and an unwise financial choice: "Mamoulian's reputation for extravagance and waste, not to mention personal difficulties, had made him unemployable. This lack of employability made his market value as a director drop drastically in the 1950s. He could now be hired at bargain rates, compared with other directors of his stature and his own past earning history."[40]

For these reasons, Freed was able to pay Mamoulian less than a third ($50,000) of the $160,000 and $170,000 he had earned as the director of his two previous musicals. Fifty grand is still, at $530,000 in 2022 dollars, nothing to sneeze at. Nevertheless, this was only marginally larger than the $40,000 Janis Paige, the recent star of *The Pajama Game* on Broadway, received for singing a couple of solo songs ("Satin and Silk" and the ludicrously shortened "Josephine") and a duet with Astaire ("Stereophonic Sound"). Astaire was paid $150,000, and in the days of unequal pay for equal work, Charisse received half as much.[41]

Mamoulian's Sixteen Production Memos and the Transformation into a Dance Musical

After persuading a reluctant Astaire that he still possessed what it took to play a romantic lead, Mamoulian got to work. By July 25, 1956, he had produced the first of sixteen production memos, all of which now reside in the Mamoulian Collection in the Library of Congress. Both the memos and the shooting stopped at the end of January 1957, and after February previews the film adaptation of *Silk Stockings* was released on July 19, one year after Mamoulian's first memo.

The memos cover an impressive range of ideas, topics, issues, and details, ranging from the minuscule to a sweeping larger vision. Since this chapter can only offer some of the highlights, it will focus on how Mamoulian went about using the talent of Astaire and Charisse to create a dance musical. His first priority, however, was to establish a love story between two sympathetic characters, Steve and Ninotchka, and to give them traits that allow viewers to "'root' for the successful outcome of their romance."[42] He did this in his first memo,

"Memorandum on the Script of *Silk Stockings*," which included twenty-eight suggested script revisions.[43]

To accomplish his most significant artistic decision, the creation of a *dance musical*, Mamoulian needed to make some changes to Ninotchka as a character and alter viewers' perceptions of her. For example, Ninotchka becomes something different after the script removed the story depicted in both the film *Ninotchka* and the stage version of *Silk Stockings* in which she killed an enemy with a bayonet. Crucial to Mamoulian's fundamental decision to emphasize dance was his wish to add a backstory for Ninotchka which explored her love of dance and music, her participation as a child in the Russian ballet, and her subsequent epiphany at the age of sixteen "that both dancing and music were a selfish indulgence—that Mother Russia and the Communist Party needed her."

Mamoulian also expressed his desire to humanize the three commissars and "get away from the conventional pattern of the vaudeville trio of clowns" by giving each "a distinct personality." Jules Munshin (Bibinski) was familiar to film audiences as a sailor in *On the Town* and a ballplayer in *Take Me Out to the Ball Game*, both from 1949 and both co-starring Frank Sinatra and Gene Kelly. In *Silk Stockings*, Bibinski was "the most frightened" commissar and the most reliant on Lenin, or at least his convenient reinterpretations of Lenin. The Yiddish actor Joseph Buloff (Ivanov), born in Lithuania, was probably best known as the Persian peddler Ali Hakim in the original stage version of *Oklahoma!*, directed by Mamoulian. In *Silk Stockings*, Mamoulian cast him as the "silent" one, who rarely goes beyond the words "noo" and "da" for most of the film until he suddenly demonstrates a latent verbal eloquence.

The best-known commissar was Peter Lorre playing Brankov against type. In 1957, Lorre, born in Hungary, was seriously ill (he died in 1964) and nearing the end of an impressive career that began when he starred as a psychologically disturbed serial killer who preys on children in Fritz Lang's first sound film *M!* (1931). Prior to *Silk Stockings*, Lorre would continue to play villains in Alfred Hitchcock's *The Man Who Knew Too Much* (1934) and in two famous films starring Humphrey Bogart, *The Maltese Falcon* (1941) and *Casablanca* (1942).

In a fascinating one-page memo dated September 14, Mamoulian prepared a list of potential actors to fill the roles of Markovitch and the three stooges (i.e., commissars). The list suggests that Mamoulian had not yet found the commissars who matched what he was looking for in the July 25 memo. The exception was the listing of a single name for the role of the Commissar of Art Markovitch, George Tobias, who also played this role on stage.[44] The potential pool of actors considered for the three Russian commissars contained thirteen names. Two were eventually cast, Lorre and Buloff.[45]

Among the candidates for the third commissar were Burl Ives, Ernie Kovacs, Charles Lawton, and Akim Tamiroff, familiar names then and to some extent today.[46] Perhaps the most provocative possibility was the last name on the list, the director Alfred Hitchcock, a choice intriguing to imagine. In the end, Mamoulian selected Munshin (not on the list), who at 5'11" offered a comic visual contrast to the diminutive Lorre (5'3") with Buloff falling somewhere in between.

The background Mamoulian explored in his memos provided the foundation he needed to execute the central departure from the stage version: the transformation of *Silk Stockings* into a dance film musical. This was the fundamental change that informed and shaped Mamoulian's subsequent directorial decisions. The addition of choreography was motivated in large part by the casting of the leading players, Astaire and Charisse, who by acclamation were two of the leading film dancers of the era. Mamoulian explains: "We can make excellent use of their common love for music and dancing—overt on the part of Steve, suppressed on the part of Ninotchka. Especially, having Astaire and Charisse in the parts, it would be a sin to let dancing be a mere ornamentation in the picture. We should make it serve some important dramatic purpose. So let us think of Astaire's and Charisse's dancing as one of the most vital and emotional factors in advancing the story."[47]

In the process of taking full advantage of the talent at his disposal, Mamoulian managed to transform and preserve the essential aspects of the stage version while retaining nearly all of Porter's songs. In the end, despite the fundamentally revised conception, only two songs were removed from the stage production, the arguably expendable Act II opener for the three commissars, "Hail, Bibinski," and the sung duet between Steve and Ninotchka that followed it on stage, "As on through the Seasons We Sail." Instead of inserting another lyrical duet, Porter replaced the latter with the lively "Fated to Be Mated," first sung by Steve then danced by Steve and Ninotchka together. The dance component of "Fated" also provided a welcome opportunity to add instrumental reprises from the songs they shared in Act I, a cha-cha version of "Paris Loves Lovers" and a jazzy dance rendition of "All of You."

At Astaire's request, Mamoulian and Porter added a solo dance for Astaire, "The Ritz Roll and Rock," as the second new musical number and placed it near the end of the film. Since Charisse had not long before been featured in a central dance version of the title song that replaced Steve's sung version and given the featured dance role in "The Red Blues," the addition of Astaire's only solo dance in the film created a belated parity with his co-lead.

"The Ritz Roll and Rock" poses a plea for timeliness in its title and lyrics. It also demonstrates early rock and roll's harmonic underpinning derived from rhythm and blues, compatibly present in Ninotchka's previous "Red Blues." The lyrics (which don't make complete prose sense) suggest that by 1957, the smart set found rock and roll "much too tame," a state of affairs that the "fancy fops and fillies" could remedy by jazzing up rock and roll and changing its name to the ritz roll and rock. Significantly, for this final number, Astaire's last solo dance in a film, Astaire resurrected his trademark costume made iconic in Berlin's "Top Hat, White Tie and Tails," from *Top Hat* (1935). As in the Berlin musical (although in this case not exclusively), Astaire was joined by a similarly attired male chorus.[48] Perhaps in keeping with Mamoulian's principle that red should be the final color audiences see in a shot, Astaire dons a red sash over his shirt and under his jacket.[49]

At the end of the dance, Astaire's hat lies on the ground. Astaire scholar John Mueller thought the hat fell off Astaire's head accidentally, an observation corroborated by Mamoulian, who later described this surprise as a "lucky accident."[50] Hermes Pan biographer John Franceschina also describes what happened to Astaire's hat as "completely by accident."[51] At the risk of contradicting Mueller, Mamoulian, and Franceschina and losing my status as a reliable narrator, I must issue a minority report and state my opinion that Astaire removed his hat *intentionally* (at least by the final take). In any event, we all agree that once the formerly stately hat reached the ground, Astaire smashed it. To reinforce this historic moment (even if no one knew this would be Astaire's final solo number in a film), his destructive, in my view pre-meditated, final action occurred firmly and precisely on the final step and final beat of the number, a fitting conclusion to Astaire's thirtieth and final major dance film.[52]

Mamoulian's July 1956 memo goes on to discuss the director's problems with the first and final sequences in the script, both of which would undergo considerable future evolution until the final cut. The early drafts of the first scene included a fair amount of narration and dialogue compared to the total absence of the latter in the final release. Eventually, instead of narration, Mamoulian wanted "a different opening which will combine imag[e]ry [*sic*] and motion." As we'll see, it would take several more months for Mamoulian to figure out how to realize this evolving vision.

For the final sequence Mamoulian proposed "two new ideas." The first idea was to have Ninotchka sent to Constantinople to retrieve the rebellious commissars and "bring them back alive, so we can have them dead." Ninotchka agrees to do this because she sees it as the best chance to save them. This revised exchange is far grimmer than either *Ninotchka* or the stage version. In the former, Ninotchka goes to Constantinople to "verify" the bad behavior of the three commissars rather than to punish them. It's not clear how Leon managed to pull enough strings to get Ninotchka out of Russia, but once she arrives, he successfully appeals to Ninotchka's desire to spare her beloved country of future embarrassment by threatening to populate the world with Russian restaurants and owners like the three commissars.

In this happy ending, not only is Ninotchka able to marry Leon, she can save her country at the same time. In the final version of the film Steve goes to Russia in order to fly Ninotchka, Markovitch, the three commissars, and their musician friends back to Paris. Once in Paris, the commissars take Ninotchka into their new nightclub, financed by Steve, who dances "The Ritz Roll and Rock" before persuading her to stay in Paris for love of Steve rather than love of country.

In Memo No. 4, "Dances in *Silk Stockings*" (August 30), Mamoulian reiterates his goal "to treat the dance as a vital and dynamic element in telling our story and expressing characters." Mamoulian proposes the elimination of one dance ("the sequence in which Steve shows Ninotchka around Paris") and proposes modifications to another six dances, not all of which would come to pass. After describing the dance for "All of You" and the conversation in which Ninotchka tells Steve about her balletic past, Mamoulian suggests that Ninotchka's private dance, in which she removes the beautiful secret clothing from hiding, including of course her new silk stockings, should resemble "a butterfly emerging from her chrysalis."[53]

Mamoulian continues his discussion of another three dance numbers in Memo No. 5 (September 18). The first of these dances follows the opening song of the show, "Too Bad." Mamoulian explains that he didn't give Astaire the opportunity for more than a dance that was "brief, colorful, and amusing" because he wanted to create a "teaser" to give viewers something to look forward to. This meant that viewers had to wait twenty-nine minutes before they heard Astaire even *sing* in a duet, "Paris Loves Lovers." Astaire's first full dance number finally occurs another six minutes later when Steve sings and dances with Peggy in "Stereophonic Sound." For Astaire's first dance number with Charisse, "All of You," viewers would need to wait until the forty-six-minute mark of a film that lasts 118 minutes.

The third dance number discussed in Memo 5 (the second was the new dance for the new song "Fated to Be Mated") was a big dance finale between Steve and Ninotchka to take place in Constantinople. Mamoulian describes in some detail what happens when Steve's verbal pleading turns to dance before he accidentally falls into the waters of the Bosporus. Ninotchka jumps in after him and the story is resolved "in comic terms and without dialogue." In contrast to his other dance descriptions, Mamoulian does not mention a specific Porter tune that would fit in this proposed context nor does he suggest that Porter write new music or recycle a song from among his past triumphs.[54]

The meeting between Ninotchka and Leon/Steve also underwent several changes between the 1939 and 1957 films. In *Ninotchka*, Leon and the beautiful Russian envoy meet cute and incognito outside the hotel. In the stage adaptation they are introduced by the commissars, and audiences soon learn Ninotchka's identity and Steve's occupation as a theatrical agent representing Boroff. Mamoulian's memos reveal that the circumstances of their meeting evolved over several months during which time Mamoulian abandoned his initial conceptionas stated in the July 25 memo when he concludes that "it is *imperative* that Canfield and Ninotchka first meet as complete strangers, knowing nothing about each other." Mamoulian is emphatic: "We must have that scene. Lubitch [sic] had a charming one, and if we don't succeed in writing a better one, we should certainly use his." This note documents Mamoulian's artistic involvement with *Ninotchka* as a model as much as the intermediary stage musical version. In Memo No. 7, Mamoulian experimented with an alternative scenario in which *Steve* knows the identity of Ninotchka but she does not know who he is.

A little more than one month before the start of shooting on November 7, Mamoulian had not yet arrived at the idea for the opening of the finished film. Following an aerial shot of Paris at night and a close shot of the electric sign of the Hotel Clarence in the October 4 Memo (No. 8), "Possible Alternate Opening for *Silk Stockings*," the camera shows a close-up of two pairs of feet sitting on a couch and a poster on the ground. After this sequence the camera dissolves to a close-up of Steve's feet getting out of an elevator and crossing the lobby. Mamoulian also considered filming additional pairs of feet, including a pair belonging to a beautiful girl and a French poodle. In the final cut we see attractive female feet (and legs) near the elevator, but only Steve's feet entering the taxi that takes him to the concert hall to catch the end of Boroff's piano recital. By beginning feet first, Mamoulian figured out how to begin *Silk Stockings* in a striking pictorial way entirely without dialogue, a gambit reminiscent of Lubitsch's stateroom sequence in *Ninotchka*.

Interestingly, Mamoulian had also focused on feet (and legs) in the opening sequence of his directorial film debut, *Applause*. Three minutes into that film the camera shows an assortment of unappealing female legs clad in white tights belonging to a small-town music hall chorus line. Soon viewers see the rest of their bodies on the burlesque stage as the dowdy and pregnant but nimble burlesque star Kitty Darling (Morgan) enters with her leading comic.[55] Whether or not Mamoulian was making a conscious reference, the focus on Astaire's feet from his hotel room to the concert hall at the outset of Mamoulian's final film turns out to be a fitting bookend to the burlesque and street walking scenes of his first film.

The comments and decisions in these memos range from significant changes such as the decisions to cut the "Josephine" number and a scene with Sonia in Russia to a wide range of dubbing details. Especially revelatory concerning the latter is the dubbing that accompanies Ninotchka as she types the notes of her first conversation with the three commissars. In Memo No. 13 (February 5, 1957) Mamoulian stated his opinion that the first try at dubbing was "too conservative" and "should sound almost like a fast, dry, machine gun firing and the typewriter bell should be short and precise (not diffused?).[56] The exaggerated sound of Ninotchka's aggressive typing reflects Ninotchka's personality before she meets and falls in love with Steve. After her transformation, the next time we see Ninotchka typing, Mamoulian asks for the following (still on Memo No. 13): "THE MUSIC OF 'ALL OF YOU' should be treated here dramatically and emotionally— it is expressive of Ninotchka's inner feelings and thoughts. Therefore, it should begin as Ninotchka starts 'typing' 'ALL OF YOU,' and not before."[57]

Reception

Freed's gamble on Mamoulian paid rich dividends. The film was a financial, critical, and popular success. According to Hugh Fordin and Mueller, the film grossed $4,417,753, which more than doubled the production costs of $1,853,463.[58] These impressive, profits fell short of other successful Freed musicals of the 1950s, *Annie Get Your Gun* (1950), *An American in Paris* (1951), and *Show Boat* (1951), all of which earned over $8 million in revenue, and *Singin' in the Rain* (1952) and *The Band Wagon* (1953), which earned, respectively, over $7 million and $5 million. Nevertheless, *Silk Stockings* deserves credit as the only one of all these acclaimed films produced within a budget under $2 million.

A telegram dated February 14, sent one day after the first preview at the Crown Theatre in Pasadena to Howard Dietz, vice president in charge of publicity at MGM, hyped the "smash audience enthusiasm" for the film.[59] Based on the polling cards, the house manager concluded that *Silk Stockings* had received the greatest reaction since *An American in Paris*. The telegram singled out Astaire and Charisse with the "highest plaudits" but also bestowing high marks for Paige and Porter's score.

The Mamoulian Collection contains reports on both the February 14 Crown Theatre previews based on 214 cards filled out by audience members and the second preview which took place on February 26 at the Picwood Theatre in West Los Angeles which collected 249 cards. The questionnaire began with the request for an overall rating from Outstanding to Poor and continued with requests to rate Astaire, Charisse, and Paige individually. Other questions asked audiences to identify the scenes they liked the most and the least and whether they would recommend the picture to their friends.

The ratings and comments in the reports support the high praise relayed in the telegram to Dietz. The vast majority of both preview audiences ranked the picture and performance from Very Good to Outstanding, and an overwhelming number of viewers recommended the picture to their friends, 140 out of 151 and 203 out of 212, respectively. Since the presence of Astaire and Charisse looms so large in our collective memory of the film, it should be noted that many viewers considered Janis Paige their favorite part of the show. Consequently, some viewers expressed their regret that "Josephine" was cut off abruptly. In both surveys, Paige received more Excellent votes than Astaire (9 more and 36 more). Despite this enthusiasm for Paige, however, Charisse was the favorite, receiving even more Excellent votes than Paige in each survey (42 and 18 more). To generalize from the many pages of comments, the dancing received by far the most enthusiastic responses from both men and women. Overall, these comments offer an enlightening window into how the film was received in its own time, at least by two attentive preview audiences.

One aspect in the reception of the film in 1957 may (or may not) be relevant for today's audience: that Astaire was perceived as too old to play a romantic lead. As one respondent stated bluntly, "Fred Astaire is too old for Miss Charisse. Gene Kelly would have been a better choice." As we know, Astaire himself was worried about this potential response, a worry he expressed to Freed when first invited to star in the film. In an effort to mollify this concern, Mamoulian promptly took the star to lunch and, according to Fordin, "told Astaire that the only reason he had accepted the assignment was because of him and Cyd Charisse."[60] After persuading Astaire that he was not too old, the director gained the star's trust, confidence, and before long, his signature. Mueller, who concluded that "Mamoulian's assurances were fully justified," conjectured that "the script may have particularly appealed to Astaire because it concerns the romance of two self-reliant grownups, getting him away from the May-September aspects of his previous few films."[61]

Mueller is alluding to Astaire's previous two films, *Daddy Long Legs* in 1955 and *Funny Face*, the latter appearing only four months before *Silk Stockings*. Both paired Astaire, fifty-eight when *Stockings* first ran in theaters, with women more than thirty years younger. Astaire's co-star in *Long Legs*, Leslie Caron, was born in 1931. *Funny Face*'s Audrey Hepburn was born in 1929 (as was Jane Powell who appeared opposite Astaire less problematically as his sister in *Royal Wedding* in 1951). For both Mueller and presumably Astaire, Charisse's birth year of 1921 was a step in the right direction. At the time of *Silk Stockings*'s release, Charisse, born the same year as Vera-Ellen, who danced with Astaire in *Three Little Words* (1950) and *The Belle of New York* (1952), was thirty-six.[62] Despite his youthful vitality as well as his extraordinary grace, combined with flawless and imaginative technique, Astaire nevertheless appeared uncomfortably older than Charisse to some members of preview audiences, an opinion shared by both men and women.

Thus, for every "Astaire is still the finest" and "Fred Astaire is still one of the outstanding performers of this day and age," there were comments along the lines of "Fred Astaire is an excellent dancer but is a little old for the lover." Among the dozen or more comments that referred to Astaire's age, even those who thought Astaire had retained his dancing prowess occasionally expressed the opinion that "Cyd Charisse could use a much younger leading man."

A Few More Words about the Music
The Three Commissars

Beyond the two principals, only four characters in the stage musical sing, Janice Dayton and the inseparable trio of commissars who sing as one.[63] The latter open each act with the lively numbers, "Too Bad" (Act I) and "Hail, Bibinski" (Act II), and toward the end of the evening the commissars are given their big song, "Siberia," the comic highlight of the evening. "Siberia" occupies a spot not unlike the "11 o'clock number" "Brush Up Your Shakespeare" for the two comic gangsters that stopped the show nightly in *Kiss Me, Kate.*[64] All the other songs are sung by Janice, Ninotchka, and Steve.

Janice/Peggy

With her three solo numbers Janice/Peggy Dayton takes the place of Ninotchka as the principal female singing lead on both the stage and film versions.[65] Her first song, "Stereophonic Sound," offers a clever text about the cutting age film techniques such as Technicolor, CinemaScope, and Stereophonic Sound (the latter word often accompanied by an echo effect that stands out on both the cast album and the film soundtrack).[66] The tune, with its many repeated notes and repeated phrases to mark the film innovations ("Cinerama, VistaVision, Superscope, Todd-AO"), is effective but upstaged by Porter's lyrics.[67]

Mamoulian made a few changes to this song for the film. First, he changed the presentation from a solo for Janice to a duet for Peggy and Steve. With Steve in the picture, naturally he added more dancing to the equation. Consequently, a completely new stanza now ends with seven repetitions of the final phrase, not with references to technical innovations but to a range of ballet dances (Russian ballet, modern ballet, English ballet, Chinese ballet, Hindu ballet, Bali ballet, or "any ballet"). Each style is marked by recognizable dance steps to match the mention of each ballet type as well as Paige's own idiosyncratic style but less accomplished technique (compared to Astaire) before two more statements of the de rigueur words "stereophonic sound."

Silk Stockings itself was filmed in "breathtaking CinemaScope" and enjoyed a wide film theater release in stereophonic sound (although it employed MGM's preferred Eastman color process known as Metrocolor rather than "glorious Technicolor"). As a result, Mamoulian exploited CinemaScope while satirizing its trendiness by showing an elongated table near the end of the dance that stretched over the fully expanded width of the screen that barely allowed Astaire and Paige to touch.

Janice's jazzy second Act I number "Satin and Silk" not only shares a stylistic similarity to "Always True to You in My Fashion" from *Kiss Me, Kate*, but the opening of its chorus also bears a distinct melodic and rhythmic musical resemblance to the beginning of that song. Her big song in the second act is "Josephine," a risqué diegetic rehearsal number extremely loosely based on the musical version of Boroff's *Ode to a Tractor*. In this musical travesty of a scene from Tolstoy's *War and Peace*, Napoleon's bride, Josephine, explains how her physical attributes, such as her "titillating thighs" and "undulating hips," led to her ascent to the throne.

In the stage version Gretchen Wyler sang the entire song. Mamoulian originally intended to film all of it as well, and a nearly five-minute cut can be heard on the expanded soundtrack recording. Memo No. 15, Item 26 (February 14) reveals that Mamoulian changed his mind at a late editing stage: "Possible elimination of cut before last of Boroff & Co.—and possible trim of 'Josephine.'" The same day in Memo No. 16, "Cuts and Corrections," Item 64, Mamoulian wrote the following directive: "'JOSEPHINE'—cut the number shorter yet—right after Janis' singing '. . . stopped Napoleon'—cut to Boroff shouting 'Stop' and etc." As a result of this final cut, what audiences saw in the finished film was reduced to a comical 1:25 minutes. Mamoulian apparently concluded that this was enough time to insult Russian culture and cause Ninotchka to abandon her budding romance with Steve and join the three commissars on their return to their homeland. In the opening 2 measures of this abbreviated song the text is reduced to the announcement of Josephine's name. Musically this amounts to three notes: G-A-flat-B (see Musical Example 5.1), which is identical to the opening of Boroff's *Ode to a Tractor*.

With its prominent "exotic" augmented second interval (ascending A-flat-B and descending B-A-flat), the tune evokes a Russia inhabited by Jews, millions of whom immigrated to the Americas in the late nineteenth and early twentieth centuries. Harold Arlen, Irving Berlin, Jerome Kern, Frank Loesser, and Richard Rodgers were all Jewish. Porter was one of the few major Golden Age songwriters who was *not*. Nevertheless, by his own admission to Rodgers in 1926, Porter had discovered that the "secret of writing hits" was to compose "Jewish tunes."[68] Rodgers notes that one of these Jewish songs was Porter's "My Heart Belongs to Daddy," the song that first made Mary Martin famous when she sang it "somewhere in Siberia" in *Leave It to Me* (1938).

Even those who question the seriousness of Porter's remark agree that when Martin chants "Da-da, da-da-da, da-da-da-ad!" the composer's treatment of the augmented second (even employing the exact pitches used in "Josephine"), might be interpreted as a Jewish signifier.[69] Thus when we hear the opening of "Ode to a Tractor," from Porter's perspective we are hearing Russian Jewish music in which Janice/Peggy Dayton recognizably channels Martin's boastful chanting about her rich sugar *daddy* (i.e., da-da-da-ad, the Russian word for "yes" combined with the English "Da-[a]d").

Example 5.1 "Josephine" (beginning) *Silk Stockings*.

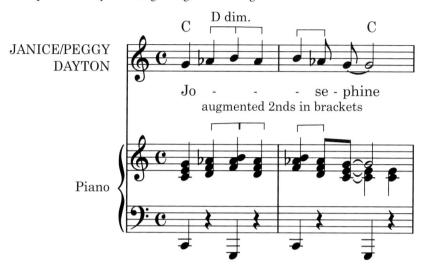

Josephine sings the augmented second no fewer than four times in the opening 2 measures, either rising or falling before reaching the third syllable of Josephine's name. This phrase, although absent in the overture of the stage version, appears briefly in the main title of the film as well as the beginning of the aborted "Josephine" number. Film audiences familiar with "Josephine" can also hear much more of this Russian Jewish tune, albeit transformed (and thus disguised) as a waltz, in the dance music for the Russian ballerinas, including Vera, the girlfriend of the newly appointed (and married) Commissar of Art Markovitch.[70] It's clear, at least in retrospect, that in this early Russian scene these dancers are rehearsing Boroff's *Ode to a Tractor* and that the work is probably a ballet. In Memo No. 16, Item 10, Mamoulian requested that the ballet music played by the rehearsal pianist (directly preceded by drums as soldiers march into the studio to remove the previous commissar of art) "should dominate and be heard very clearly" and should carry on "throughout the whole scene (no interludes)."[71] Unfortunately, the otherwise nearly comprehensive soundtrack does not include this interesting foreshadowing of "Josephine."

Ninotchka and Steve

Hildegarde Neff was apparently selected for the stage role of Ninotchka in large part because she was the closest approximation of the great Greta Garbo to be found. Indeed, Neff's acceptable singing voice (in the 1960s she became a popular cabaret singer), credibly resembles what Garbo *might* have sounded like had she been asked to sing in *Ninotchka*. Neff's vocal acumen was not unlike the functional singing of Yul Brynner as the King in *The King and I* (1951) or Rex Harrison as Henry Higgins in *My Fair Lady* (1956). Among female leads, perhaps the closest parallel was Rosalind Russell's foghorn baritone as Ruth in the film version of *Wonderful Town* (1953), who talks as much as sings "One Hundred Ways to Lose a Man." The uncertainty of Neff as a vocalist was reason enough for the stage Ninotchka to be assigned less music than Janice Dayton (Wyler), but it also makes sense dramatically since she would not feel the need to sing until she was in love. The delay of "Without Love" thus made both practical and dramatic sense. In any event, by letting Charisse's Ninotchka dance to "Silk Stockings" *before* she sings "Without Love," audiences are persuaded of her emotional transformation without her having to sing about it.

The way Porter and Feuer used Neff to depict the central character was ingenious and effective in its own way. Although she is assigned only one song of her own toward the end of Act I, "Without Love," and one duet with Steve near the beginning of Act II, "As on through the Seasons We Sail" (dropped from the film), Ninotchka receives a significant musical opportunity in the opening duet with Steve, "Paris Loves Lovers," and her brief musical introduction to Steve's "All of You," "It's a Chemical Reaction, That's All."

On both stage and screen the first chorus of "Paris Loves Lovers" belongs to Steve. Also, in both versions Steve sings the verse and chorus, after which the future lovers engage in verbal rather than musical banter. This leads to a return of the verse (Steve alone) followed by two choruses. In the first chorus Steve sings the melody, conveniently divided into short phrases (three notes or sometimes a note or two more) separated by pauses, each of which is followed by an instrumental tag.[72] In the second chorus, Ninotchka uses the counter line music of the tag for a long list of five- or six-syllable one-word commentaries ("capitalistic," "characteristic," sensualistic," "atheistic," "imperialistic," "pessimistic," "anti-communistic," "militaristic," "collectivistic," and "totalitarianistic.").

The idea of one character singing terms of endearment and the other rejecting them is similar in style if not content with what occurs in the first act finale of *Kiss Me, Kate* where Kate angrily responds to Petruchio's request to "Kiss me, Kate/Darling, devil divine" with the counter-request that he "Kindly drop dead!" In *Silk Stockings* this technique is effective because Ninotchka gets to sing a little, while Steve, played on stage by the pleasing baritone Ameche and on film by the pleasant and inimitable Astaire, gets to shine vocally.

The chorus in the film version of "Paris Loves Lovers" is the same as in the stage version. The verse offers one fascinating difference. In the first part of both versions Steve becomes Johnny One Note singing twenty-two F-naturals in a row, after which he soars with a dramatic melody for the remaining 4 measures on the words "No city but this, my friend, no city I know/Gives romance such a

Example 5.2a "Paris Loves Lovers" (beginning of verse) in *Silk Stockings*

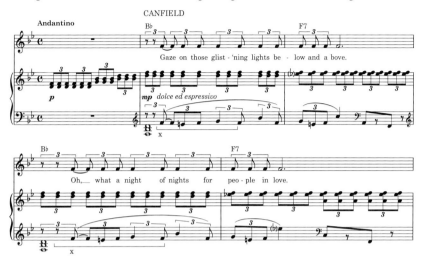

Example 5.2b "Paris Loves Lovers" (beginning chorus) in *Silk Stockings*.

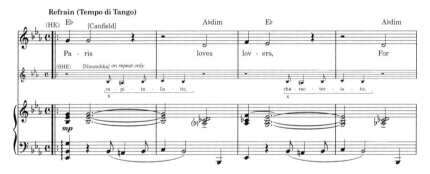

chance to grow and grow." But only in the stage version does the orchestra accompany the monotone vocal line with a musical foreshadowing of the *counter line*. The distinctive musical line will return in the first chorus in the orchestra and the repeat of the chorus when it is sung by Ninotchka. In Musical Example 5.2a and b, the parallels between the verse and chorus are placed in brackets and marked with an "X."

Immediately prior to "Paris," Ninotchka finally sings a song on her own, if only for a grand total of forty-six seconds, "It's a Chemical Reaction, That's All," which displays the simplicity of a limerick and a narrative flavor of Reverend Moon's "Be Like the Blue Bird" from *Anything Goes*.[73] The B section of this AAB miniature begins with a short waltz (still the central love trope in the 1950s) for the duration of a single phrase, appropriately on the words, "Say in love with you I fall." In *Ninotchka*, the title character agrees that Leon's "general appearance is not distasteful," but responds clinically to his question about whether he might be falling in love with her: "You are bringing in wrong values. Love is a romantic designation for a most ordinary biological, or shall we say chemical process. A lot of nonsense is talked and written about it."[74] In *Silk Stockings* Ninotchka *sings* her lecture to Steve when they return to his room after sharing a meal and an afternoon of sightseeing.

"Without Love," Ninotchka's one full-fledged solo number in the stage and film version is an effective ballad. The verse that lasts twenty-three measures begins in a dark F minor for the first eight measures before the F minor harmony underneath the words "How little I knew until very lately" turns into A-flat major to support the contrasting sentiment, "You opened my eyes to joys which had missed me." The song is in an AB form comprised of two 16-measure phrases that feature a prominent rising half-step in every phrase for the first 20 measures. As Ninotchka's passion grows in intensity, the half-steps also gradually ascend from G-sharp to D: G-sharp-A, A-B-flat, C-sharp-D. According to his early biographer and friend George Eells, "Without Love" was "the number Cole considered the best in the show."[75] Unfortunately, the message of this beautiful song ("For a woman to a man is just a woman,/But a man to a woman is her life") is destined to remain an embarrassment for the foreseeable future.

In the stage version, Porter assigned Steve (Ameche) two of the show's finest ballads, one in each act. The first is the show's biggest hit "All of You." Much has been written about the accomplished and apt lyrics of this song, including its pervasive monosyllabic simplicity (63 out of its 68 words) and the suggestive lyrics of Steve's full tour of Ninotchka's body from mouth to south (lyrics considered problematic to the Production Code). Porter's choice of words also ably employ theatrical agent lingo, such as when Steve expresses his desire to "gain complete *control*" and "handle even the heart and *soul*" of Ninotchka and his plea for her to love "a small percent" of him.[76] The music, arranged in an ABAC form is striking rhythmically by the way nearly every measure (19 out of 24) is filled for its first three (out of 4) beats with a dotted half-note on pitches that gradually rise five notes up a scale from an A-flat to an E-flat, the high note arriving fittingly on the climactic "small percent." See Figure 5.5.

Between "Siberia" and "The Red Blues" in the stage version, Steve sang his big second act ballad, the title song "Silk Stockings," which corresponds in its placement, sentiment, and minor mode to the moment Fred Graham sings of his anticipated loss of Lilli Vanessi in "So in Love" from *Kiss Me, Kate* and like its predecessor also in the minor (Russian/Jewish) mode. In the lyrics to the stage version, Steve, who has just learned about Ninotchka's return to Russia, laments

Fig. 5.5 "All of You." Fred Astaire (Steve Canfield) and Cyd Charisse (Ninotchka) in the film *Silk Stockings* [50:11]. Screenshot.

his loss and the memories evoked by the symbolic silk stockings. The song serves a far different purpose in the film version, one of Mamoulian's most memorable alterations to the dramatic structure and mode of presentation. Instead of placing it in the latter moments of the second act, Mamoulian moved "Silk Stockings" to the virtual center between "Satin and Silk" and "Without Love," a little past the hour mark. More important than its new placement was Mamoulian's decision to replace a *song* that Steve sings to Ninotchka with a *dance* that allows Ninotchka to express her private emotions alone.

As with much else in Mamoulian's film, the source of Ninotchka's dance can be traced to a scene in the Lubitsch film, this time when Ninotchka removes an absurd hat she has hidden in her room, the same hat she had earlier derisively dismissed with the question, "How can such a civilization survive which permits women to put things like that on their head" (shown in Figure 5.1).[77] In Eugene Loring's choreographic treatment, Charisse retrieves a stashed cache of under and over garments, most notably the silk stockings. Beginning with what sounds like an alto flute mixed with strings, the soft and subtle orchestrations of a beguine (a Porter specialty)—and later a brief but decisive waltz rhythm during the B section of the third chorus—accompany what many consider one of the finest solo dance performances in a film musical. Although he doesn't single out Charisse's solo in "Silk Stockings," this is clearly what film critic David Thomson had in mind when he wrote that Mamoulian's film "has some of the best intimate dances in the history of the musical."[78] The extended private moment, which lasts a generous 4.5 minutes, conveys Ninotchka's joy and delight in getting in touch with her potential for romance and beauty, and it is indeed a treasured moment in the history of the film musical.[79] See Figure 5.6.

Porter's predilection for the minor mode and what it might have meant to him was noted earlier, and even those who dismiss a Russian or Jewish connection

Fig. 5.6 Ninotchka (Cyd Charisse) admires her new silk stockings in the film *Silk Stockings* [65:54]. Screenshot.

accept the fact that Porter used the minor mode probably more than any of the other great songwriters of his generation. Less frequently mentioned is Porter's frequent practice of suddenly swerving to the *major* during his minor mode songs to mark an emotional change (and vice versa). Thus as with "So in Love" and other Porter romantic ballads, "Silk Stockings" starts and stays mainly in the minor mode but switches to the major at key moments, such as at the dramatic end of both the second and the final A sections of its AABA form. Melodically, just as "All of You" marks a gradual rising melodic trajectory, "Silk Stockings" presents a gradual mournful mostly chromatic descent of a sixth from A-flat to C (A-flat-G-F-E-E-flat-D-C). Porter also chose to unify the song in the B section by maintaining most of the rhythms of the A section. The stage version included a verse (removed in the film), which brought back Steve's music full circle when it recycled the idea of repeated notes from the verse of "Paris Loves Lovers."[80]

Critical Assessments

"*Silk Stockings.*" Ariana DeBose's response to the question, "What is your favorite film musical"?
—*20 Questions in 2 Minutes with Ariana DeBose* (2021)

Two New York opening night reviewers of the Broadway production noted the relative absence of dance, although one of them, Richard Watts, commented favorably on the work of choreographer Loring, who also staged the show.[81] From Walter Kerr's perspective, *Silk Stockings* had "almost no dances at all and it frequently lags for the lack of them."[82] This is where Mamoulian came to the rescue with his Big Idea to transform the dance-deprived stage version of *Silk Stockings* into a dancing vehicle for Astaire and Charisse. In a 1964 interview, Mamoulian explained his rationale and purpose: "I had two of the best dancers in the world, and what interested me was to give greater importance to the dancing than to the action proper, which was merely a repeat of *Ninotchka*. The psychological and dramatic development existed only in the dances."[83]

Mamoulian's idea to add a backstory about Ninotchka's early but long-since dormant love for ballet offered a believable rationale for the character played by Charisse. This plausibility contrasts with Charisse's role as Fiona in the film version of *Brigadoon* the previous year in which her formidable ballet skills are inexplicable. In an example of life imitating art, Charisse herself had joined the Ballet Russe de Monte Carlo at the age of fourteen, an experience that may have helped her to credibly establish Ninotchka's ballet roots and undergo a transformation from a communist official into a modern Western European woman through the medium of dance. Film musical historian Roy Hemming offered high praise for Charisse's performance: "When it comes to the dances, Charisse is in a class by herself—bringing [to] them an élan and electricity that makes her performance possibly the best-*danced* leading role anyone has done in a Hollywood musical."[84] That Hemming considered the partnership an equal one is implied when he wrote that Astaire's "dances in *Silk Stockings* remain among the best of his entire MGM career."[85]

Praise for the film can be traced to Bosley Crowther's enthusiastic plea in his *New York Times* contemporary review that "there should be legislation requiring that Fred Astaire and Cyd Charisse appear together in a musical picture at least once every two years."[86] For those familiar with both the stage work and the film, the film is regularly regarded more highly, an unusual comparative assessment that possibly contributed to the conspicuous future absence of the stage version from the Broadway repertoire.

In a thoughtful discussion of how a film can express ideological content, film critic Robin Wood offers *Silk Stockings* as a significant cultural and artistic model of its genre. In a rich examination, he explores four of its central "ideological impulses": the ideological superiority of capitalism over communism; the ideological role of women as objects of men's status and desires (see "Without Love"); "the validation of 'entertainment' as against 'art'" ("Josephine" vs. *Ode to a Tractor*); and "the opposition between an inhibiting depersonalizing system and freedom, self-expression, spontaneity."[87] What resolves and liberates these oppositions is, of course, dance. Wood also makes the point that Charisse's solo dance to "Silk Stockings" "gives unified expression to all four simultaneously," and more generally, that the vitality of the musical numbers "transcend their local ideological functions."[88]

Early in his essay, Wood states that aside from Tom Milne's unique "eloquent defense," *Silk Stockings* remains "a sadly underestimated, unjustly denigrated film."[89] During the course of his review, Wood perches dangerously on a critical limb: "Heretically, and despite Garbo, the Lubitsch touch, and the laughing scene, I enjoy *Silk Stockings* more than I enjoy *Ninotchka*—largely because of the extra dimension given by the musical numbers (or certain aspects of them), a dimension that affects the meaning and values of the film."[90] In his 1969 survey of Mamoulian's films, Milne goes still further than Wood in his positive assessment of *Silk Stockings*: "Perhaps, one day, critics, historians and those who write about the cinema will at last realize that it is one of the great musicals."[91]

More than fifty years since Milne expressed this view, this day may have arrived. How else to explain the pronouncement of the singing and dancing actress Ariana DeBose, who offered her interviewer the standard response of *Singin' in the Rain* when requested to name her favorite movie musical, but asked to return to this question at the end of the interview to clarify that actually *Silk Stockings* was *really* her favorite?[92]

Postscript: Adapting the Non-Musical Film after *Silk Stockings*

In addition to its endearing intrinsic qualities, *Silk Stockings*, as noted at the outset of this chapter, was important as one of the first stage musicals to use a non-musical film as its primary source. As shown in Table 5.4, "Stage Musicals Based on Films from *The King and I* to *The Producers*," Broadway adaptations of non-musical films since then have become increasingly ubiquitous and increasingly successful. Led by Walt Disney's film adaptation of *Beauty and the Beast* (5,341 performances) and the still-running (as of this writing) *The Lion King* (9,731 performances), twenty-two Broadway shows in the 1990s were adapted from non-musical or musical films. The new millennium launched an even greater proliferation of mainly non-musical film adaptations: twenty-six in the 2000s and forty-six in the 2010s. The exponential rise and kudzu-like growth of this subgenre is so extraordinary that the total of such adaptations in the 2010s alone equals the total of *all* stage adaptations from *Silk Stockings* to *The Producers*.

Some of these stage musicals have proved successful. In fact, they comprise nine of the twenty-five longest-running musicals of all time. Twenty of the approximately 150 adaptations so far have also enjoyed Broadway runs of 1,000 performances or more, and eighteen have received the Tony Award for Best Musical.[93] *Silk Stockings* may not have run forever as a hundred of Porter's friends

Table 5.4 Stage Musicals Based on Films from *The King and I* to *The Producers*.

The 1950s [7]

1952	**The King and I [1951] (1,246 performances) [based primarily on the film, *Anna and the King of Siam*, 1946] [Winner: Best Musical]**[a]
1953	*Hazel Flagg* (Film: *Nothing Sacred*, 1937) (190 performances) [not nominated]
1954	*Fanny* (based primarily on the film, *Fanny*, 1932)[b] (888 performances) [not nominated]
1955	*Silk Stockings* (Film: *Ninotchka*, 1939) (478 performances) [not nominated]
1957	**My Fair Lady [1956] (2,717 performances) [based significantly on the film, *Pygmalion*, 1938] [Winner: Best Musical]**[c]
1958	*Oh, Captain* (Film: *The Captain's Paradise*, 1953) (192 performances) [nominated]
1959	*Destry Rides Again* (Film: *Destry Rides Again*, 1939)[d] (473 performances) (not nominated]

The 1960s [12]

1960	**The Sound of Music [1959] (1,448 performances) [partially based on the film *Die Trapp-Familie*, 1956] [Winner: Best Musical, tied with *Fiorello!* (1959)]**[e]
1961	*Carnival* (Film: *Lili*, 1953) [nominated]
	Donnybrook! (Film: *The Quiet Man*, 1952) [not nominated]
1963	*Here's Love* (Film: *The Miracle on 34th Street*, 1947) [not nominated]
1964	*She Loves Me* [1963] (Film: *The Shop around the Corner*, 1940) [nominated][f]
1965	*Anya* (Film: *Anya*, 1956) [not nominated]
1966	*Sweet Charity* (Film: *Nights of Cabiria*, 1957) [nominated]
1967	*Henry, Sweet Henry* (Film: *The World of Henry Orient*, 1964) [not nominated]
1968	*Ilya Darling* (Film: *Never on Sunday*, 1960) [nominated]
	Golden Rainbow (Film: *A Hole in the Head*, 1959) [not nominated]
1969	*Promises, Promises* [1968] (Film: *The Apartment*, 1960) (1,281 performances) [nominated]
	La Strada (Film: *La Strada*, 1954) [not nominated]

The 1970s [13]

1970	**Applause (896 performances) (Film: *All about Eve*, 1950) [Winner: Best Musical]**
	Georgy (Film: *Georgy Girl*, 1966) [not nominated]
	Look to the Lilies (Film: *Lilies of the Field*, 1963) [not nominated]
1972	*Sugar* (Film: *Some Like It Hot*, 1959) [not nominated]

(*continued*)

Table 5.4 Continued

1973	*A Little Night Music* (500 performances) (Film: *Smiles of a Summer Night*, 1955) [Winner: Best Musical]
	Gigi (Film: *Gigi*, 1958) [not nominated]
1975	*Shenandoah* (Film: *Shenandoah*, 1965) (1,050 performances) [nominated]
1978	*On the Twentieth Century* (Film: *Twentieth Century*, 1934) [nominated]
	King of Hearts (Film: *King of Hearts*, 1977) [not nominated]
1979	*Ballroom* [1978] [Television: *Queen of the Stardust Ballroom*, 1975] [nominated]
	Carmelina (Film: *Buona Sera, Mrs. Campbell*, 1969) [not nominated]
	Saravà (Film: *Dona Flor and Her Two Husbands*, 1976) [not nominated]
	The Umbrellas of Cherbourg (Film: *The Umbrellas of Cherbourg* (Film: 1964) [not nominated]
The 1980s [15]	
1981	**42nd Street (1980) (1980: 3,486 performances; 2001 revival: 1,524 performances] (Film: *42nd Street*, 1933) [Winner: Best Musical]**
	Woman of the Year (Film: *Woman of the Year*, 1942) [nominated]
1982	**Nine (732 performances) (Film: *8½*, 1963) [Winner: Best Musical]**
	Little Shop of Horrors (Film: *Little Shop of Horrors*, 1960) [not nominated]
	Seven Brides for Seven Brothers (Film: *Seven Brides for Seven Brothers*, 1954) [not nominated]
1983	*Dance a Little Closer* (Film: *Idiot's Delight*, 1936) [not nominated]
1984	*La Cage aux folles* [1983] (Film: *La Cage aux Folles*, 1978)[g] [Winner: Best Musical]
1985	*Singin' in the Rain* (West End, 1983) (Film: *Singin' in the Rain*, 1952) [not nominated]
1986	*Raggedy Ann* (Film: *Raggedy Ann and Andy: A Musical Adventure*, 1977) [not nominated]
	Smile (Film: *Smile*, 1975) [not nominated]
1988	**The Phantom of the Opera (13,981 performances) [partially based on the silent film *The Phantom of the Opera*, 1925] [Winner: Best Musical]**
	Carrie (Film: *Carrie*, 1976) [not nominated]
	Legs Diamond (Film: *The Legend of Legs Diamond*, 1960) [not nominated]
1989	*The Baker's Wife* (West End) (Film: *The Baker's Wife*, 1938) [not nominated]
	Metropolis (West End) (Film: *Metropolis*, 1927) [not nominated]

Table 5.4 Continued

The 1990s [22]	
1990	*Grand Hotel* [1989] (Film: *Grand Hotel*, 1932) (1,017 performances) [nominated]
	Meet Me in St. Louis [1989] (Film: *Meet Me in St. Louis*, 1944 [nominated]
1991	*Nick and Nora* (Film: *The Thin Man*, 1934) [not nominated]
1992	*My Favorite Year* (Film: *My Favorite Year*, 1982) (not nominated]
1993	*The Goodbye Girl* (Film: *The Goodbye Girl*, 1977) [nominated]
	The Red Shoes (Film: *The Red Shoes*, 1948) [not nominated]
1994	**Passion (280 performances) (Film: *Passione d'Amore*, 1981) [Winner: Best Musical]**
	Beauty and the Beast (Film: *Beauty and the Beast*, 1991) [nominated]
1995	**Sunset Boulevard (West End, 1993 [1,530 performances]; Broadway, 1994 [977 performances]) (Film: *Sunset Boulevard*, 1950) [Winner: Best Musical]**
	Victor/Victoria (Films: 1982; *Viktor und Viktoria*, 1933) [not nominated]
1996	*Big* (Film: *Big*, 1988) [not nominated]
	The Fields of Ambrosia (Film: *The Traveling Executioner*, 1970) [not nominated]
	Martin Guerre (West End, 1996) (Film: *The Return of Martin Guerre*, 1982) [not nominated]
	State Fair (Films: *State Fair*, 1945 and *State Fair*, 1962) [not nominated]
	Scrooge (West End) (Film: *Scrooge*, 1970) [not nominated]
	State Fair (Films: 1945 and 1962) [not nominated]
	Whistle Down the Wind (West End) (Film: 1961) [not nominated]
1998	**The Lion King [1997] (9,731 performances, still running as of this writing) (Film: *The Lion King*, 1994) [Winner: Best Musical]**
	Dr. Doolittle (West End) [Film: *Dr. Doolittle*] [not nominated]
	Footloose (Film, *Footloose*, 1984) [not nominated]
	High Society (Film: *High Society*, 1956) [not nominated]
1999	*Saturday Night Fever* (Film: *Saturday Night Fever*) [not nominated}
The 2000s [the first three out of 26]	
2001	**The Producers (2,502 performances) (Film: *The Producers*, 1968) [Winner: Best Musical]**
	The Full Monty [2000] [Film: *The Full Monty*, 1997] [nominated]
	Peggy Sue Got Married (West End, 2001) (Film: *Peggy Sue Got Married*, 1986) [not nominated]

(continued)

Table 5.4 Continued

ᵃ After prompting from Gertrude Lawrence, who wanted to play Anna Leonowens in a musical adaptation of *Anna and the King of Siam*, Rodgers and Hammerstein arranged a private screening
of the 1946 non-musical film starring Irene Dunne and Rex Harrison. Realizing that it "had the
making of a beautiful musical play," Rodgers and Hammerstein soon began to work on *The King
and I* as a star vehicle for Lawrence (Rodgers, *Musical Stages*, 270). Despite the recognized pri-
macy of this film in the genesis of this show, the original posters, credit lines, and most subsequent
references, including *New Grove*, repeat the incorrect rubric, "based on the novel, *Anna and the
King of Siam*, by Margaret Landon," rather than acknowledging its indebtedness to the film script
by Talbot Jennings and Sally Benson (Shooting Final, October 15, 1945). Not only does the musical
borrow much of its plot structure from the film and even the king's famous "et cetera, et cetera, et
cetera," a number of passages from the screenplay are quoted verbatim in Hammerstein's libretto.

ᵇ The film *Fanny* from 1961 directed by Joshua Logan was not a musical film, but the title song was
used over the main title, and the composer Harold Rome used material from the stage musical for
the underscoring.

ᶜ While George Bernard Shaw's play *Pygmalion* (1913) was the central source of *My Fair Lady*, the
latter borrowed considerably from Shaw's *Pygmalion* screenplay published in 1941, which included
reworked versions of five film scenes not part of the original play. These additions are discussed in
Block, *Enchanted Evenings*, 267–68 and Donald P. Costello, *The Serpent's Eye: Shaw and the Cinema*
(Notre Dame, IN: University of Notre Dame Press, 1965), 53–68. On the genesis of *My Fair Lady* as
a whole, see Dominic McHugh, *Lovely: The Life and Times of "My Fair Lady"* (New York: Oxford
University Press, 2012).

ᵈ The film *Destry Rides Again* was preceded by a 1930 novel written by Max Brand, but its connection
to this source is limited to its title.

ᵉ Despite its origins in Baroness Maria von Trapp's 1949 autobiography, *The von Trapp Family
Singers*, Howard Lindsay and Russel Crouse adopted material from the German film *Die Trapp-
Familie* (1956), including the captain's whistling for his children, the idea to make play clothes from
curtains, and the Trapp Family performance song contest at the Kaltzberg (i.e., Salzburg) Festival
[1937].

ᶠ Although the official credit line for *She Loves Me* was "based on a play by Miklós László" [*Parfumerie*
or *Perfume Shop*], librettist Joe Masteroff's main source was Samson Raphaelson's screenplay to
Lubitsch's *The Shop Around the Corner*. In fact, Raphaelson had also distanced himself from László's
play: "Nothing, not one scene, not one line of dialogue, coincides with the film" (Michael D. Rinella,
Margaret Sullavan: The Life and Career of a Reluctant Star [Jefferson, NC: McFarland, 2019], 130).
Philip Lambert clarifies that although Masteroff "worked primarily from Raphaelson's screen-
play," in a number of places he "either incorporates ideas from László [which he did 'not recall
ever reading' and thus learned about from a collaborator] or develops new elements of his own"
(Lambert, *To Broadway, To Life!: The Musical Theater of Bock and Harnick* [New York: Oxford
University Press, 2011], 112–13).

ᵍ *La Cage aux folles* was restricted from using the 1978 film version. Consequently, the stage adaptation was based entirely on the 1973 stage play by Jean Poiret.

- *The listings in Table 5.4 show the year the musical appeared on Broadway or the West End, the film
it was based on, and whether the stage show was nominated for a Tony Award for Best Musical.*
- *The musicals in bold type received the Tony Award for Best Musical.*

had hoped, but this gem of a show (and film) helped to plant a seed for the future. That future is now, as non-musical films have replaced plays, novels, short
stories, and original properties as the major source for Broadway shows. In short,
the hyped phrase "read the book, see the movie" has been replaced with a new
reality, "see the movie, see the musical."

6

Something to Dance About

West Side Story on Stage and Screen

There was one area where we did break ground, and this is in the
subject matter. That was the beginning of it being OK to die, to be
raped, to be murdered in a musical.

—Arthur Laurents on the PBS television series,
Broadway: The American Musical

Introducing a Stage and Film Classic

The 1957 Broadway stage version of *West Side Story* arrived in the latter part of
one of the Golden Age's most glorious and memorable decades, a decade that
began with *Guys and Dolls* and *The King and I* and concluded with *Gypsy* and
The Sound of Music. Its film arrival in September 1961 followed a parade of popular and (relatively) faithful 1950s adaptations, including *Annie Get Your Gun*,
Kiss Me Kate,[1] *Guys and Dolls*, and four musicals explored in earlier chapters of
A Fine Romance (*Call Me Madam*, *Brigadoon*, *Oklahoma!*, and *Silk Stockings*).
Other financially lucrative and often critically successful film adaptations of the
era were *The Pajama Game* and *Damn Yankees*, based on recent stage hits by
Richard Adler and Jerry Ross in 1954 and 1955 and filmed in close succession in
1957 and 1958, and four films based on Rodgers and Hammerstein stage classics
(*Oklahoma!*, *Carousel*, *The King and I*, and *South Pacific*).

The last item on this impressive list, the long-awaited 1958 film version of
South Pacific (1949), although relentlessly criticized for its unsubtle use of color
filters, nonetheless offered a stunningly cinematic vision (filmed on location on
the Hawaiian island of Kauai and the Fiji Islands) and a nearly complete score
with the rejected stage song ("My Girl Back Home") serving as a welcome la-
gniappe. Like other musicals of its time, it also retained major remnants from the
stage version, this time its original stage director and co-librettist, Joshua Logan,
the original Bloody Mary, Juanita Hall (dubbed by the London Mary, Muriel
Smith), and Ray Walston, who played Mr. Applegate (i.e., the devil) on stage and
film in *Damn Yankees* and Luther Billis in *South Pacific*'s touring and London
companies.[2]

A Fine Romance. Geoffrey Block, Oxford University Press. © Oxford University Press 2023.
DOI: 10.1093/oso/9780197501733.003.0006

West Side Story was famously eclipsed by *The Music Man* as the Best Musical of 1957 at the Tony Awards. It was also *only* the twelfth longest-running show of the 1950s, behind such enduring favorites as *My Fair Lady*, *The Sound of Music*, *The Music Man*, *The King and I*, and *Guys and Dolls*. Still, four years after its Broadway debut, *West Side Story* was a promising prospect for a film adaptation. Continuing in the spirit of 1950s film adaptations, studio executives were confident that the enterprise would be more likely to succeed commercially as well as artistically if the adaptation preserved as much as possible of its stage libretto, lyrics, music, and especially Jerome Robbins's original choreography.

The film version of *West Side Story*, co-directed by Robert Wise and Robbins, turned out to be both a (mostly) faithful and comprehensive adaptation of a stage musical and an unprecedentedly popular financial bonanza. But it delivered far more. Although, as we will note, the film, like its stage source, is not without controversies, it nonetheless enjoyed a popularity, a critical acclaim, and an unprecedented destiny not shared by any of its 1940s and 1950s predecessors. According to Richard Barrios, "where a *South Pacific* (1958) or a *My Fair Lady* (1964) will eternally be 'the film of the show,' *West Side Story* stands on in its inherent merit and impact as well as that of its material."[3]

Despite its fidelity, what film viewers saw was not quite the same as what they witnessed on stage. In particular, although Ernest Lehman's screenplay retained much, perhaps even most, of Arthur Laurents's book verbatim, it rearranged the dramatic and musical narrative that came between the first five songs and the final three. Leonard Bernstein's score naturally adhered to the new order, but aside from the removal of the "Somewhere Ballet," the acclaimed score itself was left mostly untouched. The decision to keep the music intact, albeit rearranged, was in the sharpest possible contrast to the merciless slashing of *On the Town*'s score only twelve years earlier (discussed in chapter 3).

The reconception of "America" required Stephen Sondheim to make significant changes to its lyrics (discussed later in this chapter), but other stage lyrics were only modestly altered to conform to film decorum and textual changes in keeping with the revised song order. Supporting its fidelity to the stage source, the film version of *West Side Story* is the only adaptation explored in *A Fine Romance* that retained its original stage director *and* its choreographer: Robbins. Proclaiming Robbins's pivotal role, the stage version credits noted that the work was "based on a conception of Jerome Robbins" (to remind everyone that it was Robbins's idea to adapt Shakespeare's *Romeo and Juliet* into a modern drama) and that the "Entire Production [Was] Directed and Choreographed by Jerome Robbins." See Figure 6.1.

Two decades earlier, in Richard Rodgers's 17½-minute ballet, "Slaughter on Tenth Avenue" in *On Your Toes* (1936), choreographer George Balanchine surpassed audience expectations concerning the extent dance could advance

Fig. 6.1 Jerome Robbins directs Carol Lawrence and Larry Kert in rehearsal for the stage production of *West Side Story* (1957). Photo by Friedman-Abeles © Billy Rose Theatre Division, The New York Public Library for the Performing Arts.

a show's plot. Less than ten years later, de Mille's dream ballets in Rodgers and Hammerstein's *Oklahoma!* (1943) and *Carousel* (1945) further enhanced the choreographic dimension, conveying the deeper psychological truths that dance and mime can provide, especially in an extended dream ballet. Soon Michael Kidd would use dance to establish the personalities, character, and idiosyncratic milieu of Damon Runyon's Runyonland in *Guys and Dolls* (1950), and Robbins himself choreographed an integral ballet in *The King and I* (1951), "The Small House of Uncle Thomas." The choreography in *West Side Story* went still further than these dance landmarks with a conceptual vision and skill in portraying dramatic action through the medium of dance and making choreography indispensable.

Tony and Maria, the modern counterparts of Romeo and Juliet, provided the main lyrical moments in songs like "Tonight," and "One Hand, One Heart," and the duet, "A Boy Like That/I Have a Love," in which Maria persuades her friend Anita (a youthful counterpart of Shakespeare's elderly Nurse) to put love ahead of her anger, grief, and hate, offers an unmistakably operatic scene. But Robbins conceived the central dramatic events through dance rather than song: the Prologue, "Dance at the Gym," the dancing component of "America," the "Cool" Fugue, and "The Rumble" in Act I, the "Somewhere Dream Ballet" and the "Taunting" of Anita in Act II. With the exception of the "Somewhere

Ballet," Robbins's dramatic use of dance would be considered essential in the metamorphosis from the theater stage to a movie screen.

West Side Story is one of the most discussed stage musicals in the scholarly and popular literature. In the new millennium alone, the stage work, the film, or both have inspired the publication of seven books.[4] As a result, scholars and general readers have learned much about the genesis of the stage and film version and their dramatic, musical, and cinematic content. All that is required here before we move on to issues of adaptation is an encapsulation of the stage and film origins and a brief discussion of the central departures from their source (Shakespeare's Romeo and Juliet, published in 1597), and from each other.

In all likelihood, many reading this paragraph know from quiz programs and crossword puzzles (if not from program notes) that once upon a time there was an East Side Story conceived by Robbins in 1949, "a modern version of Romeo and Juliet set in slums at the coincidence of Easter-Passover celebrations."[5] Robbins (1918–1998) was able to interest playwright and screenwriter Laurents (1917–2011) in writing the book on this subject and Bernstein (1918–1990), his collaborator on Fancy Free, On the Town, and Facsimile, to compose its music.[6] Due to various individual commitments, the trio didn't seriously return to their "Romeo" project until 1955. By then, they "abandoned the whole Jewish-Catholic premise as not very fresh" in favor of "two teen-age gangs, one the warring Puerto Ricans, the other self-styled 'Americans,'" the Sharks and the Jets.[7]

Soon Robbins made a persuasive case for a larger dance component, starting with the transformation of the opening Prologue (originally conceived as a traditional song and dance number), into a pathbreaking dance-only opener during which the Jets and the Sharks fight a battle that paralleled the skirmish between Shakespeare's warring families, the Montagues and the Capulets. Since the increased role of dance necessitated a far more extensive musical score than originally planned, Bernstein, who wanted to write all the lyrics, realized he needed a co-lyricist, a task assigned in November 1955 to Stephen Sondheim (1930–2021), then twenty-five. Over the next few months, Bernstein would assign Sondheim the sole responsibility for the vast majority of lyrics that remained.

In adapting Shakespeare's play, Laurents's libretto reflects the result of considerable collaborative discussion that necessitated at least eight extant libretto drafts completed between January 1956, two months after Sondheim joined the entourage, to July 1957, one month before opening night.[8] Following a casting search that lasted for months, Robbins insisted on and was granted what was then an unprecedented eight-week rehearsal schedule (twice the usual length).

Laurents's libretto displays two significant dramatic departures from Shakespeare's plot. The first was the substitution of fate with free will when

Laurents replaced the tragic coincidences that prevented the news of Juliet's magic sleep from reaching Romeo in time. Consequently, Shakespeare's Romeo was led to think that the sleeping Juliet was dead and took his own life in despair. In Laurents's libretto, Anita, having barely survived the sexual aggression of the Jets during her attempt to deliver a message from Maria to Tony, instead deliberately asks Doc (Friar Lawrence) to convey the false message that Maria is dead. In response, Tony, with nothing to live for, runs out into the deserted New York streets to ask Chino (Paris) to "get me, too." Moments after Tony finds Maria and realizes that she *is* alive, Chino fulfills Tony's death wish. Years later, Laurents expressed his pride that he had come up with a "believable substitute for the philter" and considered this solution "better than the original story."[9]

The second major departure from Shakespeare was the decision to let Maria live after she and Tony are allowed to sing a few phrases of "Somewhere" before Tony dies from the gunshot wound inflicted by Chino. Robbins credited Richard Rodgers for keeping Maria alive when he said that "she's dead already, after this all happens to her."[10] The first two libretto drafts follow Shakespeare and included Maria's suicide (erroneously thinking that Tony, like Juliet's Romeo, was dead, she plunges a pair of dressmaking shears into her stomach). If *West Side Story* were Wagner's *Tristan and Isolde*, Maria would have no choice but to sing a Liebestod over Tony's dead body, as Isolde did in Tristan's dying arms.[11]

Actually, an aria for Maria was the plan, and the four collaborators unanimously agreed it was Bernstein's duty to convert the prose speech Laurents wrote for Maria into music. Bernstein was unable to comply. In a 1984 interview, the composer recalled that he made four or five attempts to create an "aria" for Maria based on Laurents's prose, but "never got past six bars with it."[12] If anyone wants to know the difference between an opera and a musical, we need look no further than Bernstein's "difficult, painful but surgically clean decision not to set it at all."[13] In a musical that contains spoken dialogue, Bernstein had the freedom to make this painful choice. In an opera, he would have been obligated to go back to the woodshed and come up with a musical solution. See Figure 6.2.

Several scholars have weighed in on the relative merits of Bernstein's decision to let Maria speak rather than to make her sing. Joseph P. Swain laments that "Maria's last speech should indeed have been her biggest aria."[14] Jon Alan Conrad considers this "failure to find music for Maria's final scene," one of the musical's 'weak points.'"[15] For an eloquent defense of Bernstein's inaction, Stephen Banfield praised *West Side Story* for providing a creative alternative, indeed a corrective to the dramaturgy of opera, by not becoming a "goddamned Bernstein opera" (to quote Bernstein) and concluded that "Maria's final speech works perfectly well as dialogue."[16] The debate will doubtless continue.

Fig. 6.2 Leonard Bernstein and the cast during the rehearsal for the stage production of *West Side Story* (1957). Photo by Friedman-Abeles © Billy Rose Theatre Division, The New York Public Library for the Performing Arts.

Differences between the Stage and Film Versions of *West Side Story*

Despite its adherence to the narrative content of its stage predecessor, the film version of *West Side Story* offers a cinematic perspective that considerably alters the theatrical experience. Two film historians enumerate differences between what happens on the stage versus the screen with Misha Berson offering eleven changes and Richard Barrios offering twice as many in an overlapping list.[17] The changes fall into four categories: (1) changes to the music (cuts, additions, and tweaking); (2) changes to the dialogue; (3) changes to the lyrics; and (4) changes in the song order. The next section will discuss each category.

1. Changes to the Music

The opening twenty minutes—filmed on location on the Upper West Side, mainly on the construction site of the future Lincoln Center—constitute perhaps the single greatest cinematic transformation of *West Side Story*'s stage version. But before viewers see "New York, New York" the screen presents the abstract graphics of the ubiquitous Saul Bass over a changing colored background that gradually metamorphoses into a clear and realistic aerial view of lower Manhattan filmed in glorious Panavision 70. Sounding underneath the graphics is a newly conceived overture. One month prior to opening night on Broadway, Bernstein explained in a letter to his wife Felicia that he had been "up all night trying to put together an overture of sorts, to carry us through until I do a real good prelude."[18]

At the end of the film overture, an unseen helicopter and its camera make their northward journey from lower Manhattan to a playground on the Upper West Side, accompanied by whistles, bongo drums, and ambient city sounds. The camera alights on the Jets, a group of street toughs, a toughness undermined by their clean-cut, preppy demeanor that might cause them to be mistaken for the dancers in the GAP jeans television commercials from 2000.[19] To make the idea of a street gang demonstrating well-executed ballet steps more credible, Robbins doubled the length of the Prologue to create a natural evolution from walking to dancing before eventually a balletic street fight ensues with the rival Sharks. To accommodate this new film requirement, Bernstein, who was contracted to write additional music as needed, added four minutes of technically new but related material to serve Robbins's expanded opening.[20] See Figures 6.3 and 6.4.

As noted earlier, the film removed no songs but omitted the musically rich "Somewhere Ballet," the only significant reduction of Bernstein's large score (a little under seven minutes). This consequential decision did not come easily. In October 1960, before the filming of "Dance at the Gym" was completed, Robbins was fired and even barred from the set due to his slow filming pace and resulting cost over-runs.[21] The question of whether to film the "Somewhere Ballet" was

Fig. 6.3 The Jets. Russ Tamblyn [Riff] and the Jets in the film *West Side Story* [7:52]. Screenshot.

Fig. 6.4 And the Sharks. George Chakiris (Bernardo) and two Sharks in the film *West Side Story* [9:27]. Screenshot.

answered when Robert Wise (1914–2005) decided to avoid additional costs and delete this elaborate second act dance number prior to filming, a victory for movie realism over theatrical fantasy.

In the stage version, the "Somewhere Ballet" begins with a duet between Tony and Maria, ending with the line, "Somewhere there's got to be some place for you and for me." It continues with a brief "Transition to Scherzo" (0:38) and "Scherzo" (1:31), both emphasizing the "Somewhere" motive. The ballet scenario then indicates that "the walls of the apartment begin to move off, and the city walls surrounding them begin to close in" and Tony and Maria overcome the gangs and violence to break through into an idyllic "world of space and air and sun." As Tony and Maria dance, stage audiences hear "Somewhere" off-stage sung by the opera singer Reri Grist, who also played Consuelo in the original production.

The stage ballet concludes with a Procession and Nightmare that starts with Tony and Maria holding hands and then leading the Jet and the Sharks. The orchestra foreshadows the future sung duet "I Have a Love" between Maria and Anita and again at the end of the film to accompany the procession of Jets and Sharks as they carry Tony's body away. The chorus of Jets and Sharks starts to sing "There's a place for us" (the opening lyric of "Somewhere") before being interrupted by the dramatic Nightmare music that supports Tony and Maria's hopeless attempt to avoid the deadly outcome that concluded the first act. The stage ballet ends with Tony and Maria clinging to one another in Maria's bedroom and singing the conclusion of "Somewhere." With the exception of the Procession motive, the film discards all of this ballet material. Instead, film viewers hear and see Tony and Maria sing "Somewhere" in an awake state in Maria's bedroom.[22]

2. Changes to the Book and Dialogue

Lehman's screenplay included a few, but only a few, lines of additional dialogue such as when, after surviving her near rape by the Jets in "Taunting," Lehman's Anita vehemently adds the words, "Don't you touch me." Lehman's film script also added the line, "Not with bullets and guns—with hate" for Maria during her final speech, replaced "I hate now" with "I have hate!" in the same speech, added a reference to Tony's ability as a street fighter, and altered the rhyming stage pledge between Tony and Riff, "sperm to worm," to the less seminal "birth to Earth."

For those attentive to such details, the film version also reversed the partners of the Jets girls Velma and Graziella (though both Velmas were played by Carole D'Andrea). On stage, Velma is paired with Riff and Graziella with Action; in the film Velma is paired with Ice and Graziella with Riff. The film version altered Diesel's name to Ice, who, as his new name suggests, appropriately leads the song "Cool" in the absence of the recently deceased Riff. Three stage Sharks (Anxious, Nibbles, and Moose) are given more authentic Latino film names (Loco, Rocco, and Del Campo). Finally, the film adds a brief appearance of the bridal shop owner, Madame Lucia, who, along with the other adults (with the exceptions of Doc, Schrank, Krupke, and Glad Hand), remains unseen onstage.

3. Changes to the Lyrics

The lyrics to *West Side* raised two red flags for the Production Code Administration (PCA), far fewer than what Cole Porter was subjected to in the film adaptations of *Kiss Me, Kate* and *Silk Stockings*. The first was a lyric Anita sang in the "Tonight Quintet" that PCA director Geoffrey M. Shurlock considered "unacceptably sex-suggestive": "Don't matter if he's tired,/As long as he's hot" (with "hot" rhyming with "what").[23] In *Finishing the Hat* Sondheim notes that he changed the offending lyric "in my best inoffensive style" with a lyric in which the word "here" replaces "hot" to rhyme with "poor dear."[24] In a memo to co-producer Walter Mirisch, Shurlock "urged" him to refrain from mentioning the term "social disease" in "Gee, Officer Krupke" on the grounds that it "could be considered offensive by many people" and "vulnerable to the charge of being in bad taste."[25]

Robbins, Wise, and Mirisch disregarded this last PCA request. They did, however, replace the word "schmuck" with "slob" as Goddard Lieberson, who produced the original cast recording, also insisted. This led to the change in the Broadway rhyme from "buck/schmuck" to "job/slob" in the film.[26] Sondheim also replaced "bastard/plastered" with "mommy/Commie" and "S.O.B/tea" with the safer, more pedestrian "me/tea." Sondheim's boldest original intention, the "expletive heard round the world" (i.e., the "F" word) remained unheard, even in the stage version.[27] Thus on the stage, in the cast recording, and in the film versions, the Jets' final message to Office Krupke remained "Krup you!"[28]

The song that underwent the most substantial lyrical reworking was "America." For the stage version, Robbins had insisted that this be performed by only the Shark girls. In the absence of male Sharks, the lyric consisted of an argument between Anita and Rosalia, in which Anita scolds her friend for preferring the crowded and poor conditions in Puerto Rico to the richer possibilities of life in America. For the film, Robbins accepted the suggestion to return to the pre-stage song and dance conception that included the Shark men and contained Sondheim's original lyrics. Instead of Anita and Rosalia, the argument in this earlier discarded and now resurrected version is between Anita and her boyfriend Bernardo. Anita still extols the virtues of life in America, but now it is her new sparring partner who calls attention to the prejudice Puerto Ricans face in their efforts to become assimilated Americans. See Figure 6.5.

The differences between the two sets of lyrics, both reprinted in *Finishing the Hat*, are considerable. They start at the very beginning of the verse when on stage Rosalia sings "Puerto Rico/You lovely island/Island of tropical breezes" and Anita responds contrarily with "Puerto Rico/You ugly island/Island of tropic diseases." For the film, Sondheim returns to his original lyric with Anita's "Puerto Rico/My heart's devotion—/Let it sink back in the ocean."[29] After the final two lines of the verse and the first four of the chorus (from "I like the island Manhattan—" to "for a small fee in America"), the two "America" lyrics for the most part go their separate ways. All that remain are a couple of related lyrics, Anita's "I know you can get on" (rhyming with "San Juan"), and the final two lines that address the

Fig. 6.5 Rita Moreno (Anita) and the Shark women with the Shark men looking on in "America" in the film *West Side Story* [54:59]. Screenshot.

possibility no one will be left to cheer the departing Rosalia/Bernardo in San Juan because all of Puerto Rico has moved to America.

4. Song Order

Compared with the "circular narratives" that director Quentin Tarantino subjects his viewers to in *Pulp Fiction* (1994)—with only one of the eight film sequences appearing in the correct chronological order—the changes in song order in the film adaptation of *West Side Story* might be considered mild.[30] Nevertheless, even though the film preserves *all* the songs, their reordering greatly influences the dramatic trajectory of what movie theater audiences experience. The only major film adaptation of a Broadway musical from the era that alters the song order to a greater extent is perhaps *Flower Drum Song* the following year, in which six of the seven major songs occur in significantly different places in the film narrative (see chapter 7).

In the film version of *West Side Story*, less than half (seven) of the sixteen musical numbers appear in their original stage order: Prologue, "Jet Song," "Something's Coming," "The Dance at the Gym," and "Maria" (the first five musical numbers) and "A Boy like That/I Have a Love" and "Taunting" (the last two songs before the Finale). The last three musical numbers of Act I on the stage ("One Hand, One Heart," "Tonight Quintet," and "The Rumble") appear in a different position relative to "Krupke" and "I Fee Pretty" but consecutively in the film.

This leaves the following departures from stage to screen (see Table 6.1, "*West Side Story*" on Stage and Screen"): (1) "Tonight" and "America" are now reversed; (2) "Gee, Officer Krupke" switches positions with "Cool," which alters its relation to "The Rumble." On stage, "Cool" appeared three numbers prior to "The Rumble"; in the film it arrives three numbers after "The Rumble" that ended Act I in the stage version; and (3) "I Feel Pretty" significantly opens Act II *after* "The Rumble." In the film, "I Feel Pretty" occurs between the newly placed "Krupke" and "One Hand, One Heart," three numbers *before* "The Rumble."

In considering the pros and cons of these changes, determined mainly by Wise in consultation with the Mirisch brothers and mostly accepted positively by critics and audiences, it is important to consider the larger context in which most stage musicals then and now are presented within a two-act structure separated by an intermission. To encourage audiences to come back for more, the first act, which in most cases occupies about two-thirds of the show, usually ends with a dramatic event that leaves the story unresolved and in need of a second act. Several bona fide gang members (non-actors) that Robbins invited to see the show on Broadway left after the first act thinking that "the rumble that left two dead bodies on stage at the Act One curtain seemed like a natural conclusion."[31]

Table 6.1 *West Side Story* on Stage and Screen.

Stage 1957	Screen 1961
Act I	Overture/Main Title (0:04)
Prologue (Instrumental) (282)	Prologue (Instrumental) (6:07)
Jet Song (Calin and Jets) (285)	Jet Song (Tamblyn and Jets) (20:53)
Something's Coming (Kert) (287)	Something's Coming (Beymer) (26:15)
The Dance at the Gym (Instrumental) (290)	The Dance at the Gym (Instrumental) (31:40)
Maria (Kert) (292)	Maria (Beymer) (44:14)
Tonight (Lawrence, Kert) (294)	**America (Moreno, Chakiris, Sharks, and Girls) (49:35)**
America (Rivera, Cooper, and Girls) (297)	**Tonight (Wood, Beymer) (57:37)**
Cool (Calin and Jets) (301)	**Gee, Officer Krupke (Tamblyn and Jets) (66:12)**
	I Feel Pretty (Wood, Grist, Cooper, and Miya) (81:45)
One Hand, One Heart (Kert, Lawrence) (306)	One Hand, One Heart (Beymer, Wood) (89:52)
Tonight Quintet (Kert, Lawrence, Rivera, Calin, LeRoy) (307)	Tonight Quintet (Beymer, Wood, Moreno, Tamblyn, Chakiris, Jets, and Sharks) (92:55)
The Rumble (Instrumental) (311)	The Rumble (Instrumental) (99:42)
Act II	
I Feel Pretty (Lawrence and the Girls) (313)	
Ballet Sequence (316)	
Transition to Scherzo (Instrumental)	
Scherzo (Instrumental)	
Somewhere (Grist)	Somewhere (Beymer, Wood) (109:12)
Procession and Nightmare (Instrumental)	
Gee, Officer Krupke (Jets) (319)	Cool (Smith and Jets) (115:52)
A Boy Like That/I Have a Love (Lawrence, Rivera) (323)	A Boy Like That/I Have a Love (Wood, Moreno) (124:42)
Taunting (Instrumental) (326)	Taunting (Instrumental) (133:30)
Finale (Lawrence, Kert) (328)	Finale (Instrumental) (143:09)

- *Numbers in parentheses in the stage column refer to page numbers in Arthur Laurents,* West Side Story, *in Great Musicals of the American Theatre, vol. 1, ed. Stanley Richards (Radnor, PA: Chilton, 1973).*
- *Dubbing Summary: (1) Marni Nixon did all the dubbing for Natalie Wood's songs and a few notes for Rita Moreno in the "Tonight Quintet"; (2) Jim Bryant did all the dubbing for Richard Beymer;*

Table 6.1 Continued

(3) Betty Wand dubbed Moreno in "A Boy Like That/I Have a Love"; and (4) Tucker Smith (Ice) dubbed for Russ Tamblyn in the "Jet Song."

• *The songs listed in bold in the screen column appear in a different order than in the stage version.*

• *Numbers in parentheses in the screen column refer to film timings.*

MAJOR SINGING AND DANCING AND SELECTED ROLES

Stage: Carol Lawrence (Maria); Larry Kert (Tony); Chita Rivera (Anita); Mickey Calin (Riff); Ken LeRoy (Bernardo); Art Smith (Doc); Reri Grist (Consuelo/A Girl); Marilyn Cooper (Rosalia); Joanne Miya [Nobuko Miyamoto] (Francisca); Lee Becker (Anybodys); David Winter (Baby John); TONY MORDENTE (A-Rab); Eddie Roll (Action); Martin Charnin (Big Deal); JAY NORMAN (replaced Eddie Verso as Juano)

Screen: Natalie Wood (Maria); Richard Beymer (Tony); Rita Moreno (Anita); Russ Tamblyn (Riff); George Chakiris (Bernardo); Simon Oakland (Schrank); Ned Glass (Doc); William Bramley (Krupke); Tucker Smith (Ice); Yvonne Othon [Wilder] (Consuelo); MORDENTE (Action); David Winters (A-Rab); Eliot Feld (Baby John); NORMAN (Pepe)

• *Names in capital letters indicate that a cast member appeared both on stage and in the film.*

Indeed, for many audience members such a disturbing conclusion to a first act marked a significant departure for a musical comedy in 1957.

Most films don't have intermissions, an omission that greatly alters the trajectory and pacing of the narrative. Instead of breaking up the viewing experience with a dramatic event, the goal was to retain the dramatic flow to the end. Ironically, the original deluxe limited engagement roadshow version of *West Side Story did* include an intermission, at least when it was shown in theaters capable of showing 70 mm. prints.[32] At the majority of theaters that did not possess this technology, the roadshow films were presented without an intermission, which in the case of *West Side Story* arrived close to the midpoint (rather than the usual two-thirds through) when Tony walks outside after the Jets' war council prior to the rumble. This earlier stopping point meant that both "The Rumble" and "I Feel Pretty" followed the Act I intermission break.

The decision to reverse "Tonight" and "America" was made over Robbins's strenuous objections.[33] The switch serves a purpose, however, by removing the first two successive "operatic" numbers ("Maria" and "Tonight"), thus offering a stronger contrast between the serious "Maria" and the musically lighter but lyrically biting "America." In the stage version, the intense earlier appearance of the Jets in "Cool" contrasted with the comical "America" for the Shark girls, whereas in the film version, the comical "Krupke" follows the romantic "Tonight" rather than "America."

The placement of "Krupke" arose in the 1985 panel discussion with the entire *West Side Story* quartet participating (Bernstein, Laurents, Robbins, and Sondheim).[34] On this historic occasion Sondheim argued that "Krupke" belonged where "Cool" had been placed (and vice versa) on the grounds that it was unlikely "a group of kids running from a double murder" would stop to sing a show-stopping "11 o'clock number."[35] Sondheim went on to explain his lack of success in persuading Laurents and Robbins to switch the numbers and how Laurents took credit for the idea and tried to sell the idea of "Krupke's" late placement under "the old Shakespearean drunken-porter principle" of breaking up a tragic story with a moment of comedy.[36] By the premiere of the stage version Sondheim changed his tune and concluded that " 'Krupke' works wonderfully in the second act."[37] This opinion was reinforced after seeing the numbers reversed in the film when he found the earlier placement far less effective and concluded that its later placement served "theatrical truth," if not "literal truth."

For the film, Wise & Co. decided to place "Krupke" far earlier in the story, right after "Tonight," with "Cool" taking "Krupke's" place after "The Rumble" and "Somewhere" (with Diesel replacing Riff who is by now dead). With Laurents literally out of the picture, Robbins now concurred with Sondheim's original view that "Krupke" worked better sooner rather than later.[38] Decades later, in an interview included in a special feature of the 2003 DVD, Sondheim recalled his initial objections in 1957 and his opinion that singing "Krupke" so late in the narrative was "just ridiculous."[39] "What they [the Jets] would do is sing 'Cool,' which is about keeping cool in a stressful situation." Sondheim continues: "Then when the movie was done, Jerry said OK. You got your wish. We'll transpose the numbers." When the time came to offer his final thoughts on the subject in *Finishing the Hat* in 2010, Sondheim was less definitive: "I'm no longer sure if it was for the better or not [the early "Krupke"], and ever since then I've been haunted by the feeling that I shouldn't have opened my mouth."[40]

Critics and scholars appear to be in agreement with the decision to exchange "Krupke" and "Cool" (with Sondheim as a definite maybe). The pros and cons of the film's placement of "I Feel Pretty" have generated less consensus. On the pro side, associate producer Saul Chaplin, who led the supervision of the overall musical component in the 1961 film, wrote in his memoir that " 'I Feel Pretty' was placed earlier so that it didn't stop the dramatic action as it had in the show."[41] Presumably this meant that Chaplin felt "I Feel Pretty" stopped the action at the beginning of Act II in the stage version because it occupied a concurrent rather than a successive position in the narrative in relation to "The Rumble." According to this line of argument, placing of "I Feel Pretty" before "One Hand, One Heart" in the film prepares viewers for the imaginary (but no less meaningful) marriage vows between Tony and Maria that create a false sense of hope for a married future and a misguided belief that love will avert a deadly gang war. Perhaps for this reason Ernesto Acevedo-Muñoz finds the earlier placement in the film "justifiable in light of María's excitement at the prospect of seeing Tony at the end of her work day."[42] While this decision is not without merit, I would argue in favor of its later stage placement, in which Maria was oblivious to the tragedy that would soon intrude on her newfound love for the man who, unbeknownst to her, has killed her brother.

For my taste, knowing what happened to Riff and Bernardo when we hear the joyous "I Feel Pretty" creates an effective and poignant irony absent in the film.[43]

In 2020, a Broadway revival was directed by Ivo van Hove and choreographed by Anne Teresa De Keersmaeker (both of whom were born in Belgium)—the first Broadway production to replace Robbins's choreography. The production made still more history (and in the process resolved placement issues) by removing Maria's 'I Feel Pretty' altogether. Although Sondheim didn't go on record concerning the merits of this decision, he has often expressed reservations that border on disdain about his lyrics for this song.[44] The gist of his criticism is that Maria doesn't possess the level of education that would enable her to sing internal rhymes like "it's *alarming* how *charming* I feel." Sondheim offers no defense for this crime against lyrical competence, but it might be said on his behalf that, other than this infraction, most of Maria's end rhymes are straightforward and appropriate to her education: "bright/tonight," "feel/real," "be/me," "key/me," and perhaps even "stunning/running" and "fine/resign." Sondheim complained at the time and many times thereafter about the "purple" patches in these and other *West Side Story* lyrics, in most cases blaming Bernstein for not letting him rewrite them.

Sondheim's indictment of the purple patches in "I Feel Pretty" (and also "Tonight") notwithstanding, the perennially clever and funny "Krupke" and the powerful emotions expressed by Maria and Anita in "A Boy Like That/I Have a Love" demonstrate the craft and range we have come to expect of Sondheim. And although some of his revised lyrics in the film may have suffered from Production Code censorship, the welcome return to his original conception of "America" effectively sharpened the contrasting views of the nationalists (Bernardo) versus the assimilationists (Anita).

A Few More Words about the Music

When it comes to the music, even those who find musicals distasteful often enjoy Bernstein's eclectic score that combines musical theater numbers like "America," "I Feel Pretty," and "Krupke" with songs that evoke opera such as "Maria," "Tonight," and "A Boy Like That/I Have a Love."[45] The dance music also offers distinctive musical styles for the Jets and the Sharks. The Jets dance to an original and idiosyncratic stylistic hybrid of bop and cool jazz, a substyle aptly labeled "crime jazz" by Phil Ford, who associates it with film noir; this is enhanced by its touch of the modernistic techniques and personal styles of Igor Stravinsky and Aaron Copland.[46] The Sharks dance to a wide range of Latinx musical genres, including the *seis*, the sole authentic example of Puerto Rican music, heard in the verse of "America."[47]

Although the Jets and Sharks inhabit separate and disparate musical spheres, in some of their musical numbers they share a common musical language. This musical sharing is most evident in the "Dance at the Gym," in which both the Jets and Sharks dance the *paso doble* and Tony and Maria dance a *cha-cha-cha* together to the music of "Maria" before Tony knows Maria's name. Soon the *cha-cha-cha* morphs into a *samba* to accompany "Maria," Tony's serenade to his new-found love.[48]

Since the film largely preserves Bernstein's stage score with its musical complexities and dramatic clarity, this chapter will only highlight a couple of musical points.[49] One of these is the significance of an ascending three-note motive, a perfect fourth followed by an augmented fourth or tritone (G-C-F-sharp), heard at the outset in the Jets gang whistle. The tritone at the end of the motive is a tense interval that evokes hate (hence the designation "hate motive"), but by re-solving the motive up a half-step to G, as it does with "Maria's" name (C-F-sharp-G), Bernstein demonstrates music's potential to serve dramatic meaning: the transformation from hate into love. Bernstein's score also exhibits dramatically meaningful thematic foreshadowing and thematic reminiscence in his use of the song "Somewhere," Tony and Maria's song of love and death.[50]

At the end of "Tonight," the omniscient orchestra foreshadows "Somewhere" (unheard by Tony and Maria) to prepare audiences for the tragic ending that will befall the star-crossed lovers. In the second act, the Procession motive that concludes the stage dream and contains "Somewhere," returns, albeit transformed, in "A Boy Like That/I Have a Love." The death Procession that closes the work eventually illuminates the profound connection between love and death associated with *Tristan und Isolde*.

From the beginning, the Mirisch brothers knew that despite his inexperience with film and his well-known reputation for perfectionism often characterized without hyperbole as sadism, Robbin's contribution was potentially invaluable to the film's success. Indeed, the dancing in the *West Side Story* film inspired awe and admiration as it did on the stage. Despite Robbins's stature and expertise, however, Walter Mirisch soon realized the financial downside of Robbin's ap-proach. To hedge his bets, the studio "concentrated on getting as many of the musical numbers shot as early in the schedule as we could" before making the drastic but not unexpected decision "to dispense with the two-director plan."[51]

As a result of this strategy, most of Robbins's filmed choreography survived his firing on the fifty-second or fifty-third day of shooting during the filming of the "Dance at the Gym" (the eventual number of shooting days came to 124).[52] Robbins's time on location may have resulted in only about forty minutes of us-able footage, but these crucial minutes include the Prologue, "America," "Cool," "I Feel Pretty," "One Hand, One Heart," and a good start with "Dance at the Gym."[53] Barrios summarizes the state of the dance filming at the time Robbins left the production: "Except for the gym sequence and the 'Somewhere' dream ballet, the remaining numbers were not heavy on dance. Essentially, Wise could direct them on his own, with Robbins's assistants helping with the staging."[54]

Critical Responses

With a few exceptions like Pauline Kael, film critics were enthusiastic about the movie adaptation of *West Side Story*. Bosley Crowther of the *New York Times* described it as "nothing short of a cinema masterpiece."[55] Stanley Kauffmann in *The New Republic* thought it was "the best film musical ever made."[56] Stanley Green in *Hi/Fi Stereo Review* subtitled his review "Hollywood's Treatment Is Better than Broadway's."[57] Arthur Knight in the *Saturday Review* thought the film "not only succeeded, it has *exceeded* the original."[58]

Perhaps the most frequently voiced criticism among these positive reviews was the casting of Richard Beymer as Tony (although one early reviewer found Beymer "equally attractive" as Maria's lover).[59] Not until 2011, however, did a "major" critic, Joan Acocella, describe Beymer as "underappreciated" in an article that also offered the by-then conventional praise of dances with the Prologue praised as "the most thrilling film dance ever made."[60] Two years before Acocella, *Variety*'s Todd McCarthy offered some sympathy for Beymer for making the best of a thankless role, blamed the "bad-mouthing" of Laurents and Sondheim for undermining the film's reputation overall, and found the film "superior to the stage show in nearly every possible way—it's more exciting, more dramatic."[61]

Despite the initial praise and growing appreciation, audiences soon began to confront a critical view of the stage work the film perpetuated: the stereotyped depiction of Latinx characters and the absence of Latinx actors in most roles. Particularly disappointing was the fact that the stage and film versions each cast only one Puerto Rican in a major role, the two Anitas, played by Chita Rivera on stage and Rita Moreno on screen.[62] As the Latinx scholar Frances Negrón-Muntaner argues, "There is no single American cultural product that haunts Puerto Rican identity discourses in the United Stage more intensely than the 1961 film, *West Side Story*."[63] The 2009 Broadway revival directed by Laurents helped a little by casting the Sharks exclusively with Latinx actors who were given lines in Spanish to speak and lyrics to sing.[64]

Some Latinx performers and scholars were less troubled by the film. The actress Jennifer Lopez loved it so much she watched it thirty-seven times, and Negrón-Muntaner seems to be alone in espousing a moral equivalence between *West Side Story* and D. W. Griffith's universally condemned racist treatment of African Americans in *The Birth of a Nation* (1915). Nevertheless, the film remains problematic for its reinforcement of such Shark cultural tropes as the Madonna (Maria)/Whore (Anita) dichotomy and for blacking up the Latinx characters, including the white actor George Chakiris, the son of Greek immigrants who played Riff in the London production. Moreno commented in a 2017 interview on National Public Radio that "it was like putting mud on my face."[65] Nevertheless, four years later Moreno defended Steven Spielberg's 2021 remake when asked for her "response to critics who say the movie shouldn't be revived at all because it brings up stereotypes, or it's not of our era in terms of its origin."[66] Moreno: "It does not bring up stereotypes. That's bull [expletive], pure and unadulterated bull [expletive]."[67]

It was also difficult to ignore the reality that *West Side Story* was not simply the first but the *only* major US film about Puerto Ricans, a movie in which all the male Latinos are members of a street gang rather than immigrants with high-paying jobs and other signs of social respectability. Viewers do see Latinas working in a thriving bridal shop, but they never meet Maria and Bernardo's parents, who, based on the dialogue, own a nearby store and are living (or aspiring to live) the American dream. Although Officer Krupke and Lieutenant Schrank are irredeemable racists who view Puerto Ricans with cruel bigotry, it doesn't seem productive to blame the film itself for the attitudes of its white inhabitants. In fact, Acevedo-Muñoz makes a strong argument that the film presents Puerto Ricans as "better articulated as characters than their white gang rivals."[68]

True, the Jets occupy more turf than the Sharks, even when they appear in the same film frame. They also dominate the Prologue and sing the "Jet Song," "Krupke," and "Cool," while the Shark men are limited to "America." On the other hand, the Shark women are featured in two musical numbers, "America" and "I Feel Pretty," while the Jets' girlfriends are few in number and barely sing or even speak. If the Shark men come across as paternalistic and condescending to their women, the misogynistic and disdainful treatment the Jets' women received from their boyfriends borders on contempt.

Acevedo-Munoz emphasizes that "in contrast to the lawlessness of the 'natives'. . . the Sharks—especially the Shark women—are productive, law-abiding, and apparently bound by ties that constitute some sense of community."[69] He also points out that "the only 'domestic' space represented in *West Side Story* is María's family apartment" and that her family exemplifies " 'good' immigrants and good Americans: hardworking, law-abiding, churchgoing, and respectful of Puerto Rico's political and constitutional status vis-à-vis the United States."[70] They even speak better English than the white characters. Nevertheless, in the end Bernardo's dystopian vision of America proves more prescient than the Jets' desire to hold on to their fiefdom and Tony's blindness to a negative outcome in his love for Maria. In short, despite some unfortunate stereotyping, compared with the Jets, the portrayal of the Sharks is the more favorable one.

In his autobiography *Original Story By* Laurents asserted that *West Side Story* broke "new musical ground in content" in that "serious subjects—bigotry, race, rape, murder, death—were dealt with for the first time in a musical as seriously as they would be in a play."[71] Laurents continued by stating that the four collaborators took "every musical theatre technique as far as could be taken" to create a work in which "scene, song and dance were integrated seamlessly . . . better than anyone ever had before."[72] Other than the addition of location shooting from every angle, the reordering of much of its musical score, and various other details discussed here, the film version of *West Side Story* preserved what Laurents considered the original show's greatest strengths, the four central and crucial creative parts of a musical: the book, the music, the lyrics, and dance.[73]

7

A (Mostly) All-Asian American Musical

Flower Drum Song from Page to Stage to Screen

Kenneth Leish: How do you feel about *Flower Drum Song* in retrospect? It was a success, [but] not of the caliber of your greatest shows.
Richard Rodgers: I like it. I liked the show when it was done. Beyond its
success, I liked the movie. I felt they did it quite well. But I've always
liked that show.

—Reminiscences of Richard Rodgers (1969)

"A Guilty Pleasure"

Both the stage and film versions of *Flower Drum Song* arrived closely on the
tennis shoe heels of the respective versions of *West Side Story*, sixteen months
later on stage and two months later on the screen. In the Preface and chapter 1,
I noted that, like *West Side Story*, the film version of *Flower Drum Song* removed
only a single song but took generous liberties with the song *ordering*. Among the
larger list of differences with its predecessor, *Flower Drum Song* was not filmed
on location—in this case, Chinatown, San Francisco. Of perhaps greater importance, in contrast to *West Side Story*, the film adaptation of *Flower Drum Song*
discarded most of the original choreography. At 133 minutes it was one of the
seven 1960s adaptations that ran close to two hours, albeit eighteen minutes
fewer than *West Side Story*, which at 151 minutes was one of the twenty remaining 1960s adaptations that ran between 2.5 and 3 hours. Finally, as we will
soon see, in contrast to *West Side Story*, which retained its pivotal stage director
and choreographer Jerome Robbins but not major cast members, *Flower Drum
Song*, like many 1950s and 1960s adaptations, retained several major players in
the transfer from stage to film.

The previous chapter noted (appropriately in a note) that *West Side Story*
was the sixth roadshow, an elite collection of films presented as limited national engagements, expensively produced and marketed, and often longer
than two hours (often with an intermission). As we learned in chapter 4, the
roadshow musical phenomenon began in 1955 with *Oklahoma!*. After three
more roadshow movies in the 1950s (*Guys and Dolls*, *South Pacific*, and *Porgy*

A Fine Romance. Geoffrey Block, Oxford University Press. © Oxford University Press 2023.
DOI: 10.1093/oso/9780197501733.003.0007

and Bess), the enthusiasm for roadshow adaptations of stage musicals peaked in the early 1960s with *West Side Story* (1961), *My Fair Lady* (1964), and *The Sound of Music* (1965).[1] In the latter half of the '60s, roadshow films were generally less successful financially and critically, although one movie, *Oliver!* (1968), gained distinction as the fourth musical film of the decade (and fourth adaptation) to receive the Academy Award for Best Picture.

On stage, *Flower Drum Song* was produced more modestly than its larger-scale predecessors by Rodgers and Hammerstein, *Oklahoma!*, *Carousel*, *South Pacific*, and *The King and I*; and unlike *Oklahoma!*, *South Pacific*, and *The Sound of Music*, the film version was not featured in the roadshow format. *Flower Drum Song*'s relative brevity and lack of spectacular scenes meant that the filmmakers were unable to rival the grandiose cinematic approach demonstrated in any of the other five Rodgers Hammerstein adaptations.

In part due to its casting difficulties, *Flower Drum Song* has also been overshadowed, not only by Rodgers and Hammerstein (R&H) classics, but also by other contemporary stage musicals such as *West Side Story*, *The Music Man*, and *Gypsy*, to name three shows that premiered between 1957 and 1959 in addition to *The Sound of Music*. Despite its lesser stature, even in its own time, its proud composer, Richard Rodgers, reserved a soft spot for *Flower Drum Song* on both stage and screen.[2] Rodgers's partner Oscar Hammerstein II, who wrote the lyrics and co-wrote the libretto with Joseph Fields (1895–1966) for the stage version, apparently did not publicly express his personal opinion. He did, however, reportedly convey to his son Jamie, the show's stage manager, that in contrast to past "unlucky flops," "some well-deserved hits," and some shows "that deserved to run better than they did," *Flower Drum Song* was "the first lucky hit I've ever had."[3]

Hammerstein's lucky hit had exactly 600 performances from December 1, 1958, to May 7, 1960, at a time when a run of this length was a hit. In chapter 6, it was noted that with its modest (by later standards) total of 732 performances, *West Side Story* was the twelfth longest-running show of the decade. In addition to its entertainment value, *Flower Drum Song* made history as the first significant musical since Rodgers and Lorenz Hart's 1928 flop *Chee-Chee* (31 performances) that was exclusively inhabited with Chinese characters, although unlike *Chee-Chee*, Rodgers's second Chinese musical was cast mostly with Asian American actors.[4] The show was adapted from C. Y. Lee's 1957 novel, the first by a Chinese American to be published by a major publishing house.[5] Both the novel and the musical are set contemporaneously in San Francisco's Chinatown. On March 24, 1960, shortly before its Broadway close, the show began a healthy London run of 464 performances concurrently with an eighteen-month American tour that played in Detroit, Cleveland, Los Angeles, San Francisco, and Chicago. The film adaptation released on November 9, 1961, made a profit of $1 million on its $4 million budget. Surprisingly, not only was *Flower Drum Song* the first Hollywood film with a nearly all-Asian cast; it would turn out to be the last until the non-musical films *The Joy Luck Club* (1993) followed twenty-five years later by *Crazy Rich Asians* (2018).

Flower Drum Song may have been a lucky hit in 1958, but its future was not so lucky. The challenge of assembling Asian casts combined with evolving ethnic sensibilities made the show a problematic one to stage. Consequently, the musical would languish for more than thirty years before a Broadway resuscitation appeared in 2002, a substantially revised version conceived by the Chinese American playwright David Henry Hwang, the author of the 1988 Broadway hit play *M. Butterfly*. Hwang's *Flower Drum Song* was a re-imagining that surpassed in scope Broadway's 1987 "revisal" of *Anything Goes* and other heavily revised revivals such as *Annie Get Your Gun* (1999) with a new book by Peter Stone. Hwang's stated goal was to write an adaptation of *Flower Drum Song* "that Hammerstein might have wanted to write had he been Asian American."[6]

Unlike *West Side Story*'s attempt to modernize Shakespeare's *Romeo and Juliet* while maintaining meaningful parallels, Hwang's *Flower Drum Song* offers a narrative that frequently severs connections with its 1958 stage source, an approach that resembles the kinds of changes we have noted in earlier chapters that film executives and directors regularly imposed on adapted stage works in the 1930s and 1940s. The difference was that Hwang retained nearly all of Rodgers and Hammerstein's songs, cutting only "The Other Generation" and even restoring "My Best Love," a song dropped during the 1958 tryouts. On the other hand, Hwang placed these songs within a reconstructed narrative and radically new dramatic contexts, including reassigning some songs to other characters.[7] Widely panned, the revisal lasted only 169 performances, and like the original production has largely vanished.[8]

Hwang's fascinating, if flawed, attempt to improve the work will not be further addressed here. Instead, this chapter will focus on the 1958 stage and 1961 film adaptations in relation to Lee's novel. Since Hammerstein died in August 1960, the screenplay was written solely by Fields, who retained much of the stage dialogue and all but one of its songs ("Like a God"). Due to these similarities, commentators regularly assert that the film constitutes "a fairly accurate re-creation of the original."[9] This conventional wisdom does not take into consideration the film's approach to song order, which goes even beyond what we observed in *West Side Story*. In assessing the consequences of this new song order, I will express the heretical view that in nearly every case the film's reordering and revised narrative constitutes a dramatic improvement over the stage original. Hwang referred to the film as "a guilty pleasure for many of us."[10] This chapter will have served its purpose if it encourages readers to enjoy this underrated movie with more pleasure and a little less guilt.

FLOWER DRUM SONG: FILM versus STAGE

Introduction

Aside from its unorthodox song order, in most respects the film adaptation of *Flower Drum Song* belongs to the Age of Fidelity in its observance of the adaptation Commandments listed in chapter 1. Fields's screenplay retained most of the stage dialogue and two generous dream ballets, "Ta's Dream" (now simply "Ballet") and "Sunday"; both of these offer new scenarios, and the former contains different musical themes. Going one further than Ethel Merman's return in *Call Me Madam*, it retained *two* original cast members in major roles, Miyoshi Umeki as Mei Li and Juanita Hall as Madam Liang.[11] It also cast Jack Soo, who played the Master of Ceremonies on the stage, as Sammy Fong, and retained Patrick Adiarte's Wang San in yet another important role.[12]

Along with these retentions came significant changes. Of particular consequence was the decision to recast the roles of Linda Low and Helen Chao, played on stage by singers Pat Suzuki and Arabella Hong, with dancers Nancy Kwan and Reiko Sato. Consequently, as with *West Side Story*, the studio followed the standard practice of dubbing, Kwan with popular singer B. J. Baker and Sato with opera singer Marilyn Horne, the latter having previously dubbed Dorothy Dandridge's voice in *Carmen Jones* (1954).[13] The fact that Chao was a seamstress made her dancing ability dramatically irrelevant, but her skills as a dancer allowed Sato to dance in her own dream ballet (on stage Hong was replaced by a dancing double). Although not required for the reconceived dream ballet (although featured in the second "Sunday" ballet), the casting of Kwan made sense since Linda was a dancer at the Celestial Gardens nightclub.[14] Despite these changes, what makes the film adaptation most unusual is the previously mentioned altered song order and, perhaps still more significantly, the revised contexts for many songs. These changes not only altered the plot sequence but the overall structural trajectory. In the next section I will discuss these departures and why they matter. See Table 7.1, "*Flower Drum Song* on Stage and Screen."

Act I on Stage and Its Film Counterpart

As with "Oh, What a Beautiful Mornin'" (*Oklahoma!*) and "Dites-Moi" (*South Pacific*), *Flower Drum Song* on the stage begins with a moment of intimacy. The setting is the home of patriarch Wang Chi-yang where his sister-in-law Madam Liang is placing a telephone order for various Chinese delicacies such as "one pound of dried snake meat," "a box of longevity noodles," and "a dozen thousand

Table 7.1 *Flower Drum Song* on Stage and Screen.

Stage 1958	Film 1961
Act I	
Overture (5)	Main Title—Overture (0:00)
You Are Beautiful (Kenney, Hall) (13)	
A Hundred Million Miracles (Umeki, Yama, Hall, Luke, and Quong) (27)	A Hundred Million Miracles (Umeki, Tong, and Chorus) (9:10)
	Fan Tan Fannie (Baker [for Kwan]) (14:13)
	The Other Generation (Fong, Hall, Adiarte) (23:37)
	A Hundred Million Miracles (Reprise) (Umeki) (31:39)
I Enjoy Being a Girl (Suzuki) (34)	I Enjoy Being a Girl (Baker [for Kwan]) (33:40)
I Am Going to Like It Here (Umeki) (47)	I Am Going to Like It Here (Umeki) (42:33)
Like a God (Kenney) (57)	
Chop Suey (Hall and Guests) (61)	Chop Suey (Shigeta, Hall, Adiarte, and Chorus) (56:05)
Don't Marry Me (Blyden, Umeki) (73)	
Grant Avenue (Suzuki and Ensemble) (77)	Grant Avenue (Baker [for Kwan] and Chorus) (72:29)
Love, Look Away (Hong) (83)	
Fan Tan Fannie (Ellis) (85)	
Gliding through My Memory (Soo) (87)	Gliding through My Memory (Sen Yung) (79:08)
	Fan Tan Fannie (Baker [for Kwan]; [Dance] (Kwan) (81:34)
Grant Avenue (abbreviated Reprise) (Suzuki) (89)	
Act II	
Introduction to Ta's Dream (Kenney) (95)	
Ta's Dream (Orchestra) (95)	
Love, Look Away (Reprise) (Hong) (99)	Love, Look Away (Horne [for Sato]) (86:07)
	Ballet (orchestra) (88:25)
The Other Generation (Hall, Luke) (102)	
You Are Beautiful (Reprise) (Kenney) (109)	You Are Beautiful (Shigeta) (98:17)

Table 7.1 Continued

Stage 1958	Film 1961
Sunday (Suzuki, Blyden) (117)	Sunday (Soo and Baker [for Kwan]) (104:22)
	Like a God [5 lines recited by a Beatnik]) (116:18)
Don't Marry Me (Reprise) (Blyden) (123)	Don't Marry Me (Soo, Umeki) (117:02)
The Other Generation (Reprise) (Children) (126)	
Procession (Orchestra) (138)	Procession (Orchestra) (126:41)
A Hundred Million Miracles (Reprise) (Ensemble) (141)	A Hundred Million Miracles (Umeki, Baker [for Kwan], and Chorus) (129:59)

- *Numbers in parentheses in the stage column refer to page numbers in Hammerstein and Fields, "Flower Drum Song" (New York: Farrar, Straus and Cudahy, 1959).*
- *Numbers in parentheses in the film refer to film timings.*

MAJOR SINGING AND DANCING AND SELECTED ROLES/ETHNICITIES

Stage: MIYOSHI UMEKI (Mei Li)) [Japanese]; Pat Suzuki (Linda Low) [Japanese American]; Ed Kenney (Wang Ta) [Hawaiian]; Arabella Hong (Helen Chao) [Chinese American]; JUANITA HALL (Madam Liang) [African American]; Larry Blyden (Sammy Fong) [American]; Ed Kenney (Wang Ta); PATRCK ADIARTE (Wang San) [Filipino]; JACK SOO (Frankie Wing); Keye Luke (Wang chi-yang); Conrad Yama (Dr. Li); Rose Quong (Liu Ma); Anita Ellis (Nightclub Singer)

Screen: UMEKI (Mei Li); Nancy Kwan (Linda Low) [Chinese European (English-Scottish)], dubbed by B. J. Baker; James Shigeta (Wang Ta) [Japanese]; Reiko Sato (Helen Chao) [Japanese], dubbed by Marilyn Horne; HALL (Madam Liang); SOO (Sammy Fong) [Japanese]; ADIARTE (Wang San); Benson Fong (Wang chi-yang); Kam Tong (Dr. Han Li); Victor Sen Yung (Frankie)

- *Names in capital letters indicate that a cast member appeared both on stage and in the film.*

year eggs."[15] Madam Liang then converses with Wang's two rebellious sons. The elder, Wang Ta, a recent out-of-work college graduate, asks Madam Liang for money to finance his blind date with Linda Low, a "tomato" who drives a Thunderbird.[16] To please Linda, Ta has memorized a Chinese poem, "You Are Beautiful." Madam Liang, who knows the poem, sings its verse. Ta takes over the main chorus, after which they sing together in harmony. Eventually, audiences will learn that the "small and shy" and "beautiful" woman described in the poem will not turn out to be the Americanized party girl Linda Low but the traditional Chinese immigrant Mei Li. In fact, at this point Ta and Mei Li have yet to meet. They will do so later in the scene shortly before Ta's date with Linda. In contrast to *West Side Story*'s Tony, who expresses his powerful feelings of love in song moments after meeting Maria in the eponymous "Maria," Ta does not realize he loves Mei Li until he learns the hard way that Linda is the wrong girl for him.

Instead of launching the story inside the Wang household, the film begins with Mei Li and her father Dr. Han Li, two stowaways on a boat from Hong Kong to San Francisco's Chinatown. Their journey is captured simply and elegantly during the overture and credits through a series of watercolors painted by the distinguished Chinese American artist Dong Kingman. The Lis have embarked on this daring adventure in order to avoid waiting the usual ten years before Mei Li (age nineteen) can legally travel to America and fulfill her role as the "picture bride" of nightclub owner Sammy Fong (identified in the libretto as "in his thirties"). It was to be an arranged marriage between a matchmaker and Sammy's traditional parents, sealed by a contract and an exchange of photographs.

On reaching Union Square a few blocks from their Chinatown destination, Mei Li, tired, broke, and hungry, takes out her flower drum and sings what will become the show's anthem, **"A Hundred Million Miracles" (screen: 9:10)**. A policeman takes father and daughter to Sammy's restaurant and nightclub, Celestial Gardens, where Sammy is about to introduce Linda Low, the star of the floorshow. Linda's **"Fan Tan Fannie" (screen: 14:13)** spices up the pervasive use of pentatonic scales associated with the Far East with enough syncopated rhythms to reveal the Americanized Linda as the polar opposite of Mei Li with her traditional Chinese folk song that dates back to the Ming dynasty (1360s to 1640s) named after the flower drum she uses to accompany herself in "A Hundred Million Miracles" on stage and screen.[17] Her signature rhythm heard in the orchestra (one eighth note-six sixteenth notes-two eighth notes) that pervades this song also serves to open the original Broadway show, revisal, and after a few seconds, the film.

The juxtaposition of these sharply contrasting songs in the movie quickly and effectively introduces the two central female characters in Ta's romantic life, not dissimilar to the later juxtaposition of Linda's "I Enjoy Being a Girl" with Mei Li's contrasting "I Am Going to Like It Here" in the stage version. The film introduction also gives Linda an early opportunity to check out her "competition" when she overhears her longtime lover Sammy pretending to express his willingness to honor the marriage proposal, a conversation that doesn't occur in the stage version. By presenting Mei Li and Linda as a variation on the widely employed male-female "dual-focus narrative," the early display of their representative personalities and songs efficiently introduces a central theme of both the stage and screen versions: the conflict between Eastern and Western cultural perspectives.[18]

Linda and Sammy have been an item for five years, but although Sammy buys Linda expensive gifts and supports her lavish lifestyle, his disinterest in marriage has led to tensions in their romance. Now that an interloper appears unexpectedly to claim her contracted bridal status, Sammy needs to do something. Fortunately, he knows that the wealthy and culturally conservative widower Wang Chi-yang is looking to match his rebellious son Wang Ta (who *thinks* he loves Linda), with a traditional Chinese bride. By introducing Linda's show number and her scene with Sammy, Mei Li, and Dr. Li at the club, the film offers a significant reordering of the stage narrative, which has remained in the home of Wang (who has by now returned from his weekly visit to the bank to change a $100 bill).[19] On stage, as soon as Ta leaves for his date with Linda, Sammy arrives with Mei Li and her father. Mei Li then entertains and delights Master Wang with "A Hundred Million Miracles" joined by Madam Liang. The film version later (31:39) offers a close facsimile of this performance when Mei Li gets an equal opportunity to win Wang over in a shortened reprise of her signature song.

But before Mei Li's domestic performance, the film inserts **"The Other Generation"** (screen: **23:37**), the first film song to take place in the Chinatown residence of Master Wang (the stage version will save this song for much later). Ta sets up the song, a march in the minor mode, when he tells his father that in America "a man picks his own wife." This breach of protocol embodies the generation gap, a central theme of Lee's novel and both the stage and film versions.[20] We hear the song twice, first inside the house where it is sung by the older generation, Wang and his sister-in-law Madam Liang. After a short pause, the younger generation continues the song on the patio followed by an elaborate dance led by Ta's even more Americanized younger brother Wang San (Adiarte), who usually wears a replica of the baseball uniform belonging to the recently arrived San Francisco Giants (formerly the New York Giants), joined by other teenagers and children. On realizing Adiarte's virtuosity as a jazz dancer, choreographer Hermes Pan gave San a more conspicuous dancing role here (and elsewhere) beyond what Adiarte (now eighteen) was given in the stage version when he was fifteen. Presented earlier in the film narrative, the song offers meaningful thematic exposition, whereas its late placement in the stage version comes across as redundant.

The next song in the stage and film version is **"I Enjoy Being a Girl"** (screen: **33:40**), perhaps the best-known and most often parodied song in the show due to its unabashed sexism.[21] In the stage version Linda sings it in the course of her date with Ta. Standing next to her Thunderbird while holding hands with Ta overlooking the Golden Gate Bridge, Linda explains that her only ambition is to attain "success as a girl."[22] She then tells Ta she would like "something around me" to alleviate the chill in the air, but instead of taking the unmistakable hint that this "something" would be Ta's arms, the clueless Ta offers to retrieve her sweater. Left alone, Linda sings "I Enjoy Being a Girl" in which she asserts and relishes her femininity and expresses her pride in her attractiveness to men.

Linda's values about being female have long since become unwelcome for an emancipated woman to espouse. Audiences today are likely to flinch when Linda sings that, while she might "glower and *bristle*" when men *whistle* at her in her bikini, she is pleased to be the object of the whistle. In the film version of "Enjoy" viewers are invited to become voyeurs as they gaze at Linda in the privacy of her bedroom looking at herself in front of three adjacent mirrors; for the most part, she is dressed in only a towel as she performs her post-shower rituals and prepares for her date with Ta.

Through the wonders of cinema each mirror reveals Linda in various poses and eventually a series of stylish clothes (including a bikini) magically replace her towel to accompany her graceful dance moves. And through the wonder of pre-recorded sound, Linda concludes the number singing a trio in harmony with her three selves (or rather dubber B. J. Baker's three selves). After Linda finishes her song and exits in the stage version, "a group of dancers" appear on stage to "demonstrate her philosophy." At the conclusion of the film number in Linda's bedroom, the camera immediately cuts to Linda and Ta sitting in Linda's Thunderbird on location overlooking the city. Their consequent dialogue in the screenplay mostly follows the stage libretto, although instead of asking Linda to marry him, Ta gives Linda his fraternity pin and they agree to go steady.

The stage and film also share the next new song, "I Am Going to Like It Here" (screen: 42:33), as well its context, the first meeting of Mei Li and Ta, after which Mei Li reveals her experience of love at first sight in a soliloquy. In contrast to Tony's response after meeting Maria in *West Side Story*, however, Mei Li never mentions Ta by name, only that "it's the father's first son I like" and that he is "the reason I love the place." The lyrics take the form of a pantoum, a verse form of apparent Malaysian origin arranged in a series of quatrains in which the second and fourth lines of a quatrain return as the first and third lines of the next quatrain. Hammerstein captures the powerful simplicity of Mei Li's emotions by using only five rhymes, and eight of the eleven rhyming words are monosyllabic: here, atmosphere, sincere; place and face; warm and storm; one and son; and anywhere and there. Mei Li's song features frequent repetitions of an augmented second interval (E-flat-F-sharp) resolving up to G combined with simple repetitive rhythms in both the melody and the accompaniment; a narrow melodic range of a sixth (with the sole exception of the penultimate note, one octave above the lowest note); and an exotic alto flute in the orchestra. It creates a conspicuous stylistic contrast, if not an authentically Chinese one, with Linda's jazzy Americanized musical language.

Before the versions next share a song, the stage version inserts "Like a God" during Ta's first conversation with Mei Li. Bending the stereotype in which Asians (especially female Asians) exude meekness and shyness, Mei Li demonstrates a bold directness when she asks Ta, "How would you ask a girl to marry you, Ta? What would you say?" In the verse of the song that directly follows, Ta tells Mei Lei he would ask whether he is the man that the woman loves. If the answer is yes, he will be transformed from a man to something "like a god," the emotional

Example 7.1a "I Am Going to Like It Here" (mm. 8-14) in *Flower Drum Song.*

response described in the lyrics of the main chorus. In a subtle musical touch, the middle section of "Like a God" begins with the opening melody of "I Am Going to Like It Here," now converted from Mei Li's exotic augmented scale (Musical Example 7.1a) to a Western scale in the minor mode (Musical Example 7.1b) but still suggesting their fundamental musical (and therefore romantic) compatibility.

Since film viewers have not yet heard Mei Li's musical soliloquy, the musical reminiscence of "Like a God" is unfortunately lost, although for attentive listeners it might serve as foreshadowing. With the return of the main theme, Ta exits in mid-song. After lip-synching to Ta's offstage completion of the melody, Mei Li sings an abbreviated second reprise of "A Hundred Million Miracles." The first occurred shortly before she met Ta while performing the Chinese ritual of beating Wang's shoulders, an activity that occurs frequently in Lee's novel.

Next in the film is **"Chop Suey"** (**screen: 56:05**), a song about cultural assimilation led by Madam Liang at her graduation from the citizenship school that prepared her to become an assimilated American. In the film, but not the stage version, the celebrants follow the song with a dance that exhibits a suey of American dance steps (square dance, waltz, swing, rock and roll, and jazz).[23] The stage lyrics contain a solitary Chinese reference, to "Peking Duck," but while expanded screen lyrics are filled with still more American cultural references they no longer contain even the single token stage reference to the popular Chinese dish. After **"Suey"** comes **"Grant Avenue"** (**screen: 72:29**), a song about the good life on this grand "Western street with Eastern manners." Compared with its

Example 7.1b "Like a God" (mm. 32-40) in *Flower Drum Song*.

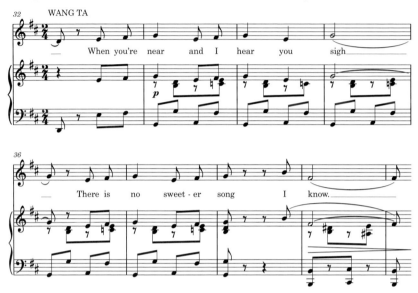

abrupt and non-integrated introduction in the stage version, Linda launches and leads a song and dance in the film that flows naturally as part of a Chinese New Year's celebration. See Figure 7.1.

Between "Chop Suey" and "Grant Avenue" the stage version inserts "Don't Marry Me," Sammy's response to Mei Li's newfound awareness that Ta loves Linda. Although Sammy isn't ready to commit to a marriage with Linda, he *knows* he would be a bad match for Mei Li and warns her that if she can't find a way to get Ta to alter his feelings, she will be stuck and miserable with the wrong man. After a short verse that begins with the words, "You are young and beautiful," a verbal rather than a musical reference to the stage version's "You Are Beautiful," Sammy provides an abundance of corroborative details to convey the ways he "will never fail to disappoint" Mei Li and why she shouldn't marry him.

The next film song is **"Gliding through My Memory" (screen: 79:08)** sung by Frankie, the Master of Ceremonies at the Celestial Gardens, as he introduces the club's audience to his Chinese female companions who impersonate women from different parts of the world. Following this musical introduction Linda reprises the provocative dance **"Fan Tan Fannie" (screen: 81:34)**.[24] In both the film and stage versions Sammy has invited the Wangs to see Linda perform at the Celestial Gardens because he knows that Ta, his conservative father, and his aunt will be attending the show that evening and that Linda's act will shock and offend everyone, including Ta, which it does. On stage, the first act concludes at the end

Fig. 7.1 Nancy Kwan (Linda Low) dancing on "Grant Avenue" in the film *Flower Drum Song* [75:39]. Screenshot.

of this performance when Linda, furious that Sammy has exposed her secret life as a Fan Tan dancer, pours a bucket of ice on his head, an action she will repeat in the film.

Act II on Stage and Its Film Counterpart

The film counterpart to Act II begins in the apartment of Helen Chao, the lonely seamstress hopelessly in unrequited love with Ta, who, distraught at finding out about Linda's profession, is drunk and vulnerable to Chao's advances. By this point in the stage version, audiences have already heard Helen's torch song "Love, Look Away" in Act I when it followed an exchange between Linda and Helen prior to the floor show at the Celestial Gardens. During the course of this stage exchange Helen learned of Sammy's plan to sabotage Linda's betrothal to Ta, who was unaware that Linda performed there. The conversation revealed that the considerably older Helen (forty-one in the novel), who has known Ta (age twenty-one) since he was a boy, must suffer her unrequited love in silence. Her only remedy is to ask, in song, for love to "look away" and set her free from the pain of rejection.

The choice to give a show's central ballad to a secondary role is fraught with peril. Rodgers and Hammerstein tried (and arguably didn't succeed) when they assigned "So Far," perhaps the most memorable song in R&H's *Allegro* (1947), to a minor character named Beulah who, after going on a single date with the protagonist Dr. Joseph Taylor, disappears forever at the end of the song. In contrast to Beulah, Helen's role is a significant one, since she provides the catalyst for Ta's realization that he truly loves Mei Li.[25]

Unfortunately, "Love, Look Away" is designed for a woman who seeks relief from emotional pain and only Helen matches this requirement. To capture Helen's longing for love to look away, Rodgers's melody and harmony set Hammerstein's lyrics on a sophisticated metaphorical level in which Helen's music seems to be searching for C minor, the harmony that will release her from her love and pain. She finds the *note* C in the melody against the G minor chord that opens each of the three A sections on the words "love, look away," "call it a day," and "love, look away," and the C minor *harmony* when the music lingers on this chord on the words "door" and "me." For a moment near the end of the song on the word "free," the climactic phrase "Leave me and set me free," the music appears to resolve to the desired key. But in the next measure, Helen's final plea, the song offers the words "look away" but without the "love." The tune's conclusion, which has saved "away" for the song's highest note (on a G) in E-flat major, suggests that love will *not* look away and that Helen's emotional suffering is destined to continue

The film omits the exchange between Helen and Linda that occurred in the stage version at the Celestial Gardens near the end of Act I, and it delays Helen's lament and departure until shortly before the dream ballet that occurs while Ta, who has passed out, is sleeping it off. The stage version also reprises "Love, Look Away" *after* the ballet, but in the film Helen sings the song for the first and only time *before* the ballet: **Love, Look Away (screen: 86:07)** and **Ballet (screen: 88:25)**. In the novel, Lee ended Helen's pain with her suicide, but in the stage and film adaptations she will simply disappear, like Beulah in *Allegro,* unexplained, immediately after she sings her poignant song that does not allow her to look away from the anguish of her unrequited love.

The Ballets present different scenarios. In the stage version, "Ta's Dream," Ta is unable to connect with the dancing doubles who represent Linda and Mei Li. Instead, Ta's dream allows him to be seduced by Helen, and the dream ends with Ta leaving with Helen to the music of "Love, Look Away."[26] The film ballet is told from the perspective of Helen, who envisions herself in a wedding gown, which is soon torn apart by male dancers dressed in black and wearing Chinese masks. At the end of the film dream ballet, stylistically a combination of ballet and jazz, Helen is unable to hold on to Ta's extended arms and falls into a watery abyss. The music concludes as it began with "Love, Look Away," which had been transformed into a waltz at the beginning of the dream. As the film dream comes to an end, this central melody returns in a fragmented and dissonant version in different keys before culminating in a jazzy version for its first two A sections and a march for the B and final A sections of a standard AABA 32-bar song form.[27]

In contrast to the events in Lee's novel, in which Helen and Ta embark on a secretive sexual affair lasting several months, Fields's *Flower Drum Song* screenplay leaves it to the audience's imagination whether any censorable activity occurred at Helen's apartment while Ta recovered from a drunken stupor.[28] According to the Hollywood Production Code Administration's benign interpretation, Fields's screenplay "clearly established that there is no illicit relationship between Helen and Ta."[29] Unfortunately, Mei Li arrives at a different conclusion when she appears at Helen's apartment the next morning to drop off Wang's coat for repairs and sees Ta's coat on a chair with the flower still attached that she pinned on his lapel in Act I.

Blissfully ignorant of what Mei Li has observed, Ta returns to his father's home to acknowledge the errors of his romantic ways and express his desire to marry Mei Li.[30] When he finds her, he sings the long-delayed **"You Are Beautiful"** **(screen: 98:17)**, the song intended for Linda early in the stage version. Now, Mei Li is the intended and rightful recipient of the words, "You are the girl I will love someday." In Henry Koster's simple and touching directorial touch, Mei Li looks away throughout the song. When it's over, Mei Li tells Ta that she saw his coat and that her hurt is so great she doesn't love him anymore. See Figure 7.2.

Meanwhile, Linda and Sammy settle their differences when Sammy spontaneously proposes marriage. Not only does Linda unhesitatingly accept the offer, but she also responds to Sammy's "We're as good as married" with "Nothing's as good as married." This leads to their bucolic duet **"Sunday" (screen: 104:22)** followed by another ballet choreographed by Pan, which begins with a dream depicting Sammy and Linda's imagined idyllic married life on a typical Sunday. The film dream continues with a series of surreal interruptions, including the arrival of two sexy female visitors, several male-female couples, and a little girl in a cowboy outfit watching a Western on television. The dream ends in wacky chaos when a cowboy and a Native American leap out of the television and initiate a madcap Mack Sennett-like chase throughout the doors and hallways of Linda and Sammy's apartment.[31]

Fig. 7.2 James Shigeta (Wang Ta) about to sing "You Are Beautiful" to Miyoshi Umeki (Mei Li) in the film *Flower Drum Song* [98: 01]. Screenshot.

In contrast to the stage version where it appeared sandwiched between "Chop Suey" and "Grant Avenue," film viewers must wait for **"Don't Marry Me"** **(screen: 117:02)** until near the end of the film when in an "11 o'clock number" (as mentioned earlier, a show-stopping number arriving late in the evening) Sammy explains why Mei Li shouldn't marry him as the camera takes the mismatched couple around Universal's soundstage scenes of Chinatown. It is well known that "Don't Marry Me" was added to the stage show during the Boston tryout when Larry Blyden, who before agreeing to replace Larry Storch (like Blyden also white), insisted on a new song for Sammy.[32] Four days later Hammerstein completed what is perhaps his funniest lyric in the R&H canon, in which Sammy offers numerous persuasive reasons for why she *shouldn't* marry him.[33] Here's a sample:

> MEI LI: I would like to know where you *go.*/I don't like a man to keep me in *doubt—*
> SAMMY: Honey, that's a thing that's easy to *know—*/You will always know where I am, I'm *out!*

When Sammy is finished, Mei Li respectfully replies, "I accept your proposal not to marry me, but you must ask my father" (74).

Immediately prior to "Don't Marry Me," Sammy and Mei Li visit a pretentious nightclub where they hear five lines of **"Like a God" (screen: 116:18)** *spoken* by Beatniks without underscoring. By this time in the stage version, Sammy and Linda have finished singing "Sunday." The stage version also offers a reprise of "Don't Marry Me," which Sammy sings to Mei Li in front of his mother. Linda makes a sudden entrance and hears Sammy's "I'm saying this because I love you, darling." At this point in the film, viewers have yet to hear "Don't Marry Me." Instead, when Linda barges into Sammy's apartment, she learns he is resigned to honoring the contract and will marry Mei Li. Coming so swiftly after "Sunday," Linda can barely control her anger in the following exchange (also heard in the stage version):

> LINDA: You are the lowest, sneakiest, slimiest—
> SAMMY: Forget the superlatives, give me a chance to explain.
> LINDA: Explain what? Half an hour ago you *had* to marry me, you couldn't live without me . . .
> SAMMY: And nothing's changed.
> LINDA: Nothing's changed! You're going to marry *her!*
> SAMMY: That's the only thing that's changed.[34]

The Novel: C. Y. Lee's *The Flower Drum Song*

In *The Flower Drum Song*, his debut novel, C. Y. Lee (1915–2018) devotes considerable attention to the love life of Master Wang Chi-yang's elder son Wang Ta, in particular the saga of three women in his life: Linda Tung (Linda Low in the musical), May Li (Mei Li in the musical), and Helen Chao. Lee also provides more space for the life and foibles of Master Wang and his sister-in-law Madam Liang than Fields and Hammerstein allowed in the stage libretto. Another Lee character, Liu Ma, "the fat, talkative woman servant, who was Liu Lung's wife and Old Master Wang's information bureau" (7), who plays a significant role in the novel's plotline, is virtually absent. Ta's often-present philosophical friend Chang has completely disappeared.

On the other hand, readers of Lee's novel will *not* meet Sammy Fong, the Americanized nightclub owner betrothed at birth to Mei Li, then living in Hong Kong. For most of the musical, the newly conceived and dramatically indispensable Sammy is in love with but has yet to commit to Linda, his Americanized Chinese girlfriend. To avoid fulfilling his family's bridal contract, Sammy tries to pass Mei Li off on Master Wang's elder son Wang Ta, but Ta, who thinks he loves Linda, isn't interested. Many plot twists later, Ta belatedly realizes he loves Mei Li, while Sammy proposes to Linda, nine years sooner than Nathan Detroit waited to finally propose to Adelaide in *Guys and Dolls*. None of this happens in Lee's novel. Although Lee's Ta eventually discovers he loves May Li, the novel fails to conform to a traditional romantic comedy marriage plot and instead leaves uncertain whether Ta may even find May Li or whether she will accept his marriage proposal if and when he does.

Stage and film audiences meet Ta's women relatively early and in quick succession. In contrast, Lee lingers on each before moving to the next. Readers first meet the party girl Linda Tung before the end of the second chapter. Three chapters later Linda introduces Ta to her "pockmarked" mah-jongg companion, Helen, whom Ta befriends for the sole purpose of learning more about Linda's mysterious "brother" (in fact another boyfriend), who supposedly has to give his consent for Linda to marry Ta. As in the musical, Lee's Linda needs this fictitious brother's approval to marry Ta, but only in the novel does Ta propose to Linda within moments of their first kiss. At the end of this chapter, Ta breaks up with Linda due to her duplicitous behavior, then immediately asks the considerably older Helen for a date. Except for a follow-up at the beginning of Part II where Ta and Chang witness the aftermath of a shooting in which "somebody shot somebody for a girl" (117), that girl being Linda, Ta's former girlfriend departs from Lee's novel by page 56 (chapter 5).[35]

In the final chapter of Part I (chapter 7), Lee relates how the lonely and desperate Helen, who clearly does *not* think of Ta as a brother, deliberately gets Ta drunk, takes off his clothes and hers, and boldly joins him in bed to begin a clandestine sexual affair lasting several months, all of which is confined to Helen's bedroom. After going through a painful "sandpaper treatment" to remove her pockmarks, Helen tricks Ta into attending her birthday party as the sole guest and proposes marriage. On the final page of Part I, Ta reads in the paper about a woman "identified as Miss Helen Chao, 41, a seamstress at Universal Clothing Factory on Stockton Street" (92) who was found washed ashore on a beach. This tragic relationship in the novel provides a backstory for "Love, Look Away" that stage and film audiences (unless they have read the novel) never hear about.

Only after Linda and Helen have departed from Ta's life is Lee ready to introduce the nineteen-year-old May Li and her father, who have been residing *legally* in the United States for three months. This occurs in chapter 3 of Part II, more than halfway through the novel. In contrast to the musical, the novel's May Li is not a picture bride betrothed at birth to a non-existent Sammy Fong. Instead, father and daughter arrive in Chinatown with a letter of introduction from an influential consul general. Before they reach their intended location, they stop and put on a flower drum show that earns them enough money for lunch.

By a stroke of fate, the house formerly owned by their contact currently belongs to Master Wang. Ta sees them in front of the house, invites them inside, and offers them a position in the household over the objections of Liu Ma, Master Wang's domestic helper. During the next few weeks Ta and May Li get to know each other. This leads to a discussion regarding the nuances of kissing in American pictures, including the distinctions between "half done" and "well-done" kissing, a discussion and activity that will be incorporated into the stage and film versions.

In the novel, Liu Ma's jealousy and enmity cause her to steal Wang's treasured gold clock and assign blame for the theft to May Li. Liu Ma also accuses May Li of stealing a pendant, an accusation resolved when Ta explains that it was a gift and that he wants to marry her. A search reveals the incriminating gold clock in May Li's bag, but Liu Ma's abused husband Liu Lung reveals the truth that it was his wife who placed it there.

Despite being proved innocent, May Li and her father are humiliated by the accusations and leave Master Wang's home, after which Ta angrily hands Lung a bamboo stick and directs him to beat his wife. Ta then leaves his father's home to search for May Li, an action that prompts Wang to finally consult a physician about his interminable cough (which appears in the stage and film versions but mainly in the novel), a sign that Wang has begun to accept Western ways. As we have seen, one year earlier *West Side Story* had stretched the boundaries of what was possible in a musical. Still, a violent shooting inspired by a male rivalry for a woman's affections (Linda), a seduction of a much younger man by a desperate pock-marked woman and her consequent suicide (Helen), and a vicious wife-beating (Liu Ma) were not the usual fare expected in a late 1950s musical and would no doubt also present situations in a film that would not be in compliance with the Production Code.

The depiction of Ta's prolonged sexual involvement with Helen and its tragic outcome posed particular problems for a musical comedy in 1958, problems not successfully resolved in the stage version and no doubt impossible to depict in a film in 1961. In the former, Ta allows himself to be seduced by Helen in his dreams but wakes up realizing that he loves Mei Li and quickly leaves Helen's apartment. The scenario of the film ballet, told from Helen's perspective, ends with her abrupt disappearance after failing to hold on to Ta's outstretched arms. Since neither the stage nor film version could reenact what happened in Helen's apartment and reveal the full extent of Helen's tragedy as conveyed in Lee's novel, the audiences for both were left potentially confused by a sad and lonely character who is given the central and most memorable romantic ballad ("Love, Look Away") before vanishing from the musical without explanation. In addition to its beauty and power, perhaps the song serves to encourage audience members to read Lee's excellent and groundbreaking novel in order to understand the song (and the show) more fully.

Postscript

Flower Drum Song has paid a stiff critical price for not displaying lofty dramatic goals, nor does it tackle provocative social issues or offer the big scenes and complex musical agendas found in *Oklahoma!*, *Carousel*, *The King and I*, and *South Pacific*. The musical does address conflicts between Eastern and Western values, the generation gap, and assimilation, but for the most part it is primarily a romantic comedy about two contrasting pairs of lovers who, after overcoming obstacles and resolving complications, succeed in finding the right partners and live happily ever after. These characters are regularly dismissed as stereotypes, perhaps because the work is so often experienced via brief excerpts on YouTube or passing references in broader discussions of the racism toward Asians so often prevalent in American popular cultural history and remains a disturbing ongoing presence in American life. But in fact, the characters in both the novel by Chinese-born Lee and the libretto and score by Fields, Hammerstein, and Rodgers possess psychological depth and are on the whole human and humorous.

Admittedly, some of the characters reinforce character traits and gendered and Asian stereotypes, in particular Mei Li's perceived meekness, Linda's sensuality, and Ta's sexual naïveté. But to their credit, Hammerstein and Fields avoided the worst stereotypes of a previous generation of Hollywood portrayals of Asian Americans. Nobody sneaks off to rot in an opium den or works in a laundry. In a 1983 interview, well after the numerous civil rights revolutions of the 1960s began, the novel's author defended the musical on cultural grounds: "I don't think there's anything against Chinese Americans or Asian Americans in it. The concept of the generation gap is definitely universal, and the families are an old-fashioned, traditional type of family."[36]

Further, if Mei Li overdoes female obsequiousness, she also demonstrates impressive resourcefulness when she appropriates a television movie plot about the illegal immigration of Latinx characters to ingeniously extricate herself from her arranged marriage with Sammy in order to marry Ta, the man she loves. It has been noted (and will be again in chapter 8) that television in the 1950s threatened the future of live theater and is recognized as a significant factor in the downfall of the studio system. For the purposes of the stage and film version of *Flower Drum Song*, however, it is a source of salvation and the means to solve an intractable problem, thus prompting Mei Li to utter the following as the final line of the musical:

MEI LI: Ta, Tomorrow we must go to the Temple of Tin How and thank the Goddess of Heaven for Television. See Figure 7.3.

Fig. 7.3 The weddings in the stage version of *Flower Drum Song*. *Center from left*: Pat Suzuki (Linda Low), Miyoshi Umeki (Mei Li), and Juanita Hall (Madam Liang). Photo by Friedman-Abeles © Billy Rose Theatre Division, The New York Public Library for the Performing Arts.

Despite the absence of long-lasting song hits, other than perhaps the controversial "I Enjoy Being a Girl" and "Love, Look Away," the *Flower Drum Song* score has been consistently underrated, but not by everyone. Ethan Mordden, for example, considers the work "superb R&H, very melodic and poetic and organized so that 'Chinese' numbers challenge 'Americanized' numbers."[37] While the stage version failed to gain a firm foothold in the Broadway canon, listeners can still savor the fine cast album and a technically accomplished and dramatically (mostly) faithful film with fine acting, singing, and dancing. And of course, the presence of a nearly all-Asian cast saves viewers from having to watch an actor like Mexican American Ricardo Montalban impersonate a Kabuki performer as he did in *Sayonara* (1957) or the Caucasian cast of Cole Porter's 1958 television musical *Aladdin* in yellowface.

A not-so-hidden agenda of this chapter is to offer some scholarly and critical PR on behalf of a film that belongs (in my view) to a select group of film musicals that arguably surpass their stage models, joining the previously discussed *Roberta*, *Call Me Madam*, and *Silk Stockings* and perhaps a handful of others not included in *A Fine Romance*. In the case of Universal-International's *Flower Drum Song*, a central reason for this verdict is not so much the realistically constructed soundstage with a Grant Avenue that rivals the verisimilitude of Disneyland's version of New Orleans architecture, or even the talented cast, but the often-overlooked imaginative and dramatically persuasive re-imagining of the stage version's song sequence and dramatic trajectory. Assuming that some directors will have future opportunities to stage this musical, the recommendation offered here is that they seriously consider adopting Fields's screenplay and the 1961 film song order instead of reviving Hwang's 2002 revisal.

8

Stretching Boundaries in the Wake of the Studio System Era

Cabaret on Stage and Screen

Putting Nazis on the stage in a musical seemed like a big enough step
at the time.

—Harold Prince, *Sense of Occasion*

The Fall of the Studio System Empire

In a 1957 *Life* magazine survey of the "glamorous era [that] ended in disaster"
(i.e., the studio system era), Eric Hodgins offered the following encapsulation: "In one fell decade Hollywood was knocked down by TV, kicked in the jaw
by a court order that broke up the profitable, monopolistic alliance between the
theater chains and the studios, and at last all but destroyed by an upheaval in
America's recreational habits."[1] A 1948 Supreme Court decision ruled against the
film studios' seemingly infallible and monolithic film and distribution model,
including the extortionist distribution practice known as block booking. In the
introductory chapter of this book, I briefly outlined how the effects of this decision led studios over the next decade to reduce their production output by half as
well as reducing its payrolls.

The shift from full-service studios like MGM to nimbler but smaller production companies diminished the power and profits of the studio moguls who
found themselves replaced by "independent producers, all-powerful agents, tax
experts, and legal wizards."[2] These independent producers and the talent they
hired were able to enter a brave new world of opportunities for innovation and
profits. The shift didn't happen overnight. Notably, MGM and the Freed Unit
continued to prosper (albeit at a slower pace and with some considerable cost-
cutting) until the end of the 1950s when *Gigi* (1958), a huge financial and critical
hit, also captured the Academy Award for Best Picture.

Several years before the Empire fell, one major film of the era discussed in *A
Fine Romance*, *Oklahoma!* (1955) (see chapter 4) had succeeded in bypassing the

A Fine Romance. Geoffrey Block, Oxford University Press. © Oxford University Press 2023.
DOI: 10.1093/oso/9780197501733.003.0008

studio system through the formation of the new production company Magna in 1952; this company combined with technological start-up Todd-AO two years later for the express purpose of producing this long-awaited film adaptation. Three years later Magna produced *South Pacific*, its second hit and last musical. In discussing *West Side Story* (chapter 6), we learned about Mirisch, another new company, formed in 1957, in large part to produce that film. Working with United Artists, Mirisch eventually produced sixty-eight films from the year of its inception through the late 1970s. After *West Side Story* only two of these films were musicals, *How to Succeed in Business without Really Trying* (1966) and *Fiddler on the Roof* (1971).

Cabaret is the third film musical explored in this survey that was produced outside of the studio system. The company that purchased the film rights for $1.5 million and then distributed the film for $5 million was called Allied Artists, which teamed up with a new television offshoot, ABC Pictures, to produce the film.[3] After producing several other successful movies, notably *Papillon* (1973) and *The Betsy* (1978), high production costs led to financial insolvency and the company's dissolution in 1979. By this time, the team of Allied/ABC had produced and distributed a grand total of one musical: *Cabaret*. By comparison, readers of *A Fine Romance* might be reminded that between 1946 and 1955, MGM produced eighty-one musicals. In the years since *The Sound of Music* (1965), the mega-hit in its day and still one of the most financially successful musicals of all time, the majority of the twelve high-profile roadshow movies that followed between *Camelot* in 1967 and *Man of La Mancha* in 1972 proved to be critically or financially disappointing compared with the successes of the early 1960s.[4]

At the end of the roadshow era, the subject of this chapter, *Cabaret*, unlike *Fiddler on the Roof*, the successful, albeit long (180 minutes) film musical also released in 1972, "was not produced, marketed, or exhibited as a roadshow."[5] The company that produced it, Allied/ABC, did not offer a production process designed for speed or efficiency. On the other hand, it did offer an experienced producer, Cy Feuer (1911–2006) introduced in chapter 5, and the freedom to produce a richly cinematic film made entirely in Germany with everything except the Kit Kat Klub filmed on location.[6] Feuer also knew enough (and knew how) to hire the best available talent for an innovative cinematic transformation of this by-now classic Broadway score by composer John Kander (b. 1927) and lyricist Fred Ebb (1928–2004): director Bob Fosse (1927-987), screenwriters Jay Presson Allen (1922-2006) and later Hugh Wheeler (1912-1987), the original stage Emcee Joel Grey (1932-) and rising star Liza Minnelli (1946-). Other indispensable contributors included film editor David Bretherton, cinematographer Geoffrey Unsworth, and art and set directors Rolf Zehetbauer, Hans Jürgen Kiebach, and Herbert Stabell. With the sole exception of Allen, who was nominated, everyone named above received an Academy Award. Not only did the film prove to be a huge and lasting hit, but it has also come to be regarded both as a milestone of musical film and a postscript to a studio era now passed.

On the Road to the Concept Musical

We have seen that librettist Arthur Laurents attributed the influence of *West Side Story* to its content rather than its form, a content that "dealt with" such topics as "bigotry, race, rape, murder, death . . . for the first time in a musical as seriously as they would be in a play."[7] Nine years later Harold Prince (1928–1919) conceived, produced, and directed *Cabaret*, a musical that took the genre forward in content *and* form. The epigraph to this chapter conveys Prince's pride that "putting Nazis on the stage in a musical seemed like a big enough step at the time."[8] A homosexual or bisexual main character would be in the show's future.[9]

Standard surveys of the Broadway musical concur with Prince that *Cabaret* also took the musical a step further toward the genre known since the late 1960s as the concept musical. Concept musicals are governed by an idea (the concept) that regularly replaces the linear narratives associated with the integrated musicals of Rodgers and Hammerstein, Lerner and Loewe, and indeed most of the hit musicals of the Golden Age from R&H's *Oklahoma!* (1943) to Bock and Harnick's *Fiddler on the Roof* (1964). At the end of this era, Jerome Robbins served as the director-choreographer of *Fiddler*, a musical which, although it presented a linear plot, anticipated *Cabaret* with "Tradition," an opening number that unified and conceptualized the show as a whole. Numerous 1950s and 1960s musicals prior to *Fiddler* also offer opening numbers that tell the audience what the show will be about.

In 1970, *Fiddler*'s producer Prince teamed up with Stephen Sondheim on the pathbreaking *Company*. The first of six Prince-Sondheim shows, *Company* eschewed a linear plot or subplot, instead offering a musical in which characters invade each other's space, the songs comment on but do not necessarily flow directly from the dialogue, and everything fits under the umbrella of the central idea, that is, the many layers inherent in the word and concept "company."[10] Most writers on the musical mark the origins of the concept musical from R&H's *Allegro* in 1947 and one year later Alan Jay Lerner and Kurt Weill's *Love Life*. By the early 1970s concept musicals such as *A Chorus Line* and *Chicago* would enter the musical theater mainstream. It is not surprising that neither *Allegro*, *Love Life*, nor *Company* were made into films. In thinking about how to adapt *Cabaret* to the screen, it is likely that Fosse understood the challenges of transforming a concept musical (even a partial concept musical like *Cabaret*) effectively to the screen.

The stage version of *Cabaret* combines past and future in a single package, a traditional book musical approach governed by integration, realism, and solid narrative as in *Fiddler* combined with a newer non-integrated, non-realistic, and non-linear concept approach soon brought into prominence by *Company*. The book songs that take place outside of the cabaret are recognizable in form and function to the book musicals of the Rodgers and Hammerstein era, while the cabaret songs comment on the book within the larger *concept* of the cabaret as it will do in future musicals in the Sondheim era. In the final song of the show, "Cabaret," which takes place in what Prince called "limbo," an alternative reality not present either in the book scenes or on the cabaret stage, the lyrics proclaim the central metaphor (i.e., concept) that "life is a cabaret." Prince also took the concept of the cabaret and used it to link the book and the cabaret scenes to deliver the message that the cabaret is not only a metaphor for "life" in general, but an embodiment of the decadence associated with the Berlin of 1929–1930 (stage) and 1931 (film) that both parallels and foreshadows what will befall Germany under Hitler within a few short years.

From Isherwood to Fosse

The starting point for the stage and film versions of *Cabaret* that would follow over the next fifty years was *The Berlin Stories* (1945) by the British writer Christopher Isherwood (1904–1986), a semi-autobiographical collection of occasionally intersecting short stories set in Berlin between 1929 and 1933 at the end of the short-lived Weimar Republic (1918–33).[11] The narrator and protagonist of the stories, the "I" in the famous phrase "I am a camera" introduced on the first page of the second collection of stories, was the author himself. The stories were loosely based on Isherwood's experiences in Berlin and the people he met there. Decades later, in his autobiography *Christopher and His Kind* (1976), which promised to "be as frank and factual as I can make it, especially as far as I myself am concerned," Isherwood attempted to separate fact from fiction and in the process reveal the identities of his fictional characters as well as his own sexual identity.[12]

Isherwood's belated revelations clear up a number of crucial matters that were either omitted or purposefully vague in the stories that inspired four significant fictional adaptations: (1) *I Am a Camera*, the Broadway play from 1951 by John Van Druten, starring Julie Harris as Sally Bowles; (2) the 1955 film adaptation of the play directed by Henry Cornelius, also starring Harris; (3) the 1966 stage musical *Cabaret* directed by Prince, which opened on November 20, 1966, and closed on September 6, 1969, after 1,165 performances; and (4) the January 1972 film adaptation of the stage musical directed by Bob Fosse. The common denominators of all these versions are the presence of a surrogate for Isherwood (with several name changes) in Berlin circa 1930, his relationship (platonic or consummated) with the colorful cabaret singer Sally Bowles (Jean Ross in real life) based on the eponymous short story, and a cabaret. The play and movie of *I Am a Camera* and Fosse's film version of *Cabaret*, but not the stage musical, are also traceable to the story, "The Landauers," which, like "Sally Bowles," appears in *Goodbye to Berlin*.[13]

The sexual identity of Christopher in *The Berlin Stories* remains undisclosed, but his friendship with Sally appears to be chaste. Although inconclusive, Sally's choice of the word "somehow" when she explains to Christopher, "Somehow, I couldn't possibly be in love with you," may offer a clue. Isherwood clears up this ambiguity in *Christopher and His Kind*: "In real life, Jean and Christopher had a relationship which was asexual but more truly intimate than the relationships between Sally and her various partners in the novel, the plays, and the films."[14] Sally does become pregnant (and has an abortion) in *Goodbye to Berlin*, but the father is Sally's casual boyfriend Klaus, not Christopher.

Since Isherwood did not clarify the sexuality of Christopher's surrogate or the nature of his relationship with Sally in *The Berlin Stories*, the play and the musical were free to have Clifford sleep with Sally (at least once), an action that resulted in pregnancy in these versions (and a hypothetical pregnancy in the case of the film version of *I Am a Camera*). Perhaps the boldest departure in the content in the Fosse film was that Clifford Bradshaw (now Brian Roberts) was bisexual, four years before Isherwood's public revelation of his own gay identity and lifestyle in *Christopher and His Kind*.

Both in *Contradictions* and *Sense of Occasion*, Prince explains that "what attracted the authors and me was the parallel between the spiritual bankruptcy of Germany in the 1920s and our country in the 1960s." In both memoirs he credits librettist Joe Masteroff for the show's title and the idea of the cabaret as "a metaphor for Germany," the foundation of the concept Prince would develop in *Cabaret*.[15] When Prince was stationed in Stuttgart in 1951, he saw a diminutive emcee perform regularly at a nightclub, and this gave him the idea of casting Joel Grey in the central role as the Emcee of the musical's Kit Kat Klub.[16] Prince's decision offered a new dramatic dimension to Isherwood's *Berlin Stories* and the *I Am a Camera* adaptations. It also introduced a future star, Grey, who would receive a Tony as Best Featured Actor in a Musical and an Oscar for Best Featured Actor in a Supporting Role.

The cabaret was more than a metaphor. It was central to the plot. In Prince's vision, the centrality of the Kit Kat Klub (with its triple initial K's likely a reference to the American racist organization the Ku Klux Klan founded in 1865) was in sharp contrast to the peripheral role cabaret life played in Isherwood's stories and the two versions of *I Am a Camera*. In fact, in 400 pages of *The Berlin Stories*, the cabaret figures in less than two when Sally's friend Fritz Wendel takes Christopher to The Lady Windermere (named after the Oscar Wilde's play *Lady Windermere's Fan*) to hear Sally Bowles, who "sang badly, without any expression," but whose "performance was, in its own way, effective because of her startling appearance and her air of not caring a curse what people thought of her."[17]

Sally continues to keep a low profile as a performer in the play version of *I Am a Camera*. Its first scene introduces a different character also named Fritz, Sally's Jewish friend who is living surreptitiously as a gentile (a character omitted from Isherwood's and Prince's versions but returning in Fosse's); he tells Christopher that Sally sings at The Lady Windermere. They never get there, however. Finally, in an early frame of the film adaptation, viewers see and hear Sally perform as badly as Isherwood described her in his *Berlin Stories*. In stark contrast, six of the fourteen songs in *Cabaret* take place in the Kit Kat Klub. Five are sung by Sally or the Emcee, alone or together, and the sixth, "Tomorrow Belongs to Me," is introduced by Klub waiters joined by the Emcee.

In a major departure from both Isherwood's stories and *I Am a Camera*, Prince adds a subplot that is for the most part a reimagined one. The subplot in *I Am a Camera* is based on Natalia Landauer, the young and beautiful daughter of a wealthy Jewish banker who appeared in "The Landauers," and the handsome gigolo Fritz Wendel who courts her for her money but falls so much in love he reveals the dangerous and well-kept secret that he is a Jew. Prince replaced the romance between Natalia and Fritz with a newly conceived secondary story based on a late-blooming romance between Christopher's landlady Fräulein Schneider (Frau Schroeder in *The Berlin Stories*) and an invented Jewish fruit vendor, Herr Schultz, who courts her with rare pineapples. When it becomes an inescapable truth to Fräulein Schneider that she will lose her license if she married Herr Schultz, she breaks off the engagement.

Prince wrote in *Sense of Occasion* that "probably the most inspired casting I've ever done was asking Lotte Lenya (1898-1981) to be a principal in the original production of *Cabaret*."[18] Lenya, Weill's widow and a theatrical legend in her own right, had starred in the late–1920s Weimar classics Weill wrote with Bertolt Brecht, *The Threepenny Opera* and *The Rise and Fall of the City of Mahagonny*. In 1954 she reprised her role in the former work in what would become the longest-running off-Broadway show up to that time (2,611 performances). In *Cabaret*, not only did Lenya enjoy a major dramatic role, but she also sang a solo song in each act, "So What?" in Act I and "What Would You Do?" in Act II. This was one song more than Clifford, the romantic male lead was given

Prince considered Lenya's second act song the "key song" of the show.[19] In addition to its importance to the dramatic meaning of the show, the *musical* question that supports Fräulein Schneider's rhetorical question in the title is aptly captured in musical rhetoric, in which nearly every phrase concludes with a questioning upward half step.[20] In addition to her two solos, Lenya was assigned two duets with Jack Gilford, the son of Romanian Jewish immigrants, who played her Jewish fiancé Herr Schultz ("It Couldn't Please Me More" and "Married" ["Heiraten" in German]). In the film version, all of these songs would vanish, and Herr Schultz's one solo song, "Meeskite" (the Yiddish word for an ugly or funny looking person), would disappear from future stage versions as well.

Prince's *Cabaret* thus consisted of two shows, one within the other: a book show that featured two pairs of romantic couples, Sally and Clifford, Fräulein Schneider and Herr Schultz, and a diegetic cabaret musical with songs performed at the Kit Kat Klub with one exception by Sally and the Emcee. After Kander and Ebb wrote "about forty-seven" songs, the 1966 stage production ended up with nine book songs (including "Tomorrow Belongs to Me" introduced at the Klub) and five cabaret songs.[21]

In the movie, the musical component was reduced to eight songs. All were diegetic, and only "Tomorrow" (77:01) was performed beyond the cabaret stage.[22] In addition to "Tomorrow," the "book" songs from the Broadway production that were sung outside of the Kit Kat Klub include Fräulein Schneider's two songs, Herr Schultz's one, and their two duets. As noted, the film removed all these songs. Also cut were Sally and Clifford's duet "Perfectly Marvelous" and Clifford's solo "Why Should I Wake Up?" (both in Act I), and the reprise of "Tomorrow Belongs to Me," which had been sung at the end of Act I led by Fräulein Kost (Fräulein Schneider's anti-Semitic boarder and a prostitute) joined by Clifford's German acquaintance Ernst Ludwig (revealed at the Schneider-Schultz engagement party to be a Nazi sympathizer), and several other guests.

When Prince wrote and spoke about his intentions, he distinguished between "real world" numbers and "metaphorical numbers illustrating changes in the German mind" (i.e., the "limbo area"). In making this distinction, Prince made it clear that some of the club numbers were "realistic numbers" that belonged to the "real world" and some were "limbo" numbers. Eventually he worked out a staging in which the limbo numbers were presented upstage in front of a silvery curtain.[23] In his "Reflections" on his *Cabaret* chapter in *Sense of Occasion* (published forty-four years after *Contradictions*), Prince explained that he placed the final number "Cabaret" in the limbo area "to dramatize Sally Bowles's knowledge that she is pregnant" and that when she sings about her friend Elsie, "she is really singing about herself, making up her mind to have an abortion."[24]

In *Contradictions*, Prince wrote that shortly before the Boston tryouts he arranged for George Abbott and Stephen Sondheim to see the show, describing them as "the two I most like to hear from at that stage."[25] Curiously, Prince does not mention in either *Contradictions* or *Sense of Occasion* that he also invited Jerome [Jerry] Robbins to a performance. We learn this from *Cabaret* choreographer Ron Field, who "was nervous about him [Robbins] seeing my work" and recalled that "Jerry thought the show was wonderful, but his strong suggestion was that any dancing that didn't take place as part of the performance at the Kit Kat Klub be cut from the show."[26] Fortunately from Field's point of view, Prince decided to reject Robbins's "scary" suggestion. Six years later Fosse went further than Robbins and removed not only the non-Klub dancing but also all but one of the non-Klub song ("Tomorrow Belongs to Me").

Cy Feuer's *Cabaret*

The film version of *Cabaret* that arrived six years after the premiere of the stage version is almost invariably thought of as "Bob Fosse's *Cabaret*" (when not referred to as Liza Minnelli's or Joel Grey's *Cabaret*). Indeed, Fosse was the director and the choreographer. He also deserves (but rarely receives) co-credit for his painstaking frame-by-frame collaborative work with Academy Award-winning film editor David Bretherton. In his description of the camerawork and editing in Minnelli's signature opening solo number, "Mein Herr," Kevin Winkler offers a telling example of how Fosse uses film to "direct the audience's attention to just the detail he wishes it to see."[27] The detail Winkler offers occurs when Fosse's "camera catches each dancer as she points up, down, and sideways" to match Ebb's lyric, "The continent of Europe is so wide, Mein Herr/ Not only up and down, but side to side, Mein Herr," a correlation that would be difficult if not impossible for stage audiences to process.[28] Film viewers can thank Fosse for the creation of such details as well as the numerous disturbing "reaction" cutaways to the Emcee's sinister and mocking facial expressions that appear often and without warning after, or even intruding within, numerous scenes and songs.

But if credit is due Fosse for so much of what film viewers witness, it was producer Cy Feuer who made three crucial non-negotiable transformative decisions *prior* to Fosse's arrival on the scene. All were in response to what Feuer didn't like about Prince's *Cabaret*. The first decision was to toss out "that soupy, sentimental, idiotic business with the little old Jewish man [Herr Schultz] courting Sally's landlady [Fräulein Schneider] by bringing her a pineapple every day." Instead, Feuer returned to the subplot of *I Am a Camera*, the love story "between a young Jewish heiress [Natalia Landauer] who cannot marry out of her faith and a gentile [Fritz Wendel]," who "really is not a gentile, but a poor Jewish schnook trying to pass."[29] The second decision was to "get straight (and this is no pun")" the "homosexual angle," in direct contrast to the stage version, in which "the exact sexual inclination of Sally Bowles's admirer is either fudged or eliminated."[30] Feuer wanted to leave no doubt about Clifford's sexual predilections.[31]

Feuer's third edict was that the film strictly enforce diegeticism (not Feuer's word), a principle introduced in this book in connection with *The Cat and the Fiddle* (chapter 2). As mentioned in that discussion, since the 1950s, diegetic has meant that the characters knew they were singing. Diegetic songs occur regularly in stage musicals but are ubiquitous in film musicals, which often preferred that characters not sing or dance unless they had a natural reason to do so as part of a performance. This last point is one reason for the popularity of film musicals about show business (think *42nd Street* and *Singin' in the Rain*). Although to a lesser extent than the stage and film versions of *The Cat and the Fiddle* and the film adaptation of *Roberta*, the other musicals explored in *A Fine Romance* also use a combination of diegetic and non-diegetic performance styles. Feuer's third decision went even further in its efforts to remove *all* non-diegetic situations: "There can be no unjustified singing on the screen. There's a reality about the movies that will not accept it. This is a show-business story and the singing takes place on the stage of the Kit Kat Klub. Period."[32]

To fulfill Feuer's conditions, Herr Schultz entirely vanished from the picture and Lotte Lenya's major acting and singing role as Fräulein Schneider (played in the film by the Austrian actress Elisabeth Neumann-Viertel) was drastically cut, including all four of her songs. Eventually Feuer allowed some fudging on his demands, such as when Brian (formerly Clifford or Cliff) was depicted, not as gay, but as bisexual—what Feuer and many others at that time, both straight and gay, referred to as a "switch-hitter." "Tomorrow Belongs to Me" was also removed from the Kit Kat Klub but was sung diegetically by a Nazi youth and older Germans drinking at an outdoor Biergarten in the countryside. What they are singing is the kind of patriotic folk anthem familiar to native Germans. It consists of a single 16-measure melody that moves mostly adjacently from one note to the next aside from a few small leaps here and there and one larger downward leap of a sixth on the word "belongs." The short, simple, repetitive, and diatonic melody (i.e., every note belonging to the key of the song) has proven so successful as a patriotic folk song that many listeners continue to be surprised to learn that Kander and Ebb wrote it.[33]

Connections between the Kit Kat Klub Songs and the Book Narrative for *Cabaret* on Stage and Screen

One of the most distinctive and imaginative features of *Cabaret* is the way the cabaret songs connect thematically with adjacent moments in the book narrative. These connections begin with "Willkommen" (2:04), the Emcee's opening number juxtaposed with extended cutaway shots of Brian arriving by train where he is welcomed by the city of Berlin. The shots continue as Brian makes his way to the boarding house where he will meet Sally (who has been seen occasionally in the number that occurred presumably earlier or later in real time but concurrently in the film). The imaginative connections in the film between the cabaret and life in other parts of Berlin will be the central focus in the following section of this chapter.

The two sets of songs, stage and film, also reflect differing approaches to integration. The book songs tend to follow the established Rodgers and Hammerstein approach. For example, when Fräulein Schneider tells her suitor, Herr Schultz, "If you bought me diamonds,/If you bought me roses" etc. "It couldn't please me more," everything she speaks is musicalized and the song flows naturally from the dialogue.[34] The cabaret songs operate differently. As we'll soon observe, instead of being marked by a gradual transition, *Cabaret*'s Kit Kat Klub songs usually begin directly after the lights dim on the previous scene. This decision inspired Prince to create other dramatic means to achieve conceptual connections between dialogue and song. See Table 8.1, "*Cabaret* (1966, 1972, and 1998)."

For the most part, Fosse follows Prince and Masteroff's approach and consistently connects the cabaret songs topically and meaningfully with the libretto narrative taking place outside of the Kit Kat Klub. The person most responsible for creating *new* connections with the reworked narrative was screenwriter Jay Presson Allen, whose previous credits included Alfred Hitchcock's *Marnie* (1964), a major overhaul of Winston Graham's 1961 novel *Marnie*, and the 1969 film adaptation of her own play, *The Prime of Miss Jean Brodie* (1966).[35] Allen recalled that she worked on the *Cabaret* screenplay for ten months, "which is a very long time for me."[36] Since she completed her draft on June 10, 1970, this would place as the starting date the previous August, several months *before* Feuer hired Fosse to direct and almost six months before the introductory meeting with Feuer, Fosse, Allen, and Kander and Ebb that Fosse noted in his diary.[37] This screenplay draft provides the clearest evidence of Allen's ideas for these connections.

"Tomorrow Belongs to Me" was moved from the cabaret to a new diegetic situation and location, and Robbins retrospectively got his wish when they cut the "Telephone Song," a plot song in which the cabaret girls made phone appointments with male customers to solicit drinks and perhaps something more. The Feuer-Fosse *Cabaret* also made a number of significant changes regarding the musical stage numbers performed at the Kit Kat Klub. For starters, the film introduced a new opening number for Sally, "Mein Herr," replacing "Don't Tell Mama." Another change was the substitution of "The Money Song," which on stage featured the Emcee and the cabaret girls, with "Money, Money" for the Emcee and Sally. It also added an untitled "slap dance" number and a Nazi

Table 8.1 *Cabaret* (1966, 1972, and 1998).

Stage 1966 and 1998 (both versions unless otherwise noted)	Film 1972 and Stage 1966/1998
Act I	
Willkommen (Grey and the Company) (415)	Willkommen (Grey) [1966 and 1998] (2:04)
So What? (Lenya) (418)	
Don't Tell Mama (Haworth and the Girls) (421)	Mein Herr (Minnelli) [new in film; also 1998] (10:56)
Telephone Song (Company) [cut in 1998] (425)	
	Bavarian Slap Dance (Grey) [new in film] (22:34)
	Maybe This Time (Minnelli) [new in film; also 1998] (45:41)
Perfectly Marvelous (Haworth, Convy) (429)	
	Money, Money (Grey, Minnelli) [new in film; also 1998] (55:45)
Two Ladies (Grey, Ehara, and O'Connor) (431)	Two Ladies (Grey and Two Ladies [1966 and 1998] (65:29)
It Couldn't Please Me More (Lenya, Gilford) (435)	
Tomorrow Belongs to Me (Grey and Waiters) (437)	Tomorrow Belongs to Me (Lambert [for Collignon] and other Germans) [1966] (77:01)
Why Should I Wake Up? (Convy) [replaced by Don't Go in 1987; cut in 1998] (438)	
The Money Song (Sitting Pretty) (Grey and the Cabaret Girls) [replaced by Money, Money in 1998] (440)	
	Tiller Girls [Goose Step] (Grey) [new in film; part of 1998 Entr'acte] (89:34)
Married (Lenya, Gilford) (443)	*Heiraten* (Married) [Greta Keller, singing on the gramophone] (91:57)
Meeskite (Gilford) [cut in 1998] (446)	
Tomorrow Belongs to Me (Reprise) (Murray, Winter, and Guests) (448)	

Table 8.1 Continued

Stage 1966 and 1998 (both versions unless otherwise noted)	Film 1972 and Stage 1966/1998
Act II	
Married (Reprise) (Gilford) (450)	
If You Could See Her (Grey and the Girls (451)	If You Could See Her (Grey and Doby) [1966 and 1998] (101:03)
What Would You Do? (Lenya) (452)	
I Don't Care Much (Emcee).[a] [cut in 1966; restored in 1987 and 1998]	
Cabaret (Haworth) (456)	Cabaret (Minnelli) [1966 and 1998] (116:27)
Finale (Convey, Haworth, Lenya, Gilford, Grey, and the Company) (460)	

[a] Fred Ebb and John Kander, *"Cabaret": The Illustrated Book and Lyrics* (New York: Newmarket, 1999), 91. [1998 libretto]

- *Numbers in parentheses in the stage column refer to page numbers in Joe Masteroff,* Cabaret, *in* Great Musicals of the American Theatre, *vol. 2, ed. Stanley Richards (Radnor, PA: Chilton, 1976).*
- *The songs listed in bold in the film column were not in the stage version.*
- *Numbers in parentheses in the film column refer to film timings.*

MAJOR SINGING AND DANCING AND SELECTED ROLES

Stage: Jill Haworth (Sally Bowles); Jack Gilford (Herr Schultz); Bert Convy (Clifford Bradshaw); Lotte Lenya (Fräulein Schneider); JOEL GREY (Master of Ceremonies [Emcee]); Peg Murray (Fräulein Kost); Edward Winter (Ernst Ludwig); Mary Ehara (one of Two Ladies); Rita O'Connor (one of Two Ladies)

Screen: Liza Minnelli (Sally Bowles); Michael York (Brian Roberts); Helmut Griem (Baron Maximilian van Heune); GREY (Emcee); Marisa Berenson (Natalia Landauer); Fritz Wepper (Fritz Wendel); Elizabeth Neumann-Viertel (Fräulein Schneider); Helen Vita (Fräulein Kost); Ralf Wolter (Herr Ludwig); Oliver Collignon [dubbed by Mark Lambert] (Hitler Youth Singer); Louise Quick (Kit Kat Dancer); Kathryn Doby (Kit Kat Dancer/Gorilla)

- *Names in capital letters indicate that a cast member appeared both on stage and in the film.*

number ("Tiller Girls") for the Emcee and the cabaret girls and gave Sally another new song, "Maybe This Time."[38]

Prior to casting for the stage version, Prince decided he didn't want to make Sally the main character. He also didn't want to follow Kander and Ebb's suggestion to cast Minnelli as Sally on the grounds that she "wasn't British" and "sang too well."[39] In contrast, Feuer thought that the American actress's talent and star appeal were perfect for the role and hired Minnelli for the film before hiring Fosse and wanted her to play an American. To accommodate Feuer's casting choice, the film switched Clifford's nationality from American to British, and cast the British actor Michael York in this role, now called Brian.

"Don't Tell Mama" (stage) and "Mein Herr" (film) (10:56)

The desire to feature Minnelli and enhance Sally's role is evident with her new opening number, "Mein Herr," which replaced "Don't Tell Mama." "Don't Tell Mama" appeared in the stage version in scene 4 when Sally (and the cabaret girls) confide to the Kit Kat Klub audience that her Mama, who thinks Sally is "living in a convent," doesn't have a clue that she works in a sleazy nightclub ("You can tell my papa, that's all right/'Cause he comes in here every night," but "Don't Tell Mama").[40] With its lively, ragtime feel, the catchy "Don't Tell Mama" is classic Kander and Ebb.

"Mein Herr" conveys a version of Sally that is different from the mischievous and devious but endearing entertainer who entreats her audience in "Don't Tell Mama." The singer of "Mein Herr" is an opportunistic and unfeeling *femme fatale*, a jaded woman who uses men for her own pleasure and then discards them. Brian challenges this self-image during an argument later in the film when he tells her she is "about as *fatale* as an after-dinner mint." What prompted this argument was Sally's claim that she has "handled Max [Maximilian van Heune, the playboy who has seduced both Sally *and* Brian] brilliantly." After the song's instrumental vamp that duplicates the opening vamp of "Willkommen" (OOM-cha-cha, OOM-cha-cha, OOM-cha-cha-cha, OOM-cha) and a talky "Ad. Lib.," the verse moves from 3 measures of tonic C minor to 6 measures of dominant (G major) before returning to C minor to begin the chorus.

The slightly askew 7 + 8-bar chorus could hardly be simpler (or more repetitive). Every phrase begins with a three-note upbeat, like the verse, first on C minor (7 measures) then on the dominant G major (8 measures). After more repetitions and a circling back to the verse, the chorus returns, this time in C *major* (7 measures) with the shared dominant on G major (8 measures). The chorus concludes on the highest and longest-held note on high C for 11 measures, supported by a C-major harmony. Despite this exciting finale, I would nevertheless contend that from a purely musical standpoint, the substitution of "Don't Tell Mama" with "Mein Herr" was not an improvement.

But it suits Minnelli perfectly and she pulls it off admirably. Her vocal skill and showmanship, matched by the ensemble dancing and riveting photography and imaginative editing, made "Mein Herr" such an inextricable part of *Cabaret* that it would return, along with "Don't Tell Mama," in the popular 1998 Broadway revival directed by Sam Mendes and in future stage productions elsewhere.[41]

"Bavarian Slap Dance"—Film Version Only (22:34)

Several minutes after the conclusion of "Mein Herr" we see a young Nazi going around taking a collection from Kit Kat Klub customers and the Klub manager roughly throwing him out. The "Bavarian Slap Dance" that follows a few minutes later (a folk-like dance apparently not by Kander) illustrates the first of numerous film examples of life imitating art. Later that night on a deserted street, the manager is brutally beaten by a gang of thugs led by the same young Nazi who had been unceremoniously removed from the Klub. The scene quickly shifts to the cabaret where the Emcee, dressed in lederhosen, performs a traditional Bavarian Slap Dance in which "he smilingly administers face and body slaps in time to the music."[42] Allen's scene directions continue: "The comic violence of this dance should play in juxtaposition to the inter-cut scenes of realistic violence. Music cuts off on each quick cut to the mugging."[43] This is precisely what viewers see on the screen. The cutaway of the Emcee crowing like a rooster at the end of the dance contributes to the cabaret-as-metaphor concept that connects what's happening in the cabaret with what's taking place in Weimar Germany in 1931.

"Maybe This Time"—Film Version Only (45:41)

According to Kaye Ballard, Kander and Ebb wrote "Maybe This Time" in 1964 at her request to sing in nightclubs. But it was Minnelli who made the song known when she recorded it the same year on her debut studio album *Liza! Liza!* Kander and Ebb introduce the song with an ascending chromatic orchestral vamp nearly identical melodically (but not rhythmically) to the first phrase of melody in "Nowadays" from *Chicago* (1975). Following the vamp, a 16-bar chorus begins in which its first 8 measures starts off like a blues with 4 measures of tonic (I chord) and 2 measures of subdominant (IV chord). Instead of continuing with the blues progression and returning to the tonic for the seventh and eighth measures, however, Kander breaks the pattern by inserting 2 more measures of IV instead.

The melody of "Maybe This Time" is perhaps even more repetitive than "Mein Herr." Other than at the ends of phrases its rhythm is the same in nearly every measure to the swing-triplets of the opening measure. In the first half of each chorus the melodic phrase consists of Do Re Mi Do, C-D-E-C in the key of C (4 measures on C and 4 measures on F, the latter F-G-A-F); in the second half, the melody focuses on a half-step turn around (e.g., B-A#-B) followed by a descent, usually a fifth. Although Kander claimed to have become absorbed in "German jazz and vaudeville songs" of the era, the style of "Maybe This Time" more closely resembles a torch song in an American 1960s nightclub than a cabaret act during the waning years of the Weimar Republic.[44] In the final chorus the orchestra takes the melody up a half-step, a ubiquitous cliché of Big Band arrangements dating back to the 1930s and 1940s.

Ethan Mordden considered the song "wrong for the character and wrong for the era."[45] Its meaning also directly contradicts the love 'em and leave 'em attitude expressed in Sally's "Mein Herr." Clearly, Sally is not as hardened by life and love as she pretends to be in her first number. In its defense, the song effectively captures the hopefulness of a woman who has found a man to comfort her and tell her she's talented when her absent father fails to show up for their planned meeting. "Maybe this time/for the first time/Love won't hurry away."

"The Money Song" (stage) and "Money, Money" (film) (55:45)

In Prince's *Cabaret*, the catalyst for the stage version of "The Money Song" (also known as "Sitting Pretty"), performed by the Emcee and the cabaret girls, occurs much later in the story than the song's film counterpart, "Money, Money." On stage (Act I, scene 9) the song follows the scene in which Ernst offers Cliff a large sum of money to retrieve a briefcase from Paris to help an unidentified cause that audiences later learn turns out to be the Nazi Party.[46] Shortly before Ernst arrives at the boarding house in Act I, Sally has informed Cliff she might be having his baby, a natural consequence of their recent decision to share the same bed and Sally's successful (and unprotected) efforts to seduce him. After Cliff accepts Ernst's request to travel to Paris, the topic of marriage enters the conversation and the trio raise a glass to the prospect of becoming rich, after which they toast using the Latin word "Prosit!," the German equivalent of "Cheers."

The lights fade and the scene immediately shifts to scene 10 at the Kit Kat Klub where an expensively dressed and bejeweled Emcee connects the two scenes with his own "Prosit!" Like Cliff, the Emcee toasts to wealth and a financial situation that finds him "sitting pretty." Also like Cliff, the Emcee's earnings are obtained by less-than-honest work. The unknowing Cliff is aiding the Nazis, and the decadent Emcee is a pimp in the business of selling girls from Russia, Japan, France, and America.

The film counterpart to "The Money Song," "Money, Money," sung and danced by the Emcee and Sally in their only duet together, is nearly a completely new version of the stage song. The chorus of the new "Money" expresses the simple belief that "Money makes the world go around." The melody features a chromatic descent on the words "makes the world" (C-C-flat-B-flat) and repeats "the world" three more times (C-flat-B-flat), perhaps to emphasize that the influence of money goes beyond the confines of the Kit Kat Klub.

In the stage version of "The Money Song" Cliff toasts the prospect of money. "Money, Money" is about money now at hand. Its appearance in the film follows naturally and immediately after Sally meets the dapper German Maximilian van Heune, who does not appear in the stage version. Max retrieves an undergarment that Sally has dropped in front of the laundry, explains to a worker that

Sally needs her clothes by Tuesday, and offers her a ride in his luxurious car. The scene quickly shifts to a close-up of the Emcee, who says "Money" followed by Sally repeating this magic word, also in close-up. The new song will follow suit. Money is the essence and meaning of the song and its mantra. "Money, Money" is so much about money that when the Emcee sings its middle section, Sally repeats the word "money" in a counter melody that consists entirely of a single pitch on the word "money" no less than FORTY-EIGHT times!

"Two Ladies" (stage and film) (65:29)

"Two Ladies" and the two restaged but musically intact stage songs that conclude the musical component of the film, "If You Could See Her" and "Cabaret," reinforce Prince's central stage concept in its intertwining the Berlin plot with the world of the Kit Kat Klub. Allen, mainly in consultation with Feuer, built on Prince's stage idea in her screenplay draft by creating situations for the cabaret songs that meaningfully connected in new and powerful ways with the songs that took place outside the cabaret. Fosse then choreographed and edited these newly contextualized musical numbers with skill and imagination.

In the stage version (Act I, scene 6), "Two Ladies" follows the scene in Fräulein Schneider's boarding house that contains the song "Perfectly Marvelous" and Cliff's decision to welcome Sally as his roommate. Whether their arrangement results in a sexual *ménage à deux* does not become clear until scene 9. The scene direction, "They are in each other's arms as the lights fade" suggests it does, as Cliff and Sally sing the final lyric of "Perfectly Marvelous" about "living together and having a marvelous time." A more sexually direct exchange begins in scene 9 when Sally and Cliff awaken after a romantic night. Cliff sings "Why Should I Wake Up?," Ernst arrives with his lucrative offer to enlist Cliff to retrieve the contraband briefcase in Paris, and the two lovebirds toast "Prosit!" to their pending riches and the possibility of marriage, all of which prepares for the Emcee's "Money Song."

The decision to become roommates, even platonic roommates sharing a bed, is a big step for Cliff, who worries that its "peculiar" nature would be difficult to explain. As soon as the lights go out after "Perfectly Marvelous," the scene shifts to the Kit Kat Klub and the song "Two Ladies." The Emcee adds sexual decadence to their decision by adding a second female roommate to create a sexually unambiguous *ménage à trois*. Cliff wasn't especially eager to have sex with even one woman. The Emcee now has two. The screenplay takes "Two Ladies" and provides a more directly meaningful narrative connection to what preceded it, an actual *ménage à trois*, albeit with one woman, Sally, and two *men*, Brian and Max. In contrast to the stage libretto, the screenplay also removes any lingering ambiguity about whether the men consummate their mutual attraction. This

Fig. 8.1 One lady (and two gentlemen). Liza Minnelli (Sally Bowles), Helmut Griem (Maximilian van Heune) [*center*], and Michael York (Brian Roberts) [*right*] in the film *Cabaret* [74:22]. Screenshot.

becomes evident when the next day Brian brandishes Max's gift of the expensive cigarette lighter he had refused to accept the day before. See Figure 8.1.

"If You Could See Her" (stage and film) (101:03)

The subplots of both the stage and film versions involve a romance between a Jew and a Gentile. In the stage version the romance is between Fräulein Schneider (Lenya) and the Jewish fruit vendor Herr Schultz (Gilford). The film pairs a more youthful Jewish heiress Natalia Landauer (Marisa Berenson) and a gigolo, Fritz Wendel (Fritz Wepper). The song, "If You Could See Her," also known as "The Gorilla Song," appears in both versions, albeit in altered narrative contexts. On stage, Fräulein Schneider expresses her realization that "one can no longer dismiss the Nazis" and the likelihood of losing her license to rent rooms if she marries a Jew. After Schultz reprises the last portion of "Married," someone off-stage throws a brick through his shop window, confirming the landlady's fears. The lights fade and "the Emcee enters, walking hand-in hand with a gorilla."

"If You Could See Her" constitutes the most direct manifestation of anti-Semitism in either version. In a song ostensibly about prejudice and intolerance, the Emcee explains that while his girlfriend may not conform to accepted societal norms, he appreciates the gorilla's attributes. For example, she reads music and unlike the Emcee neither smokes nor drinks. After the Emcee sings a chorus of the tune in its original duple meter, the orchestra repeats the tune as a waltz (triple meter), evoking the romance of Johann Strauss Jr.'s nineteenth-century Vienna.[47] After placing an engagement ring on the gorilla's nose, the Emcee delivers the punch line that proved controversial to influential members of the Jewish community in 1966: "If you could see her through my eyes she wouldn't look Jewish at all!" To save the show from closing, Prince replaced this provocative and misunderstood line with the innocuous "she isn't a meeskite at all!" a decision he would continue to view as the right one.[48] See Figures 8.2 and 8.3.

We have noted that Fritz, initially interested only in Natalia's money, soon falls in love. Although Natalia comes to realize that Fritz's love is genuine and she feels the same, religious differences and the undeniable rise of anti-Semitism and the Nazis, who kill her dog, prompt her to break things off. Heartbroken by Natalia's rejection, Fritz confesses to Brian that he is a Jew passing as a Gentile and afraid to share this secret with the Jewish woman he loves. The camera then shifts to the Kit Kat Klub for "If You Could You See Her." The music and dance are the same as on stage, but between the waltz and the final four lines of the song in the film, the Emcee speaks rather than sings to the audience as he pleads for understanding. The film uses the original final line ("She wouldn't look Jewish at all"), but because of worries about pressure to replace it, Fosse directed Grey to speak the line so that it could be more easily changed if required.

In one of the most powerful moments of film editing, the camera swiftly cuts from the Emcee's final spoken line to Fritz banging on the door of the Landauer home waking up her family in the middle of the night. When Natalia finally opens the door, Fritz announces, "I'm a Jew." The camera immediately cuts to

Fig. 8.2 Joel Grey and Gorilla in the stage version of *Cabaret*. Photofest.

Fig. 8.3 Joel Grey and Gorilla in the film *Cabaret* [105:26]. Screenshot.

a Jewish wedding where Natalia and Fritz exchange vows and seal their doom. Knowing what we know will soon happen to millions of Jews, the romance and marriage between the young Jewish couple is especially poignant and chilling.

"Cabaret" (stage and film) (116:27)

The stage show evolved considerably from its original idea that the Emcee introduce the show with a group of songs. Kander and Ebb called these the "Berlin Songs."[49] Gradually, the original nine "Berlin Songs" were reduced to five. Two of these, "Two Ladies" and "Tomorrow Belongs to Me," were eventually integrated into the stage narrative, and a third song "I Don't Care Much," dropped from the original production, was later added for the 1987 Prince and 1998 Mendes revivals (also London 2012 and New York 2014) where it was sung by the Emcee. The self-consciously operatic "Angel of Love" was dropped prior to the first script draft.

The remaining song, "I Never Loved a Man as Much as Herman," was intended for two Chinese girls and contains a number of Asian musical stereotypes. As far as I can determine, it has previously gone unnoticed that a portion of "Herman" made a guest appearance in the song "Cabaret." This is the part of the song where Sally digresses to sing about her friend Elsie, who despite an early death from pill-taking and drinking was fondly remembered as "the happiest corpse I'd ever seen." The "Elsie" interlude appears as a contrasting musical sidebar between two AABA choruses in which nearly every measure of the A sections displays syncopated rhythmic patterns associated with ragtime: m. 1 short LONG short/ m. 2 short LONG short/m. 3 short short short LONG/m. 4 LONG, tied from the previous measure.[50] The first three phrases of the "Elsie" section share the identical rhythmic pattern of 11 successive quarter notes as the song about Herman and the pitches for the first 9.

It was previously mentioned that according to Prince, when Sally steps through the glittering silver curtain leading to limbo to sing her final number "Cabaret" alone downstage, she is singing about her abortion rather than her friend Elsie.[51] In the film version, significantly the only cabaret song that focuses exclusively on the performer without camera intrusions of Berlin life or even cutaways to the audience, the abortion is a fait accompli. Sally and Brian have already parted ways. Like their aborted romance, Brian's return train to Cambridge has left the station.

Final Thoughts on the Notion of Life as a Cabaret

Despite its modernity, Fosse's *Cabaret* did not violate all the Commandments of screen adaptation. In fact, the film conspicuously observed two Commandments: first when it cast Joel Grey as the Emcee, and second when it engaged the Broadway songwriting team, Kander and Ebb, to write the new songs. Perhaps the Feuer-Fosse approach to adaptation was not so radical after all. For example, when Hollis Alpert praised the film in the *Saturday Review* because it allowed only performers who are *supposed* to sing the opportunity to do so, he could have been writing about nearly any Fred Astaire and Ginger Rogers movie.[52] To give Alpert the benefit of the doubt, when he praised this feature of Fosse's *Cabaret* as "clearly an innovation," perhaps he meant that characters who didn't *play* singers in the stage version should forfeit their right to sing in a film adaptation. Either way, Albert concluded that the creators of the film version of *Cabaret* "not only improved on the original, they have brilliantly transformed it."[53]

Even Pauline Kael liked the film. The critic who dismissed *West Side Story* for lacking an "HONEST routine" like Donald O'Connor's "Make 'Em Laugh" from *Singin' in the Rain*, praised Fosse's *Cabaret* as "the first really innovative movie musical in many years."[54] Kael was especially appreciative that the film "violates the pseudo-naturalistic tradition . . . which requires that the songs appear to grow organically out of the story." For Kael, "*Cabaret* is a great movie musical, made, miraculously, without compromises," despite the fact that it falls short of an "ideal musical," which "would include far more dancing."

Fosse had his own strong ideas about how to adapt *Cabaret*, but he never wavered from Prince's overriding concept that Sally/Minnelli belted out in the song "Cabaret." For Prince, Fosse, and later Mendes, "life *is* a cabaret," a mirror to the Nazi menace about to overtake Germany and a major part of the problem. Particularly through the use of often disturbing close-ups of the Emcee at strategic moments throughout the film, Fosse succeeds in equating the cabaret with the menace. Nevertheless, while this conceit is highly effective from an artistic standpoint it arguably misrepresents historical cabaret life by depicting cabarets as the embodiment of a social decadence that parallels the moral depravity of the Nazi regime. Indeed, seeing the men in Nazi uniforms dispersed among the cabaret audience was a powerful image at the end of both the stage and film versions.

The Prince-Fosse-Mendes interpretation of the cabaret as a breeding ground for anti-Semitism that contributed to the rise of Hitler has been challenged by Linda Mizejewski who argues that cabarets "were actually points of resistance" and that "cabaret humor often took on the Nazis as their targets of satire."[55] Before the cabarets were shut down shortly after Hitler became chancellor in 1933, they were more often raided for satirizing the Nazis than for their complicity in the rise of Nazism and the escalation of anti-Semitism. Audiences and critics generally accept the Prince and Fosse premise, although Stephen Farber criticized the film's conceit of implying "a simple causal relationship between decadence and totalitarianism."[56] Despite this reservation, Farber liked the film, concluding that "even with its PG rating, *Cabaret* deserves to be called the first adult film musical."[57] Both the stage and film versions offer a brief moment of satire directed against the Nazis. On the stage, this occurs in the goose-stepping Nazi parody that opens Act II in which the Emcee in drag and fellow cabaret girls perform a martial version of "Tomorrow Belongs to Me." In Fosse's *Cabaret*, the goose-stepping number appears at the end of "Tiller Girls," when a song medley is followed by military drumming and the appearance of the Emcee, also in drag, who lets out a prolonged and manic laugh.[58]

At the outset of this chapter, I recalled Laurents's historical verdict that *West Side Story* influenced the course of musical theater history, not because of its technical features, but for its content as the first musical to consider so many "serious subjects."[59] Indeed, not only did *Cabaret* break new artistic ground on the journey to the concept musical, but it also seriously incorporated previously unexplored topics, including anti-Semitism and abortion. Despite this new boldness, *Cabaret*'s male protagonist, three years before Stonewall, was as straight as he was in the stage and film versions of *I Am a Camera*, or, for that matter, as straight as Christopher in Isherwood's *Berlin Stories.* Prince didn't think Broadway audiences were ready for this next step, but in his "Reflections" in *Sense of Occasion* he wrote that "were I to do *Cabaret* now, I would take the opportunity, as Fosse did in the film, to restore the original gay subplot."[60]

In its structural approach to the musical, Fosse's *Cabaret* was not unlike a 1930s film adaptation of a stage show in which the producer and director felt free to discard half or more of the Broadway score and limit the number of singers to as few as two stars. But just as the stage versions of *West Side Story* and *Cabaret* went further than their stage predecessors in tackling previously unexplored content, this return to earlier film conventions in the adaptation of *Cabaret* was more than matched by its provocative subject matter. And as we have seen, the film version and future stage revivals not only introduced Nazis and abortion but also explored homosexuality and bisexuality, one of Feuer's pre-conditional mandates. Allen's readiness to comply, which predated Fosse's hiring, is perhaps most strikingly evident in the following exchange from her June 10, 1970, screenplay draft as Sally and Brian discuss their relationship with the playboy Maximilian van Heune (then named Lothar):

> SALLY: Lothar's everything you're not! He's worldly and rich and suave and divinely sexy! He really appreciates a woman's body . . .
> BRIAN: Oh fuck Lothar! [61]
> SALLY (shouts): I *do*!
> BRIAN (shouts back): So do *I*!

Allen retained this wording and most of the surrounding exchange in a Revised Draft dated December 30, 1970. But since Allen had signed up for only one draft and had other commitments, Hugh Wheeler was called in (at Allen's suggestion) to take over the revisions in places where Fosse found fault with Allen's original version.[62] The Final Draft of "A Screenplay by Jan [*recte* Jay] Presson Allen and Hugh Wheeler" of February 15, 1971, included the following significant revision of the two 1970 drafts, changes presumably courtesy of Wheeler:

SALLY: You can't stand it because Maximilian's everything you're not! He's worldly and rich and suave and divinely sexy! He really appreciates a woman.

BRIAN: He appreciates a man too.

SALLY (after a pause—stunned): You mean, you and Max!

BRIAN (savagely quiet): Me and Max.[63]

As it turned out, Wheeler's sanitized changes to the Final Draft were not the last word. Sometime during the shooting of the film Fosse decided to revisit Allen's earlier draft, although softening her word for the sexual act both Sally and Brian separately performed with Maximilian from "fuck" to "screw." No doubt the reason for the expurgated language was to avoid the potential economic consequence of a PG-13 or R rating (it ended up as PG), a self-censorship not unlike the decision to substitute the words "Krup you!" as the punch line to "Gee, Officer, Krupke" in *West Side Story*.[64] But even the substitution of the word "screw" for "fuck" and the fact that it was uttered by a bisexual male protagonist was shocking in 1972. Brian might have said "screw Maximilian," but for a film musical in 1972, this was truly a big f***ing deal, or to use an expression memorably uttered by then Vice President Joe Biden, a BFD.

After Fosse's *Cabaret*, the sexuality of the male protagonist continued to evolve. Prince's 1987 Broadway revival contained a whiff of bisexuality, but by the time the Mendes revival arrived in London (1993) and New York (1998), Clifford is a confirmed bisexual. In real life Isherwood did not out himself as a gay man until his 1976 memoir, *Christopher and His Kind*. Like the fictional "Sally Bowles," the singing career of Jean Ross, Isherwood's real life platonic friend who inspired the fictional Sally, is notably smaller than the featured musical role played by Sally in the musical version, a single visit to Lady Windermere's. The non-fictional Christopher's preferred nightclub venues were instead primarily "boy bars" such as the Cozy Corner, where he could satisfy his sexual preference for younger men from the working class.

On one of the special features of the *Cabaret* DVD released in 2003, Marty Baum, the executive producer for ABC pictures which had teamed with Allied Artists to produce the film, recalled his "fondest memory" of working on the movie.[65] The incident occurred in 1972 after one of the two Westwood screenings (January 21 or 22, 1972), several weeks before the film's formal premiere in New York on February 13. Prior to the screening someone had pointed out that Isherwood happened to be sitting next to him. After the screening Baum vividly recalled overhearing the original Christopher: "And when the lights went up, I was watching Isherwood, and he turned to the man next to him and his response was, 'What a goddam lie! I never slept with a woman in my life!'"[66]

Coda: Not So Happily Ever After *Cabaret*

After *Cabaret*, film adaptations entered a period of semi-hibernation and relative obscurity.[67] It was not until decades later that another film adaptation, *Chicago* (2002), based on another Kander and Ebb show and directed by Rob Marshall, achieved both critical acclaim and earned the first Best Picture Oscar for a musical after a thirty-four-year drought. As before, for the next few decades nearly all hit musicals after *Cabaret* found their way onto film (see Appendix 4). And as with stage to film production cycles in previous decades, most of the dozen stage musicals that were hits in the 1960s and 1970s and that appear on the list of 1970s films took between three and ten years to get from stage to screen. Two exceptions were *Evita* (1979), which took seventeen years to arrive in 1996, and the off-Broadway hit *The Fantasticks* that ran for forty-two years (1960–2002) and filmed two years before closing. The early norms were reversed in the 1980s and 1990s when only *five* hit musicals based on 1970s and 1980s stage musicals were adapted into films, four in the 1980s (*Annie*, *The Best Little Whorehouse in Texas*, *A Chorus Line*, and *Little Shop of Horrors*), and *Evita* in the 1990s.

In the 1960s, especially in the early 1960s, film adaptations of stage musicals were a financial and critical force to be reckoned with. An unprecedented four adaptations won the Academy Award for Best Picture: *West Side Story* (1961), *My Fair Lady* (1964), *The Sound of Music* (1965), and *Oliver!* (1968). Seven film adaptations were among the top thirty-five earners for the decade, with *The Sound of Music* and *My Fair Lady* ranking number 1 and 5, respectively. *West Side Story* was the highest-earning film to appear in 1961. Moving on to the 1970s, *Fiddler on the Roof* was the top money maker in 1971, and *Grease*, which made roughly $360 million on its $6 million investment, was the top earner in 1978 and the third most financially lucrative film of any type for the decade overall. After *Grease*, no film adaptations can be found on lists of top money makers for their decade.

Most of the film adaptations after *Cabaret* made money, but few, if any, earned critical acclaim.[68] Some films conspicuously suffered both financial injury and critical insult. For example, *Mame* (1974) lost nearly half of its $12 million budget. A few years later, although it soon "acquired canonical status as a classic film musical in the African American community," *The Wiz* (1978) lost $3 million on its $24 million dollar budget.[69] *A Chorus Line* (1986) lost about $11 million on its $25 million dollar investment. *Hair* (1979), an imaginative restructuring of the stage musical directed by Miloš Forman took some critical abuse at the time but eventually earned $27 million on its $11 million investment. The film version of *Annie* made an impressive total of $7 million, but to attain this sum Columbia paid a whopping $57 million, which made future investors think twice about taking part in such a risky business. Fourteen years later, wisely banking on the critic-proof Madonna, *Evita* netted $86 million on its $55 million investment despite mixed reviews.

Following the success of *Chicago*, film adaptations in the 2000s and 2010s started to appear in greater numbers (nine adaptations of hit shows in the 2000s and four in the 2010s).[70] The time lag from stage to screen would also increase exponentially. Of the four longest-running shows from the 1980s that were eventually filmed, the *swiftest* turnover from stage to screen was sixteen years for the then still-running *The Phantom of the Opera*. The longest delay was *Cats*, thirty-seven years, which for many disappointed critics and viewers was not nearly long enough. Several hit shows from the 1980s and 1990s, many of which some were based on dramatic movies (an increasingly common phenomenon in the twenty-first century as observed in chapter 5), have as of this writing yet to be remade as film musicals. Most of these shows with unmade films lasted more than 1,000 performances in their Broadway runs: *La Cage aux Folles*, *Sunday in the Park with George*, *Big River*, *Me and My Girl*, *Grand Hotel*, *City of Angels*, *Miss Saigon*, *Kiss of the Spider Woman*, *Sunset Boulevard*, and *Jekyll and Hyde*.

In the wake of *A Chorus Line* and other money-losing films, producers and their sponsors frequently decided not to risk the considerable sums necessary only to achieve comparatively modest profits, especially when compared to blockbusters like the *Star Wars* franchise. Of the five film adaptations of the longest-running Broadway shows from the 1980s and 1990s, the *cheapest* film to produce, *Rent*, cost $40 million, which made $8.4 million. The most expensive film, *Cats*, cost at least $80 million and according to *Wikipedia* perhaps as much as $100 million to produce. Most of the major studios have by now been acquired by large media conglomerates, such as the purchase of MGM by Amazon in 2021, albeit in a deal that for good or ill did not include MGM films made prior to 1986.[71]

As I was completing *A Fine Romance* in 2021, film adaptations of Lin-Manual Miranda's *In the Heights* (2008) directed by Jon M. Chu (*Crazy Rich Asians*), *Dear Evan Hansen* (2016), directed by Stephen Chbosky, and *Tick. . . BOOM!* (2001), directed by Miranda, had recently arrived in movie theaters that began to re-open during the waxing and waning COVID-19 pandemic. They also became instantly available for streaming. At the end of the year, audiences witnessed a second film version of *West Side Story*, this time directed by Steven Spielberg with Tony Kushner as his screenwriter, featuring the original Anita, Rita Moreno, in a significant newly conceived role (discussed briefly in chapter 6). As of this writing, film adaptations of the Broadway shows *Wicked* (2003), *The Little Mermaid* (2008), and *Matilda* (2013) are also in the works.

So the future of film adaptations might be bright after all. In fact, after several decades of gloom and imagined doom that following the film adaptation of *Cabaret* in 1972, the complicated fine romance between Broadway and Hollywood has matured, changed, and indeed—endured. The odd, endearing, and by now well-seasoned couple appears destined to live and love (and fight) another day.

Stage and Screen Musicals Discussed in
A Fine Romance

A. Stage Musicals Discussed in *A Fine Romance*

	Composer	Lyricist	Librettist	Producer	Director	Choreographer
SHOW BOAT (1927)	Kern	Hammerstein	Hammerstein	F. Ziegfeld	Z. Colvan; Hammerstein (uncredited)	S. Lee
THE CAT AND THE FIDDLE (1931)	Kern	Harbach	Harbach	M. Gordon	J. Ruben	A. Rasch
ROBERTA (1933)	Kern	Harbach	Harbach	M. Gordon	H. Short (uncredited)	J. Limon; J. Lonergan (uncredited)
CABIN IN THE SKY (1940)	Duke	J. Latouche	L. Root	A. Lewis; V. Freedley	G. Balanchine; Lewis	Balanchine; K. Dunham
OKLAHOMA! (1943)	Rodgers	Hammerstein	Hammerstein	Theatre Guild	Mamoulian	De Mille
ON THE TOWN (1944)	Bernstein	B. Comden; A. Green	Comden/Green	O. Smith; P. Feigay	G. Abbott	J. Robbins
BRIGADOON (1947)	Loewe	A. J. Lerner	Lerner	C. Crawford	R. Lewis	J. Kennedy
CALL ME MADAM (1950)	Berlin	Berlin	H. Lindsay; R. Crouse	L. Hayward	Abbott	Robbins
SILK STOCKINGS (1955)	Porter	Porter	S. Kaufman; L. McGrath; A. Burrows	C. Feuer; E. Martin	Feuer	E. Loring
WEST SIDE STORY (1957)	Bernstein	S. Sondheim	A. Laurents	R. Griffith; H. Prince	Robbins	Robbins; P. Gennaro
FLOWER DRUM SONG (1958)	Rodgers	Hammerstein	Hammerstein; J. Fields	Rodgers; Hammerstein; Fields	G. Kelly	C. Haney
CABARET (1966)	Kander	Ebb	J. Masteroff	Prince	Prince	R. Field

B. **Screen Adaptations Discussed in *A Fine Romance***

	Additional Composer	Additional Lyricist	Screenwriter	Producer	Director	Choreographer
SHOW BOAT (1936)	Kern	Hammerstein	Hammerstein	C. Laemmle Jr.	J. Whale	L. Prinz
THE CAT AND THE FIDDLE (1934)			B. & S. Spewack	B. Hyman	W. K. Howard	A. Rasch
ROBERTA (1935)	Kern	D. Fields	Harbach	P. Berman	W. A. Seiter	H. Pan, F. Astaire (uncredited)
CABIN IN THE SKY (1943)	Arlen	E. Y. Harburg	J. Schrank	A. Freed	V. Minnelli	B. Berkeley (uncredited)
OKLAHOMA! (1955)			S. Levien; W. Ludwig	A. Hornblow	F. Zinnemann	De Mille
ON THE TOWN (1949)	R. Edens	B. Comden; A. Green	Comden/Green	Freed	G. Kelly; S. Donen	Kelly and Donen
BRIGADOON (1954)			Lerner	Freed	Minnelli	Kelly
CALL ME MADAM (1953)	Berlin	Berlin	A. Sheekman	S. C. Siegel	W. Lang	R. Alton
SILK STOCKINGS (1957)	Porter	Porter	L. Gershe; L. Spiegelgass; H. Kurnitz (uncredited)	Freed	R. Mamoulian	Loring; Pan (uncredited)
WEST SIDE STORY (1961)	Bernstein	S. Sondheim	E. Lehman	R. Wise	Wise; Robbins	Robbins
FLOWER DRUM SONG (1961)			Fields	R. Hunter; Fields	H. Koster	Pan
CABARET (1972)	Kander	Ebb	J. P. Allen; H. Wheeler (uncredited)	Feuer	B. Fosse	Fosse

Stage and Screen Sources Discussed in *A Fine Romance*

BRIGADOON (Broadway 1947; MGM 1954)

LIBRETTO: Alan Jay Lerner, *Great Musicals of the American Theatre Volume One*, ed. Stanley Richards. Radnor, PA: Chilton, 1973.

SCREENPLAY: Lerner.

VOCAL SCORE: Lyrics by Lerner; music by Frederick Loewe. Miami: Belwin, 1947, 1967, 1975.

AUDIO RECORDINGS: (a) Original 1947 Broadway Cast (Masterworks Broadway, 1988); (b) 1954 Original Motion Picture Soundtrack (Turner Broadcasting, 1996). (c) 1992 Studio Cast, John McGlinn, conductor (EMI, 1992).

VIDEO: MGM 1954 (108 minutes). Directed by Vincente Minnelli. Produced by Arthur Freed. Turner Entertainment and Warner Bros. Entertainment, 2005.

CABARET (Broadway 1966; Allied Artists and ABC 1972)

SOURCES: *The Berlin Stories* by Christopher Isherwood (1945). New York: New Directions, 1963; *I Am a Camera* by John Van Druten. New York: Dramatists Service, 1951.

LIBRETTO: (a) Broadway 1966: Joe Masteroff, *Great Musicals of the American Theatre Volume Two*, ed. Stanley Richards. Radnor, PA: Chilton, 1976; (b) Broadway 1966: *American Musicals: The Complete Book and Lyrics of Eight Broadway Classics 1950–1969,* ed. Lawrence Maslon, Library of America (LOA #254). New York: Penguin Random House, 2014; (c) Broadway 1998: *Cabaret: The Illustrated Book and Lyrics.* New York: Newmarket, 1999.

SCREENPLAY: (a) Jay Presson Allen, First Draft, June 10, 1970. Formerly distributed by Script City; (b) *Cabaret,* "A Screenplay by Jan [*recte* Jay] Presson Allen and Hugh Wheeler," Final Draft, February 15, 1971; Revised April 15, 1971, Hugh Wheeler Collection #1417, Box 44E, Howard Gotlieb Archival Research Center, Boston University.

VOCAL SCORE: Lyrics by Fred Ebb; music by John Kander. *The Complete "Cabaret" Collection.* Milwaukee: Hal Leonard, 1966, 1972, 1998. Songs from the 1966 original Broadway production, the 1972 film score, and the 1998 Broadway revival.

AUDIO RECORDINGS: (a) Original 1966 Broadway Cast (Sony Music Entertainment 1966, 1998); (b) 1972 Original Soundtrack (MCA 1980; reissued, Hip-O, 2006); (c) 1993 Studio Cast, John Owen Edwards, conductor (Jay Productions, 1999).

VIDEO: Allied Artists and ABC 1972 (124 minutes). Directed by Bob Fosse. Produced by Cy Feuer. ABC Pictures and Warner Bros. Entertainment, 2000.

CABIN IN THE SKY (Broadway 1940; MGM 1943)

LIBRETTO: Lynn Root. John Latouche Lyrics and Scripts, Billy Rose Theater Division, New York Public Library #4552. Latouche Estate, Gift of Gore Vidal, 1970.

SCREENPLAY: Joseph Schrank (Marc Connelly uncredited). September 21, 1942; revised October 20, 1942.

VOCAL SCORES: (a) 1940 Broadway: Lyrics by John Latouche; music by Vernon Duke. "Cabin in the Sky"; "Taking a Chance on Love," Miller Music 1940; "Honey in the Honeycomb," EMI Miller Catalog and Alfred Publishers, 1940, *Broadway Vamps & Sirens: Classic Songs of Feminine Seduction,* Van Nuys, CA: Alfred Publishing, 2008; (b) 1943 MGM: "Happiness Is a Thing Called Joe" (lyrics by E.Y. Harburg; music by Harold Arlen), New York: Leo Feist, 1942; "That's Why They Call Me Shine" (lyrics by Cecil Mack; music by Ford Dabney), New York: Gotham-Attuck Music Co., 1910.

AUDIO RECORDINGS: (a) Original 1940 Broadway Cast: Overture (Max Meth, conductor), "Taking a Chance on Love," Honey in the Honey Comb," "Cabin in the Sky," and "Love Turned the Light Out" (Ethel Waters), AEI-CD 1979 and 1994; (b) 1942 Film Soundtrack (The Sound Track Factory, 1999); (c) 1963 New York Revival Cast Recording (Angel, 1993); (c) 2000 Musical Revue: *Taking a Chance on Love—The Lyrics and Life of John Latouche* (includes seven selections from *Cabin in the* Sky) (Original Cast Records, 2000).

VIDEO: MGM 1943 (99 minutes). Directed by Vincente Minnelli. Produced by Arthur Freed. Turner Entertainment and Warner Bros. Entertainment, 2006.

CALL ME MADAM (Broadway 1950; 20th Century-Fox 1953)

LIBRETTO: Howard Lindsay and Russel Crouse, London, Irving Berlin, Ltd., 1956.

SCREENPLAY: Arthur Sheekman, Shooting Final, September 5, 1952. Distributed by Script Fly, 1953.

VOCAL SCORE: Lyrics and music by Irving Berlin. London, Irving Berlin, LTD, 1952.

AUDIO RECORDINGS: (a) Original 1950 Broadway Cast and Studio Cast Recording, 1950 and Film Soundtrack 1953 (Naxos, 2006); (b) 1950 Studio Recordings with Dinah Shore and Ethel Merman (Prism Leisure, 1950); (b) 1995 Original New York Cast Recording, City Center's Encores! (with Tyne Daly), Rob Fisher, Musical Director (DRG 1995).

VIDEO: 20th Century-Fox 1953 (117 minutes). Directed by Walter Lang. Produced by Sol C. Siegel. 20th Century-Fox for Home Entertainment, 2004.

THE CAT AND THE FIDDLE (Broadway 1931; MGM 1934)

LIBRETTO: Otto Harbach.

SCREENPLAY: Bella and Samuel Spewack (1933).

VOCAL SCORE: Lyrics by Harbach; music by Jerome Kern. New York: T. B. Harms, 1932.

AUDIO RECORDINGS: (a) 1932 London: Jerome Kern in London Original Cast Recordings (with Peggy Wood singing "She Didn't Say Yet," "Try to Forget," "A New Love Is Old," and "The Night Was Made for Love"), LP (Monmouth Evergreen, 1972); (b) Americans in London in the 1930s, CD (includes all of [a] plus additional instrumental selections conducted by Hyam Greenbaum and the Palace Theatre Orchestra; (c) Jerome Kern Overtures, National Philharmonic Orchestra. John McGlinn, conductor (Entr'acte to act II) (EMI, 1989); (d) 2006 Studio Recording: The Comic Opera Guild, Adam Aceto, Artistic Director (complete two-piano recording that closely follows the published Vocal Score and includes narration between scenes), 2 CDs (The Comic Opera Guild, 2006).

VIDEO: MGM 1934 (92 minutes). Directed by William K. Howard. Produced by Bernard Hyman. Warner Bros. Archive, 2013.

FLOWER DRUM SONG (Broadway 1958; Universal 1961)

SOURCE: *The Flower Drum Song* by C. Y. Lee. New York: Penguin, 1957.

LIBRETTO: (a) Broadway 1958: Oscar Hammerstein II and Joseph Fields. New York: Farrar, Straus and Cudahy, 1959; (b) 2002 Revival: David Henry Wang. New York: Theatre Communications Group, 2003.

SCREENPLAY: Fields.

VOCAL SCORES: Lyrics by Hammerstein; music by Richard Rodgers. (a) Vocal Score, Broadway 1958: New York: Williamson Music, 1958, 1959; (b) Vocal Selections, 2002 Revival: New York: Williamson and Milwaukee: Hal Leonard, 2002 (includes "My Best Love," dropped from the 1958 production).

AUDIO RECORDINGS: (a) Original 1958 Broadway Cast (Columbia, 1958); (b) 1961 Film Soundtrack (MCA 1960); (c) 2002 New Broadway Cast Recording (DRG, 2003).

VIDEO: Universal 1961 (133 minutes). Directed by Henry Koster. Produced by Ross Hunter and Joseph Fields. Universal Studios, 2006.

OKLAHOMA! (Broadway 1943; Magna 1955)

SOURCE: *Green Grow the Lilacs* by Lynn Riggs. New York: Samuel French, 1930, 1931.

LIBRETTO: Oscar Hammerstein II. *6 Plays by Rodgers and Hammerstein*. New York: Modern Library, 1959.

SCREENPLAY: Sonya Levien and William Ludwig, Final Script, June 1, 1954. Formerly distributed by Script City.

VOCAL SCORE: Lyrics by Hammerstein; music by Richard Rodgers. New York: Williamson Music, 1943.

AUDIO RECORDINGS: (a) Original 1943 Broadway Cast (MCA, 1943, 1945); (b) 1955 Film Soundtrack (Capitol, 1955; reissued Angel, 1993); (c) 1979 Broadway Revival (Sony 2012); (e) 1998 Royal National Theatre Recording (First Night, 1998); (f) 2019 Broadway Revival (Decca, 2019).

VIDEO: Magna 1955 (145 minutes). Directed by Fred Zinnemann. Produced by Arthur Hornblow Jr. 2 DVDs. Twentieth Century Fox Entertainment, 2005.

ON THE TOWN (Broadway 1944; MGM 1949)

LIBRETTO: Betty Comden and Adolph Green. *The New York Musicals of Comden & Green.* New York: Applause, 1997.

SCREENPLAY: Comden and Green. February 24, 1949 Draft. Formerly distributed by Script City.

VOCAL SCORES: (a) 1944 Broadway: Lyrics by Comden and Green; music by Leonard Bernstein. Boosey & Hawkes, Leonard Bernstein Music Publishing, 1997; (b) 1949 MGM: Additional lyrics by Comden and Green and music by Roger Edens. "Count on Me," "Main Street," and "You're Awful." New York: M. Witmark, 1950 (also "On the Town" and "Prehistoric Man").

AUDIO RECORDINGS: (a) 1960 Original Cast Studio Recording (with John Reardon replacing John Battles), Leonard Bernstein, conductor (Columbia, 1960); (b) 1949 Film Soundtrack (Delta Leisure Group, 2010); 1992 Live Recording, Michael Tilson Thomas, conductor (Deutsche Grammophon, 1993).

VIDEO: MGM 1949 (98 minutes). Directed by Gene Kelly and Stanley Donen. Produced by Arthur Freed. Turner Entertainment and Warner Bros. Entertainment, 2008.

ROBERTA (Broadway 1933; RKO 1935)

SOURCE: *Gowns by Roberta* by Alice Duer Miller. New York: Dodd, Mead, 1933.

LIBRETTO: Otto Harbach. New York: T. B. Harms, 1933.

SCREENPLAY: Sam Mintz and Jane Murfin (Allan Scott uncredited), Revised Final Script, November 27, 1934. New Dorothy Fields lyrics and Jerome Kern music for "Lovely to Look At" and reworked Fields lyrics for "I Won't Dance."

VOCAL SCORES: Lyrics by Harbach; music by Kern. New York: T. B. Harms; London: Chappell, 1933, 1950.

AUDIO RECORDINGS: (a) 1935 Film Soundtrack: *Fred Astaire & Ginger Rogers at RKO.* Songs: "Let's Begin" (Fred Astaire, Johnny ["Candy"] Candido, and Gene Sheldon); "I'll Be Hard to Handle" (Ginger Rogers); and "I Won't Dance" (Astaire and Rogers), 2 CDs. (Turner Classic Movies Music, 1998); (b) 2014 Studio Cast, Rob Berman, conductor, 2 CDs. (New World Records, 2014).

VIDEO: RKO 1935 (105 minutes). Directed by William A. Seiter. Produced by Pandro S. Berman. Turner Entertainment and Warner Bros. Entertainment, 2006.

SHOW BOAT (Broadway 1927; Universal 1936)

SOURCE: *Show Boat* by Edna Ferber. Garden City, NY: Doubleday, 1926.

LIBRETTO: Oscar Hammerstein II. *American Musicals: The Complete Books and Lyrics of Eight Broadway Classics 1927–1949* ed., Lawrence Maslon. Library of America (LOA #253). New York: Penguin Random House, 2014.

SCREENPLAY: Hammerstein.

VOCAL SCORES: Lyrics by Hammerstein; music by Jerome Kern; (a) Harms Co., 1927; (Broadway 1927); (b) Chappell & Co. and T. B. Harms Co., 1928 (London 1928); (c) The Welk Music Group, 1927 (Broadway 1946).

AUDIO RECORDINGS: (a) Original London Cast 1928, with Paul Robeson, Jules Bledsoe, and Edith Day (Pearl Gemm, 1994); (b) Original London Cast 1928: *Show Stoppers: Various Historic Victor Recordings,* with Robeson and Helen Morgan (BMG, 1989); (c) The Ultimate *Show Boat* (Original, Revival, and Studio Cast Anthology), 2 CDs. (Pearl, 2007); (d) 1988 Studio Cast, John McGlinn, conductor, 2 CDs (EMI/ ANGEL, 1988); (e) 1994 Broadway Revival (Live Entertainment of Canada, 1994).

VIDEO: (a) Universal 1936 (113 minutes). Directed by James Whale. Produced by Carl Laemmle Jr. The Criterion Collection 1021, 2 DVDs. Turner Entertainment and Warner Bros. Home Entertainment, 2020. Special Features include excerpts from the sound prologue and 20 minutes of silent excerpts from the 1929 film version with audio commentary by Miles Kreuger; (b) MGM 1951 (108 minutes). Directed by George Sidney. Produced by Arthur Freed. Turner Entertainment and Warner Bros. Home Video, Entertainment, 2000.

SILK STOCKINGS (Broadway 1955; MGM 1957)

SOURCE: *Ninotchka* (MGM 1939) (110 minutes). Directed by Ernst Lubitsch. Charles Brackett, Billy Wilder, and Walter Reisch, *Ninotchka.* New York: Viking, 1972.

LIBRETTO: George S. Kaufman, Leueen McGrath, and Abe Burrows.

SCREENPLAY: Leonard Gershe and Spigelgass (Harry Kurnitz uncredited).

VOCAL SCORES: Lyrics and music by Cole Porter: (a) *Music & Lyrics by Cole Porter.* New York: Chappell, n.d. ("All of You"; "As on through the Seasons We Sail"; "Stereophonic Sound"); (b) *Music & Lyrics by Cole Porter Volume Two.* New York: Chappell, n.d. (""Paris Loves Lovers"; "Satin and Silk"; "Silk Stockings"; "Siberia"; "Without Love"); (c) Vocal Selection ("Silk Stockings"; "The Ritz Roll and Rock"; "Paris Loves Lovers"; "All of You"; "Fated to Be Mated"; "Without Love"; "Siberia").

AUDIO RECORDINGS: (a) Original 1955 Broadway Cast (BMG, 1955); (b) 1957 Original Motion Picture Soundtrack (Turner Entertainment, 2002).

VIDEO: MGM 1957 (118 minutes). Directed by Rouben Mamoulian. Produced by Arthur Freed. Turner Entertainment and Warner Home Video, 2003.

WEST SIDE STORY (Broadway 1957; Mirisch-Seven Arts 1961)

SOURCE: *Romeo and Juliet* by William Shakespeare (1595).

LIBRETTO: Arthur Laurents. (a) *Romeo and Juliet/West Side Story.* New York: Dell, 1965); (b) *Great Musicals of the American Theatre Volume One,* ed. Stanley Richards. Radnor, PA: Chilton, 1973).

SCREENPLAY: Ernest Lehman, *West Side Story,* Special Edition, DVD Collector's Set, MGM, 2003.

VOCAL SCORE: Lyrics by Stephen Sondheim; music by Leonard Bernstein: G. Schirmer and Chappell, 1957 and 1959.

FULL SCORE: (a) Chappell, 1957 and 1959; (b) Full Score, Leonard Bernstein Publishing Co. (HPS 1176). New York: Jalni Publications and Boosey & Hawkes, 1994.

AUDIO RECORDINGS: (a) Original 1957 Broadway Cast (Columbia, 1957); (b) 1961 Film Soundtrack (Columbia, 1961; reissued 1992); (c) 1985 Studio Cast, Leonard Bernstein, Conductor. 2 CDs. (Deutsche Grammophon, 1985).

VIDEO: Mirisch-Seven Arts 1961 (151 minutes). Directed by Robert Wise and Jerome Robbins. 2 DVDs. Produced by Wise. MGM Home Entertainment, 2003.

Unless otherwise indicated, the audio recordings refer to a single CD and the videos to a single DVD.

Selected Stage Musicals and Their Screen Adaptations (1920–2021)

1920s	STAGE MUSICALS	SCREEN ADAPTATIONS
1920	*Sally* (570)	1929 First National Pictures
1924	*Rose-Marie* (557)	1936 and 1954 MGM
	The Student Prince (608)	1954 MGM
1925	*The Vagabond King* (511)	1930 and 1956 Paramount 1930
	Sunny (517)	1930 First National Pictures and 1941 RKO
1926	*The Desert Song* (471)	1929, 1943, and 1953 Warner Bros.
1927	*Rio Rita* (494)	1929 RKO
	Good News (551)	1947 MGM 1947
	Funny Face (244)	1957 Paramount
	Show Boat **(575)**	**1936 Universal**; 1951 MGM
1928	*The New Moon* (509)	1940 MGM
1930s	**STAGE MUSICALS**	**SCREEN ADAPTATIONS**
1930	*Flying High* (357)	1931 MGM
	Girl Crazy (272)	1943 MGM
1931	***The Cat and the Fiddle*** **(395)**	**1934 MGM**
1932	*Music in the Air* (342)	1934 Fox
1933	***Roberta*** **(295)**	**1935 RKO**
1934	*Anything Goes* (420)	1936 Paramount
1935	*Porgy and Bess* (124)	1959 Samuel Goldwyn
1936	*On Your Toes* (315)	1939 Warner Bros.
1937	*Babes in Arms* (289)	1939 MGM
1938	*I Married an Angel* (338)	1942 MGM
	Hellzapoppin (1,404)	1941 Universal
1939	*Du Barry Was a Lady* (408)	1943 MGM
1940s	**STAGE MUSICALS**	**SCREEN ADAPTATONS**
1940	*Louisiana Purchase* (444)	1941 Paramount
	Cabin in the Sky **(156)**	**1943 MGM**
	Panama Hattie (501)	1942 MGM

	Pal Joey (374)	1957 Columbia
1941	*Lady in the Dark* (467)	1944 Paramount
	Let's Face It! (547)	1943 Paramount
1942	*This Is the Army* (113)	1943 Warner Bros.
1943	*Something for the Boys* (422)	1944 20th Century-Fox
	Oklahoma! (2,212)	**1955 Magna**
	One Touch of Venus (567)	1948 Universal
	Carmen Jones (502)	1954 20th Century-Fox
	Mexican Hayride (481)	1948 Universal-International
1944	*Song of Norway* (860)	1970 Cinerama
	On the Town (463)	**1949 MGM**
1945	*Up in Central Park* (504)	1948 Universal
	Carousel (890)	1956 20th Century-Fox
1946	*Call Me Mister* (734)	1951 20th Century-Fox
	Annie Get Your Gun (1,147)	1950 MGM
1947	*Finian's Rainbow* (725)	1968 Warner Bros.-Seven Arts
	Brigadoon (581)	**1954 MGM**
1948	*Where's Charley?* (792)	1952 Warner Bros.
	Kiss Me, Kate (1,070)	1953 MGM
1949	*South Pacific* (1,925)	1958 20th Century-Fox
	Gentlemen Prefer Blondes (740)	1953 20th Century-Fox
1950s	**STAGE MUSICALS**	**SCREEN ADAPTATIONS**
1950	**Call Me Madam** (644)	**1953 20th Century-Fox**
	Guys and Dolls (1,200)	1955 Goldwyn
1951	*The King and I* (1,246)	1956 20th Century-Fox
1953	*Can-Can* (892)	1960 20th Century-Fox
	Kismet (583)	1955 MGM
1954	*The Pajama Game* (1,063)	1957 Warner Bros.
1955	**Silk Stockings** (478)	**1957 MGM**
	Damn Yankees (1,019)	1958 Warner Bros.
1956	*My Fair Lady* (2,717)	1964 Warner Bros.
	Li'l Abner (693)	1959 Paramount
	Bells Are Ringing (924)	1960 MGM
1957	**West Side Story** (732)	**1961 Mirisch-Seven Arts**
		2021 Amblin Entertainment
	The Music Man (1,375)	1962 Warner Bros.
1958	**Flower Drum Song** (600)	**1961 Universal**
1959	*Gypsy* (702)	1962 Warner Bros.
	The Sound of Music (1,443)	1965 20th Century-Fox

1960s	STAGE MUSICALS	SCREEN ADAPTATIONS
1960	*Bye Bye Birdie* (607)	1963 Columbia
	The Unsinkable Molly Brown (532)	1964 MGM
	The Fantasticks (17,162)	2000 United Artists
	Camelot (873)	1967 Warner Bros.-Seven Arts
1961	*How to Succeed in Business Without Really Trying* (1,417)	1966 Mirisch-United Artists
1962	*A Funny Thing Happened on the Way to the Forum* (964)	1966 United Artists
	Stop the World—I Want to Get Off (555)	1966 Warner Bros.
1963	*Oliver!* (774)	1968 Columbia
1964	*Hello, Dolly!* (2,844)	1969 20th Century-Fox
	Funny Girl (1,348)	1968 Columbia
	Fiddler on the Roof (3,242)	1971 Mirisch-United Artists
	Half a Sixpence (512)	1967 Paramount British Pictures
1965	*Man of La Mancha* (2,328)	1972 United Artists
1966	*Sweet Charity* (608)	1969 Universal
	Mame (1,508)	1974 Warner Bros.
1966	**Cabaret (1,165)**	**1972 Allied Artists & ABC**
1968	*Hair* (1,750)	1979 United Artists
1969	*1776* (1,217)	1972 Columbia
1970s	**STAGE MUSICALS**	**SCREEN ADAPTATIONS**
1972	*Grease* (3,388)	1978 Paramount
1973	*A Little Night Music* (600)	1977 Sascha-Wien
1975	*The Wiz* (1,672)	1978 Motown Productions
1975	*A Chorus Line* (6,137)	1985 Embassy & PolyGram
	Chicago (898)	2002 Miramax
1977	*Annie* (2,377)	1982 Columbia
1978	*The Best Little Whorehouse in Texas* (1,703)	1982 Distributed by Universal
1979	*Sweeney Todd* (557)	2007 DreamWorks/Warner Bros.
	Evita (1,567)	1996 Hollywood Pictures
1980s-1990s	**STAGE MUSICALS**	**SCREEN ADAPTATIONS**
1981	*Dreamgirls* (1,522)	2006 DreamWorks/Paramount
1982	*Nine* (732)	2009 Weinstein Co.
	Little Shop of Horrors (2,209)	1986 Distributed by Warner Bros.
	Cats (7,485)	2019 Distributed by Universal
1987	*Les Misérables* (6,680)	2012 Distributed by Universal

	Into the Woods (764)	2014 Walt Disney Pictures
1988	The Phantom of the Opera (13,981)	2004 Warner Bros.
1996	Rent (5,124) Chicago (revival) (10,114)[1]	2005 Columbia 2002 Miramax
1998	Hedwig and the Angry Inch (857)	2001 Fine Line Features
	Cabaret (revival) (2,377)	**1972 Allied Artists & ABC**
2000-21	**STAGE MUSICALS**	**SCREEN ADAPTATIONS**
2001	The Producers (2,502)	2005 Universal/Columbia
	Tick, Tick . . . BOOM! (215)	2021 Netflix/Imagine Entertainment
	Mamma Mia! (5,758)	2008 Universal
2002	Hairspray (2,642)	2007 New Line Cinema
2003	Wicked (6,836)[2]	2024 and 2025 Universal/Marc Platt Productions
2005	Jersey Boys (4,642)	2014 Distributed by Warner Bros.
	The Color Purple (910)	2023[3] Distributed by Warner Bros.
2008	The Little Mermaid (685)	2023 Walt Disney Pictures
	In the Heights (1,184)	2021 Distributed by Warner Bros.
2013	Matilda (1,555)[3]	
2016	Dear Evan Hansen (1,672)	2021 Universal

[1] As of October 2, 2022.

[2] As of October 2, 2022.

[3] Opened in London's West End in 2011 where it is still running as of January 2023.

• Musicals and their film adaptations discussed in "A Fine Romance" are highlighted in bold.
• The numbers in parentheses that follow the stage musicals indicate the number of performances during their initial Broadway run.

Selected Screen Adaptations of Stage Musicals (1930–2023)

1930s (18)	
1930	*Whoopee!* (Samuel Goldwyn) [1928]
1931	*Flying High* (MGM) [1930]
1934	**The Cat and the Fiddle** (MGM) **[1931]**
	Evergreen (Gaumont-British) [1930 London]
	The Merry Widow (MGM) [1907]
	The Gay Divorcee (RKO) [1932]
	Music in the Air (Fox) [1932]
	Sweet Adeline (Warner Bros.) [1929]
1935	**Roberta** (RKO) **[1933]**
	Naughty Marietta (MGM) [1910]
1936	*Rose Marie* (MGM) [1924]
	Anything Goes (Paramount) [1934]
	Show Boat (Universal) **[1927]**
1937	*Maytime* (MGM) [1917]
	The Firefly (MGM) [1912]
1938	*Sweethearts* [MGM) [1913]
1939	*Babes in Arms* (MGM) [1937]
	On Your Toes Warner Bros.) [1936]
1940s (16)	
1940	*Too Many Girls* (RKO) [1939]
1941	*Louisiana Purchase* (Paramount) [1940]
	Hellzapoppin (Universal) [1938]
1942	*I Married and Angel* (MGM) [1938]
	Panama Hattie (MGM) [1940]
1943	**Cabin in the Sky** (MGM) **[1940]**
	Let's Face It (Paramount) [1941]
	This Is the Army (Warner Bros.) [1942]
	Du Barry Was a Lady (MGM) [1939]
	Girl Crazy (MGM) [1930]
1944	*Lady in the Dark* (Paramount) [1941]

	Something for the Boys (20th Century-Fox) [1943]
1948	*Up in Central Park* (Universal) [1945]
	One Touch of Venus (Universal) [1943]
	Mexican Hayride (Universal-International) [1943]
1949	**On the Town (MGM) [1944]**
1950s (20)	
1950	*Annie Get Your Gun* (MGM) [1946]
1951	*Call Me Mister* (20th Century-Fox) [1946]
1952	*Where's Charley?* (Warner Bros.) [1948]
1953	**Call Me Madam (20th Century-Fox) [1950]**
	Gentlemen Prefer Blondes (20th Century-Fox) [1949]
	Kiss Me Kate (MGM) [1948]
1954	**Brigadoon (MGM) [1947]**
	Carmen Jones (20th Century-Fox) [1943]
1955	**Oklahoma! (Magna) [1943]**
	Guys and Dolls (Samuel Goldwyn [1950]
	Kismet (MGM) [1953]
1956	*Carousel* (20th Century-Fox) [1945]
	The King and I (20th Century-Fox) [1951]
1957	**Silk Stockings (MGM) [1955]**
	The Pajama Game (Warner Bros [1954]
	Pal Joey (Columbia) [1940]
1958	*South Pacific* (20th Century-Fox) [1949]
	Damn Yankees (Warner Bros.) [1955]
1959	*Porgy and Bess* (Samuel Goldwyn) [1935]
	Li'l Abner (Paramount) [1956]
1960s (20)	
1960	*Can-Can* (20th Century-Fox) [1953]
	Bells Are Ringing (MGM) [1956]
1961	**West Side Story (Mirisch-Seven Arts) [1957]**
	Flower Drum Song (Universal) [1958]
1962	*The Music Man* (Warner Bros.) [1957]
	Gypsy (Warner Bros.) [1959]
1963	*Bye Bye Birdie* (Columbia) [1960]
1964	*The Unsinkable Molly Brown* (MGM) [1960]
	My Fair Lady (Warner Bros.) [1956]
1965	*The Sound of Music* (20th Century-Fox) [1959]
1966	*How to Succeed in Business without Really Trying* (Mirisch-United Artists) [1961]
	Stop the World—I Want to Get Off (Warner Bros) [1962]

	A Funny Thing Happened on the Way to the Forum (United Artists) [1962]
1967	*Camelot* (Warner Bros.-Seven Arts) [1960]
	Half a Sixpence (Paramount British Pictures) [1964]
1968	*Finian's Rainbow* (Warner Bros-Seven Arts) [1947]
	Funny Girl (Columbia) [1964]
	Oliver! (Columbia) [1963]
1969	*Sweet Charity* (Universal) [1966]
	Hello, Dolly! (20th Century-Fox) [1964]
1970s (12)	
1970	*On a Clear Day You Can See Forever* (Paramount) [1965]
	Song of Norway (Cinerama) [1944]
1971	*Fiddler on the Roof* (Mirisch-United Artists) [1964]
1972	**Cabaret (Allied Artists & ABC) [1966]**
	1776 (Columbia) [1969]
	Man of La Mancha (United Artists) [1965]
1974	*Mame* (Warner Bros.) [1966]
1975	*Rocky Horror Picture Show* (Michael White) [1975]
1977	*A Little Night Music* (Sascha-Wien) [1973]
1978	*Grease* (Paramount) [1972]
	The Wiz (Motown Productions [1975]
1979	*Hair* (United Artists) [1968]
1980s and 1990s (5)	
1982	*Annie* (Columbia) [1977]
	The Best Little Whorehouse in Texas (distributed by Universal) [1978]
1985	*A Chorus Line* (Embassy & Polygram) [1975]
1986	*Little Shop of Horrors* (distributed by Warner. Bros.) [1982]
1996	*Evita* (Hollywood Pictures) [1979]
2000s (10)	
2001	*Hedwig and the Angry Inch* (Fine Line Features) [1998]
2002	*Chicago* (Miramax) [1975]
2004	*The Phantom of the Opera* (Warner Bros.) [1988]
2005	*Rent* (Columbia) [1996]
	The Producers (Universal/Columbia) [2001]
2006	*Dreamgirls* (DreamWorks/Paramount) (1982)
2007	*Hairspray* (New Line Cinema) [2002]
	Sweeney Todd (DreamWorks/Warner Bros.) [1979]
2008	*Mamma Mia!* (Universal) [2001]
2009	*Nine* (Weinstein Co.) [1982]

2010s (4)	
2012	*Les Misérables* (distributed by Universal) [1987]
2014	*Jersey Boys* (distributed by Warner Bros.) [2005]
	Into the Woods (Walt Disney Pictures) [1987]
2019	*Cats* (distributed by Universal) [1982]
2020s (8)	
2021	*Dear Evan Hansen* (Universal) [2016]
	In the Heights (distributed by Warner Bros.) [2008]
	Tick, Tick. . . BOOM! (Netflix/Imagine Entertainment) [2001]
	***West Side Story* (Amblin Entertainment) [1957]**
2022	*Matilda* (distributed by Sony Pictures) [2013]
2023	*The Little Mermaid* (Walt Disney Pictures) [2008]
	The Color Purple (distributed by Warner Bros.) [2005]
2024 and 2025	*Wicked* (Universal/ Marc Platt Productions) [2003]

- *Film adaptations discussed in A "Fine Romance" are highlighted in bold.*

Notes

Preface

1. Geoffrey Block, *Enchanted Evenings: The Broadway Musical from "Show Boat" to Sondheim and Lloyd Webber* (New York: Oxford University Press, 1997; rev. 2nd ed. 2009).

2. Geoffrey Block, "Refashioning *Roberta*: From Novel to Stage to Screen," in *The Oxford Handbook of Musical Theatre Screen Adaptations*, ed. Dominic McHugh (New York: Oxford University Press, 2019), 29–53; "Is Life a Cabaret? *Cabaret* and Its Sources in Reality and the Imagination," *Studies in Musical Theatre* 5/2 (2011): 163–80.

3. "Broadway" refers to New York City's theater district, which is located in Midtown Manhattan on or near Broadway (a broad street that travels through most of Manhattan from north to south). The boundaries of the theater district portion of this long street range from West 54th (north), West 40th (south), Sixth Avenue (east), and Eighth Avenue (west). "Hollywood" is the conventional metonym for the film studios located in the Hollywood area of Los Angeles in the years encompassed in *A Fine Romance* and the films that were made there.

4. McHugh, "Introduction," in *The Oxford Handbook of Musical Theatre Screen Adaptations*, 19–24.

5. David Bordwell, Janet Staiger, and Kristin Thompson, *The Classical Hollywood Cinema: Film Style & Mode of Production to 1960* (New York: Columbia University Press, 1985).

6. Nevertheless, eleven of the American Film Institute's (AFI's) Top 25 list of film musicals are adaptations, including four of the film adaptations explored in *A Fine Romance* (#2 *West Side Story*; #5 *Cabaret*; #19 *On the Town*; and #24, the 1936 version of *Show Boat*).

7. Adaptation theory has inspired an impressively extensive literature. Some widely discussed and cited studies include Deborah Cartmell and Imelda Wheelan, *Screen Adaptation: Impure Cinema* (Houndmills, Basingstoke: Palgrave Macmillan, 2010); Linda Hutcheon, with Siobhan O'Flynn, *A Theory of Adaptation*, 2nd ed. (London: Routledge, 2013); Thomas Leitch, ed., *The Oxford Handbook of Adaptation Studies* (New York: Oxford University Press, 2017); Julie Sanders, *Adaptation and Appropriation*, 2nd ed. (London: Routledge, 2016). Before this one, however, the only book devoted to film adaptations of film musicals is *The Oxford Handbook of Musical Theatre Screen Adaptations*, edited by Dominic McHugh.

8. David L Kranz, "Trying Harder: Probability, Objectivity, and Rationality in Adaptation Studies," 77–102, in *The Literature/Film Reader: Issues in Adaptation*, ed. James M. Welsh and Peter Lev (Lanham, MD: Scarecrow, 2007), quote on 98,

9. Ibid., 99. For readers unfamiliar with the term, according to *Wikipedia*, hermeneutics is "the branch of knowledge that deals with interpretation, especially of the Bible or literary texts."

10. Thomas Leitch, "Twelve Fallacies in Contemporary Adaption Theory," *Criticism* 45/2 (Spring 2003), 149–71, quote on 153.

11. Ibid.

12. Ibid. The pioneering musical film historian Rick Altman traces the origins and ideology of films' "privileging of vision over all other senses," especially at the expense of music. Nearly twenty years before Leitch, Altman calls this privileging the "ontological fallacy," a fallacy in which "film is a visual medium and that the images must be/ are the primary carriers of the film's meaning and structure." Altman, "The Evolution of Sound Technology," 44–53, in *Film Sound: Theory and Practice*, ed. Elisabeth Weis and John Bolton (New York: Columbia University Press, 1985), quotations on 45 and 51.

13. Jesse Green, "Sondheim Dismembers 'Sweeney,'" *New York Times*, December 16, 2007. Sondheim's distaste for musical films extends far beyond adaptations of stage musicals. In fact, in his interview with Green, Sondheim can only name three praiseworthy musicals of any type, all of which appeared between 1930 and 1932: *Under the Roofs of Paris* [Sous le Toits de Paris]; *The Smiling Lieutenant,* and *Love Me Tonight.* The only adaptation that he consistently found worthy was Tim Burton's 2007 adaptation of *Sweeney Todd,* which Sondheim considered "the first musical that has ever transferred successfully to the screen." Norman Lebrecht, "When a Movie Outshines the Outstanding Original," *Scena,* February 12, 2008.

14. Stage to film: *Cabin in the Sky* (George Balanchine and Katherine Dunham [uncredited] replaced by Busby Berkeley [uncredited]); *On the Town* (Robbins replaced by Gene Kelly and Stanley Donen); *Call Me Madam* (Robbins replaced by Robert Alton); *Brigadoon* (de Mille replaced by Kelly); *Silk Stockings* (Eugene Loring retained but with the addition of Hermes Pan and Fred Astaire [uncredited]); *Flower Drum Song* (Carol Haney replaced by Pan); and *Cabaret* (Ron Field replaced by Bob Fosse).

15. Information about the creative figures behind the twelve musicals explored in *A Fine Romance* (composers, lyricists, librettists, screenwriters, producers, directors, choreographers) can be readily consulted in Appendix 1. Source information on each work is contained in Appendix 2, Appendix 3 provides a more comprehensive chronological listing of stage musicals and their film adaptations from the 1920s to the present organized around the stage shows, and Appendix 4 offers a comparable listing from the 1930s to the present organized around the films. A comparative song list for each of the selected twelve shows and films receives its own table in the chapter where it is discussed.

16. See the citations in the bibliography of critical studies by Rick Altman, Bruce Babington and Peter William Evans, Jeanine Basinger, Steven Cohan, Jane Feuer, Bill Marshall and Robynn Stilwell, and Susan Smith. A new series as of this writing, *Oxford's Guides to Film Musicals*, consists of studies of individual original film musicals, some of which will be written by musicologists, the latest group of scholars to till the fertile field of film studies. Although the use of the word "musical" in this

series does not distinguish between *original* film musicals and film *adaptations*, all volumes in the series will consider the former sub-genre exclusively.

17. For a worthwhile critical survey that continues to espouse the conventional critical disdain towards film adaptations, see Jeanine Basinger, *The Movie Musical!* (New York: Knopf, 2019).

18. McHugh, *The Oxford Handbook of Musical Theatre Screen Adaptations.*

19. Mordden, *When Broadway Went to Hollywood* (New York: Oxford University Press, 2016); Barrios, *Must-See Musicals 50 Show-Stopping Musicals We Can't Forget* (Philadelphia: Running Press, 2017). Included among Barrrios's 50 selections are 22 of the AFI's 25 Top 25. *A Fine Romance* examines 6 of Barrios's 19 adaptations: *Show Boat* (1936); *Cabin in the Sky* (1943); *On the Town* (1949); *Oklahoma!* (1955); *West Side Story* (1961); and *Cabaret* (1972).

20. In addressing the American Musicological Society in 1964 Kerman wrote that critical insight "has never been easy to define, and it has always been as urgent as it is problematic." The reason he considered it urgent was "because criticism is the way of looking at art that tries to take into account the meaning it conveys, the pleasure it initiates, and the value it assumes, for us today." Joseph Kerman, "A Profile for American Musicology," *Journal of the American Musicological Society* 18 (1965): 61–69; reprinted in *Write All These Down: Essays on Music* (Berkeley: University of California Press, 1994), 3–11, quotation on 5.

21. Ralph Waldo Emerson, Harvard Divinity School Address, July 15, 1838.

Chapter 1: The Hollywood Studio System and a Brief Survey of Film Adaptations from *Show Boat to Cabaret*

1. Well-known early song interpolations in shows composed mostly by others include Kern's "How'd You Like to Spoon with Me?" (*The Earl and the Girl*, 1905), Rodgers and Hart's "Any Old Place with You" (*A Lonely Romeo*, 1919), and Gershwin's first hit "Swanee" with lyrics by Irving Caesar (added to the road tour of *Sinbad* in 1919).

2. Richard Rodgers, *Musical Stages: An Autobiography* (New York: Random House, 1975; repr. New York: Da Capo, 1995, 2000), 95–96. An anonymous reviewer of this chapter stated that the *New York Times* pre-announced in a short item the week before Belle Baker introduced "Blue Skies" on the opening night of Rodgers and Hart's *Betsy*, December 28, 1926, that Berlin was writing a song for the show. Unable to locate this announcement, I will for the moment take Rodgers at his word that he was surprised to hear this future hit for the first time on opening night when he witnessed Berlin taking a bow from the enthusiastic audience. The practice of interpolation continued to linger. In 1941, Rodgers (a "silent partner" as a co-producer) himself composed the music and co-wrote the lyrics (with Hugh Martin) for an interpolated song, "The Guy Who Brought Me," in Martin and Ralph Blane's *Best Foot Forward*.

3. The American village, which possessed "antique taste and a limited appetite for novelty," was Mordden's third, and most important, audience. The first was "the more

sophisticated audience of the theatre capitals," while the second "dwelled in the towns of the interior: less sophisticated but occasionally adventurous." Ethan Mordden, *When Broadway Went to Hollywood* (New York: Oxford University Press, 2016), 31.

4. See "Studio System," *Wikipedia*, https://en.wikipedia.org/wiki/Studio_system.

5. In 1934, MGM had 4,000 people on their payroll, including 61 contracted stars and feature players, 17 directors, and 51 writers. John Douglas Eames, *The MGM Story: The Complete History of Fifty-Four Roaring Years* (New York: Crown, 1979), 8.

6. The Lubitsch films starring Chevalier and/or Macdonald are *The Love Parade* in 1929 (both), *Monte Carlo* in 1930 (MacDonald without Chevalier), *The Smiling Lieutenant* in 1931 (Chevalier without MacDonald), *One Hour with You* in 1932 (both), and *The Merry Widow* in 1934 (both). *Love Me Tonight* (1932) was the lone Chevalier-MacDonald pairing directed by Mamoulian.

7. Temple was born with blond hair, but by the time she was a teenager it had evolved into reddish-brown. The other Fox blondes remained that way, either by nature or nurture.

8. Thomas Schatz, *The Genius of the System: Hollywood Filmmaking in the Studio Era* (New York: Pantheon, 1988), 447.

9. Ibid.

10. According to Lee Davis, "Even when other films lost money, the Freed Unit musicals returned an average of 250 percent in profits to the studio." Quoted in Peter Hay, *MGM: When the Lion Roars* (Atlanta: Turner, 1991), 219.

11. Freed remarked: "I prefer to do original material. About the only times I did a stage play is when Metro owned it." John Kobal, *People Will Talk* (New York: Knopf, 1985), 651.

12. Pan was also credited as the choreographer for the film versions of *Roberta* and *Flower Drum Song*.

13. Two non-musical Freed films followed *Bells Are Ringing*: *The Subterraneans* and *The Light in the Piazza* both released the same day, February 7, 1962).

14. Eric Hodgins, "Amid Ruins of an Empire a New Hollywood Arises, *Life*, June 10, 1957, 160.

15. Block booking forced theaters to purchase many films, even when a given block contained only one desirable film. While block booking eventually was declared illegal as a result of a 1948 Supreme Court settlement, the concept would continue well into the future when stage theater owners regularly required patrons to purchase tickets for a group of shows in order to obtain a ticket to a hit show.

16. Hay, *When the Lion Roars*, 313. Bosley Crowther notes that when Dore Schary took over as MGM's president in 1951, "the studio had some 4,000 employees" [same number as in 1934, see note 5]. Crowther, *The Lion's Share* (New York: Garland, 1985), 301.

17. Earl Hess and Pratibha A. Dabholkar, *Gene Kelly: The Making of a Creative Legend* (Lawrence: University Press of Kansas, 2020) 290.

18. Musical genres other than revues are often referred to as "book shows" because they usually contain dialogue that advances a story (i.e., the book or libretto) rather than self-contained skits and songs. Two 1930s musical revues surpassed 1,000

performances, *Hellzapoppin* (1938) (1,404 performances) and *Pins and Needles* (1937) (1,108 performances).

19. The partnership began with *Lady, Be Good!* (1924) and continued with *Oh, Kay!* (1926), *Funny Face* (1927), and *Girl Crazy* (1930). The Astaires starred in the first three of this quartet of shows.

20. Lindsay and Russel Crouse would go on to write the books for *Call Me Madam* and *The Sound of Music*. For an explanation of what led to the replacement of Bolton and Wodehouse and how the libretto was altered, see Geoffrey Block, *Enchanted Evenings: The Broadway Musical from "Show Boat" to Sondheim and Lloyd Webber* (New York: Oxford University Press, 2009), 42–43.

21. "Kate the Great," a song about the sexual proclivities of Catherine the Great, had to go because, as its orchestrator Hans Spialek recalled, Merman refused to sing a number she considered "durrty." Apparently the offending line that Merman reportedly did not think suitable for her mother to hear was "She made the maid who made the room." John McGlinn, "The Original 'Anything Goes'—a Classic Restored," jacket notes to the studio recording of *Anything Goes* conducted by McGlinn, EMI Records, 1989, 33.

22. Future film viewers rarely got even this much chance to see Merman repeat a leading stage role in a film. Despite an impressive number of stage hits and several film appearances (the latter mainly as a featured singer), a perceived lack of Hollywood glamour denied Merman the opportunity to duplicate her starring stage roles in the film adaptations of *Annie Get Your Gun* (1950) and *Gypsy* (1962). After Paramount's *Anything Goes*, her only chance to star in a film version of one of her hits was the 1953 film adaptation of *Call Me Madam* discussed in chapter 3.

23. "Night and Day" lost on its own merits in 1932, but by 1941 it would not have been eligible for a best song Oscar since it was not written exclusively for a film.

24. Both the 1934 stage version and much of the 1956 *Anything Goes* remake take place on an ocean liner and star Bing Crosby. That's about it. This lack of correspondence is only marginally greater than the connections between the Gershwins' 1927 stage hit *Funny Face* in its 1957 MGM film adaptation. Another film with relatively few plot connections to its stage source is the newly conceived 1931 hit *The Band Wagon* with lyrics by Howard Dietz and music by Arthur Schwartz both in its Broadway stage version and its 1953 MGM film, which includes some shared songs and the fact that the Broadway versions were composed by Dietz and Schwartz and both starred Fred Astaire. I have nevertheless included it in Table 1.2 to show that a 1950s stage adaptation might roam even further afield from its stage source than a 1930s film adaptation.

25. Block, *Enchanted Evenings*, 165–66.

26. Allison Robbins, "Rescoring *Anything Goes* in 1930s Hollywood," 613–33, in McHugh, *The Oxford Handbook of Musical Theatre Screen Adaptations* (New York: Oxford University Press, 2019).

27. Two years before *Anything Goes* Crosby became a top 10 box-office film attraction for the first time, a distinction he would retain every year between 1940 and 1954, reaching number 1 status from 1944 to 1948. Eventually, Crosby made over sixty-three

movies, most of them musicals. Basinger, *The Movie Musical!* (New York: Knopf, 2019), 138.

28. The Merman-Gaxton songs make up nearly half the grand total of eleven songs used in the stage version. The others are "Bon Voyage" and "Where Are the Men?" for the sailors and passengers and the sea chantey, "There'll Always Be a Lady Fair" for the sailors in Act I, "Public Enemy Number One" for the Captain and Purser, "Be Like the Bluebird" for Victor Moore, and "The Gypsy in Me" for Hope in Act II, played by Bettina Hall, who had starred in the stage version of *The Cat and the Fiddle.*

29. The 1936 film didn't completely discard "All through the Night" and "Blow, Gabriel, Blow." Instrumental fragments of both followed the twenty seconds of the title song.

30. See Table 27.1 in Robbins, "Rescoring *Anything Goes,*" 619.

31. Two years later, the prolific Carmichael would compose the music to "Heart and Soul" and "Two Sleepy People" with lyrics by Frank Loesser (before "Loesser" became "greater" known as the composer of *Guys and Dolls* for the stage in 1950).

32. Robbins discusses the contexts for Crosby's three solo songs in "Rescoring *Anything Goes,*" 625–26. Crosby also starred in Paramount's 1956 remake where he would sing Porter's "You're the Top" with Mitzi Gaynor, "All through the Night" as a solo, and two of the three Sammy Cahn-James Van Heusen interpolations, "Ya Gotta Give the People Hoke" and "A Second Hand Turban and Crystal Ball" with Donald O'Connor (see Table 1.2).

33. "*Anything Goes,*" Paramount 1936 and 1956. Decca CD 2004.

34. The two songs retained in the *Babes in Arms* film were "Where or When" and the title song. Among the deleted songs were "I Wish I Were in Love Again," "Way Out West," "My Funny Valentine," "Johnny One Note," "All at Once," and "The Lady Is a Tramp." Five of these seven song hits were eventually seen and given the star treatment a decade later when sung by Betty Garrett, Judy Garland, Mickey Rooney, and Lena Horne, in the fictionalized biopic of Rodgers and Hart, *Words and Music* (1948).

35. For more on *Love Me Tonight,* see Geoffrey Block, *Love Me Tonight,* Oxford's Guides to Film Musicals (New York: Oxford University Press, forthcoming).

36. Only three 1938 movies, *You Can't Take It with You,* *The Adventures of Robin Hood,* and *Boys Town,* made more money than *Alexander's Ragtime Band* that year. The other cavalcade film musicals based on songs by Berlin were *Easter Parade* (1948) and *There's No Business Like Show Business* (1954).

37. Future chapters will make the case that the casting of Astaire and Rogers in *Roberta,* O'Connor and Vera-Ellen in *Call Me Madam,* Astaire and Charisse in *Silk Stockings,* and Kwan and Sato in *Flower Drum Song* was imaginative and effective.

38. Dunne starred in five films with scores by Kern. In addition to *Show Boat* and *Roberta* these include *Sweet Adeline* (the only other adaptation), *High, Wide and Handsome* (1937), and *Joy of Living* (1938).

39. Arlen-Harburg: "Happiness Is a Thing Called Joe," *Cabin in the Sky*; Carmichael-Heyman: "Moonburn," *Anything Goes*; Carmichael-Adamson: "When Love Goes Wrong," *Gentlemen Prefer Blondes*; and Whiting-Robin: "Sailor Beware," *Anything Goes.*

40. In contrast, the two film adaptations of Berlin musicals, *Louisiana Purchase* (1941) and *This is the Army* (1942), contain scores entirely by Berlin.

41. The film version removed the exclamation point.

42. Universal also changed the name of "Foolish Heart" to "Don't Look Now" and replaced Ogden Nash's imaginative lyrics.

43. Foster Hirsch, *Kurt Weill on Stage* (New York: Knopf, 2002), 238. A third Hollywood adaptation of a musical composed by Weill was *Knickerbocker Holiday* (1944), which appeared on film one month after *Lady in the Dark*. Like *One Touch of Venus*, the film version of *Knickerbocker*, starring Nelson Eddy, retained only three songs, including the famous "September Song." Since the contract negotiations of *Knickerbocker Holiday* did not contain a non-interpolation clause, the studio was free to interpolate new songs by Styne, Sammy Cahn, and lesser-known studio composers.

44. In his pathbreaking synthesis of the "Golden Age" Kim Kowalke extends the era to *Hair* in 1968. Kowalke, "Theorizing the Golden Age Musical: Genre, Structure, Syntax," *Gamut* 6/2 (2013), 133-84, *Special Feature—A Music-Theoretical Matrix: Essays in Honor of Allen Forte Part V*. In his earlier formation of a Broadway canon (i.e., musicals that serve as "models of excellence"), Lehman Engel pushed the boundaries still further at both ends, now beginning before *Oklahoma!* (1943) with *Pal Joey* (1940) and continuing through Stephen Sondheim's *Company* (1970) and *A Little Night Music* (1973) with *Cabaret* as "a strong runner-up to the list of 'best' shows." Engel, *The American Musical Theater* (New York: Collier, 1975), 35–36. See also Geoffrey Block, "The Broadway Canon from *Show Boat* to *West Side Story* and the European Operatic Ideal," *Journal of Musicology* 11/4 (Fall 1993), 525–44. Most of the shows discussed by these authors were hits in their day, which Kowalke usefully defines as shows in which "their producers recouped their investments" (Kowalke, "Theorizing the Golden Age Musical"), 135.

45. On the history of the cast album, see Laurence Maslon, *Broadway to Main Street: How Show Tunes Enchanted America* (New York: Oxford University Press, 2018).

46. The screen arrivals of the stage revue *Hellzapoppin* and the book shows, *I Married an Angel*, and *Du Barry Was a Lady* from late in the 1930s were filmed in a four-year span—from Broadway to screen—thus moving into the 1940s. The major exception to the three-year norm for a 1930s film was *Girl Crazy*, which took more than a decade for its film adaptation.

47. Victor Moore also played the ineffectual and ignored vice president Alexander Throttlebottom in *Of Thee I Sing* and Moonface Martin in *Anything Goes*, both roles teamed with Gaxton, who plays the male lead opposite Merman on stage in the latter. Moore can also be seen on screen in Astaire and Rogers's *Swing Time* (1936).

48. The "1996 Original New York Cast Recording" was recorded under the direction of Rob Fisher. DRG 94766. The 1975 Goodspeed Opera House in East Haddam Connecticut production did not lead to a commercial recording.

49. Some examples of film rights expenditures for musicals discussed in *A Fine Romance* include *Show Boat* ($65,000 for the 1929 film version), Miles Kreuger, *"Show Boat": The Story of a Classic American Musical* (New York: Oxford University Press, 1977), 76; *Cabin in the Sky* ($40,000), Anonymous, *Hollywood Reporter* (April 14,

1942), 2; *On the Town* ($250,000), Hugh Fordin, *M-G-M's Greatest Musicals: The Arthur Freed Unit* (New York: Da Capo, 1996), 258; *Oklahoma!* ($1 million), "Bought by Magna Theatre Corp., Up Bid's for Stage Plays," *Variety* (September 23, 1953), 3; *West Side Story* ($350,000), Richard Barrios, *"West Side Story": The Jets, the Sharks, and the Making of a Classic* (Philadelphia: Running Press, 2020), 24; and *Cabaret* ($1.5 million), "'Cabaret' Film Rights at AA's [Allied Artists] Peak $1.5-Mil," *Variety*, May 28, 1969, 1. For *My Fair Lady*, see Dominic McHugh, *Loverly: The Life and Times of "My Fair Lady"* (New York: Oxford University Press, 2012), 181; for *The Music Man*, see Barrios, *"West Side Story,"* 24.

50. Barrios, *Must-See Musicals: 50 Show-Stopping Movies We Can't Forget* (Philadelphia: Running Press, 2020), 123. "When Love Goes Wrong," recorded by the cast originals Marilyn Monroe and Jane Russell (Eileen Wilson dubbed Russell's voice on the soundtrack), was one of the twenty Carmichael songs selected in the American Songbook Series produced by the Smithsonian Collection of Recordings, Sony 1993.

51. The major cut songs were "I'm a Bad, Bad Man" (Frank Butler), "Moonshine Lullaby" (Annie and the kids), and "I Got Lost in His Arms" (Annie and ensemble). The other deleted songs are the two duets for Winnie and Tommy, "I'll Share It All with You" and "Who Do You Love, I Hope," which over the years have more often than not been deleted from stage revivals as well, along with the young lovebirds who sang them.

52. Although *West Side Story* and *Flower Drum Song* retain nearly all of their stage scores, they both take considerable liberties with the sequence of these songs. The consequences and wisdom of these decisions will be discussed in the chapters devoted to these shows.

53. The following musicals listed in Table 1.2 added at least one song by the *original* songwriters: *Call Me Madam, Kiss Me Kate, Guys and Dolls, Kismet, Anything Goes, Silk Stockings, Pal Joey, South Pacific, Damn Yankees, L'il Abner, Can-Can, Bells Are Ringing, The Music Man, Jumbo, Bye Bye Birdie, The Unsinkable Molly Brown*, and *The Sound of Music*. The three exceptions are *Gentlemen Prefer Blondes* (three songs by Carmichael and Adamson), the 1956 remake of *Anything Goes* (two songs by Cahn and Van Heusen), and *Jumbo* (one song by Edens). Two other related points: (1) Irving Berlin, Frank Loesser, Cole Porter, and Meredith Willson wrote the lyrics as well as the music in these films; and (2) Rodgers wrote the lyrics as well as music for the two new songs in *The Sound of Music* in the absence of Hammerstein, who died in 1960.

54. Among the sixteen 1950s stage musicals listed in Appendix 3, perhaps only *Can-Can, Kismet, Silk Stockings, Gypsy*, and *The Sound of Music* did not retain a major star, director, or choreographer from the original stage version in the film adaptation.

55. The three retentions from stage to film were Officer Krupke (William Bramley), Gee-Tar (Tommy Abbott), and Velma (Carole D'Andrea). Ernesto R. Acevedo-Muñoz, *"West Side Story" as Cinema: The Making and Impact of an American Masterpiece* (Lawrence: University Press of Kansas, 2013), 37. A fourth actor, Jay Norm, played Juano on stage and Pepe in the film.

56. Abbott and Logan were also the co-librettists of their respective musicals.

57. Producer Prince soon concluded that he closed *West Side Story* prematurely and brought the show back after a year-long national tour for an additional 249 performances.

58. The 1998 revival is surpassed only by Kander and Ebb's *Chicago*, as of this writing second only to *The Phantom of the Opera* as the longest-running musical, original or revival. In contrast, the 2009 revival of *West Side Story* ran only 66 performances longer than the 1957 production.

59. Commentary in *Broadway: The American Musical*, "Episode Five; Tradition (1957–1970), PBS Home Video 2004.

60. Foster Hirsch, *Harold Prince and the American Musical Theatre* (New York: Applause, 2005), 66. In his later reflections, Prince added the following: "Were I to do *Cabaret* now, I would take the opportunity, as Fosse did in the film, to restore the original gay subplot. . . . But putting Nazis on the stage in a musical seemed like a big enough step at the time." Harold Prince, *Sense of Occasion* (New York: Applause, 2017), 138.

61. The other top five film musicals in the AFI list were *Singin' in the Rain* (#1), *The Wizard of Oz* (#3), and *The Sound of Music* (#4). The film versions of *West Side Story* and *Cabaret* were also added to the National Film Registry, *Cabaret* in 1995 and *West Side Story* in 1997, with the 1936 *Show Boat* (1996) in between and later followed by three other film musicals discussed in *A Fine Romance*: *Oklahoma!* (2007), *Flower Drum Song* (2008), and *Cabin in the Sky* (2020). *Ninotchka*, the non-musical film that inspired *Silk Stockings* was added in 1990.

Chapter 2: Surviving in the 1930s Movie Studio Jungle: Jerome Kern and *Show Boat, The Cat and the Fiddle*, and *Roberta*

1. The ballet music that Victor Herbert's composed for the stage show was also assigned to another composer for the film.

2. *Swing Time*, with lyrics by Fields, starred Astaire and Rogers and included "Pick Yourself Up," "The Way You Look Tonight," and the song that inspired the title of this book, "A Fine Romance." *You Were Lovelier*, with lyrics by Johnny Mercer, starred Astaire and Rita Hayworth and included "Dearly Beloved," "I'm Old Fashioned," and the title song; *Cover Girl*, with lyrics by Ira Gershwin, starred Gene Kelly and Hayworth and included "Long Ago and Far Away"; *High, Wide and Handsome*, with lyrics by Hammerstein, was directed by Rouben Mamoulian, starred Irene Dunne, and offered "Can I Forget You?" and "The Folks Who Live on the Hill."

3. Roy Hemming, *The Melody Lingers On: The Great Songwriters and Their Movie Musicals* (New York: Newmarket, 1986), 93. See also Geoffrey Block, "Refashioning *Roberta*: From Novel to Stage to Screen," in *The Oxford Handbook of Musical Theatre Screen Adaptations*, ed. Dominic McHugh (New York: Oxford University Press, 2019), 29–53.

4. Major productions include New York (1927, 1932, 1946, 1956–57, 1983, and 1994) and London (1928, 1943, 1971, 1989–90, and 1998).

5. For information on several of these productions, see Todd Decker, *"Show Boat": Performing Race in an American Musical* (New York: Oxford University Press, 2013). A pioneering predecessor to Decker is Miles Kreuger, *"Show Boat": The Story of a Classic American Musical* (New York: Oxford University Press, 1977). Kreuger surveys the novel; the 1927, 1932, and 1946 Broadway productions; the three films; and several other productions that appeared in New York and London between 1954 and 1971.

6. Decker, *Show Boat": Performing Race in an American Musical*, 249.

7. Some of these shows featured Black writers as well as performers: *Raisin* was based on Lorraine Hansberry's play *A Raisin in the Run*; Charlie Smalls was the main composer for *The Wiz*, and Luther Vandross contributed "Everybody Rejoice"; Fats Waller composed the music for *Ain't Misbehavin'*; and Brenda Russell and Stephen Bray were two of the three composer-lyricists for *The Color Purple*.

8. Decker, *"Show Boat": Performing Race in an American Musical*, 5. In addition to compiling this list, Decker footnotes a group of "commercially non-hit shows with interracial casts": *Great Day* (1929); *Kwamina* (1961); *1600 Pennsylvania Avenue* (1976); *Grind* (1985); *Marie Christine* (1999); *Caroline, or Change* (2004); and *The Scottsboro Boys* (2010). To this list might be added *The Wild Party* (2000) (68 performances) with music by Michael John LaChiusa, directed by the African American director George C. Wolfe.

9. Despite her unpleasant nature and negative character, Parthy does, however, deserve some credit for quickly sizing up Ravenal as the charming but weak man he was.

10. Gary Giddins, "Rollin' on the River," *Show Boat*, The Criterion Collection 1021, DVD Edition (2020), n.p.

11. Decker, *"Show Boat,"* 195.

12. Jeanine Basinger, *The Movie Musical* (New York: Knopf, 2019), 336–37.

13. Letter from Hammerstein to Carl Laemmle Jr., October 1, 1935, Oscar Hammerstein II Collection 1847–2000, Library of Congress, General Correspondence and Business Papers, 1917–1998, Box 63, Folder 5. Many thanks to Mark Eden Horowitz for making Hammerstein's letters available to me prior to the publication of Mark Eden Horowitz, compiled and ed., *The Letters of Oscar Hammerstein II* (New York: Oxford University Press, 2022), 98.

14. Ibid.

15. Kreuger, *"Show Boat": The Story of a Classic American Musical*, 50. Mordden notes but does not document Kreuger's claim that Hammerstein came to regret his decision to bring Ferber's Ravenal back from the dead. Mordden, *Make Believe: The Broadway Musical in the 1920s* (New York: Oxford University Press, 1997), 211.

16. This chapter does not discuss stage revivals or screen versions such as the still-often shown 1951 MGM version. The 1929 film, based on Ferber's novel, was mainly a silent film but also included a prologue consisting of songs performed by Morgan, Jules Bledsoe, and Tess Gardella from the Broadway cast. The Criterion Collection *Show Boat* includes four songs from the prologue and twenty minutes of excerpts from the silent portion with audio commentary by Kreuger.

17. A sung version of "Why Do I Love You?" was filmed but cut a few days before the film was released (Kreuger, *"Show Boat": The Story of a Classic American Musical*,

136). The song returns as underscoring when Ellie reads Ravenal's farewell letter to Magnolia in the lowly Chicago boarding house.

18. Basinger, *The Movie Musical!*, 341. Viewers also have Whale to thank for not allowing Morgan to sing sitting on top of a piano, her trademark in *Show Boat* on stage and throughout her cabaret career.

19. Decker, "*Show Boat*," 153.

20. Letter from Breen (Production Code Administration) to Harry Zehner (Universal), October 17, 1935, *Show Boat*, Production Code Files, Margaret Herrick Library, Los Angeles (quoted in Decker, "*Show Boat*," 149–50).

21. Oscar Hammerstein, "Notes on Lyrics," in *Lyrics* (New York: Simon & Schuster, 1949; expanded and ed., William Hammerstein (Milwaukee, WI: Hal Leonard, 1985), 39.

22. Chappy Gardner, "Along the Rialto," *Pittsburgh Courier*, February 4, 1928 (quoted in Decker, "*Show Boat*," 102).

23. The term "colored" remained the most respectful term until the 1960s when it was replaced by "Black" or African American. For this reason, "colored" was used when naming the National Association for the Advancement of Colored People when it was founded in 1909. On the other hand, the word "nigger" was already considered less respectful than "colored" before the Civil War, "recognized as opprobrious" by 1904, and "an insult" in the first edition of H. W. Fowler's *A Dictionary of Modern English Usage* (Oxford: Clarendon Press, 1926). See also "They Are Only 'Niggers' in the South," *Seattle Republican*, October 14, 1904, Image 5, and John McWhorter, "How the N-Word Became Unsayable," *New York Times,* April 30, 2021. The offensive word was used several other times in *Show Boat*, not only by Julie's vindictive admirer Pete and Sheriff Vallon, but also by Queenie.

24. Miles Kreuger, "Some Words about 'Show Boat," *Show Boat*, conducted and directed by John McGlinn, EMI Records CDS 7 49108 2 (1988), 23. After considering "brothers all work," the Hal Prince production of 1994 returned to "colored folks" used in the 1936 film.

25. Letter from Hammerstein to James Whale, March 16, 1936, Oscar Hammerstein II Collection, Library of Congress, Box 63, Folder 5. Horowitz, *The Letters of Oscar Hammerstein II,* 117.

26. Letter from James Whale to Oscar Hammerstein, March 17, 1936, Oscar Hammerstein II Collection, Library of Congress, Box 63, Folder 5. Horowitz, *Letters of Oscar Hammerstein II,* 119.

27. Kreuger, 1989 audio commentary, *Show Boat*, The Criterion Collection 1021, DVD Edition (2020).

28. Ibid.

29. Decker, "*Show Boat*," 150. Basinger made note of the eye rolling, but incorrectly attributed it to Dunne in this number, rather than to McDaniel's eye roll in response to Morgan's singing which precedes the dancing (Dunne doesn't roll her eyes until "Gallivantin' Around"); Without expressing an opinion Basinger notes that it [eye rolling] "is often seen as offensive" (Basinger, *The Movie Musical!*, 339).

30. Giddins, "Rollin' on the River," n. p.

31. Shana L. Redmond, 2020 commentary in *Show Boat*, The Criterion Collection.

32. "After the Ball" composed by Charles K. Harris in 1892, was likely the most commercially successful song of its era and a song that the Trocadero audience would certainly know. Perhaps not coincidentally, John Philip Sousa's band performed it daily at the Chicago World's Fair of 1893, and it was also performed in the opening Fair setting of *Show Boat*'s second act. Peter Gammon, *The Oxford Companion to Popular Music* (New York: Oxford University Press, 1991).

33. Letter from Hammerstein to Whale, November 18, 1935. Oscar Hammerstein II Collection, Library of Congress, Box 63, Folder 5. Horowitz, *Letters of Oscar Hammerstein II*, 107.

34. Kreuger, 1989 audio commentary, *Show Boat*, The Criterion Collection, and Redmond, 2020 commentary in *Show Boat*, The Criterion Collection.

35. Peter Stansfield, "From the Vulgar to the Refined: American Vernacular and Blackface Minstrelsy in *Showboat* [*sic*], in *Musicals: Hollywood and Beyond*, ed. Bill Marshall and Robynn Stilwell (Portland, OR: Intellect, 2000), 147.

36. Ibid., 149.

37. Ibid.

38. Ibid., 153.

39. Stephen Banfield, *Jerome Kern* (New York: Yale University Press, 2006), 254–55.

40. Readers might recall Kim Kowalke's definition of a hit in chapter 1 as a show in which "their producers recouped their investments." Kowalke, "Theorizing the Golden Age Musical," 135.

41. The title *The Cat and the Fiddle* derives from the opening line of the sixteenth-century English nursery rhyme, "Hey diddle diddle, the cat and the fiddle." The libretto doesn't spell things out about the identity of the cat and the fiddle, but it is possible that "cat" might be a reference to the 1920s slang phrase "cool cat," in which case Shirley is the cat. Although "fiddle" is a less long-haired term for violin (after all, the nursery rhyme isn't "The Cat and the Violin"), Victor would be the logical choice, even though it is Odette and her character Pierrot who actually play the violin.

42. Wood, best known to musical film buffs for her role as the Mother Abbess in *The Sound of Music* (1965), recorded four songs from the 1932 London production: "She Didn't Say 'Yes,'" "Try to Forget," "A New Love Is Old," and "The Night Was Made for Love." *Jerome Kern in London Original Cast Recordings*, LP Monmouth Evergreen MES17054 (1972) and *Americans in London in the 1930s*, CD, *Encore* ENBO-CD-3/ 92 (ALB-1427). The latter recordings also include additional instrumental selections conducted by Hyam Greenbaum and the Palace Theatre Orchestra.

43. Edward Baron Turk, *Hollywood Diva: A Biography of Jeanette MacDonald* (Berkeley: University of California Press, 1998), 135.

44. For a significant scholarly exception, see the thorough and perceptive discussion in Banfield, *Jerome Kern*, 179–98.

45. *Sweet Adeline* was performed at *Encores!* in 1997 and *Music in the Air* in 2006. Other musicals explored in this volume that were performed at *Encores!* include the two musicals discussed in chapter 2, *On the Town* (2008) and *Call Me Madam* (1994 and 2019), and *Cabin in the Sky* (2016) in chapter 4.

46. "'Cat and the Fiddle' in a Concert Version," *New York Times*, March 21, 1990, Section C, 15.

47. *Jerome Kern Overtures*, National Philharmonic Orchestra, conducted by John McGlinn, EMI Records CDC 7 49630 2 (1989).

48. For a complete two-piano recording of a 2006 performance that closely follows the published Vocal Score (T. B. Harms, 1932) and includes narration between scenes, see The Comic Opera Guild, Adam Aceto, Artistic Director, 2 CDs B003CIR WSK (2006). The DVD of the film version was released in 2013 by Warner Archive BOOCZQWYP4.

49. For more on the term integration as it applies to musicals, see Geoffrey Block, "Integration," in *The Oxford Handbook of the American Musical*, ed. Raymond Knapp, Mitchell Morris, and Stacy Wolf (New York: Oxford University Press, 2011), 97–110; repr.in *Histories of the Musical Vol. 1*, eds. Knapp, Morris, and Wolf (New York: Oxford University Press, 2018), 153-75.

50. Louis R. Reid, "Composing While You Wait," *Dramatic Mirror*, June 2, 1917, 5 (quoted in Block, "Integration," note 49).

51. Ethan Mordden, *Sing for Your Supper: The Broadway Musical in the 1930s* (New York: Palgrave Macmillan, 2005), 221.

52. For an informed discussion of how musical theater and film scholars have misinterpreted Aristotle's use of "diegesis" and "diegetic" and gave it new meaning, see Stefano Castelvecchi, "On 'Diegesis' and 'Diegetic': Words and Concepts," *Journal of the American Musicological Society* 73, no. 1 (Spring 2020): 149–71. Bruce F. Kawin extends the meaning of diegeticism to encompass all sounds (not only songs) that are "capable of being heard by the real or fictive inhabitants of the filmed world, whether or not it was recorded during production." Bruce F. Kawin, *How Movies Work* (New York: Macmillan, 1987), 539.

53. Banfield, *Jerome Kern*, 179.

54. George Meader sang with the Metropolitan Opera from 1921 until 1932, his final two years coinciding with his Broadway role in *The Cat and the Fiddle*, which closed that year.

55. The numbers in parentheses following the quoted dialogue here and elsewhere in this section refer to page numbers in the unpublished libretto.

56. MacDonald found this reunion "particularly absurd" and did her best to have it reshot. According to her biographer Edward Baron Turk, MacDonald succeeded in getting producer Bernie Hyman to film an alternative closing scene. For the final cut, however, Hyman disregarded MacDonald's wishes and kept the original ending, a decision that created considerable long-term ill will between the producer and the star. Turk, *Hollywood Diva*, 139.

57. Banfield reprints the music of the final four lines sung by Shirley and Victor, which followed the first 4 measures of "One Moment Alone." Banfield, *Jerome Kern*, 197 (Vocal Score, 177–79).

58. The names of the themes used here are taken from Banfield's thematic table which is organized into three groups: "Brussels street themes," "Shirley's (and American

themes),” and “Victor’s (and Pierrot) themes.” Banfield offers incipits for twenty-four themes, which include the major song titles (see Banfield, *Jerome Kern*, 190–92).

59. A siciliana is a slow eighteenth-century instrumental movement or aria that customarily begins with an upbeat and features the same dotted rhythms in 6/8 time found at the bottom of *The Cat and the Fiddle* Vocal Score, 22 (Musical Example 2.1a).

60. The introduction appears several times in its chordal form and provides the subject for a quasi-fugue directly after its first appearance. Victor closes the fugue exposition with two G major chords to which Shirley responds argumentatively with two B minor chords. After four such chordal disagreeable exchanges between G major and B minor, Victor returns to the chordal version while Shirley plays a countermelody above. If anyone reading this note doesn’t have the DVD of *The Cat and the Fiddle* handy, the chordal opening fanfare of Victor’s operetta is the same as the first music heard over the credits in the widely available Kern biopic *Till the Clouds Roll By* (1946).

61. Block, *Enchanted Evenings*, contains a musical illustration of the transformation of “Can’t Help Lovin’ Dat Man” from the original song to the ragged version (28–29). Another example in *Show Boat* is “It’s Getting Hotter in the North,” the first of many ideas for a finale, which consists of a jazzy transformation of Magnolia’s piano theme.

62. Letter from James Wingate to E. J. Mannix, August 10, 1933, *The Cat and the Fiddle*, Production Code Files, Margaret Herrick Library, Los Angeles. Although Wingate mentions various other lines for removal and the scene when Victor holds up a funeral in respect to religious ceremonies (a scene that also remained in the final film), he didn’t suggest the removal of an early morning conversation in which Shirley, still in bed, shares her overtly sexual dream in which Victor is wearing nothing under his “golden jacket.”

63. The memo is dated three days before the film’s release and only a few weeks before Breen took over as the new director of the Production Code. Letter from Breen to Louis B. Meyer, February 13, 1934, Production Code Files, Margaret Herrick Library, Los Angeles. According to Breen biographer Thomas Doherty, “after only two months on the job, Breen had rejected six pictures—as many as had been rejected under [Colonel Jason S.] Joy and Wingate together during the previous three years.” Thomas Doherty, *Hollywood’s Censor: Joseph I. Breen & the Production Code Administration* (New York: Columbia University Press, 2007), 63. The minor breach Breen alludes to occurred after Victor’s angry “deep breath as if swearing in silence” when the taxi driver responded: “That’s not true. My mother was a lady.” *The Cat and the Fiddle*, Screenplay by Bella and Samuel Spewack, May 13, 1933 through September 27, 1933. Production Files (508-f.C-425), 12, Margaret Herrick Library. The Spewacks are best known as the co-librettists to *Kiss Me, Kate* (1948) with lyrics and music by Cole Porter.

64. Letter from Breen to L. B. Mayer, April 19, 1937, *The Cat and the Fiddle*, Production Files, Margaret Herrick Library.

65. Future chapters will explore three other film adaptations on this exclusive list: *Call Me Madam*, *Silk Stockings*, and *Flower Drum Song*. The relatively less attention paid to *Roberta* in this chapter in no way reflects the author’s opinion that it occupies a

position of less importance or is a less successful film adaptation of a Kern musical, but is instead entirely due to the fact that I have discussed the stage and screen versions elsewhere in some detail. For an expanded discussion of *Roberta*, upon which the present chapter is based, see Block, "Refashioning *Roberta*," especially 29-53.

66. *Roberta* is one of two Astaire-Rogers films in which they play characters who have known each other before the film begins. The second was *Follow the Fleet* (1936), which also features the non-singing Randolph Scott as the secondary leading male.

67. Arlene Croce, *The Fred Astaire & Ginger Rogers Book* (New York: Outerbridge & Lazard, 1972), 47.

68. In the film, Minnie was played by Helen Westley, who the following year would play Parthy in the film version of *Show Boat*, another non-singing role.

69. After Huck sings a chorus, he introduces a roster of well-known popular singers of the day to continue the song he started, including Bing Crosby, Ruth Etting, Ethel Merman, Rudy Vallee, Morton Downey, Arthur Tracy, and Helen Morgan. Each of these singers, some still well known today, are impersonated by a cast member listed by name, both in the libretto and the Vocal Score (e.g., Alan Jones as Downey and Fred MacMurray as Vallee).

70. Block, "Refashioning *Roberta*," 43–44.

71. Hemming, *The Melody Lingers On*, 93.

Chapter 3: Challenging the Hollywood Studio Model: *On the Town* versus *Call Me Madam*

1. In 1934 Paramount paid $85,000 for the rights to *Anything Goes* plus 10% gross in rentals if they surpassed the million mark (Allison Robbins, "Rescoring *Anything Goes* in 1930s Hollywood," in *The Oxford Companion of Musical Theatre Screen Adaptations*, ed. Dominic McHugh [New York: Oxford University Press, 2019], 621). Thirteen years later MGM paid a record $650,000 for the film rights to *Annie Get Your Gun* (Laurence Bergreen, *As Thousands Cheer: The Life of Irving Berlin* [New York: Viking, 1990], 460). Adjusted for inflation the film adaptation of *Anything Goes* would have cost a little over $145,000 in 1950.

2. For indispensable historical background and musical and cultural analysis of the stage versions as well as insightful commentary on the film adaptations of *On the Town* and *Call Me Madam*, see Carol J. Oja, *Bernstein Meets Broadway: Collaborative Art in a Time of War* (New York: Oxford University Press, 2014) and Jeffrey Magee, *Irving Berlin's Musical Theater* (New York: Oxford University Press, 2012).

3. Major *On the Town* revivals include West End (1963), Broadway (1971, 1998, 2014), English National Opera (2007), New York City Center *Encores!* (2008), and London's Regents Park (2017). The innovative but short-lived 1998 Broadway revival was directed by the prominent African American director George C. Wolfe. "The Three Dance Episodes, consist of "The Great Lover Displays Himself" (one portion of the musical's fourth ballet, "The Subway Train to Coney Island" and "The

Dream Coney Island"), "The Lonely Town Pas de Deux" (the second ballet), and "Times Square: 1944" (the finale to Act I). According to Steven Suskin, Hershy Kay was the exclusive arranger of the "'serious' ballet sequences," including the material in the Dance Episodes. Steven Suskin, *The Sound of Broadway Music: A Book of Orchestrators and Orchestrations* (New York: Oxford University Press, 2009), 48, 497.

4. Otis L. Guernsey Jr., ed., in *Broadway Song and Story: Playwrights/Lyricists/ Composers Discuss Their Hits* (New York: Dodd, Mead, 1985), 6.

5. Oliver Smith, the scene designer and co-producer (an unusual combination) had designed *Rosalinda* in 1942. After *On the Town* he went on to design some of the most memorable shows of the next three decades: *Gentlemen Prefer Blondes* (1949); *My Fair Lady* (1956); *Candide* (1956); *West Side Story* (1957); *Flower Drum Song* (1958); *The Sound of Music* (1959); and *Hello, Dolly!* (1964). The only Bernstein musical that he did not work on was *Wonderful Town* (1953). Smith also designed the sets for the film adaptations of *Guys and Dolls* (1955), *Oklahoma!* (1955), and *Porgy and Bess* (1959), and the original film musical *The Barkleys of Broadway* (1953).

6. Guernsey, *Broadway Song and Story*, 7; Hugh Fordin, *M-G-M's Greatest Musicals: The Arthur Freed Unit* (New York: Ca Capo, 1996), 258.

7. Guernsey, *Broadway Song and Story*, 14.

8. In *Ball Game*, Comden and Green wrote the lyrics only for most of the songs (with music by Edens), and Harry Tugend and George Wells wrote the screenplay.

9. Thomas S. Hischak, *Through the Screen Door* (Lanham, MD: Scarecrow, 2004), 15.

10. Clive Hirschhorn, *The Hollywood Musical* (New York: Crown,1981), 308–9.

11. Guernsey, *Song and Story*, 7. Abbott would continue to direct shows until his death at 107 in 1995.

12. Ibid, 9.

13. John Kobal, *People Will Talk* (New York: Knopf, 1985), 651.

14. Stephen M. Silverman, *Dancing on the Ceiling: Stanley Donen and His Movies* (New York: Knopf, 1996), 108.

15. Decca recorded only six songs, no more than three of which featured members of the original cast, and Mary Martin recorded two others. Laurence Maslon, *Broadway to Main Street: How Show Tunes Enchanted America* (New York: Oxford University Press, 2918), 75.

16. Will Friedwald, *Sinatra! The Song Is You: A Singer's Art* (Chicago: Chicago Review Press, 2018), 268–69. Sinatra and Kelly had previously played sailors in *Anchors Aweigh* (MGM 1945).

17. Silverman, *Dancing on the Ceiling*, 111.

18. "Presentation of Miss Turnstiles," ten minutes into the film version, included only one theme from the stage version of this ballet, but instead used music by Bernstein from other parts of *On the Town* (mainly "The Great Lover").

19. Other *On the Town* songs in minor include most of Gabey's "Lonely Town" and Pitkin's "I Understand" and in *West Side Story*, "Jet Song" and "A Boy Like That." In *Silk Stockings* Porter used the minor mode in the verse of "Without Love" (the chorus is major) and most of the title song before it concludes in the major. The issue of Porter and his predilection for the minor mode will be revisited in chapter 5.

20. Letter from Joseph I. Breen to L. B. Meyer, February 23, 1949, Production Files, Margaret Herrick Library, Los Angeles.

21. Jack Gottlieb, *Working with Bernstein* (New Haven, CT: Yale University Press, 2013), 214.

22. Oja, *Bernstein Meets Broadway*, 111–12.

23. Although Bernstein receives no official credit, the 1997 vocal score includes the words "additional lyrics by Leonard Bernstein" in a font as large as that received by Comden, Green, Robbins, and six orchestrators. This rubric refers to the generally accepted fact that Bernstein wrote the lyrics to "I Can Cook Too," directly acknowledged in the credits on Nancy Walker's 1945 release of the song. Bernstein's long-time assistant Jack Gottlieb confirms this authorship and goes further in stating that Bernstein also "wrote the words for the refrain on 'New York, New York.'" Gottlieb, *Working with Bernstein*), 44.

24. It's possible but probably unlikely that Freed requested a Code review of the lyrics to "I Can Cook Too," but in any event I was unable to locate such a request in the Production Files at the Margaret Herrick Library.

25. In contrast to the stage version with its strong interracial presence in the dancing chorus throughout, the Club Dixieland scene in the film is the first time viewers witness any African American performers.

26. Gerald Mast, *Can't Help Singin': The American Musical on Stage and Screen* (Woodstock, NY: Overlook, 1987), 239. Although Thomas S. Hischak describes the Edens songs as "mediocre," he makes a partial exception for "Prehistoric Man," which in his view "came close to the quality of the original songs." Hischak, *Musicals in Film: A Guide to the Genre* (Westport, CT: Greenwood, 2016), 201.

27. Richard Rodgers, *Musical Stages* (New York: Random House, 1975), 175.

28. Humphrey Burton, *Leonard Bernstein* (New York: Doubleday, 1994), 193.

29. Silverman, *Dancing on the Ceiling*, 111.

30. Kobal, *People Will Talk*, 650.

31. *On the Town*, 1949 Original Soundtrack, Delta Leisure Group CD6808 (2010).

32. Earl Hess and Pratibha A. Dabholkar, *Gene Kelly: The Making of a Creative Legend* (Lawrence: University Press of Kansas, 2020), 228. In describing the pains, both literal and metaphorical, that Kelly took during the filming, Hess and Dabholkar note that the final scene alone took twenty-six painful takes to satisfy him (Ibid., 230). Based on a 1985 interview, Sheryl Flatow concludes that *On the Town* "signaled the coming of age of Kelly and the wholly integrated dance musical and is, without a doubt, the pivotal movie of his career (and as a result, his favorite)." Flatow, "Through a Lens Brightly," *Ballet News,* April 1985, 11–14, 30; quotation on 11. xxx

33. *On the Town*, Screenplay, February 24, 1949, 69.

34. The photograph is reprinted in Fordin *M-G-M's Greatest Musicals*, 266 and Richard Barrios, *Must-See Musicals: 50 Show-Stopping Movies We Can't Forget* (Philadelphia: Running Press, 2017), 97

35. *On the Town*, Screenplay, February 24, 1949, 69. Formerly distributed by Script City.

36. Ibid.

37. Silverman, *Dancing on the Ceiling*, 112.

38. Microsoft Windows 7 Startup Sound. https://youtu.be/095XUIKnQSY.
39. Although Bernstein's intentions are unknown, it is striking that the four-note "New York, New York" motive is identical to the central motive of Jean Sibelius's Fifth Symphony in E-Flat Major, Op. 82 (1915; rev. 1916 and 1919). Also suggestive rather than conclusive is the fact that when Bernstein met Green for the first time in 1937 at Camp Onota in northwest Massachusetts, the Sibelius Fifth was one of the musically knowledgeable Green's favorite compositions and Bernstein didn't know it. This would change that evening when Green performed the work for Bernstein with "funny and odd full-orchestra phonographic sounds" of his own making. Burton, *Leonard Bernstein*, 39. After this performance Bernstein became a life-long convert to the work and eventually recorded it with the New York Philharmonic in 1966.
40. Fordin, *M-G-M's Greatest Musicals*, 267.
41. Beth Genné, *Dance Me a Song* (New York: Oxford University Press, 2018), 211.
42. Ibid.
43. Ibid.
44. I trust that readers won't mind my repeating the definition of a cavalcade musical offered in chapter 1, that is, a film musical that features an anthology of previously composed songs. Once again the three Berlin cavalcade musical films are *Alexander's Ragtime Band* (1938), *Easter Parade* (1948), and *There's No Business Like Show Business* (1954). While emphasizing earlier songs, all three also offered Berlin songs expressly written for these films.
45. At a fundraising rally for Eisenhower at Madison Square Garden on February 8, 1952, Berlin sang "*I Like Ike*," a retitled version of "*They Like Ike*" that soon became a major campaign slogan for the Eisenhower presidential campaign. Bergreen, *As Thousands Cheer*, 508–9.
46. "Truman Wrote of '48 Offer to Eisenhower," *New York Times*, July 11, 2003.
47. See Robert Kimball and Linda Emmet, eds., *The Complete Lyrics of Irving Berlin* (New York: Knopf, 2001), 76–77, for a comparison between the 1913 and revised film lyrics, which do not appear in the September 4, 1952, screenplay.
48. In the stage version, Kenneth was appointed in an act of nepotism, whereas in the film he earns his position as press attaché by demonstrating his knowledge of Lichtenburg and by immediately proving his usefulness to Sally. This change makes Kenneth more sympathetic and endearing and, along with his new dancing skills, it's hard not to root for a happy ending in his pursuit of the princess.
49. Bentley, who played the Brunette in *Fancy Free*, was long associated with Robbins, including as Chita Rivera's replacement in the role of Anita in the initial run of *West Side Story* (July 1958 to March 1959).
50. George Abbott, *"Mr. Abbott"* (New York: Random, House, 1963). 227.
51. Deborah Jowitt, *Jerome Robbins: His Life, His Theater, His Dance* (New York: Simon & Schuster, 2004), 175.
52. Ibid.
53. During the Boston tryouts of *Madam*, Robbins also dropped "Free," a song written for Merman that was not a dance number. It returned a few years later with a new title and new Berlin lyrics as "Snow" in the film *White Christmas* (1954).

54. To be more precise, the main melody of the music began multiple phrases on a single pitch over continuously changing harmonies.
55. Fordin, *M-G-M's Greatest Musicals*, 233–34.
56. Jowitt, *Jerome Robbins*, 175.
57. Gerald Bordman and Thomas S. Hischak, eds., *The Oxford Companion to American Theatre*, 3rd ed. (New York: Oxford University Press, 2004), 23.
58. John Martin, "The Dance: Revue Style," *New York Times*, February 18, 1940, 136.
59. "The Ocarina" occurs much later in the film (60:00), a few minutes after the first rendition of "You're Just in Love."
60. Between 1914 and 1966, Berlin composed fifteen counterpoint songs, none of which gained a foothold in the repertoire comparable to his first and last efforts and "You're Just in Love." The first was "Play a Simple Melody" composed for Berlin's debut full-length show *Watch Your Step* (1914). The last was "An Old-Fashioned Wedding," introduced by Merman and Bruce Yarnell at the 1966 Lincoln Center revival of *Annie Get Your Gun*. "Wedding," which proved to be the composer's final song before retiring from show business, was later added to the 1999 Broadway revival. Here's a list of the counterpoint songs Berlin composed between these bookends: "When I Get Back to the U.S.A" [combined with "My Country 'tis of Thee"], *Stop! Look! Listen* (1915); "Kiss Once More," *The Century Girl* (1916); "I'll See You in C-U-B-A," *Ziegfeld Midnight Frolic* (1919) and *Blue Skies* (Paramount, 1946); "Pack Up Your Sins and Go the Devil," *The Music Box Revue of 1922*; "Climbing Up the Scale," *The Music Box Revue of 1923*; "The Call of the South" [combined with "Old Folks at Home"], *The Music Box Revue of 1924*; "Drinking Song" [combined with "Stars and Stripes Forever" and "Dixie"], *Face the Music* (1932); "Debts" [combined with "Star Spangled Banner"], *As Thousands Cheer* (1933); "Blue Skies," *Blue Skies* (1946) [film]; "Extra! Extra!" *Miss Liberty* (1949); "You're Just in Love," *Call Me Madam* (1950); "Dallas," *Sentimental Guy* (1955) [unfinished musical]; and "Empty Pockets Filled with Love," *Mr. President* (1962). Magee, *Irving Berlin's Musical Theater*, 23. Although less complete overall, Henry Hewes's list contains "Climbing Up the Scale," which is not included in Magee's list (Hewes, "Mr. American Music," *Saturday Review*, October 1, 1966, 36, 80). I have a helpful anonymous reviewer to thank for the inclusion of "I'll See you in C-U-B-A."
61. The correlation between love and sickness in "You're Just in Love" is not unlike Rodgers and Hart's "It's Got to Be Love" from *On Your Toes*, in which a young woman realizes that what she feels has "got to be love" (because "it couldn't be tonsillitis").
62. Sally's telephone conversations with Truman with their references to his daughter Margaret's attempts at a singing career, were a running gag both on stage and screen. On stage, a Truman look alike made an appearance every night during the show's run; in the film, Truman's *hands* make an appearance playing his famous "Missouri Waltz" on the piano.
63. Arthur Sheekman, *Call Me Madam*, screenplay, Shooting Final, September 5, 1952, 108–9.
64. Richards is also Charisse's voice on "Baby, You Knock Me Out" in *It's Always Fair Weather* (1955).

65. Letter from Joseph I. Breen to Colonel Jason S. Joy, April 30, 1952, William "Billy" Gordon Papers, *Call Me Madam*, Margaret Herrick Library, Los Angeles. In the same letter Breen reminded Joy "the Production Code makes it mandatory that the intimate parts of the body—specifically the breasts of women—be fully covered at all times." In other letters Breen also requests changes to two song lyrics, the removal of references to an affair and panties in "The Hostess with the Mostes" (letter of November 26, 1951) and the words "hell" and "damn" in "Mrs. Sally Adams" (letter of June 12, 1952).

66. Although circumspect about his sexual identity, de Wolfe, who died in 1974 at the dawn of a new era of self-acceptance, was widely assumed and later identified as gay in published memoirs and articles.

67. The costumes for *The King and I* earned Sharaff the Tony Award one year before the film version of *Call Me Madam*. She was also nominated sixteen times for her film costumes, winning for *An American in Paris*, *The King and I*, *West Side Story*, *Cleopatra*, and *Who's Afraid of Virginia Woolf?*.

68. In the course of the song on both stage and screen, Berlin inserts the first 4 measures of Berlin's "God Bless America."

69. Howard Lindsay and Russel Crouse, *Call Me Madam* (New York: Irving Berlin Music, 1956), 64.

70. Sheekman, *Call Me Madam*, screenplay, 123.

71. Zoë Heller, "What Are We Meant to Get Out of Movies Based on Short Stories and Novels?" *New York Times*, December 24, 2013.

Chapter 4: 1940s Stage Musicals and Their Screen Adaptations: *Cabin in the Sky*, *Brigadoon*, and *Oklahoma!*

1. *Cabin* closed 156 performances later on March 8, 1941. *Porgy and Bess* ran 124 performances during its initial 1935 run and 286 performances during its 1942 revival.

2. In addition to *Hallelujah*, the two Hollywood films featuring a Black cast prior to *Cabin in the Sky* were *Hearts in Dixie* (Fox, 1929) and *Green Pastures* (Warner Bros., 1936). Alongside these high-profile films, Oscar Micheaux (among others) served Black moviegoers with independently produced features). The successful gangster drama *Dark Manhattan* (1937), produced by a new independent company, demonstrated the renewed commercial potential of "race films"; see https://tcm.com/tcmdb/title/72304/dark-manhattan#articles-reviews?articleId=17723. See also Cara Caddoo, *Envisioning Freedom: Cinema and Building of Modern Black Life* (Cambridge, MA: Harvard University Press, 2014

3. "Taking a Chance on Love," "Cabin in the Sky," "Honey in the Honeycomb," and "Love Turned the Light Out"; conductor Max Meth included a chorus of "My Old Virginia Home" in the Overture (AEI-CD 017 [1994]). The 1964 New York Revival Cast Recording offered the following additional songs: "The General's Song" [retitled

"Make Way"]; "Pay Heed" [retitled "The Man Upstairs"]; "Do What You Wanna Do"; "It's Not So Bad to Be Good"; "Love Me Tomorrow"; "Savannah," and several songs dropped from the original Broadway production (Angel ZDM 0777 7 64892 2 3 [1993]). A recording of the revue *Taking a Chance on Love* (2000) reinstated "In My Old Virginia Home" and the deleted song "Little Poppa Satan." A complete film soundtrack, including released and unreleased song material and Roger Edens's underscoring, was released in 1999, and a DVD with special features followed in 2006.

4. On post-Broadway performances (as well as a reliable survey of the original stage work) see Howard Pollack, *The Ballad of John Latouche: An American Lyricist's Life and Work* (New York: Oxford University Press, 2017). Selections from the 2016 *Encores!* can be viewed on YouTube.

5. Talley Beatty, interview with Zita Allen, in *Artists and Influences* (New York: Hatch Billops Collection, 1981), 11–12; quoted in Carol J. Oja, *Bernstein Meets Broadway: Collaborative Art in a Time of War* (New York: Oxford University Press, 2014), 164.

6. Hugh Fordin, *M-G-M's Greatest Musicals: The Arthur Freed Unit* (New York: Da Capo, 1996), 74. The film version of *Green Pastures* (Warner Bros. 1936), based on Marc Connelly's Pulitzer Prize–winning first all-Black play on Broadway in 1930 (with spirituals arranged by Johnson), featured alumni who would reunite in the film version of *Cabin*, including its playwright and co-director Connelly, who served as an uncredited screenwriter for the *Cabin* screenplay: Eddie Anderson as Little Joe; Rex Ingram as the Lord (Lucifer Jr. on both stage and screen); Oscar Polk in the double role of the Deacon and Fleetfoot; and Willie Best as the Second Idea Man at the Hotel Hades.

7. The majority of requested script changes are located in June 29 and August 24, 1942, memos from Joseph I. Breen to MGM's L. B. Mayer. Requests to change lyrics appear in memos from Breen to Mayer July 6 ("Li'l Black Sheep") and September 8 ("Ain't It de Truth"). Breen's rejection of "Jezebel Jones" is recorded on a memo dated September 25. Production Files, Margaret Herrick Library, Los Angeles.

8. In the stage version, Georgia finds the ticket crumpled on the ground at Little Joe's backyard; in the film she picks it up outside Joe's place of employment before she goes to see Joe in his backyard.

9. In the film, it is Petunia's plea to the Lord rather than the General's decision that leads to the destruction of Jim Henry's sinful club.

10. In an apparent contradiction, shortly before Little Joe receives heavenly judgment, the stage libretto he makes it clear that he *does* recall the earlier deathbed battle between the General and Lucifer.

11. The character singing "Supper Time" was a woman whose husband has been lynched and won't be coming home for dinner.

12. Donald Bogle explains that the problem occurred at the film's conclusion when "the Black characters assumed that the tailcoat with all the money that had fallen out of an airplane had in fact been dropped from the Lord." Bogle, *Heat Wave: The Life and Career of Ethel Waters* (New York: Harper-Collins, 2011), 177.

13. The budget for *Cabin* was $662,142 (Fordin, *M-G-M's Greatest Musicals*, 76). According to James Naremore, *Cabin* was "the lowest-budgeted musical in the history of the Freed unit." Naremore, "Uptown Folk: Blackness and Entertainment in *Cabin the Sky*," in *Representing Jazz*, ed. Krin Gabbard (Durham: Duke University Press, 1995), 175. Minnelli's next film, *Meet Me in St. Louis* one year later, cost $1,707.561 to produce (Fordin, *M-G-M's Greatest Musicals*, 118).

14. Presumably not by coincidence, a Little Joe is a term used in craps for a "hard four" throw of the dice (i.e., 2-2 rather than 3-1 or 1-3).

15. A common misrepresentation of this line is "Play it again, Sam."

16. Anderson's raspiness was allegedly due to the permanent vocal strain he suffered when selling newspapers during his youth. The film is unusual for its time in that none of the voices were overdubbed by playback singers.

17. In addition to Horne, the Black artists featured in *Stormy Weather* included Bill Robinson, Cab Calloway, Fats Waller, Ada Brown, the Nicholas Brothers, and the Dunham Dancers and Dooley Wilson from the stage version of *Cabin*.

18. Donald Bogle, *Toms, Coons, Mulattoes, Mammies, and Bucks* (New York: Bloomsbury Academic, 2016), 25–28 (McKinney), 112–19 (Horne), and 149–58 (Dandridge)

19. "Taking a Chance on Love," a popular song standard from its time to ours, was a late addition for Waters to sing in Act I, adapted from an unused song called "Fooling Around with Love" that Duke had composed using lyrics by Ted Fetter. The majority of the song's lyrics, including four new choruses, were by Latouche, who nonetheless shared the copyright credit with Fetter. In the film (but not the stage) version, Waters follows Horne with a reprise of "Honey in the Honeycomb."

20. Harburg had turned down the offer to compose the lyrics for the original score because he didn't think Duke was the right composer for a work of *Cabin*'s potential social significance. The five unused film songs were "Ain't It de Truth" for Georgia, later reused for Horne in *Jamaica* (1957); "Some Folk Work (Is You Man or Mule?)" (context unknown); "Petunia's Prayer" for Petunia; "Jezebel Jones" for Georgia; and "I Got a Song" for Domino, reused in *Bloomer Girl*. Lyric sheets for all these songs as well as the three used songs submitted between July 2 and October 21, 1942, are located in the Production Files, Margaret Herrick Library, Los Angeles. MGM submitted them for approval to the Production Code Administration in the following order: "Li'l Black Sheep" and "Some Folk Work" (July 2); "Happiness is Jes' a Thing Called Joe" and "I Got a Song" (August 1); "Life's Full of Consequence" [title and lyrics designated "Life's Full o' Consequence] (August 7); "Ain't It de Truth" (September 4; revised September 8 and 11); "Li'l Black Sheep" (revised September 14); "Petunia's Prayer" (September 15); "Jezebel Jones" (September 21); "Cabin in the Sky" and Prologue to "Shine" and "Shine" (September 25 and 29); "Honey in the Honeycomb" (September 27); "Taking a Chance on Love" (October 21).

21. *Cabin in the Sky*, Sound Track Factory.

22. The Hall Johnson Choir replaced the stage version's J. Rosamond Johnson Singers.

23. The extensively revised lyrics dated September 14, 1942, included changes that honored the Code request to delete "Li'l black sheep found my door/Double bed ain't single no more" and without prompting replaced the word "soul" with "sin" in the second line of the song, "With his sins washed whiter den foam."

24. Naomi André writes expressively and personally about her "complicated relationship loving and being frustrated" by *Porgy and Bess* with its "many complicated and tender issues around representation of African Americans." André, "Complexities in Gershwin's *Porgy and Bess*," in *The Cambridge Companion to Gershwin*, ed. Anna Harwell Celenza (Cambridge: Cambridge University Press, 2019), quotations on 194 and 192.

25. Kwame Anthony Appiah, "Cultural Borrowing Is Great: The Problem Is Disrespect," *Wall Street Journal*, September 19, 2018. Appiah discusses cultural appropriation more fully in *The Lies That Bind: Rethinking Identity* (New York: Liveright, 2019).

26. Rob Weinert-Kendt, "Expanding the Range of the Musical," *New York Times*, January 2, 2022.

27. Arlen, who was Jewish and the son of a Cantor, composed the music to three shows with mostly Black casts: *St. Louis Blues* (1946), *House of Flowers* (1954), and *Jamaica* (1957); *Bloomer Girl* (1944) also included a subplot about a slave played by Wilson.

28. Horne's associations with Arlen would continue into the 1950s with Arlen and Harburg's *Jamaica*.

29. Edward Jablonski, *Harold Arlen: Happy with the Blues* (Garden City, NY: Doubleday, 1961), 68. Harburg, who wrote the lyrics for Arlen's *Cabin* songs in the film, spoke of his collaborator's "synthesis of Negro rhythms and Hebraic melodies." Harold Meyerson and Ernie Harburg, *Who Put the Rainbow in "The Wizard of Oz"?* (Ann Arbor: University of Michigan Press, 1993), 176.

30. The stage version also included the traditional gospel hymn "Holy unto the Waters" followed directly in Act I by "Dem Bones," a well-known spiritual composed by James Weldon Johnson and J. Rosamond Johnson (the latter also cast as Brother Green).

31. The form of the song is A (16) A (20), in which the second A extends the standard 32 measures to 36. With the exception of 4 measures (measures 12–15), every 4-bar phrase begins with a three-note ascending pickup (most often D#-E-G-C) with the C sounding on the downbeat on the main notes (the first syllable of "Happiness," then "smile" and "sigh"). The first 3 measures of each 4-bar phrase consist entirely of quarter notes, while the fourth measure arrives on a whole note that lingers an extra beat before the next pickup.

32. See Susan Smith's discussion of this performance in *The Musical: Race, Gender and Performance* (London: Wallflower, 2005), 29–38.

33. Note that for the film's second chorus Petunia sings the lyrics of the stage version's *third* chorus.

34. Vernon Duke, *Passport to Paris* (Boston: Little, Brown, 1955), 390. For more on the influence of African dance in Dunham's work see Joanna Dee Das, *Katherine Dunham: Dance and the African Diaspora* (New York: Oxford University Press, 2017).

35. Brian Harker, *Sportin' Life: John W. Bubbles, An American Classic* (New York: Oxford University Press, 2022. In the film, "Buck" also played the postal delivery man who delivered the sweepstakes ticket to Little Joe and was given a couple of lines at the beginning of "Shine" before retreating into the background as Bubbles's barely audible piano accompanist.

36. John Mueller argues that in the blackface tribute to Bill Robinson from the racially controversial "Bojangles of Harlem" number in *Swing Time* (1936), Astaire

models his tap-dancing more closely on Bubbles's technique and style than the intended and far-better known honoree. Mueller, *Astaire Dancing: The Musical Films* (New York: Wings, 1985), 108. Dance scholar Beth Genné shows photos of Bubbles as he slides across the dance floor on one foot. Genné, *Dance Me a Song: Astaire, Balanchine, Kelly, and the American Film Musical* (New York: Oxford University Press, 2018), 32f. Although uncredited, Busby Berkeley is recognized as "Shine's" choreographer. Berkeley biographer Jeffrey Spivak notes that "as he climbs the stairs to his exit, a visual clue to the director's identity is seen in the perfectly framed hand shadows on the wall over Sublett's (Bubbles's) shoulder, a Buzz Berkeley signature device that he used with effectiveness." Jeffrey Spivak, *Buzz: The Life and Art of Busby Berkeley* (Lexington: The University Press of Kentucky, 2011), 194.

37. Based on the Local Censor Board files contained in the Production Files in the Margaret Herrick Library, Georgia's underwear and accompanying suggestive comment provoked several theater owners to request the removal (of the latter): Ontario, Canada (March 9, 1943); Maryland (April 12 and November 14); Massachusetts (April 12); Ohio (April 19); and India (November 9).

38. When "Ain't It de Truth" was first submitted, the Code's Breen found the line "you will be S.O.L" [i.e., shit outta luck] "unacceptable, because of its vulgarity" (September 8, 1942). In a second memo to Mayer one day later Breen wrote that the line "love is cash and carry" was "unacceptable because of its sex suggestiveness." Curiously, even though MGM failed to remove the second lyric, on September 14 Breen was "happy to report" that the lyrics were up to Code requirements.

39. As a welcome bonus, the film soundtrack contains Duke Ellington and His Orchestra playing the unused "My Old Virginia Home" and "Love Me Tomorrow." In its role as Bubbles's backup orchestra on "Shine," in one shot Ellington can clearly be seen behind Bubbles.

40. Ramon Lewis, "'Cabin' Picture Called Insult," *Amsterdam News*, June 13, 1943, 17.

41. Hobe [Morrison], "*Cabin in the Sky*," *Variety*, February 10, 1943.

42. Thomas M. Pryor, "'Cabin in the Sky,' a Musical Fantasy, with Ethel Waters, at Loew's Criterion," *New York Times*, May 28, 1943, 19.

43. James Naremore, "Uptown Folk," 187. In 2020, the Library of Congress added the film adaptation of *Cabin in the Sky* to the National Film Registry.

44. See Kara Gardner, *Agnes de Mille: Telling Stories in Broadway Dance* (New York: Oxford University Press, 2016), especially the chapters on *Oklahoma!*, *Carousel*, and *Brigadoon*.

45. Although she needed to make changes to fit the new format, much of de Mille's choreography for the Civil War ballet in *Bloomer Girl* was preserved on the television broadcast, *Producers Showcase* (NBC, February 28, 1956). The production also featured several dancers from the 1944 Broadway production including James Mitchell. Gardner, *Agnes de Mille*, 80.

46. Colin McArthur, "*Brigadoon*," "*Braveheart*" *and the Scots* London: I. B. Taurus, 2003), 64.

47. Prior to her career as a choreographer, de Lappe danced the role of the "Dream Ballet" Laurey in the long-running original West End production (1,543 performances) that opened in 1947.

48. Kara Gardner, *Agnes de Mille*, 110.

49. Vincente Minnelli, with Hector Arce, *I Remember It Well* (Garden City, NY: Doubleday, 1974), 279.

50. In *The Complete Lyrics of Alan Jay Lerner*, edited and with annotations by Dominic McHugh and Amy Asch (New York: Oxford University Press, 2018), 52, McHugh labels this October 14, 1953, screenplay as L3: MGM Final Screenplay, Alan Jay Lerner Collection, Library of Congress (72 pages). It is located in Box 1, Folder 1, where it is marked "temporary complete." I am grateful to Broomfield-McHugh for making this version available to me. Not examined for this study is the copy in the Margaret Herrick Library, which contains a complete composite screenplay of approximately 160 pages dated between October 14, 1953, and March 10, 1955 (the filming stopped on March 17). The Margaret Herrick Library in Los Angeles also houses a number of earlier screenplay versions that go back as far as November 1951.

51. Production Files, Margaret Herrick Library.

52. Breen continues: "The effort on her part is made to seem highly romantic, and hence is completely in violation of Code requirements" and "this objectionable flavor would have to be removed before the scene could be approved in the finished picture." Letter from Joseph Breen to Dore Schary, November 2, 1953, Production Files, Margaret Herrick Library, Los Angeles.

53. In Meg's defense, one day per century is not a lot of time to acquire a husband.

54. In the stage version, Jeff impulsively sticks out his foot and Beaton dies when he falls on a rock.

55. The film also omitted the dance music that followed the vocal component of "Come to Me," at seven minutes (in the studio recording conducted by John McGlinn from 1992) the longest dance segment in the show. Most of this dance music uses "Come to Me," but other sections include new music. The theme labeled *Più calmo* at rehearsal N of the Vocal Score (93) was used to underscore Mr. Lundie's story of Brigadoon. It can be heard on the 1996 soundtrack's "Talk to the Dominie." Ethan Mordden notes that this melody can also be heard on the 1947 cast album. Mordden, *When Broadway Went to Hollywood* (New York: Oxford University Press, 2016), 200n4.

56. The verse, recorded but not filmed, can be heard on a twenty-five-second outtake in the CD soundtrack.

57. Susan Smith, "*Brigadoon* and Its Transition to MGM Dance Musical," in *The Oxford Handbook of Musical Theatre Screen Adaptations*, ed., Dominic McHugh (New York: Oxford University Press, 2019), 395-421.

58. Kelly noted in an interview that "the music in *Brigadoon* generally was on the slow side," and that this slowness led to the cutting of a number he filmed with Charisse (presumably "From This Day On") as well as other solo numbers." Jerome Delamater, *Dance in the Hollywood Musical* (Ann Arbor, MI: UMI Research Press, 1981), 217.

59. Ibid., 416.

60. It was also a financial disappointment. Earl Hess and Pratibha A. Dabholkar report that despite mixed reviews, the film made $3.3 million on $2.3 million, "not enough to offset the cost of advertising and marketing now that the studio no longer owned the distribution outlets." Hess and Dabholkar, *Gene Kelly: The Making of a Creative Legend* (Lawrence: University Press of Kansas, 2020), 293.

61. Mark Griffin, *A Hundred or More Hidden Things: The Life and Films of Vincente Minnelli* (New York: Da Capo, 2019), 168.
62. Alvin Yudkoff, *Gene Kelly: A Life of Dance and Dreams* (New York: Backstage Books, 1999), 230.
63. Ibid.
64. Most recently, Grayson had starred in the remakes of *Show Boat* (1951), *Roberta* (retitled *Lovely to Look At* [1952]), *The Desert Song* (1953), and *Kiss Me Kate* (1953).
65. In MGM's *On the Town*, Kelly also transformed a singing role into a dancing one, but *On the Town* was already primarily a dance musical on the stage. Similarly, although the central romantic couple was a singing one, the stage version of *Brigadoon* fully merited the appellation "dance musical."
66. See Gardner, *Agnes de Mille*, 21–46, and Tim Carter, *Oklahoma!: The Making of an American Musical*, rev. ed. New York: Oxford University Press, 2020, *passim*.
67. Warren Hoffman offers a more sinister subtext to explain *why* the lyrics in "The Farmer and Cowman" advocate that "territory folks should stick together": "They share a common enemy: the Indian." Hoffman, *The Great White Way: Race and the Broadway Musical* (New Brunswick, NJ: Rutgers University Press, 2014), 64.
68. Todd S. Purdum, "The *Hamilton* of World War II," *New York Times*, March 31, 2018.
69. Richard Rodgers, *Musical Stages: An Autobiography* (New York: Random House, 1975; repr. New York: Da Capo, 1995, 2000), 227.
70. The summary of the principles of integration discussed here is derived from Block, "Integration," 97–110, in *The Oxford Handbook of the American Musical*, ed. Raymond Knapp, Mitchell Morris, and Stacy Wolf (New York: Oxford University Press, 2011), 97-110, especially 98-99; repr. in *Histories of the Musical: An Oxford Handbook of the American Musical, Volume 1*, ed. Knapp, Morris, and Wolf (New York Oxford University Press, 2018), 153–75, especially 155–57.
71. Rodgers, *Musical Stages*, 219. See also Rodgers, "Introduction (with Oscar Hammerstein) to *The Rodgers and Hammerstein Song Book* (New York: Simon and Schuster, 1958), 6–9; repr. Block, *The Richard Rodgers Reader* (New York: Oxford University Press, 2002), 281-84. In both cases, Rodgers inserted a musical illustration in his own hand, the first 2 measures in the *Song Book* in F major and the first A section (8 mm.) in G major in *Musical Stages*. Since Rodgers rarely wrote or spoke about his musical intentions, it is noteworthy that he did so here (and twice), however briefly.
72. Rodgers, *Musical Stages,* 219.
73. A touring company played in 128 cities throughout nearly all of the show's initial run through May 1948 and a little beyond (October 15, 1943, to June 11, 1949). Following the show's closing, it would go on to tour in another 253 cities, including Montreal and Berlin, from August 25, 1949, to May 1, 1954. Stanley Green, ed., *Rodgers and Hammerstein Fact Book* (New York: Lynn Farnol, 1980), 519. By then, Rodgers and Hammerstein were finally ready to negotiate a film deal.
74. AO stands for America Optical Company.

75. For more on roadshows, see chapter 6, which includes a list of the twenty roadshow film adaptations of Broadway stage musicals from 1955 to 1972 starting with *Oklahoma!*. For an invaluable discussion of the roadshow in the 1960s and early 1970s see Matthew Kennedy, *Roadshow!: The Fall of Film Musicals in the 1960s* (New York: Oxford University Press, 2014).

76. *Brigadoon* had also been filmed twice in direct succession. It was released in CinemaScope but also filmed in Wide Screen. Both versions of *Oklahoma!* are contained on the 2-DVD 50th Anniversary Edition released by 20th Century-Fox along with audio commentary and featurettes on the two technologies in 2005.

77. Rodgers and Hammerstein had hoped to cast Charlotte Greenwood as Aunt Eller in 1943, but she was contractually unavailable.

78. Gene Nelson later played Buddy in the original 1971 Broadway production of *Follies*.

79. Letter from Joseph Breen to Arthur Hornblow, April 9, 1954, Motion Picture Association of America (MPAA), Production Code Administration records, Production Files, Margaret Herrick Library, Los Angeles. In a June 18 letter to Breen, Hornblow refers to the revised final script of June 1 and specifies how the new script complies with Breen's April 9 suggestions.

80. The Claremore train station was filmed in Elgin, about fifty miles north.

81. Smith, "*Brigadoon* and Its Transition to MGM Dance Musical," 395–96.

82. Richard Barrios, *Must-See Musicals: 50 Show-Stopping Movies We Can't Forget* (Philadelphia: Running Press, 2017), 144 and 145.

83. Mordden, *When Broadway Went to Hollywood*, 192.

84. Rick Altman, *The American Film Musical* (Bloomington: Indiana University Press, 1989), 196. In his pioneering study, Altman uses the film version of *Oklahoma!* as a detailed paradigm of the characteristics that define the folk musical as a subgenre of musical film. Interestingly, in his analysis, Altman mentions a cinematic element, Jud's profile blocking out half the frame of a shot, a visual device that "encapsulates Jud's role as a dark shadow" over the narrative.

85. Ibid., 196–97.

86. Gerald Mast, *Can't Help Singin': The American Musical on Stage and Screen* (Woodstock, NY: Overlook, 1987), 216–17.

87. Jeanine Basinger, *The Movie Musical!* (New York: Knopf, 2019). See Block, "*The Movie Musical!* Jeanine Basinger (2019)," *Studies in Musical Theater* 14/1 (2020): 230–233.

88. It was previously noted in chapter 2 that Basinger singles out for praise the "intensity," "purity," and *absence* of "camera tricks" in the filming of Helen Morgan's singing of "Bill" in the Universal 1936 *Show Boat*. Basinger, *The Movie Musical!*, 340.

89. As an example of a critical double standard, the minimal camera work Fred Astaire required for his films with Ginger Rogers has gained wide praise. With a minimum of editing and about one cutaway per dance, Astaire launched a revolution in which he insisted on a full-figure shot for an entire dance. Mueller, *Astaire Dancing*, 26-29.

90. Basinger, *The Movie Musical!*, 488.

91. Jesse Green, "The Bumpy Road from Broadway to Hollywood," *New York Times*, December 20, 2020.

Chapter 5: More Than a "Chemical Reaction": The Romance between *Ninotchka* and *Silk Stockings* on Stage and Screen

1. Dominic McHugh, "'And I'll Sing Once More': A Historical Overview of the Broadway Musical on the Silver Screen," in *The Oxford Handbook of Musical Theatre Screen Adaptations*, ed. Dominic McHugh (New York: Oxford University Press, 2019), 17. See also the section "Other Continuities from Stage to Screen" and Table 1.2, "Deleted and Added Songs in 31 Selected Musical Film Adaptations from 1950 to 1965," in chapter 1 of this volume.

2. Charles Brackett, Billy Wilder, and Walter Reisch, *Ninotchka* (New York: Viking, 1972), 60.

3. Joseph McBride, *How Did Lubitsch Do It?* (New York: Columbia University Press, 2018), 3–6. Alex Ross, "Laughter in the Dark: The Subtly Incisive Film Comedy of Ernst Lubitsch," *The New Yorker,* August 15, 2022.

4. Pyotr (Peter) Ilyitch were also the first and middle names of the well-known Russian composer Tchaikovsky.

5. Scott Eyman, *Ernst Lubitsch: Laughter in Paradise* (New York: Simon & Schuster, 1993), 274.

6. Maurice Zolotow, *Billy Wilder in Hollywood* (New York: Limelight, 1987), 75. As a contemporary sign of its acclaim, *Ninotchka* was nominated for Academy Awards for Best Picture, Best Actress, Best Screenplay, and Best Original Story, although it lost out to *Gone with the Wind* and Scarlett O'Hara (Vivian Leigh) in the first three categories and to *Mr. Smith Goes to Washington* in the fourth. It was not the best year to compete for an Oscar. In addition to the *Gone with the Wind* juggernaut, *Ninotchka* faced unusually strong competition from other notable films, including *Dark Victory*, *Destry Rides Again*, *Goodbye, Mr. Chips*, *Of Mice and Men*, *Stagecoach*, *The Wizard of Oz*, and *Wuthering Heights*.

7. Andrew Sarris, ed., *Interviews with Film Directors* (Indianapolis: Bobbs-Merrill, 1967), 284.

8. Zolotow, *Billy Wilder in Hollywood*, 79.

9. A few years later, Lengyel wrote the screenplay for Lubitsch's *To Be or Not to Be* (1942).

10. Curiously, the German actor cast as the bumbling Marxist emissary Buljanoff, Felix Bressart, bore a striking physical resemblance to the comical exponent of Marxism, Groucho Marx. Bressart, a Jewish immigrant who arrived in 1938, would also be cast in Lubitsch's *The Shop around the Corner* (1940) and *To Be or Not to Be*.

11. Brackett, Wilder, and Reisch, *Ninotchka*, 60.

12. Many audience members would immediately realize that Janice is a *cinematique à clef* for the All-American swimming champion Esther Williams, who starred in numerous commercially successful swimming pictures such as *Million Dollar Mermaid* (1952). In *Neptune's Daughter* (1949), she got out of the pool long enough to sing (without dubbing) Frank Loesser's Academy Award-winning song, "Baby, It's Cold Outside," with Ricardo Montalban. As portrayed both on the stage (Janice) and film (renamed Peggy) this character, newly added to *Silk Stockings,* appeared in so many

swimming pictures (including one called *Neptune's Mother*) that her right ear keeps getting plugged up. When we first meet her, she tells reporters she will be making her "first serious, non-swimming" picture based on a book she just heard about called *War and Peace* ("Of course, that title will have to go").

13. Act II, scene 3, 20.

14. Ibid.

15. Brackett, Wilder, and Reisch, *Ninotchka*, 24. The scholarly consensus is that "almost all the anti-Soviet jokes came from Wilder." Zolotow, *Billy Wilder in Hollywood*, 81.

16. McBride, *How Did Lubitsch Do It?*, 374.

17. Nick Smedley, *A Divided World: Hollywood Cinema and Émigré Directors in the Era of Roosevelt and Hitler 1933–1948* (Bristol: Intellect, 2011), 206.

18. Its run, while successful, fell far short of the biggest hit that season, the still-revived *Damn Yankees* (1,019 performances), and noticeably short of another currently little-known musical, *Fanny* (888 performances), from earlier in the season. On the other hand, it fell only a little shy of Feuer and Martin's most recent hit *The Boy Friend* (485 performances) and conspicuously outlasted two of its contemporaries, *Peter Pan* (152 performances) and *House of Flowers* (165 performances).

19. By way of comparison, *Damn Yankees* managed to thrive without enjoying a single rave review. Steven Suskin, *Opening Night on Broadway: A Critical Quotebook of the Golden Era of the Musical Theatre, "Oklahoma!" (1943) to "Fiddler on the Roof" (1964)* (New York: Schirmer Books, 1990), 618–20.

20. After *Silk Stockings*, Porter would complete the scores to two more films over the next three years, *High Society* and *Les Girls*, and the two new songs for the film adaptation of *Silk Stockings*, before ending his long career with *Aladdin* in 1958, a ninety-minute television musical.

21. Malcolm Goldstein, *George S. Kaufman: His Life, His Theater* (New York: Oxford University Press, 1979), 442–45; Scott Meredith, *George S. Kaufman and His Friends* (Garden City, NY: Doubleday, 1974), 615–18; Rhoda-Gale Pollack, *George S. Kaufman* (Boston: Twayne, 1988), 121–23; Abe Burrows, *Honest, Abe: Is There Really No Business Like Show Business?* (Boston: Little, Brown, 1980), 259–74; Cy Feuer, with Ken Gross, *I Got the Show Right Here* (New York: Simon & Schuster, 2003), 199–208.

22. Geoffrey Block, *Enchanted Evenings: The Broadway Musical from "Show Boat" to Sondheim and Lloyd Webber* (New York: Oxford University Press, 1997; rev. 2nd ed., 2009), 237–38.

23. Suskin, *Opening Night on Broadway*, 620,.

24. Ibid. As we'll note in discussing the film version of *Cabaret* (chapter 8), Feuer also came close to firing Bob Fosse in 1971.

25. Cliff Eisen and Dominic McHugh, eds., *The Letters of Cole Porter* (New Haven, CT: Yale University Press, 2019), 450. I would like to thank Dominic Broomfield-McHugh for generously making available all the Porter letters cited in this chapter prior to their publication.

26. Ibid., 483.

27. Ibid., 488 and 489.

28. Ibid., 491.

29. The Kaufman letters and Porter's notes on "Siberia's" lyrics are located in the Porter Collection of the Library of Congress; some facsimiles were reprinted in *Cole*, ed., Robert Kimball (New York: Holt, Rinehart & Winston, 1971), 240–41. Mark Eden Horowitz discusses Kaufman's letters in "Cole Porter's Papers," in *A Cole Porter Companion*, ed. Don M. Randel, Matthew Shaftel, and Susan Forscher Weiss (Urbana: University of Illinois Press, 2016), 314–15.

30. Feuer, *I Got the Show Right Here*, 200–201.

31. Hildegard Knef, *The Gift Horse: Report on a Life* (New York: McGraw Hill, 1970), 286 (the pun intended in the title stems from the fact that "Knef" is the German word for "horse"). In another diary entry from February 16 (eight days before opening night), Knef describes a chaotic rehearsal process in which "several scenes from the original version have been reintroduced" (313).

32. Mueller states that after Burrows replaced Kaufman and MacGrath, "several scenes from the original script were reinserted, and the resulting mix was apparently about half Burrows and half Kaufman-MacGrath." See Mueller, *Astaire Dancing: The Musical Films* (New York: Wings, 1985), 388. Fortunately, Mueller's assertion can be tested by consulting the Kaufman-MacGrath libretto in the Cole Porter Collection of the Library of Congress, Box 25, Folders 1–2, although space does not permit a discussion in this chapter beyond the evolution of the songs. The final libretto that incorporates the combined contributions of Kaufman-MacGrath and Abe Burrows is located in Folder 3. Kaufman and MacGrath retained writing credit and kept on receiving their original share of performance royalties, and Porter paid Burrows out of his own share of royalties. See the business correspondence at the New York Public Library, Abe Burrows Papers Box 29, Folder 12, *Silk Stockings* contracts.

33. Robert Kimball, *The Complete Lyrics of Cole Porter* (New York: Vingate, 1984), 445–51.

34. For a discussion of Production Code problems with Porter's lyrics for the 1953 film adaptation of *Kiss Me, Kate*, see Block, *Enchanted Evenings*, 317–18.

35. Letter from Geoffrey Shurlock to Dory Schary, May 6, 1956, Production Files, Margaret Herrick Library, Los Angeles. In 1956, Shurlock was relatively new to the position, having replaced the formidable and long-reigning Joseph I. Breen two years earlier. Meanwhile, Schary was on the way out and would be fired a few months later.

36. Many in the audience would likely recall that several months before the stage opening of *Silk Stockings* Monroe sang and danced the lines "She started the heat wave/By letting her seat wave" in *There's No Business Like Show Business* (20th Century-Fox, December 1954) from Irving Berlin's "Heat Wave" (a song originally performed by Ethel Waters in the 1933 Broadway revue *As Thousands Cheer*).

37. Although *The Gay Desperado* (1936) contains a considerable amount of music, it is not usually regarded as a musical.

38. Tom Milne, *Mamoulian* (Bloomington: Indiana University Press, 1969), 51. See also Block, *Love Me Tonight* (New York: Oxford University Press, forthcoming).

39. Mark Spergel, *Reinventing Reality—The Art and Life of Rouben Mamoulian* (Metuchen, NJ: Scarecrow, 1993), 218.

40. Ibid.

41. Ibid.
42. Rouben Mamoulian, "Memorandum [No. 1] on the Script of *Silk Stockings*," 2, Mamoulian Collection, Library of Congress, July 25, 1956.
43. The title page of the MGM file copy of the script I am using is marked "okayed by Arthur Freed" and delivered "from the following writer: Leonard Gershe 10-8-56." On the next pages the script is marked as completed on November 6. This working script also contains a considerable amount of additional revisions and replacement pages inserted from November to January.
44. Starting as the Russian visa official who refused Leon's travel to Russia in *Ninotchka*, Tobias ended up as the only actor to appear in the 1939 film and both versions of *Silk Stockings*.
45. Although Buloff was listed as Joe Bulow, they are almost certainly the same person, since Buloff's name at birth was Jósef [Joe] Bulow.
46. Twenty years earlier Tamiroff was cast as a decadent villain in Mamoulian's *High, Wide and Handsome*.
47. Mamoulian, "Memorandum [No. 1])," 6–7, Mamoulian Collection, Library of Congress.
48. Mueller points out that Astaire had avoided his top hat and tails trademark in his two most recent films (*Daddy Long Legs* and *Funny Face*), 399. See Mueller, *Astaire Dancing*, 399.
49. James R. Silke, *Rouben Mamoulian "Style Is the Man,"* The American Film Institute, 1971, 25–26; Eric Sherman, *Directing the Film: Film Directors and Their Art* (Los Angeles: Acrobat, 1976), 131.
50. Mueller, *Astaire Dancing*, 399.
51. John Franceschina, *Hermes Pan: The Man Who Danced with Fred Astaire* (New York: Oxford University Press, 2012), 201.
52. Eleven years later Astaire danced less extensively in Francis Ford Coppola's adaptation of *Finian's Rainbow* (1968). *Silk Stockings* also marked Cyd Charisse's final appearance in a Hollywood musical, the final dance musical produced by Freed, and of course the last film directed by Mamoulian.
53. Mamoulian's statement that they *could* use "Silk Stockings" here, followed by his suggestion that Porter would want to write new lyrics, creates a mystery as to why *any* lyrics would be needed for her private dance.
54. Two early Porter hits, "I've Got You under My Skin" and "Easy to Love," both from *Born to Dance* (1936), were used in the film version as underscoring. The former can be heard in the Hotel Lobby just before the commissars first meet Ninotchka; the latter song, which serves as the seduction music Steve plays on the radio before Ninotchka sings "It's a Chemical Reaction, That's All," can be heard on the 2002 film soundtrack.
55. Much later in *Applause* we see the comely legs and feet of Kitty's daughter April, who is mistaken for a street walker. Soon April is accosted by three pairs of anonymous masculine feet and rescued by another pair of feet that belong to a young sailor who will soon sweep April off hers.

56. Mamoulian Collection, Library of Congress, Memorandum No. 13, February 4, 1957, 2.

57. Ibid., 4. The rhythm of Ninotchka's blissful typing after her dance with Steve resembles the opening lyric of "All of You," "I love the looks of you." Her typing in her new love-sick state presents the sharpest possible contrast to the machine-gun like typing earlier in the film.

58. Hugh Fordin, *M-G-M's Greatest Musicals: The Arthur Freed Unit* (New York: Da Capo), 452; Mueller, *Astaire Dancing*, 411. Mamoulian biographer David Luhrssen reinforces Fordin and Mueller: "Mamoulian worked with great efficiency, editing as he shot, delivering the movie at a cost of under $2 million. After its release on July 18, *Silk Stockings* would gross over $4 million during its initial run and, during its six weeks at Radio City Music hall, became the biggest-grossing musical ever to play the venerable theater." Luhrssen, *Mamoulian: Life on Stage and Screen* (Lexington: University Press of Kentucky, 2013), 138.

59. Telegram from Dan Terrell to Howard Dietz, February 14, 1957, Mamoulian Collection, Library of Congress.

60. Fordin, *M-G-M's Greatest Musicals*, 443-44.

61. Mueller, *Astaire Dancing*, 388.

62. Prior to the 1950s, Astaire's dancing partners ranged in age from twelve and thirteen years younger (Ginger Rogers and Eleanor Powell) to eighteen and nineteen years younger (Joan Fontaine, Lucille Bremer, and Rita Hayworth). The only major dance partner senior to Fred was his sister Adele (1896–1981), Fred's dance partner in vaudeville and on the stage (but not film) for twenty-seven years, who retired from show business in 1932 to marry Lord Charles Cavendish.

63. This section focuses (although not exclusively) on Porter's lyrics and music rather than on the dancing component led by Eugene Loring, who choreographed the non-Astaire numbers, and Hermes Pan, who collaborated with Astaire on the choreography of Astaire's dances as he had been doing since the Fred and Ginger films in the 1930s. For a brief but informative and insightful discussion of what happens in each dance number of *Silk Stockings*, the indispensable source remains Mueller's *Astaire Dancing*, 391–99.

64. For more on "Siberia," see "The Genesis" section of *"Silk Stockings": The Musical* earlier in this chapter.

65. On stage, Janice was played by Gretchen Wyler, the *second* assigned understudy, initially for an ailing Yvonne Adair and then for Sherry O'Neil, who surreptitiously abandoned the show to audition for another play. Wyler appeared frequently on Broadway in the fifties but mainly as an understudy (Adelaide in the original *Guys and Dolls*) or replacement cast member for stars such as Gwen Verdon (Lola in *Damn Yankees*) and Chita Rivera (Rose in *Bye Bye Birdie*).

66. In Memorandum No. 16 (February 14, 1957) Mamoulian made the following specification: "The word stereophonic is sung fourteen times—play the effect on 1st, 2nd, and 3rd 'stereophonic' and then the last 'stereophonic' preceding the dance."

67. Curiously, "Stereophonic Sound" was not included among the seven song selections published in connection with the release of the film ("Silk Stockings," "Paris Loves Lovers," "All of You," Without Love," and "Siberia" from both the stage and film and

the two newly added film songs, "Fated to Be Mated," and "The Ritz Roll and Rock"). Other songs from the show were published in *Music and Lyrics by Cole Porter*, "All of You," "As on through the Seasons We Sail," and "Stereophonic Sound" in volume 1 and "Silk Stockings," "Without Love," "Satin and Silk," "Paris Loves Lovers," and "Siberia" in volume 2. Indeed it's "too bad" that in contrast with many shows of the era, neither a vocal score nor a libretto of *Silk Stockings* was published. On the bright side, with the exception of the Entr'acte the cast album is complete as is the film soundtrack released in 2002

68. Richard Rodgers, *Musical Stages: An Autobiography* (1975; reprinted New York: Da Capo, 1995), 88.

69. For a rich discussion of Jewish signifiers in the American songbook, see Jeffrey Magee, "Irving Berlin's 'Blue Skies': Ethnic Affiliations and Musical Transformations, *Musical Quarterly* 84/4 (Winter 2000): 537-80, especially 539-52. On the influence of Jewish music on Porter, including a plausible source for Martin's "Da-da" passage, see Jack Gottlieb, *Funny, It Doesn't Sound Jewish: How Yiddish Songs and Synagogue Melodies Influenced Tin Pan Alley, Broadway, and Hollywood* (Albany: State University of New York in association with the Library of Congress, 2004), 186–92.

70. On stage, Vera was played by Julie Newmar, 5 ft., 11 in., a rising singer and dancer recently seen as one of the seven brides in the film *Seven Brides for Seven Brothers* (1954) and on stage in the small but conspicuous role of Stupefyin' Jones in *L'il Abner* in 1956 (as well as the 1959 film adaptation).

71. Mamoulian Collection, Library of Congress, Memorandum No. 16, February 14, 1957, 2.

72. These tags are not unlike the famous orchestral tags that follow many of the phrases in Berlin's "Cheek to Cheek," which Astaire danced with Ginger Rogers in *Top Hat* (1935). In "Cheek" we hear "Heaven" (orchestra: DUM dee DUM) "I'm in Heaven" (orchestra: DUM dee DUM).

73. Even with her vocal limitations, which surpassed those of Neff, "Chemical Reaction," unlike "Without Love," was a song that Cyd Charisse *could* have sung in the film as we can hear in Charisse's unused demo recorded on November 6 during the early days of the shooting. Carol Richards, the voice of Charisse in the film versions of *Brigadoon*, *Deep in My Heart* (1954), and *It's Always Fair Weather* (1955), and Vera-Ellen in *Call Me Madam* (1953) before that, recorded "Chemical Reaction" on October 31 and November 6. Both the Charisse and Richards versions can be heard on the 2002 soundtrack.

74. Brackett, Wilder, and Reisch, *Ninotchka*, 37.

75. George Eells, *The Life That Late He Led: A Biography of Cole Porter* (New York: G. P. Putnam's Sons, 1967), 292; see also McBrien, *Cole Porter: A Biography* (New York: Knopf, 1998), 357. Eells notes that Kaufman's "plan to have Miss Neff talk-sing her songs in the [Marlene] Dietrich manner was not as effective as expected," 292.

76. This description of the lyrics is based on Fred Lounsberry's analysis excerpted in Stephen Citron's *Noel and Cole: The Sophisticates* (New York: Oxford University Press, 1993), 245.

77. Brackett, Wilder, and Reisch, *Ninotchka*, 25.

78. David Thomson, *The New Biographical Dictionary of Film* (New York: Alfred A. Knopf, 2002), 557.

79. Milne makes a persuasive parallel between Ninotchka's dance and Garbo's famous "bedroom-stroking sequence in *Queen Christina* [from 1933, also directed by Mamoulian] on which it is obviously patterned." Milne, *Mamoulian*, 151.

80. This chapter has room for only a few words about "Fated to Be Mated," the first new song added to the film version and one which Mamoulian planned in great detail. The number begins with Steve singing the tune before Ninotchka joins him in a dance that includes reprises of "Paris Loves Lovers" and "All of You." In striking contrast to these two reprised songs, the beginning of each A section of "Fated" consists of three groups of four notes on four syllables all on quarter notes (such as "We were fated"), all in a narrow range, and all separated by a pause of equal value. Halfway through the B section, Porter returns to the rhythms of the words "we were fated to be mated" and the pitches as well for "we were fated."

81. Richard Watts Jr., "Kidding the Muscovites to Music," *New York Post*, February 25, 1955.

82. Walter F. Kerr, "*Silk Stockings*," *New York Herald Tribune*, February 25, 1955.

83. Jean Douchet and Bertrand Tavernier, *Positif 64/65* (1964), 69, trans. in Tom Milne, *Mamoulian*, 149.

84. Roy Hemming, *The Melody Lingers On: The Great Songwriters and Their Movie Musicals* (New York: Newmarket, 1986), 179.

85. Ibid.

86. Bosley Crowther, "The Screen: *Silk Stockings* Arrives." *New York Times*, July 18, 1957.

87. Robin Wood, ""Art and Ideology: Notes on *Silk Stockings*," *Film Comment 11/3* (May/June 1975), 28-31, quotation on 30.

88. Ibid., 31.

89. Ibid., 28.

90. Ibid., 31.

91. Milne, *Mamoulian*, 160.

92. DeBose, self-described as queer and Afro-Latina, was cast as Anita in Steven Spielberg's 2021 remake of *West Side Story*. Sixty years after Rita Moreno (also Anita) made history as the first Latina to receive the Oscar for Best Supporting Actress, DeBose, the first openly queer person of color to receive an Oscar, revealed that history can both repeat itself and also move on.

93. Since 2001, seven of the twenty-four nominated stage adaptations of non-musical films have received the Tony Award for Best Musical.

Chapter 6: Something to Dance About: *West Side Story* on Stage and Screen

1. The film eschews the comma after "me" employed in the Broadway title.

2. See Appendix 4 for a list of twenty significant film adaptations in the 1950s and another twenty in the 1960s.

3. Richard Barrios, *"West Side Story": The Jets, The Sharks, and the Making of a Classic* (Philadelphia: Running Press, 2020).

4. Mary E. Williams, ed., *Readings on "West Side Story"* (San Diego: Greenhaven, 2001); Nigel Simeone, *Leonard Bernstein: "West Side Story"* (New York: Routledge, 2009); Barry Monush, *"West Side Story": Music on Film* (Milwaukee: Limelight, 2010); Misha Berson, *Something's Coming, Something Good: "West Side Story" and the American Imagination* (Milwaukee: Applause, 2011); Elizabeth A. Wells, *"West Side Story" as Cinema: The Making and Impact of an American Masterpiece: Cultural Perspectives on an American Musical* (Lanham, MD: Scarecrow, 2011); Ernesto R. Acevedo-Muñoz, *"West Side Story" as Cinema: The Making and Impact of an American Masterpiece.* Lawrence, KS: University Press of Kansas, 2013; and Barrios, *"West Side Story."*

5. Bernstein's post-dated January 6, 1949, entry in a *West Side Story* log. The full log with its eleven brief entries through August 20, 1957, the last entry dated one day after opening night of the musical's Washington, DC, tryout, was published in Bernstein, *Findings* (New York: Simon & Schuster, 1982), 147–50. On the "Excerpts from a West Side Log" and the genesis of *West Side Story*, see Simeone, *Leonard Bernstein: "West Side Story,"* 17–52.

6. After *West Side Story*, Robbins and Bernstein would collaborate for a fifth and final time on the ballet *Dybbuk* (1974).

7. Bernstein, *Findings*, 148.

8. For a brief discussion of eight libretto drafts, see Block, *Enchanted Evenings: The Broadway Musical from "Show Boat to Sondheim and Lloyd Webber* (New York: Oxford University Press, 1997; 2nd ed, 2009), 286–90 and 293–94.

9. Otis L. Guernsey Jr., ed., *Broadway Song & Story: Playwright/Lyricists/Composers Discuss Their Hits* (New York: Dodd, Mead, 1985), 47.

10. Ibid., 43.

11. In the stage version, Tony dies while singing "Somewhere" whereas in the film, in contrast to Tristan and most opera characters, he doesn't sing as much as a single note before expiring, much less an aria.

12. Humphrey Burton, *Leonard Bernstein* (New York: Doubleday, 1994), 275; see also Guernsey, *Broadway Song & Story*, 44.

13. Burton, *Leonard Bernstein*, 275.

14. Joseph P. Swain, *The Broadway Musical: A Critical and Musical Survey* (New York: Oxford University Press, 1990; 2nd ed., Lanham, MD: Scarecrow, 2002), 245.

15. Jon Alan Conrad, *"West Side Story," The New Grove Dictionary of Opera* (1992), Oxford Music Online, https://doi-org.ezproxy.ups.edu:2443/10.1093/gmol/978156 1592630.article.0009114.

16. Stephen Banfield, *Sondheim's Broadway Musicals* (Ann Arbor: University of Michigan Press, 1993), 37. For more on this issue, see Block, *"Sondheim's Broadway Musicals* by Stephen Banfield," *Journal of the Royal Musical Association* 121/1 (1996), 20–27.

17. Berson, *Something's Coming, Something Good*, 175–77; Barrios, *"West Side Story,"* 143–44.

18. Nigel Simeone, ed., *The Leonard Bernstein Letters* (New Haven, CT: Yale University Press, 2013), Letter from Leonard Bernstein to Felicia Bernstein, August 15, 1957,

371. Whether the Broadway show included Bernstein's overture during its opening run is not firmly established in the literature, but in any event an overture never made it to either the cast recording or Bernstein's definitive 1985 recording, both of which open with the Prologue. The Broadway premiere took place on September 26, 1957, and closed on June 27, 1959, after 732 performances. Following a national tour, Hal Prince, who thought he had closed the show too soon, brought the show back to Broadway on April 27, 1960, where ran another 249 performances before closing on December 10.

19. The ads appeared in three 30-second spots, one each to the music of "America," "Cool," and "Mambo" with added slogans such as "When you're a jean" and "Are you a jean or a khaki?" According to Misha Berson, Irene Sharaff, who designed the costumes for both the stage and film versions, requested that for the latter the Jets' jeans be made of "a specially treated and dyed [elastic] fabric to accommodate the exertions of their dancing—an expenditure of $75 per pair," roughly $748 in 2022 money (Berson, *Something's Coming*, 77).

20. Citing the contract from February 21, 1961, Barrios notes that Bernstein was paid an additional $7,500 for this new four-minute extension (Barrios, *"West Side Story,"* 143). Bernstein was also asked to supply an extended *West Side Story* medley to accompany Saul Bass's stylish end credits, in which simulated graffiti is displayed on realistic urban backdrops.

21. Barrios, *"West Side Story,"* 106–8.

22. In addition to the differences discussed in this section Barrios notes a number of details in the musical distribution in the "Tonight Quintet" (Barrios, *"West Side Story,"* 144).

23. Letter from Geoffrey M. Shurlock to Walter M. Mirisch, *West Side Story* Censor Reports, June 28, 1960, Margaret Herrick Library, Los Angeles. Regarding the nomenclature of the "Quintet," Sondheim corrects the record by pointing out that "this 'Quintet' is actually a quartet, since both Maria and Tony sing the same melodic line." Stephen Sondheim, *Finishing the Hat: Collected Lyrics (1954–1981) with Attendant Comments, Principles, Heresies, Grudges, Whines and Anecdotes* (New York: Knopf, 2010), 47.

24. Sondheim, *Finishing the Hat*, 44. In printing the revised lyrics in *Finishing the Hat* Sondheim rhymes "poor dear" with "near," which contradicts both Lehman's screenplay (conveniently included with the 2003 DVD), and more important, with the fact that Rita Moreno (in a non-dubbed portion of the song) clearly sings "here," not "near." One wonders precisely how to interpret Sondheim's remark about the revised lyric, "Even Oscar might have winced," but it seems unlikely Hammerstein would have taken it as a compliment.

25. Letter from Geoffrey M. Shurlock to Walter M. Mirisch, *West Side Story* Censor Reports, August 3, 1960, Margaret Herrick Library, Los Angeles.

26. In *Finishing the Hat* Sondheim recalled that shortly after Lieberson informed him that "schmuck" would have to go, he came up with "dough" and "schmo" about an hour before the song was recorded for the cast album. He also expressed his opinion

that the lyric for the movie version, "job" and "slob," "improved it a bit" (Sondheim, *Finishing the Hat*, 51).

27. Ibid.

28. Sondheim credits Bernstein with coming up with "Krup you!" which according to Sondheim "may be the best lyric line in the show" (ibid.).

29. Sondheim, *Finishing the Hat*, 40–42. By returning to the original verse, Sondheim removed the offending line about Puerto Rico and tropical diseases he refused to change in the stage version. In the earlier complaint, which arrived one day after opening night, Dr. Howard A. Rusk of the Rusk Institute explained in an editorial published in the *New York Times*, "The Facts Don't Rhyme," that tropical diseases in Puerto Rico were a thing of the past (Berson, *Something's Coming*, 98; Sondheim, *Finishing the Hat*, 42).

30. Fiona A. Villella, "Circular Narratives: Highlights of Popular Cinema in the '90s," *Senses of Cinema* 3 (February 2000), https://sensesof cinema.com/2000/feature-articles/circular/.).

31. Berson, *Something's Coming*, 148.

32. Roadshow films were reserved for limited engagements designed to attract audiences interested in a more theatrical cinematic experience. They were deluxe in every way, expensive, long enough to warrant an intermission, with only one or two showings a day, and included souvenir programs to purchase, an occasion worth dressing up for and for turning off the television for a few hours. Starting in 1955 with *Oklahoma!* and *Guys and Dolls*, *West Side Story* was the sixth roadshow film adapted from a stage musical. After the extraordinary success of the films *My Fair Lady* and *The Sound of Music*, eight less successful roadshow film adaptations followed before the enterprise collapsed under its own weight. *A Fine Romance* includes two of the twenty roadshow film adaptations shown from 1955 to 1972: *Oklahoma!* and *West Side Story*. The list of all twenty that follows does not include *Silk Stockings*, *Flower Drum Song*, or *Cabaret*. Here is the list: *Oklahoma!* and *Guys and Dolls* (1955); *South Pacific* (1958); *Porgy and Bess* (1959); *Can-Can* (1960); *West Side Story* (1961); *My Fair Lady* (1964); *The Sound of Music* (1965); *Half a Sixpence* and *Camelot* (1967); *Oliver!*, *Finian's Rainbow*, and *Funny Girl* (1968); *Paint Your Wagon*, *Sweet Charity*, and *Hello, Dolly!* (1969); *Song of Norway* (1970); *Fiddler on the Roof* (1971); *1776* and *Man of La Mancha* (1972). Matthew Kennedy offers a critical discussion of roadshow musicals focused mainly between 1965 and 1972, see Kennedy, *Roadshow!: The Fall of Film Musicals in 1960s* (New York: Oxford University Press, 2014). For a complete list of roadshow films in all genres see "Roadshow Theatrical Release," https://en.wikipedia.org/wiki/Road show_theatrical_release.

33. Based on my reading of the literature, Robbins was the only person involved in the project to object to this change.

34. Guernsey, *Broadway Song & Story*, 40–54.

35. Ibid., 50. In case you are a reader unfamiliar with the term "11 o'clock number" and happen to be reading this chapter out of the conventional order (like many of the songs in the film adaptation of *West Side Story*), I will restate that this term refers to

a show-stopping song designed to wake up audiences toward the end of an evening, which in the old days occurred about 11:00 P.M.

36. Ibid.

37. Ibid.

38. Jerome Robbins to Robert Wise, April 12, 1961, Box 37, Folder 10, "Jerome Robbins," Wise Collection.

39. *West Side Memories*, "Special Feature," DVD 2003.

40. Sondheim, *Finishing the Hat*, 52.

41. Saul Chaplin, *The Golden Age of Movie Musicals and Me* (Norman: University of Oklahoma Press, 1994), 179.

42. Acevedo-Muñoz, "West Side Story," 106.

43. Incidentally, "I Feel Pretty" is one of only three *West Side Story* songs to avoid conspicuous use of the tritone (the others are "America" and "Somewhere"). Helen Smith plausibly posits that its absence in "Pretty" may be attributed to the fact that "Maria is in her own dream world about Tony, and is not thinking about reality [i.e., tritones] at all" (Smith, *There's a Place for Us: the Musical Theatre Works of Leonard Bernstein* [Burlington, VT: Ashgate, 2011], 153).

44. Sondheim, *Finishing the Hat*, 47–50.

45. The 1957 cast album sold well, lasting 191 weeks on the Billboard charts reaching as high as #5 in 1962, the same year it attained gold record status. By then the film soundtrack with Marni Nixon's voice dubbing Natalie Wood (Maria), Jim Bryant dubbing Richard Beymer (Tony), and Betty Wand dubbing for Rita Moreno (Anita) in "A Boy Like That/I Have a Love" (Moreno did her own singing for "America"), had already shot up to No.1, where it stood for fifty-four weeks, the longest-running No. 1 album to date. Curiously, the stage songs inspired only a handful of recordings during the years that immediately followed the release of the original cast album. In his DVD interview on *West Side Memories*, Sondheim notes that only two established popular singers risked recording a song from the show, Dinah Shore ("Tonight") and Johnny Mathis ("Maria"). Misha Berson adds a Sammy Davis Jr. medley to this short list (Berson, *Something's Coming*, 182–83). Sondheim recalled in a 1964 interview that *West Side Story* produced no hit songs because "everybody said they couldn't hum the score" (Laurence Maslon, *Broadway to Main Street: How Show Tunes Enchanted America* [New York: Oxford University Press, 2018], 145). It took the popularity and exposure of the 1961 film version to create a barrage of previously unrecognized hits and a hummable soundtrack that reached No. 1, eventually becoming the best-selling album of the 1960s.

46. Phil Ford, "Jazz Exotica and the Naked City," *Journal of Musicological Research* 27 (2008), 113–33, especially 117–18. See also Katherine Baber, *Leonard Bernstein and the Language of Jazz* (Urbana: University of Illinois Press, 2019), 155–84.

47. Latinx styles in *West Side Story* include the *mambo* and *cha-cha-cha* (Cuba), the *paso doble* and *cachucha* (Spain), the *huapango* (Mexico), and *samba* (Brazil). It might be noted here that throughout *A Fine Romance* instead of Hispanic I am using the terms Latino/Latina (singular) and Latinx (plural), which are widely used in the academy. I have included the *samba* in a list of Latinx styles because Brazil is located in Latin

America, even though the primary language of Brazil is Portuguese and the vast majority of Brazilians are not Hispanic (by definition Spanish speaking). Beginning with the 2000 US Census the identifier "Hispanic" has been changed to "Spanish/Hispanic/Latino."

48. The film critic Pauline Kael famously wrote in her widely quoted, aggressively ignorant review that Bernstein's musical score was "so derivative that, as we left the theater, and overheard some young man exclaiming 'I could listen to that music forever,' my little daughter answered 'We *have* been listening to it forever.'" *Chacun à son goût.* If you permit me to interject my own *goût* on this point, it would be that despite the breathtaking eclecticism of Bernstein's score, the result is invariably Bernstein's own.

49. For a survey of the musical content of *West Side Story* and Bernstein's dramatic use of musical motives (including the use of the tritone, foreshadowing, and borrowing), see Block, *Enchanted Evenings*, 279–308.

50. Ibid., 296–300.

51. Walter Mirisch, *I Thought We Were Making Movies, Not History* (Madison: University of Wisconsin Press, 2008), 126. A few years earlier the two-director plan had proved successful with *The Pajama Game* (1957) and *Damn Yankees* (1958) in which Stanley Donen staged the music numbers and George Abbott the book scenes. Gene Kelly and Stanley Donen also successfully shared directing-choreography responsibilities in the film version of *On the Town* (see chapter 3).

52. Acevedo-Muñoz, *"West Side Story,"* 49.

53. Barrios, *"West Side Story,"* 108.

54. Ibid., 108. In his interview from *West Side Memories*, Wise recalled that the only dance assistant who left with Robbins was Howard Jeffrey. Not only did all the other assistants remain, but the "Dance at the Gym" choreography was unchanged from the stage version, and Wise brought Robbins back, both for additional editing and later for the Academy Awards.

55. Bosley Crowther, "'West Side Story' Arrives," *New York Times*, October 19, 1961.

56. Stanley Kauffmann, "The Asphalt Romeo and Juliet," *New Republic*, October 23, 1961, 28–29.

57. Stanley Green, "'West Side Story'—The Film Version," *Hifi/Stereo Review*, January 1962, 65.

58. Arthur Knight, "Movies: Romeo Revisited," *Saturday Review*, October 14, 1961, 40

59. James Powers, "*West Side Story*," *Hollywood Reporter*, September 22, 1961.

60. Joan Acocella, "City Lights," *New Yorker*, November 28, 2011.

61. Todd McCarthy, "Jets Have Their Way Onscreen: 'West Side Story' Screen Version Underrated," *Variety*, June 4, 2009.

62. Jay Norman, who played the role of Juano on stage and Pepe in the film, was partly Puerto Rican (Barrios, *"West Side Story,"* 48).

63. Frances Negrón-Muntaner, "Feeling Pretty: *West Side Story* and Puerto Rican Identity Discourses, *Social Text* 63 18/2 (Summer 2000), 83.

64. Due to some grumbling, some of these Spanish additions, which were prepared by Lin-Manuel Miranda, were reduced during the course of the run.

65. Barrios, *"West Side Story,"* 184.

66. Melena Ryzik, "Rita Moreno and Ariana DeBose: From One Anita to Another," *New York Times*, December 15, 2021.

67. Ibid. The Spielberg 2021 remake (see the Postscript, note 73 below) continued the controversies inspired by the van Hove Broadway production of 2020. In fact, much of the reception in the Latinx community to the stage and film version has been more negative than Moreno's perspective (see Yarimar Bonilla, "*The West Side Story* Remake We Didn't Need," *New York Times* December 19, 2021 and Andrea González-Ramírez, "*West Side Story* Can't Be Saved," *New York Times*, December 13, 2012). In the panel discussion, "The Great 'West Side Story' Debate," Carina de Valle Schorske expressed her desire for the Spielberg remake "to flop so we can move on." In contrast, playwright Matthew López confessed having a "bifurcated mind" in which "there's a part of me that really loves *West Side Story* and a part of me that really hates that I love *West Side Story*" (Jesse Green et. al, "The Great 'West Side Story' Debate," *New York Times*, December 1, 2021). The Black scholar and opinion writer John McWhorter finds that the Puerto Rican characters "are depicted richly and sympathetically, even if not as much so as our current values would urge" (McWhorter, "Why I Still Love *West Side Story*," *New York Times*, January 22, 2012). Most of the negative response to Spielberg's remake ignores the artistic component (the focus of this chapter), although Jesse Green, while acknowledging in the "Debate" that "all art is political, yes, and deserves to be judged as such . . . art is not *just* political, and deserves to be judged on other grounds, too." One reader's letter to the newspaper went further than Green in its complaint that the "Debate" was "about 90 percent politics and 10 percent art." (

68. Acevedo-Muñoz, "*West Side Story,*" 168.

69. Ibid., 156.

70. Ibid. 160.

71. Arthur Laurents, *Original Story By: A Memoir of Broadway and Hollywood* (New York: Knopf, 2000), 347. See also Laurents's remarks in this chapter's epigraph spoken on *Broadway: The American Musical*, "Episode Five; Tradition (1957–1970), PBS Home Video 2004.

72. Laurents, *Original Story By,* 348.

73. Postscript: This chapter was completed prior to the arrival of the 2021 film remake directed by Steven Spielberg and with a new screenplay by Tony Kushner. Since perhaps a plurality of those reading this footnote may be familiar with one or more movies directed by Spielberg, I will mention only the two films that received the Academy Award's Best Picture Oscars and for which Spielberg received the Oscar for Best Director: *Schindler's List* (1993) and *Saving Private Ryan* (1998). Kushner, best known for his two-part play, *Angels in America* (1990, 1991), also collaborated on a musical with composer Jeanine Tesori, *Caroline, or Change* (2002). Tesori, who later composed *Fun Home* (2015), served as the voice coach for the Spielberg-Kushner *West Side Story* remake.

Since a discussion of this film is beyond the scope of this survey, I will resist the temptation to go much beyond expressing my agreement with NPR that it serves "as both an affectionate tribute and a gentle corrective" to the 1961 film original, to acknowledge the new film as a significant addition to the *West Side Story* saga (https://

npr.org/2021/12/09/1062380664/steve-spielbergs-west-side-story-review, and to offer four observations germane to this chapter: (1) the Spielberg-Kushner remake for the most part returns to the song order of the stage version; (2) the remake reinstates "I Feel Pretty," which as noted earlier was removed from the 2020 revival directed by van Hove; (3) by virtually unanimous consent (in my view inexplicably and unfairly) the actor who played the thankless role of Tony (Ansel Elgort), like Richard Beymer in 1961, receives the largest share of negative criticism; and (4) instead of merely appearing in a cameo "walk-on," the ninety-year old Moreno is featured in a newly conceived and important role as Doc's widow, Valentina, who is entrusted with delivering and thus usurping Tony and Maria's central song "Somewhere."

I conclude this Postscript by noting two exceptions to observation number 1. The first is the earlier placement of "Gee, Officer Krupke" as in the 1961 film, although now after the stage's "Tonight"–"America" sequence instead of the "America"–"Tonight" 1961 film sequence. In an effective new touch, Spielberg inserted the "Transition to Scherzo" portion of the "Somewhere" ballet into a "morning after" the evening's fire escape scene (Shakespeare's balcony scene) not present either on the stage or in the 1961 film. Another departure from the stage order is the placement of "One Hand, One Heart" before rather than after "Cool."

Chapter 7: A (Mostly) All-Asian American Musical: *Flower Drum Song* from Page to Stage to Screen

1. For more on roadshows, see chapter 6 (especially note 32), which includes a list of the twenty film adaptations of Broadway stage musicals from 1955 to 1972 starting with *Oklahoma!* For a reliable survey of roadshow films of various types (focusing on the years between 1965 and 1972, see Matthew Kennedy, *Road-Show! The Fall of Film Musicals in the 1960s* (New York: Oxford University Press, 2014).

2. See the chapter epigraph. *Reminiscences of Richard Rodgers* (Oral History Collections of Columbia University, 1969), Interviews with Kenneth Leish, 348; reprinted in Geoffrey Block, ed., *The Richard Rodgers Reader* (New York: Oxford University Press, 2002), 318.

3. Hugh Fordin, *Getting to Know Him: A Biography of Oscar Hammerstein II* (New York: Ungar, 1977), 342.

4. According to David H. Lewis, twelve of the forty-six original cast members were Chinese (Lewis, *Flower Drum Songs: The Story of Two Musicals* [Jefferson, NC: McFarland, 2006], 69). Two Chinese actors were cast in major roles, Arabella Hong as Helen Chao and Keye Luke ("No. 1 Son" in seven Charlie Chan movies of the 1930s) as Wang Chi-yang. *Flower Drum Song (FDS)* was one of several plays and films with Asian themes during the late 1950s and early 1960s: *Sayonara* (film 1957) with *Flower Drum Song*'s Miyoshi Umeki, who received the Oscar for Best Supporting Actress; *The World of Suzie Wong* (play 1958; film 1960), starring *FDS*'s Nancy Kwan; *A Majority of One* (play 1959; film 1961); and *Rashomon* (a 1959 play

based on the 1950 Japanese film directed by Akira Kurosawa (starring Claire Bloom and Rod Steiger made up in "yellowface"). The original cast of *FDS* also included one white actor, Larry Blyden (Sammy Fong) and one African American, Juanita Hall (Madam Liang), the latter also cast in the film.

5. Farrar, Straus and Cudahy, reprinted in a 2002 Penguin edition that includes an Introduction by David Henry Hwang. For the record, in contrast to the stage and film versions, the novel is preceded by "The."

6. Henry David Hwang, "Introduction," *The Flower Drum Song* (New York: Theatre Communications Group, 2003), xi.

7. One striking example of a new context was the decision to place "Chop Suey," Madam Liang's celebration of assimilation, into a stage act in which Sammy Fong (the stage persona of Wang Chi-yang and no longer a separate character) made a kitschy entrance inside an extra-large take-out container of Chinese food surrounded by female dancing containers and men impersonating gigantic chopsticks. Unfortunately, in his attempt to remove Asian stereotypes, Hwang inexplicably added a gay one in the new character Harvard, a costume designer. Ben Brantley's *New York Times* review referred to Harvard as a "swishy" gay character that inspired the kind of humor found in sitcoms like *Will and Grace*: "Mr. Hwang has said that in researching this show, he 'began to realize that one generation's breakthroughs often become the next generation's stereotypes.' Evidently, some breakthroughs turn into stereotypes faster than others" (Brantley, "New Coat of Paint for Old Pagoda," *New York Times*, October 18, 2002).

8. For a representative critical view of Hwang's revisal, see Warren Hoffman, *The Great White Way: Race and the Broadway Musical* (New Brunswick, NJ: Rutgers University Press, 2014), 196–201; for a more sympathetic assessment, see Dan Bacalzo, "A Different Drum: David Henry Hwang's Musical 'Revisal' of *Flower Drum Song*," *Journal of American Drama and Theatre* 15/2 (Spring 2003): 71–83.

9. Thomas S. Hischak, *Through the Screen Door* (Lanham, MD: Scarecrow, 2004), 45).

10. Hwang, "Introduction," x.

11. Juanita Hall, an African American actress and the only member of the film cast in yellowface, is probably best known as the Tonkinese character Bloody Mary in the stage and film versions of *South Pacific*. Kathryn Edney explores the impact of Hall's casting in *Flower Drum Song* on the Black community during the civil rights era. Kathryn Edney, "'Integration through the Wide Open Back Door': African Americans Respond to *Flower Drum Song* (1958)," *Studies in Musical Theatre* 4/3 (2010), 261–72.

12. The Japanese American Soo, born Goro (later Jack) Suzuki, changed his name when he performed regularly in Chinese nightclubs prior to being cast in *Flower Drum Song*. Aside from playing Sammy Fong, Soo is best known as a regular in the popular television program *Barney Miller* (1975–79). At the age of thirteen, the Filipino-born Adiarte was cast as the king's oldest son Prince Chulalongkorn in the film adaptation of *The King and I* (1956).

13. Concerning the substitution of Horne's voice for Dandridge and examples of white singers dubbing Black actors in *Carmen Jones*, see Jeff Smith, "Black Faces, White

Voices: The Politics of Dubbing in *Carmen Jones*," *Velvet Light Trap* 51 (Spring 2003), 29–42.

14. The discussion of *Oklahoma!* in chapter 4 noted that Bambi Linn (Dream Laurey) and James Mitchell (Dream Curly) doubled for Joan Roberts and Alfred Drake, respectively, in the dream ballet "Laurey Makes Up Her Mind."

15. Oscar Hammerstein and Joseph Fields, *Flower Drum Song* (New York: Farrar, Straus and Cudahy, 1959), 9–10. Madame Liang repeats these identical requests when she is introduced a little later in the screenplay.

16. A "tomato" was a slang term for an attractive young woman. It dates back to the 1920s and remained in wide circulation in the 1950s.

17. The "Fannie" in "Fan Tan Fannie" was spelled "Fanny" in the original Broadway libretto and vocal score and film soundtrack but "Fannie" on the original cast album and the libretto and cast album of the Hwang revisal. The present chapter uses "Fannie" throughout, the spelling Hammerstein used when he published the lyrics in 1959. Amy Asch, ed., *The Complete Lyrics of Oscar Hammerstein* (New York: Knopf, 2008), 390.

18. Rick Altman, *The American Film Musical* (Bloomington: Indiana University Press, 1989), 16–20.

19. In the novel, stage, and film versions, Wang is robbed on the way home. In the novel, Wang saw the robber but was unable to describe him, because "all foreigners look alike" (35) (in the stage and film versions this line was changed to "all white men look alike" [17]). Stage audiences only hear about the robbery, whereas film viewers witness the robbery in progress, which takes place at Wang's front door. Thus, only film viewers see that the robber is white (the only white character in the movie).

20. In an extensive interview published in 2004, C. Y. Lee conveyed his intention to follow the writing advice of a professor to use "the material you are most familiar with" and "to find a conflict." Lee "found two conflicts: the cultural conflict; the other is the generation gap." Interview with Andrew Shin, "'Forty Percent Is Luck': An Interview with C. Y. (Chin Yang) Lee," *Melus* 29/2 (Summer 2004): 77–104; quotation on 88.

21. For a summary of the subordination of women as well as sexism and misogyny in the early 1960s, see Louis Menand, *The Free World: Art and Thought in the Cold War* (New York: Farrar, Straus and Giroux, 2021), 542–59.

22. The screenplay repeats Linda's ambition "to be a success as a girl" instead of pursuing a singing career. Another scene goes beyond the stage libretto in cringe-worthiness with Master Wang's response when Mei Li brings him breakfast in bed and takes the initiative to clean his water pipe: "Personally, I never fully approved of the old custom of drowning daughters." The cavalier callousness of this remark recalls Ninotchka's verdict that the recent mass trials were "a great success" because they would result in "fewer but better Russians." As noted in chapter 5, Ninotchka's assessment was mercifully *removed* from both the stage and film versions of *Silk Stockings* (Charles Brackett, Billy Wilder, and Walter Reisch, *Ninotchka* (New York: Viking, 1972), 24.

23. The novel and stage work appeared only a few years after the US Congress passed the Immigration and Nationality Act of 1952. Since 1943, only about 100 people from China had been allowed to immigrate to the United States each year. Although the

Act of 1952 continued to limit visas from each Asian country, it did eliminate laws that prevented Asians from becoming naturalized citizens. Madam Liang was among the first group of Chinese immigrants to take advantage of this opportunity.

24. In the stage version, "Fan Tan Fannie" is sung at the Celestial Gardens, not by Linda (Suzuki) but by a "girl singer" (Anita Ellis) who accompanies "a chorus of girls in idealized coolie costumes." After Frankie's "Gliding through My Memory," Linda concludes Act I with an abbreviated reprise of "Grant Avenue."

25. I know I promised not to discuss Hwang's revisal, but I can't resist noting that even commentators highly critical of Hwang's altered narrative seldom complain that he assigned "Love, Look Away" to Mei Li and removed Helen's character entirely.

26. Assuming the Vocal Score (116–29) accurately conveys what was heard on the stage, the music of "Ta's Dream" contains the following musical medley: "You Are Beautiful"; "Grant Avenue"; "A Hundred Million Miracles" (opening rhythm); "I Am Going to Like It Here"; "Chop Suey" (fragments); "Grant Avenue"; "Chop Suey" (fragments); and "Love, Look Away."

27. Between the framing statements of "Love, Look Away," the film ballet presents the B section of "You Are Beautiful" as a waltz and jazzy trumpet fragments of "Fan Tan Fannie." The film ballet appears on the soundtrack (MCA Records), the longest cut on the album at 5:02 minutes.

28. Due to censorship issues, the film version of *South Pacific* was similarly altered to imply that "nothing happened" between Lt. Joseph Cable and Liat. Geoffrey Block, *Richard Rodgers* (New Haven, CT: Yale University Press, 2003), 154–56.

29. *Flower Drum Song,* Motion Picture Association of America (MPAA), Production Code Administration records, Production Files, Margaret Herrick Library, Los Angeles.

30. In the stage version Ta humbly begs forgiveness for his behavior; the film goes further when Ta calls himself a fool, which inspires a sentimental but moving response from his father: "Knowing you are a fool is the beginning of wisdom. Now I have my son back."

31. John Franceschina, *Hermes Pan: The Man Who Danced with Fred Astaire* (New York: Oxford University Press, 2012), 232–33. The stage libretto includes a longer exchange between Sammy and Linda prior to the song. One change in the screenplay seems to be for the sake of the Production Code. In both the stage and film versions Linda enters Sammy's apartment unannounced in the presence of his judgmental parents which prompts Sammy to ask, "What's the idea of barging in?" On stage, Linda responds with her own question, "Why should I ring the bell when I've got a key?" In the film, Linda doesn't have a key, a detail that might well have been censored as too suggestive.

32. Blyden was then married to Carol Haney, the show's choreographer.

33. According to Amy Asch, "Hammerstein wrote the lyric in about four days" (Asch, *The Complete Lyrics of Oscar Hammerstein,* 389). In his autobiography Rodgers stated that "Oscar simply put the dialogue into a lyric," but clearly it wasn't that simple. Rodgers doesn't mention how many days it took his partner to perform this simple task, but the composer does say that he worked out the music on a piano he "discovered in the Shubert Theatre's ladies' lounge," which suggests that he completed his

work with his typical swiftness. Richard Rodgers. *Musical Stages: An Autobiography* (New York: Random House, 1975), 295.

34. Hammerstein and Fields, *Flower Drum Song,* 124–25. This exchange is repeated word for word in the screenplay but not the song, which will be heard three minutes after viewers see the opening of a wedding notice, "Doctor Han Li, Former Professor of Philosophy, Peking University" (1:53:37). David Lewis states, albeit without evidence, that "Sunday" was the only number in the Broadway version staged by director Kelly rather than choreographer Carol Haney (Lewis, *Flower Drum Songs*, 58). According to Earl J. Hess and Pratibha A. Dabholkar, after discussing the choreography with Haney, Kelly "left her alone to work out the numbers," several of which contained "traditional Chinese movements," presumably including "Sunday." Hess and Dabholkar, *Gene Kelly: The Making of a Creative Legend* (Lawrence: University Press of Kansas, 2020), 314.

35. One final reference to Linda appears in chapter 8 of Part II when Ta's friend Chang reports that Linda had been expelled from Chinatown and is free-lancing in Los Angeles.

36. Sheri Tan, "'Flower Drum' Critics Haven't Read Script," *Asian Week*, March 31, 1983, 4. In this March interview, the one the following week (April 7, 1983, 14), and again in his lengthy 2004 interview with Andrew Shin, "Forty Percent Is Luck," 85, Lee states that the novel was set in the 1930s, a surprising (and erroneous) assertion often repeated by commentators on the musical. While few details establish a particular decade, one unmistakable clue that places the story in the 1950s appears early in the novel (page 16), when a minor character, Mary, tells Ta on a date she wants to see Alfred Hitchcock's *Rear Window* which came out in 1954. It would also be unlikely to see a television in a home in the 1930s.

37. Ethan Mordden, *Rodgers & Hammerstein* (New York: Harry N. Abrams, 1992), 198.

Chapter 8: Stretching Boundaries in the Wake of the Studio System Era: *Cabaret* on Stage and Screen

1. Eric Hodgins, "Amid Ruins of an Empire a New Hollywood Arises," *Life*, June 1957, 146. Hodgins was the source in chapter 1 of the fact that in 1957 independents produced fifty percent of all movies in the United States (Ibid. 160).

2. Ibid., 146.

3. June Skinner Sawyers, *Cabaret FAQ: All That's Left to Know about the Broadway and Cinema Classic* (Milwaukee: Applause, 2017), 182.

4. *The Sound of Music*—although it was distributed by 20th Century-Fox and is usually identified by this logo, it was produced by Argyle Enterprises, Inc., a company founded in 1963. *Cabaret* may have been Allied's only musical, but *The Sound of Music* proved to be Argyle's only major film of *any* genre.

5. Matthew Kennedy, *Roadshow: The Fall of Film Musicals in the 1990s* (New York: Oxford University Press, 2014), 257. Although *Cabaret* didn't belong in a list of roadshow musicals by studio and release years in the United States from 1965 to 1972, Kennedy

included it due to "its importance in the history of film musicals and its release within the roadshow era" (Ibid, 257). See chapter 6 (especially note 32) for more on the roadshow phenomenon.

6. The Klub was filmed on a set constructed in Berlin's Bavarian Studios.

7. Arthur Laurents, *Original Story By: A Memoir of Broadway and Hollywood* (New York: Knopf, 2000), 347.

8. Prince, *Sense of Occasion* (Milwaukee: Applause, 2017), 138. It was noted in chapter 1 that Prince "felt at the time that audiences had enough to handle—two doomed romances, Nazis, Sally's abortion without inflicting Isherwood's homosexuality on them as well" (Foster Hirsch, *Harold Prince and the American Musical Theatre* [New York: Applause, 2005], 66).

9. In *Contradictions*, Prince stated his conviction "that the musical comedy audience required a sentimental heterosexual love story" (Prince, *Contradictions* [New York: Dodd, Mead, 1974], 134; repr. *Sense of Occasion* [New York: Applause, 2017], 133. Christopher Isherwood similarly refrained from disclosing the sexual identity of his narrator and alter ego, also named Clifford, in his *roman à clef*, *The Berlin Stories* (1945) (New York: New Directions, 1963). These stories were a principal source for John Van Druten's 1951 Broadway play *I Am a Camera* and its 1955 film adaptation and later *Cabaret*. Isherwood eventually acknowledged his homosexuality in *Christopher and His Kind: 1929–1939* (New York: Farrar, Straus and Giroux, 1976, ten years after the stage version of *Cabaret*.

10. For a brief introduction to the concept musical, see Geoffrey Block, "Integration," in *The Oxford Handbook of the American Musical*, ed. Raymond Knapp, Mitchell Morris, and Stacy Wolf, (New York: Oxford University Press, 2011), 104–6

11. Isherwood published a first set of stories in 1935 under two titles, *Mr. Norris Changes Trains* in England and *The Last of Mr. Norris* in the United States; a second volume of stories, *Goodbye to Berlin*, appeared in 1939. The two sets of stories were published together as *The Berlin Stories* in 1945 (New York: New Directions, 1963). Some material in this chapter is derived from my essay, "Is Life a Cabaret?: *Cabaret* and Its Sources in Reality and the Imagination," *Studies in Musical Theatre* 5/2 (2011): 163–80.

12. Isherwood, *Christopher and His Kind*.

13. "Sally Bowles" was also published separately in 1937.

14. Isherwood, *Christopher and His Kind,* 63. Isherwood does mention, however, that "on at least one occasion, because of some financial or housing emergency, they shared a bed without the least embarrassment."

15. Prince, *Contradictions*, 126; *Sense of Occasion*, 127.

16. *Contradictions*, 126-27; repr. in *Sense of Occasion*, 128.

17. Isherwood, *Goodbye to Berlin*, 25.

18. Prince, *Sense of Occasion*, 285.

19. "Kit Kat Klub Memory Gallery: The Film's Stars and Creators Reminisce about Making Movie History," *Cabaret*, DVD (Warner Bros., 2003).

20. In an ironic twist, the ends of many phrases in "Willkommen" share this rising half step, as do several phases in "Married/Heiraten," Fräulein Schneider's duet with Herr Schultz.

21. Otis L. Guernsey Jr., ed., *Broadway Song and Story: Playwrights/Lyricists/Composers Discuss Their Hits* (New York: Dodd, Mead, 1985), 139.

22. *The Complete "Cabaret" Collection* (Milwaukee: Hal Leonard, 1966, 1998), includes vocal scores for the 1966 Original Broadway Production, Additional Songs for the 1972 Film Score and 1998 Revival, and three 1966 Production Cut-Outs.

23. For color photos of the limbo area and photos of other scenes from the original stage version, see Frank Rich, with Lisa Aronson, *The Theatre Art of Boris Aronson* (New York: Knopf, 1987), 187–99. See also the song animations from the 1966 stage version created by Doug Reside, curator of the Billy Rose Theater Division, New York Public Library, in Jesse Green, "Reanimating *Cabaret*, One Frame at a Time," *New York Times*, April 14, 2021.

24. Prince, *Sense of Occasion*, 137.

25. Prince, *Contradictions*, 135; repr. in *Sense of Occasion*, 134.

26. Guernsey, *Broadway Song and Story*, 149.

27. Kevin Winkler, *Big Deal: Bob Fosse and Dance in the American Musical* (New York: Oxford University Press, 2018), 149.

28. Ibid.

29. Cy Feuer, with Ken Gross, *I Got the Show Right Here: The Amazing, True Story of How an Obscure Brooklyn Horn Player Became the Last Great Broadway Showman* (New York: Simon & Schuster, 2003), 242.

30. Ibid., 240–41.

31. Feuer thought that Van Druten's Clifford in *I am a Camera* was gay, but in Winkler's assessment, "the character was neutered" sexually (Winkler, *Big Deal*, 142).

32. Feuer, *I Got the Show Right Here*, 241.

33. In her study of "Tomorrow," Susanne Scheiblhofer notes that "several people have searched for the Nazi and/or German folk original, refusing to give up when their research ends with Kander and Ebb." Scheiblhofer, "'Tomorrow Belongs to Me': The Journey of a Show Tune from Broadway to *Rechtsrock*," *Studies in Musical Theatre* 11/1 (2017), 5–22; quotation on 11.

34. The introduction of "It Couldn't Please Me More" is not unlike what happens in *Oklahoma!* when Ado Annie converses with Laurey and tells her friend she knows she just can't kiss any man who asks: "Yeow, they *told* me . . ." But with her next words, "It ain't so much a question of not knowin' whut to do," Annie has imperceptibly changed her mode of communication from dialogue to song and the verse of "I Cain't Say No" has begun.

35. When asked in an interview whether she contributed to visual ideas in the film, Allen replied that normally she didn't do this. An exception to this general rule was the scene directions she included prior to the filming of "Tomorrow," in which she instructed the camera to gradually descend from a Nazi youth's face to reveal his Sam Browne belt and swastika at the Biergarten (Allen, *Cabaret*, First Draft, June 10, 1970, 98 [unpublished]). "Jay Presson Allen: Writer by Default," interview with Pat McGilligan, *Backstory 3: Interviews with Screenwriters of the 1960s* (Berkeley: University of California Press, 1997), 35.

36. Judith Crist, *Take 22: Moviemakers on Moviemaking* (New York: Continuum, 1991), 305.

37. Bob Fosse Daily Diary, Bob Fosse and Gwen Verdon Collection, Library of Congress, Box 55G.

38. The Tiller girls were English dancers who were popular nightclub entertainers in the Weimar Republic.

39. Prince, *Contradictions*, 126; repr. in *Sense of Occasion*, 128. Prince went on to express his opinion that the casting of Minnelli in the film was flawed. According to Winkler, after working with Minnelli on their first major musical, *Flora, The Red Menace*, produced by Prince, for which Minnelli received the Tony Award for Best Actress at the age of nineteen, Kander and Ebb "lobbied hard" to cast Minnelli as Sally in the stage version (Winkler, *Big Deal*, 143).

40. For the 1966 libretto, see Joe Masteroff, *Cabaret* (New York: Random House, 1967); repr. in Stanley Richards, ed. *Great Musicals of the American Theatre Volume Two* (Radnor, PA: Chilton, 1976), 411–60.

41. For the 1998 libretto, see Joe Masteroff, *"Cabaret": The Illustrated Book and Lyrics* (New York: Newmarket, 1999).

42. Allen, *Cabaret*, First Draft, June 10, 1970, 21. The literature explored for this chapter does not clarify whether Kander composed the slap dance, which in any event does not appear on the film soundtrack.

43. Ibid.

44. John Kander and Fred Ebb, as told to Greg Lawrence, *Colored Lights: Forty Years of Words and Music, Show Biz, Collaboration, and All That Jazz* (New York: Faber and Faber, 2003), 63. A little later in this oral history, Kander expressed to Lenya his concern that he would be accused of "cribbing from Kurt Weill" in his 1966 score (69). Kander took great comfort when Lenya assured him she heard "Berlin," not "Kurt" in his songs. In an earlier essay, I wrote that modern and future audiences not familiar with German jazz of the 1920s are potentially destined to "hear the Berlin of 1929 as imagined by Kander by way of Weill" and that "the seldom heard sound of 1920s German jazz will probably appear increasingly inauthentic" (Block, "Is Life a Cabaret?" *Cabaret* and Its Sources in Reality and the Imagination," *Studies in Musical Theatre* 5/2 [2011], 173).

45. Ethan Mordden, *Open a New Window: The Broadway Musical in the 1960s* (New York: Palgrave, 2001), 159.

46. Ernst was the German whom Clifford met on the train when he arrived in Berlin in the stage version; Ernst told him about Fräulein Schneider's boarding house and later became one of Clifford's English students. The scene with Ernst appears in Allen's First Draft but not in the film.

47. In musical theater and film as well in Germany and America during the time *Cabaret* takes place, triple meter evoked love, such as when Magnolia and Ravenal declared their love at the end of Act I by singing "You Are Love" in *Show Boat* (1927) or when Marlene Dietrich sang "Falling in Love Again" in Josef Von Sternberg's classic German film *The Blue Angel* (1930). This is a good opportunity to mention that Dietrich's "Falling in Love Again" provided the model for Minnelli's costume in "Mein Herr."

Both singers possess a similar sartorial splendor with their bowler hat, stockings with garters, boots, and chair props.

48. Prince, *Contradictions*, 137; repr. in *Sense of Occasion*, 135.

49. James Leve, *Kander and Ebb* (New Haven, CT: Yale University Press, 2009), 41.

50. This is how the accents match the words (with the LONGS placed in CAPS): m. 1 "What GOOD is/m. 2 sit-TING a- / m. 3 –lone in your ROOM" with "ROOM" held through m. 4

51. Prince, *Sense of Occasion*, 137.

52. Hollis Alpert, "Willkommen, Bienvenue, Welcome!" *Saturday Review*, March 4, 1972, 66.

53. Ibid.

54. Pauline Kael, "Grinning," *New Yorker*, February 19, 1972; repr. in *For Keeps* (New York: Plume, 1994), 430–33.

55. Linda Mizejewski, *Divine Decadence: Fascism, Female Spectacle, and the Makings of Sally Bowles* (Princeton, NJ: Princeton University Press, 1992), 27. See also Block, "Is Life a Cabaret?"

56. Stephen Farber, "'Cabaret' May Shock Kansas. . . ," *New York Times*, February 20, 1972, D1.

57. Ibid.

58. In Allen's screenplay, the scene directions follow the stage version that opens Act II with the Emcee revealed as one of the girls, the military drums, the martial version of "Tomorrow Belongs to Me," and the goose-stepping.

59. Laurents, *Original Story By*, 247. In making this assertion Laurents neglects to note *West Side Story*'s technical contribution in increasing the role of dance as the center for dramatic action.

60. Prince, *Sense of Occasion*, 138. Since no version of Christopher or Clifford was gay, it's not clear what Prince means by "the original gay subplot." Perhaps he is referring to the fact that Isherwood's sexuality was known, even if all of his literary surrogates were heterosexual prior to the Fosse version.

61. Allen, *Cabaret*, First Draft, 101.

62. Although Wheeler revised Allen's work and even made changes on the production set, the Writers Guild determined that since more than two-thirds of Allen's screenplay remained unchanged, Allen had the right to deny Wheeler's listing as a co-author. After the Writers Guild denied appeals from Fosse, Feuer, and Marty Baum to reverse this decision, Wheeler became formally credited as "research consultant." Radie Harris, "Hugh Wheeler Role in 'Cabaret' Told," *The Hollywood Reporter*, April 5, 1972, 6. Harris gives Wheeler the title of "rehearsal consultant," but "research consultant" is correct.

63. *Cabaret*, "A Screenplay by Jan [*recte* Jay] Presson Allen and Hugh Wheeler," Final Draft, February 15, 1971; Revised April 15, 1 971, Alternate Page 101, Hugh Wheeler Collection #1417, Box 44E, Howard Gotlieb Archival Research Center, Boston University.

64. In his autobiography, Michael York relates how he and Minnelli were forced against their will to change the original word and tried to no avail to "screw" up the filming

of the bowdlerized version in order to retain it. York, *Accidentally on Purpose* (New York: Simon & Schuster, 1991), 276.

65. "Kit Kat Klub Memory Gallery."

66. Ibid.

67. For a helpful survey of what happened to musical film adaptations after *Cabaret*, see the sections aptly titled "Decline: The 1970s to the 1990s" and "Renaissance in the New Millennium." Dominic McHugh, "'And I'll Sing Once More': A Historical Overview of the Broadway Musical on the Silver Screen," in *The Oxford Handbook of Musical Theatre Screen Adaptations*, ed. Dominic McHugh (New York: Oxford University Press, 2019), 19–24.

68. The present author attempted to make a case on behalf of one frequently maligned adaptation from the 1970s, *A Little Night Music*, directed by Prince, which was produced in 1977 four years after the stage hit but not released until 1978. Block, "A Sad and Listless Affair": The Unsung Film Adaptation of Sondheim's *A Little Night Music*," in *Sondheim in Our Time and His*, ed. W. Anthony Sheppard (New York: Oxford University Press, 2021), 277–306.

69. Ryan Bunch, "'Ease on Down the Road': Black Routes and the Soul of *The Wiz*," 183–204, in *Adapting "The Wizard of Oz": Musical Versions from Baum to MGM and Beyond*, ed. Danielle Birkett and Dominic McHugh (New York: Oxford University Press 2019), quotation on 183; La Donna L. Forsgren, "*The Wiz* Redux; Or Why Queer Black Feminist Spectatorship and Politically Engaged Popular Entertainment Continue to Matter," *Theatre Survey* 60/3 (September 2019), 325–54.

70. *Chicago* (2002); *The Phantom of the Opera* (2004); *Rent* (2005); *The Producers* (2005); *Dreamgirls* (2006); *Hairspray* (2007); *Sweeney Todd* (2007); *Mamma Mia!* (2008); *Nine* (2009); *Les Misérables* (2012); *Jersey Boys* (2014); *Into the Woods* (2014); and *Cats* (2019).

71. Brooks Barnes et al., "James Bond, Meet Jeff Bezos: Amazon makes $8.45 Billion Deal for MGM," *New York Times*, May 26, 2021, B1. MGM films released before May 1986 are owned by Warner as part of its ownership of Turner Entertainment Co.

Selected Bibliography

Abbott, George. "*Mr. Abbott.*" New York: Random House, 1963.

Acevedo-Muñoz, Ernesto R. "*West Side Story as Cinema: The Making and Impact of an American Masterpiece.* Lawrence: University Press of Kansas, 2013.

Acocella, Joan. "City Lights." *New York,* November 28, 2011.

Adams, Dean. "*The Producers* and *Hairspray*: The Hazards and Rewards of Recursive Adaptation." In *The Oxford Handbook of Musical Theatre Screen Adaptations*, edited by Dominic McHugh, 591–612. New York: Oxford University Press, 2019.

Altman, Rick. "The Evolution of Sound Technology." In *Film Sound: Theory and Practice*, edited by Elisabeth Weis and John Bolton, 44–53. New York: Columbia University Press, 1985.

Altman, Rick. *The American Film Musical.* Bloomington: Indiana University Press, 1989.

André, Naomi. "Complexities in Gershwin's *Porgy and Bess.*" In *The Cambridge Companion to Gershwin*, edited by Anna Harwell Celenza, 182–196. Cambridge: Cambridge University Press, 2019.

Appiah, Kwame Anthony. "Cultural Borrowing Is Great: The Problem is Disrespect." *Wall Street Journal*, September 19, 2018.

Appiah, Kwame Anthony. *The Lies That Bind: Rethinking Identity*. New York: Liveright, 2019.

Asch, Amy, ed. *The Complete Lyrics of Oscar Hammerstein II*. New York: Knopf, 2008.

Atkinson, Brooks. "Hollywood Dough: A Theatre Financed by the Screen Raises Several Questions." *New York Times*, November 10, 1935, X1.

Baber, Katherine. *Leonard Bernstein and the Language of Jazz.* Urbana: University of Illinois Press, 2019.

Babington, Bruce, and Peter William Evans, eds. *Blue Skies and Silver Linings: Aspects of the Hollywood Musical.* Manchester: Manchester University Press, 1985.

Bacalzo, Dan. "A Different Drum: David Henry Hwang's Musical 'Revisal' of *Flower Drum Song.*" *Journal of American Drama and Theatre* 15/2 (Spring 2003): 71–83.

Banfield, Stephen. *Sondheim's Broadway Musicals.* Ann Arbor: University of Michigan Press, 1993.

Banfield, Stephen. *Jerome Kern.* New Haven, CT: Yale University Press, 2006.

Barrios, Richard. *Must-See Musicals: 50 Show-Stopping Movies We Can't Forget.* Philadelphia: Running, 2017.

Barrios, Richard. "*West Side Story*": The Jets, The Sharks, and the Making of a Classic. Philadelphia: Running Press, 2020.

Basinger, Jeanine. *The Movie Musical!.* New York: Knopf, 2019.

Beatty, Talley. Interview with Zita Allen in *Artists and Influences.* New York: Hatch Billops Collection, 1981; available online in "Black Thought and Culture."

Bernstein, Leonard. *Findings.* New York: Simon & Schuster, 1982.

Berson, Misha. "A Drum with a Difference." *American Theatre* 19/2 (February 2002): 14–17, 76.

Berson, Misha. *Something's Coming, Something Good: "West Side Story" and the American Imagination*. Milwaukee: Applause, 2011.

Block, Geoffrey. "The Broadway Canon from *Show Boat* to *West Side Story* and the European Operatic Ideal." *Journal of Musicology* 11/4 (Fall 1993): 525–44.

Block, Geoffrey. "*Sondheim's Broadway Musicals* by Stephen Banfield." *Journal of the Royal Musical Association* 121/1 (1996): 20–27.

Block, Geoffrey. *Enchanted Evenings: The Broadway Musical from "Show Boat" to Sondheim and Lloyd Webber.* New York: Oxford University Press, 1997; rev. 2nd ed., 2009.

Block, Geoffrey. "Integration." In *The Oxford Handbook of the American Musical*, edited by Raymond Knapp, Mitchell Morris, and Stacy Wolf. New York: Oxford University Press, 2011, 97-110; repr. in *Histories of the Musical Vol. 1*, eds. Knapp, Morris, and Wolf. New York: Oxford University Press, 2018, 153–75.

Block, Geoffrey. "Is Life a Cabaret? *Cabaret* and Its Sources in Reality and the Imagination." *Studies in Musical Theatre* 5/2 (2011): 163–80.

Block, Geoffrey. "Refashioning *Roberta*: From Novel to Stage and Screen." In *The Oxford Handbook of Musical Theatre Screen Adaptations*, edited by Dominic McHugh, 29–54. New York: Oxford University Press, 2019.

Block, Geoffrey. "*The Movie Musical!* by Jeanine Basinger (2019)." *Studies in Musical Theater* 14/1 (2020), 230–233.

Bogle, Donald. *Heat Wave: The Life and Career of Ethel Waters.* New York: Harper-Collins, 2011.

Bordman, Gerald. *Jerome Kern: His Life and Music.* New York: Oxford University Press, 1980.

Bordwell, David, Janet Staiger, and Kristin Thopson. *The Classical Hollywood Cinema: Film Style & Mode of Production to 1960.* New York: Columbia University Press, 1985.

Brackett, Charles, Billy Wilder, and Walter Reisch. *Ninotchka.* New York: Viking, 1972.

Brantley, Ben. Review of *Flower Drum Song*, "New Coat of Paint for Old Pagoda." *New York Times*, October 18, 2002.

Bukatman, Scott, "*A Day in New York: 'On the Town' and 'The Clock.'*" In *City That Never Sleeps: New York and the Filmic Imagination*, edited by Murray Pomerance, 32–39. New Brunswick, NJ: Rutgers University Press, 2007.

Burrows, Abe. *Honest, Abe: Is There Really No Business Like Show Business?* Boston: Little, Brown, 1980.

Burton, Humphrey. *Leonard Bernstein.* New York: Doubleday, 1994.

Carter, Tim. "*Oklahoma!" The Making of an American Musical.* Revised edition. New York: Oxford University Press, 2020.

Cartmell, Deborah, and Imelda Wheelan. *Screen Adaptation: Impure Cinema.* Houndmills, Basingstoke: Palgrave Macmillan, 2010.

Castelvecchi, "On 'Diegesis' and 'Diegetic': Words and Concepts." *Journal of the American Musicological Society* 73, no. 1 (Spring 2020): 149–71.

Chaplin, Saul. *The Golden Age of Movie Musicals and Me.* Norman: University of Oklahoma Press, 1994.

Cheng, Anne Anlin, "Beauty and Ideal Citizenship: Inventing Asian America in Rodgers and Hammerstein's *Flower Drum Song*." In *The Melancholy of Race: Psychoanalysis, Assimilation, and Hidden Grief*, edited by Anne Anlin Cheng. New York: Oxford University Press, 2001, 31–63.

Citron, Stephen. *Noel and Cole: The Sophisticates.* New York: Oxford University Press, 1993.

Clark, Randy. "Bending the Genre: The Stage and Screen Versions of *Cabaret*." *Literature Film Quarterly* 19/1 (1991): 51–59.

Cohan, Steven, ed. *Hollywood Musicals: The Film Reader*. London: Routledge, 2002.

Conrad, Jon Alan. "*West Side Story.*" *The New Grove Dictionary of Opera* (1992), Oxford Music Online, https://doi-org.ezproxy.ups.edu:2443/10.1093/gmol/9781561592630.article.0009114.

Croce, Arlene. *The Fred Astaire & Ginger Rogers Book*. New York: Outerbridge & Lazard, 1972.

Crowther, Bosely. "The Screen: *Silk Stockings* Arrives." *New York Times*, July 18, 1957.

Crowther, Bosely. "'West Side Story' Arrives." *New York Times,* October 19, 1961.

Crowther, Bosley. *The Lion's Share*. New York: Garland, 1985.

Das, Joanna Dee. *Katherine Dunham: Dance and the African Diaspora*. New York: Oxford University Press, 2017.

Deaville, James. "The Many Lives of *Flower Drum Song* (1957–2002): Negotiating Chinese American Identity in Print, on Stage, and on Screen." In *China and the West: Music, Representation, and Reception*, edited by Yang Hon-Lun and Michael Saffle, 119–36. Ann Arbor: University of Michigan Press, 2017.

Decker, Todd. "*Show Boat*": *Performing Race in an American Musical*. New York: Oxford University Press, 2013.

Decker, Todd. *Astaire by Numbers: Time & the Straight White Male Dancer*. New York: Oxford University Press, 2022.

Delamater, Jerome. *Dance in the Hollywood Musical*. Ann Arbor, MI: UMI Research Press, 1978.

Doherty, Thomas. *Hollywood's Censor: Joseph I. Breen & the Production Code Administration*. New York: Columbia University Press, 2007.

Duke, Vernon. *Passport to Paris*. Boston: Little, Brown, 1955.

Dyer, Richard. "The Colour of Entertainment." In *Musicals: Hollywood & Beyond*, edited by Bill Marshall and Robynn Stilwell, 23–50. Portland, OR: Intellect, 2000.

Eames, John Douglas, *The MGM Story: The Complete History of Fifty-Four Roaring Years*. New York: Crown, 1979.

Edney, Kathryn, "'Integration through the Wide Open Back Door': African Americans Respond to *Flower Drum Song* (1958)." *Studies in Musical Theatre* 4/3 (2010): 261–72.

Eells, George. *The Life That Late He Led: A Biography of Cole Porter*. New York: G. P. Putnam's Sons, 1965.

Eisen, Cliff, and Dominic McHugh, eds. *The Letters of Cole Porter*. New Haven, CT: Yale University Press, 2019.

Engel, Lehman. *The American Musical Theater*. New York: Collier, 1975.

Eyman, Scott. *Ernst Lubitsch: Laughter in Paradise*. New York: Simon & Schuster, 1993.

Felschow, Laura E. "Broadway Is a Two-Way Street: Integrating Hollywood Distribution and Exhibition." *Creative Commons* 6/1 (2019), accessed April 17, 2021.

Feuer, Cy, with Ken Gross. *I Got the Show Right Here: The Amazing, True Story of How and Obscure Brooklyn Horn Player Became the Last Great Broadway Showman*. New York: Simon & Schuster, 2003.

Feuer, Jane. *The Hollywood Musical*. Second edition. Bloomington: Indiana University Press, 1993.

Flinn, Caryl. *Brass Diva: The Life and Legends of Ethel Merman*. Berkeley: University of California Press, 2007.

Ford, Phil. "Jazz Exotica and the Naked City." *Journal of Musicological Research* 27 (2008): 113–33.

Fordin, Hugh. *Getting to Know Him: A Biography of Oscar Hammerstein II*. New York: Ungar, 1977.

Fordin, Hugh. *M-G-M's Greatest Musicals: The Arthur Freed Unit*. New York: Da Capo, 1996.

Franceschina, John. *Hermes Pan: The Man Who Danced with Fred Astaire*. New York: Oxford University Press, 2012.

Gardner, Kara. *Agnes de Mille: Telling Stories in Broadway Dance*. New York: Oxford University Press, 2016.

Garebian, Keith. *The Making of "Cabaret."* Second Edition. New York: Oxford University Press, 2011.

Genné, Beth. *Dance Me a Song: Astaire, Balanchine, Kelly, and the American Film Musical*. New York: Oxford University Pres, 2018.

Giddins, Gary. "The Mother of Us All." In *Riding on a Blue Note: Jazz and American Pop*, 3–13. Oxford: Oxford University Press, 1981.

Giddins, Gary. "Rollin' on the River," n.p. *Show Boat* 1936, The Criterion Collection, Warner Bros. 1936 and Turner Entertainment, 2020.

Goldstein, Malcolm. *George S. Kaufman: His Life, His Theater*. New York: Oxford University Press, 1979.

Gottlieb, Jack. *Funny, It Doesn't Sound Jewish: How Yiddish Songs and Synagogue Melodies Influenced Tin Pan Alley, Broadway, and Hollywood*. Albany: State University of New York in association with the Library of Congress, 2004.

Green, Jesse. "Sondheim Dismembers 'Sweeney.'" *New York Times,* December 16, 2007.

Green, Jesse. "The Bumpy Road from Broadway to Hollywood." *New York Times,* December 20, 2020.

Green, Jesse. "Reanimating *Cabaret,* One Frame at a Time." *New York Times,* April 14, 2021.

Green, Jesse, et. al. "The Great 'West Side Story' Debate." *New York Times,* December 1, 2021.

Green, Stanley. "'West Side Story'—The Film Version." *HiFi/Stereo Review,* January 1962, 65.

Green, Stanley, ed. *Rodgers and Hammerstein Fact Book*. New York: Lynn Farnol, 1980.

Green, Stanley. *Encyclopedia of the Musical Film*. New York: Oxford University Press. 1981.

Green, Stanley. *Hollywood Musicals Year by Year*. Third edition. Revised and updated by Barry Monush. New York: Applause Theatre and Cinema Books, 2010.

Green, Stanley. *Broadway Musicals Show by Show*. Eighth edition. Revised and updated by Cary Ginell. New York: Applause Theatre and Cinema Books, 2014.

Griffin, Mark. *A Hundred or More Hidden Things: The Life and Films of Vincente Minnelli*. New York: Da Capo, 2010.

Guernsey, Otis L., ed. *Broadway Song and Story: Playwrights/ Lyricists/ Composers Discuss Their Hits*. New York: Dodd, Mead, 1985.

Hammerstein, "Notes on Lyrics." In *Lyrics*. New York: Simon & Schuster, 1949; expanded and ed., William Hammerstein. Milwaukee, WI: Hal Leonard, 1985.

Harker, Brian. *Sportin' Life: John W. Bubbles, An American Classic*. New York: Oxford University Press, 2022.

Harvey, Stephen. *Directed by Vincente Minnelli*. New York: Museum of Modern Art and Harper & Row, 1989.

Hay, Peter. *MGM: When the Lion Roars*. Atlanta: Turner, 1991.

Hemming, Roy, *The Melody Lingers On: The Great Songwriters and Their Movie Musicals*. New York: Newmarket, 1986.

Hess, Earl, and Pratibha A. Dabholkar. *Gene Kelly: The Making of a Creative Legend*. Lawrence: University Press of Kansas, 2020.

Hill, Constance Valis. "Collaborating with Balanchine on *Cabin in the Sky*." In *Kaiso! Writing By and About Katherine Dunham*, edited by Vèvè A. Clark and Sara E Johnson, Studies in Dance History, 235–47. Madison: University of Wisconsin Press, 2005.

Hill, Constance Valis. "*Cabin in the Sky*: Dunham's and Balanchine's Ballet (Afro) Americana." *Discourses in Dance* 3/1 (2005): 59–71.

Hirsch, Foster. *Harold Prince and the American Musical Theatre*. New York: Cambridge University Press, 1989.

Hischak, Thomas S. *Through the Screen Door: What Happened to the Broadway Musical When It Went to Hollywood*. Lanham, MD: Scarecrow, 2004.

Hischak, Thomas S. *The Rodgers and Hammerstein Encyclopedia*. Westport, CT: Greenwood, 2007.

Hischak, Thomas S. *The Jerome Kern Encyclopedia*. Lanham, MD: Scarecrow, 2013.

Hoffman, Warren. *The Great White Way: Race and the Broadway Musical*. New Brunswick, NJ: Rutgers University Press, 2014.

Hodgins, Eric. "Amid the Ruins of an Empire a New Hollywood Arises." *Life*, June 1957, 146-50+

Horowitz, Mark Eden. "Cole Porter's Papers." In *A Cole Porter Companion*, edited by Don M. Randel, Matthew Shaftel, and Susan Forscher Weiss, 307–18. Urbana: University of Illinois Press, 2016.

Horowitz, Mark Eden, compiled and ed. *The Letters of Oscar Hammerstein II*. New York: Oxford University Press, 2022.

Hutcheon, Linda, with Siobhan O'Flynn. *A Theory of Adaptation*. Second edition. London: Routledge, 2013.

Hwang, David Henry. "A New Musical by Rodgers and Hwang." *New York Times*, October 13, 2002; revised as the "Introduction" in *Flower Drum Song*, ix–xiv. New York: Theatre Communications Group, 2003.

Jablonski, Edward. *Harold Arlen: Happy with the Blues*. Garden City, NY: Doubleday, 1961.

Jablonski, Edward. *Irving Berlin: American Troubadour*. New York: Henry Holt, 1999.

Jacobs, Lea. "Hollywood Institutions: Industry Self-Regulation and the Problem of Textual Determination." *The Velvet Light Trap: A Critical Journal of Film and Television* 23 (Spring 1989): 4–15.

Johnson, David T. "Adaptation and Fidelity." In *The Oxford Handbook of Adaptation Studies*, edited by Thomas Leitch, 87–100. New York: Oxford University Press, 2017.

Jowitt, Deborah. *Jerome Robbins: His Life, His Theater, His Dance*. New York: Simon & Schuster, 2004.

Kander, John, and Fred Ebb, as told to Greg Lawrence. *Colored Lights: Forty Years of Words and Music, Show Biz, Collaboration, and All That Jazz*. New York: Faber and Faber, 2003.

Kaplan, James. *Irving Berlin: New York Genius*. New Haven, CT: Yale University Press, 2019.

Kauffmann, Stanley. "The Asphalt Romeo and Julie." *New Republic*, October 23, 1961, 28–29.

Kennedy, Matthew, *Roadshow! The Fall of Film Musicals in the 1960s*. New York: Oxford University Press, 2014.

Kerr, Walter F. "*Silk Stockings*." *New York Tribune*, February 25, 1955.

Kimball, Robert, ed. *Cole*. New York: Holt, Rinehart & Winston, 1971.

Kimball, Robert, ed. *The Complete Lyrics of Cole Porter*. New York: Vintage, 1984.

Kimball, Robert, and Linda Emmet, eds. *The Complete Lyrics of Irving Berlin*. New York: Knopf, 2001.

Knapp, Raymond, Mitchell Morris, and Stacy Wolf, eds. *The Oxford Handbook of the American Musical*. New York: Oxford University Press, 2011; repr. in *Histories of the Musical: An Oxford Handbook of the American Musical*, ed. Knapp, Morris, and Wolf. New York Oxford University Press, 2018.

Knee, Adam, "Doubling, Music and Race in *Cabin in the Sky*." In *Representing Jazz*, edited by Krin Gabbard, 193–204. Durham, NC: Duke University Press, 1995.

Knef, Hildegard. *The Gift Horse: Report on a Life*. New York: McGraw Hill, 1970.

Knight, Arthur. "Movies: Romeo Revisited." *Saturday Review*, October 14, 1961, 40.

Kobal, John. *People Will Talk*. New York: Knopf, 1985.

Kowalke, Kim H. "Theorizing the Golden Age Musical: Genre, Structure, Syntax." *Gamut: Online Journal of the Music Theory Society of the Mid-Atlantic* 6/2, Article 6 (2013), 133–84.

Kranz, David L. "Trying Harder: Probability, Objectivity, and Rationality in Adaptation Studies." In *The Literature/Film Reader: Issues in Adaptation*, edited by James M. Welsh and Peter Lev, 77–102. Lanham, MD: Scarecrow 2007.

Kraut, Anthea. "Between Primitivism and Diaspora: The Dance Performances of Josephine Baker, Zora Neale Hurston, and Katherine Dunham." *Theatre Journal* 55/3 (October 2003): 433–50.

Kreuger, Miles. Audio commentary from 1989, *Show Boat* 1936, The Criterion Collection, Warner Bros. 1936 and Turner Entertainment, 2020.

Kreuger, Miles. *"Show Boat": The Story of a Classic American Musical*. New York: Oxford University Press, 1977.

Kunze, Peter C. "Belles Are Singing: Broadway, Hollywood, and the Failed *Gone with the Wind* Musical." *Historical Journal of Film, Radio, and Television* 38/4 (2018): 787–807.

Laurents, Arthur. *Original Story By: A Memoir of Broadway and Hollywood*. New York: Knopf, 2000.

Lawrence, Greg. *Dance with Demons: The Life of Jerome Robbins*. New York: Berkeley, 2001.

Lee, Josephine. "'Something Beyond and Above': David Henry Hwang's Revision of *Flower Drum Song*." In *The Theatre of David Henry Hwang*, edited by Esther Kim Lee, 129–41. London: Bloomsbury Methuen, 2015.

Lee, Robert G. *Orientals: Asian Americans in Popular Culture*. Philadelphia: Temple University Press, 1999.

Leitch, Thomas. "Twelve Fallacies in Contemporary Adaptation Theory." *Criticism* 45/2 (Spring 2003): 149–71.

Leitch, Thomas. ed. *The Oxford Handbook of Adaptation Studies*. New York: Oxford University Press, 2017.

Leve, James. *Kander and Ebb*. New Haven, CT: Yale University Press, 2009.

Lewis, David H. *Flower Drum Songs: The Story of Two Musicals*. Jefferson, NC: McFarland, 2006.

Luhrssen, David. *Mamoulian: Life on Stage and Screen*. Lexington: University Press of Kentucky, 2013.

Ma, Sheng-mei. "Rodgers and Hammerstein's 'Chopsticks' Musicals." *Literature/Film Quarterly* 31/1 (2003): 17–26.

McArthur, Colin. *"Brigadoon," "Braveheart, and the Scots: Distortions of Scotland in Hollywood Cinema.* London: I. B. Tauris, 2003.

McBride, Joseph. *How Did Lubitsch Do It?* New York: Columbia University Press, 2018.

McBrien, William. *Cole Porter: A Biography*. New York: Knopf, 1998.

McCarthy, Todd. "Jets Have Their Way Onscreen: 'West Side Story' Screen Version Underrated." *Variety,* June 4, 2009.

McConachie, Bruce. "Theatre and Film in Evolutionary Perspective." *Theatre Symposium* 19 (2011): 129–47.

McGlinn, John. "The Original 'Anything Goes'—a Classic Restored." Jacket notes to the studio recording conducted by McGlinn, 1989, 29-34.

McHugh, Dominic. "'And I'll Sing Once More': A Historical Overview of the Broadway Musical on the Silver Screen." In *The Oxford Handbook of Musical Theatre Screen Adaptations*, edited by Dominic McHugh, 13–27. New York: Oxford University Press, 2019.

McHugh, Dominic. ed. *The Oxford Handbook of Musical Theatre Screen Adaptations*. New York: Oxford University Press, 2019.

McHugh, Dominic, and Amy Asch, eds. *The Complete Lyrics of Alan Jay Lerner*. New York: Oxford University Press, 2018.

McWhorter, John. "How the N-Word Became Unsayable." *New York Times*, April 30, 2021.

McWhorter, John. "Why I Still Love *West Side Story*," *New York Times,* January 22, 2022.

Magee, Jeffrey. "Irving Berlin's 'Blue Skies': Ethnic Affiliations and Musical Transformations." *Musical Quarterly* 84/4 (Winter 2000): 537–80.

Magee, Jeffrey. *Irving Berlin's American Musical Theater*. New York: Oxford University Press 2012.

Maltby, Richard. "The Production Code and the Hays Office." In *History of the American Cinema Volume 5, Grand Design: Hollywood as a Modern Business Enterprise 1930–1939*, edited by Tino Balio, 37–72. New York: Charles Scribner's, 1993.

Marshall, Bill, and Robynn Stilwell, eds. *Musicals: Hollywood & Beyond*. Portland, OR: Intellect, 2000.

Maslon, Laurence. *Broadway to Main Street: How Show Times Enchanted America*. New York: Oxford University Press, 2018.

Mast, Gerald. *Can't Help Singin': The American Musical on Stage and Screen*. Woodstock, NY: Overlook, 1987.

Mast, Gerald, and Bruce F. Kawin. *The Movies: A Short History*. Revised and updated. Boston: Allyn and Bacon, 1996.

Menand, Louis. *The Free World: Art and Thought in the Cold War*. New York: Farrar, Straus and Giroux, 2021.

Meredith, Scott. *George S. Kaufman and His Friends*. Garden City, NY: Doubleday, 1974.

Meyerson, Harold, and Ernie Harburg. *Who Put the Rainbow in "The Wizard of Oz?": Yip Harburg, Lyricist*. Ann Arbor: University of Michigan Press, 1993.

Milne, Tom. *Mamoulian*. Bloomington: Indiana University Press, 1969.

Minnelli, Vincente, with Hector Arce. *I Remember It Well*. Garden, NY: Doubleday, 1974.

Mirisch, Walter. *I Thought We Were Making Movies, Not History.* Madison: University of Wisconsin Press, 2008.

Mizejewski, Linda. *Divine Decadence: Fascism, Female Spectacle, and the Makings of Sally Bowles*. Princeton, NJ: Princeton University Press, 1992.

Monush, Barry. *"West Side Story": Music on Film*. Milwaukee: Limelight, 2010.

Mordden, Ethan. *The Hollywood Musical*. New York: St. Martin's, 1981.

Mordden, Ethan. *The Hollywood Studios: House Style in the Golden Age of the Movies.* New York: Knopf, 1988.

Mordden, Ethan. *Rodgers & Hammerstein.* New York: Harry N. Abrams, 1992.

Mordden, Ethan. *Make Believe: The Broadway Musical in the 1920s.* New York: Oxford University Press, 1997.

Mordden, Ethan. *Coming Up Roses: The Broadway Musical in the 1950s.* New York: Oxford University Press, 1998.

Mordden, Ethan. *Beautiful Mornin': The Broadway Musical in the 1940s.* New York: Oxford University Press, 1999.

Mordden, Ethan. *Open a New Window: The Broadway Musical in the 1960s.* New York: Oxford University Press, 2001.

Mordden, Ethan. *One More Kiss: The Broadway Musical in the 1970s.* New York: Oxford University Press, 2003.

Mordden, Ethan. *The Happiest Corpse I've Ever Seen: The Last Twenty-Five Years of the Broadway Musical.* New York: Oxford University Press, 2004.

Mordden, Ethan. *Sing for Your Supper: The Broadway Musical in the 1930s.* New York: Palgrave Macmillan, 2005.

Mordden, Ethan. *When Broadway Went to Hollywood.* New York: Oxford University Press, 2016.

Mueller, John. *Astaire Dancing: The Musical Films.* New York: Wings, 1985.

Naremore, James. "Uptown Folk: Blackness and Entertainment in *Cabin in the Sky.*" In *Representing Jazz,* edited by Krin Gabbard, 169–92. Durham, NC: Duke University Press, 1995.

Negrón-Muntaner, Frances. "Feeling Pretty: *West Side Story* and Puerto Rican Identity Discourses." *Social Text* 18/2 (Summer 2000): 83–106.

Norton, Richard C. *A Chronology of American Musical Theater.* Volume 2, *1913–1952,* and Volume 3, *1952–2001.* New York: Oxford University Press, 2002.

Oja, Carol J. *Bernstein Meets Broadway: Collaborative Art in a Time of War.* New York: Oxford University Press, 2014.

Parkinson, David. *The Rough Guide to Film Musicals.* London: Penguin, 2007.

Pollack, Howard. *The Ballad of John Latouche: An American Lyricist's Life and Work.* New York: Oxford University Press, 2017.

Pollack, Rhoda-Gale. *George S. Kaufman.* Boston: Twayne, 1988.

Prince, Harold. *Contradictions: Notes on Twenty-six Years in the Theatre.* New York: Dodd, Mead, 1974.

Prince, Harold. *Sense of Occasion.* New York: Applause, 2017.

Propst, Andy. *They Made Us Happy: Betty Comden and Adolph Green's Musicals and Movies.* New York: Oxford University Press, 2019.

Purdom, Todd S. *Something Wonderful: Rodgers and Hammerstein's Broadway Revolution.* New York: Henry Holt, 2018.

Purdom, Todd S. "The *Hamilton* of World War II." *New York Times,* March 31, 2018.

Rich, Frank, with Lisa Aronson. *The Theatre Art of Boris Aronson.* New York: Knopf, 1987.

Robbins, Allison, "Rescoring *Anything Goes* in 1930s Hollywood." In *The Oxford Handbook of Musical Theatre Screen Adaptations,* edited by Dominic McHugh, 613–33. New York: Oxford University Press, 2019.

Rodda, Arlene. "*Cabaret*: Utilizing the Film Medium to Create a Unique Adaptation." *Literature Film Quarterly* 22/1 (1994): 36–41.

Rodgers, Richard. *An Autobiography.* New York: Random House, 1975; repr. New York: Da Capo, 1995, 2000.

Ross, Alex. "Laughter in the Dark: The Subtly Incisive Film Comedy of Ernst Lubitsch." *The New Yorker,* August 15, 2022.

Ryzik, Melena. "Rita Moreno and Ariana DeBose: Fro One Anita to Another." *New York Times,* December 15, 2021.

Sanders, Julie. *Adaptation and Appropriation.* Second edition. London: Routledge, 2016.

Sandoval-Sánchez, Alberto. *José, Can You See? Latinos on and off Broadway.* Madison: University of Wisconsin Press, 1999.

Sawyers, June Skinner. *Cabaret FAQ: All That's Left to Know about the Broadway and Cinema Classic.* New York: Applause, 2017.

Schatz, Thomas. *The Genius of the System: Hollywood Filmmaking in the Studio Era.* New York: Pantheon, 1988.

Schickel, Richard. *The Men Who Made the Movies.* New York: Atheneum, 1975.

Seifert, Marsha. "Image/Music/Voice: Song Dubbing in Hollywood Musicals." *Journal of Communication* 45/2 (Spring 1995): 44–64.

Shearer, Martha, "The Party's Over: *On the Town, Bells Are Ringing*, and the Problem of Adapting Postwar New York." In *The Oxford Handbook of Musical Theatre Screen Adaptations*, edited by Dominic McHugh, 85–106. New York: Oxford University Press, 2019.

Shin, Andrew. "Forty Percent Is Luck": An Interview with C.Y. (Chin Yang) Lee. *Melus* 29/2 (Summer 2004): 77–104.

Silverman, Stephen M. *Dancing on the Ceiling: Stanley Donen and His Movies.* New York: Knopf, 1996.

Simeone, Nigel. *Leonard Bernstein: "West Side Story."* Farnham, UK: Ashgate, 2009.

Simeone, Nigel, ed. *The Leonard Bernstein Letters.* New Haven, CT: Yale University Press, 2013.

Smedley, Nick. *A Divided World: Hollywood Cinema and Émigré Directors in the Era of Roosevelt and Hitler 1933–1948.* Bristol: Intellect, 2011.

Smith, Helen. *There's a Place for Us: The Musical Theatre Works of Leonard Bernstein.* Farnham, UK: Ashgate, 2011.

Smith, Jeff. "Black Faces, White Voices: The Politics of Dubbing in *Carmen Jones.*" *Velvet Light Trap* 51 (Spring 2003): 29–42.

Smith, Susan. *The Musical: Race, Gender and Performance.* London: Wallflower, 2005.

Smith, Susan. "*Brigadoon* and Its Transition to MGM Dance Musical: Adapting a Stage Show for Star Dancers." In *The Oxford Handbook of Musical Theatre Screen Adaptations*, edited by Dominic McHugh, 395–422. New York: Oxford University Press, 2019.

Sondheim, Stephen. *Finishing the Hat: Collected Lyrics (1954–1981) with Attendant Comments, Principles, Heresies, Grudges, Whines and Anecdotes.* New York: Knopf, 2010.

Spergel, Mark. *Reinventing Reality—The Art and Life of Rouben Mamoulian.* Metuchen, NJ: Scarecrow, 1993.

Spivak, Jeffrey. *Buzz: The Life and Art of Busby Berkeley.* Lexington: The University Press of Kentucky, 2011.

Stansfield, Peter. "From the Vulgar to the Refined: American Vernacular and Blackface Minstrelsy in *Showboat* [*sic*]." In *Musicals: Hollywood and Beyond,* edited by Bill Marshall and Robynn Stilwell. Portland, OR: Intellect, 2000.

Suskin, Steven. *Opening Night on Broadway: A Critical Quotebook of the Golden Era of the Musical Theatre, "Oklahoma!" (1943) to "Fiddler on the Roof" (1964).* New York: Schirmer, 1990.

Swain, Joseph P. *The Broadway Musical: A Critical and Musical Survey.* New York: Oxford University, 1990; 2nd ed., Lanham, MD: Scarecrow, 2002.

Tan, Sheri. "'Flower Drum' Critics Haven't Read Script." *Asian Week*, March 31, 1983, 4.

Taves, Brian. "Production Trends: Musicals." In *History of the American Cinema Volume 5, Grand Design: Hollywood as a Modern Business Enterprise 1930–1939*, edited by Tino Balio, 211–35. New York: Charles Scribner's, 1993.

Thomson, David. *The New Biographical Dictionary of Film.* New York: Knopf, 2002.

Tropiano, Stephen. *Music on Film: "Cabaret."* Milwaukee: Hal Leonard, 2011.

Turk, Edward Baron. *Hollywood Diva: A Biography of Jeanette MacDonald.* Berkeley: University of California Press, 1998.

Villella, Fiona A. "Circular Narratives: Highlights of Popular Cinema in the '90." *Senses of Cinema* 3 (February 2000). https://sensesofcinema.com/2000/feature-articles/circular/,

Wada, Karen. "Afterword." In *Flower Drum Song* (New York: Theatre Communications Group, 2003), 99–115.

Waters, Ethel, with Charles Samuels. *His Eye Is on the Sparrow: An Autobiography.* Garden City, NY: Doubleday, 1951.

Watts, Richard Jr. "Kidding the Muscovites to Music." *New York Post,* February 25, 1955.

Wells, Elizabeth A. *"West Side Story": Cultural Perspectives on an American Musical.* Lanham, MD: Scarecrow, 2011.

Wilder, Alec. *American Popular Song: The Great Innovators 1900–1950.* New York: Oxford University Press, 1972.

Williams, Mary E., ed. *Readings on "West Side Story."* San Diego: Greenhaven, 2001.

Winkler, Kevin. *Big Deal: Bob Fosse and Dance in the American Musical.* New York: Oxford University Press, 2018.

Woll, Allen. *Black Musical Theatre: From "Coontown" to "Dreamgirls."* Baton Rouge: Louisiana State University Press, 1989.

Wood, Robin. "Art and Ideology: Notes on *Silk Stockings*." *Film Comment* 11/3 (May/June 1975: 28-31.

Yudkoff, Alvin. *Gene Kelly: A Life of Dance and Dreams.* New York: Backstage Books, 1999.

Zolotow, *Billy Wilder in Hollywood.* New York: Limelight, 1987.

Index

racial stereotypes
  in *Cabin in the Sky* (stage and screen
    adaptation), 109, 110, 123, 126
  in *Flower Drum Song* (stage and screen
    versions), 221–22, 308n.7
  as reflected in language, 277n.23
  in *Show Boat* (stage and screen versions), 27,
    28, 29, 31, 26, 39, 41, 42
  in *Tales of Manhattan*, 113
  in *West Side Story* (stage and screen versions),
    201–2
Rainger, Ralph, 9
Raisin (stage musical), 28
Raitt, John, 19
Rall, Tommy, 95
Redmond, Shana, 38, 41
Reisch, Walter, 149
Rent (screen adaptation), 248
Revuers, The, 70
Richards, Carol, 103, 129
Rise and Fall of the City of Mahagonny, The
  (Weill/Brecht), 229
Rivera, Chita, 201
RKO, 2, 3. See also *Roberta*
roadshow musical films, 204–5, 303n.32
Robbins, Allison, 8
Robbins, Jerome, xvii, xxi, 77, 87, 230–31
  as choreographer, 70, 95, 96
  as choreographer for *West Side Story* (stage
    and screen versions), 23, 95, 186, 200–201
  as co-director of *West Side Story* (screen
    adaptation), 186, 200–201
  and *Fancy Free* (ballet), 70
  and *Fiddler on the Roof* (screen adaptation),
    226
  Oscar awarded to, 24
  and screen adaptation of *The King and I*, 23
  and screen adaptation of *West Side Story*,
    23, 23
  and stage version of *Call Me Madam*, 95, 96
  and stage version of *West Side Story*, 24
  Tony Award presented to, 24
  See also *On the Town*
Roberta (1935 screen adaptation), xvi–xvii,
  xviii, xx, 3, 12, 13, 17, 62–63, 232
  critical assessment of, 65, 68
  diegeticism in, 64, 65
  orchestral underscoring in, 63, 65
  song interpolations in, 13, 65
  songs altered in, 64–65
  songs cut from, 27
  songs from, 64–67; "Don't Ask Me Not to
    Sing," 47, 63, 64; "Hot Spot," 63; "I'll Be

Hard to Handle," 27, 62, 64; "Indiana," 14,
64, 65; "I Won't Dance," 27, 62, 63–64, 65;
"Let's Begin," 27; "Lovely to Look At," 27,
63, 64, 65; "Russian Song," 64, 65; "Smoke
Gets in Your Eyes," 27, 63, 65; "The Touch
of Your Hand," 65; "Yesterdays," 27, 63, 65;
"You're Devastating," 63, 65
  success of, 61, 65, 67
  See also *Lovely to Look At*
Roberta (stage musical), xvi, xxi, 12, 61, 62
  diegeticism in, 64
  songs from, 64–67; "Don't Ask Me Not to
    Sing," 63; "Hot Spot," 63; "I'll Be Hard to
    Handle," 64; "Madrigal," 63; "Something
    Had to Happen," 63
Roberti, Lyda, 62
Robeson, Paul
  in *Show Boat* (screen adaptation), 29, 31,
    32, 38
  in *Tales of Manhattan*, 113
Robin, Leo, 9, 10, 13, 18
Rodgers, Richard, xvii, 1–2, 10, 78, 84, 104, 172
  and *Chee-Chee*, 205
  and *Love Me Tonight*, 162
  screen adaptations of stage scores by, 11
  See also *Flower Drum Song* (screen
    adaptation); *Flower Drum Song* (stage
    musical); *Oklahoma!* (screen adaptation);
    Oklahoma! (stage musical)
Rogers, Ginger, 3, 11–12, 15
  in *Roberta* (screen adaptation), 62, 65
Romberg, Sigmund, 1, 8
Romeo and Juliet (Shakespeare)
  as source for *West Side Story*, 186
Rosalie (original film musical), 8
Ross, Jean, 228, 246
Ross, Jerry, 185
Rousseau, Jean-Jacques, xv
Royal Wedding (original film musical), 170
Run Little Chillun (Broadway play), 35
Rusk, Howard A., 303n.29
Russell, Jane, 18
Russell, Rosalind, 91, 174
Ryskind, Morrie, 43

Saddler, Donald, 95
St. John, Howard, 19
St. Louis Woman (stage musical), 162
Sally (screen adaptation), 26
  songs from: "Look for the Silver Lining," 26;
    "Wild Rose," 26
Sanders, George
  in *Call Me Madam* (stage musical), 103